Firearms

A Global History to 1700

This book is a history of firearms across the world from the 1100s up to the 1700s, from the time of their invention in China to the time when European firearms had surpassed all others. It asks why it was the Europeans who perfected firearms when it was the Chinese who invented them, but it answers this question by examining how firearms were used throughout the world. Early firearms were restricted to infantry and siege warfare, limiting their use outside of Europe and Japan. Steppe and desert nomads imposed a different style of warfare on the Middle East, India, and China – a style with which firearms were incompatible. By the time that better firearms allowed these regions to turn the tables on the nomads, Japan's self-imposed isolation left Europe with no rival in firearms design, production, or use, with consequences that are still with us today.

Kenneth Chase is an attorney at the law firm of Cleary, Gottlieb, Steen and Hamilton. He received his Ph.D. in East Asian Languages and Civilizations from Harvard University and his J.D. from Stanford Law School.

Firearms

A Global History to 1700

KENNETH CHASE

CAMBRIDGE
UNIVERSITY PRESS

PUBLISHED BY THE PRESS SYNDICATE OF THE UNIVERSITY OF CAMBRIDGE
The Pitt Building, Trumpington Street, Cambridge, United Kingdom

CAMBRIDGE UNIVERSITY PRESS
The Edinburgh Building, Cambridge CB2 2RU, UK
40 West 20th Street, New York, NY 10011-4211, USA
477 Williamstown Road, Port Melbourne, VIC 3207, Australia
Ruiz de Alarcón 13, 28014 Madrid, Spain
Dock House, The Waterfront, Cape Town 8001, South Africa

http://www.cambridge.org

First published 2003

Printed in the United States of America

Typeface Sabon 10/13 pt.   *System* LATEX 2$_\varepsilon$ [TB]

A catalog record for this book is available from the British Library.

Library of Congress Cataloging in Publication Data
Chase, Kenneth Warren.
Firearms : a global history to 1700 / Kenneth W. Chase.
p.   cm.
Includes bibliographical references and index.
ISBN 0-521-82274-2 (hardback)
1. Firearms – History.   I. Title.
UD390 .C43   2003
623.4'42 – dc21   2002041026

ISBN 0 521 82274 2 hardback

In Memoriam
Warren Chase

(1934–2000)

How, foul and pestilent discovery,
Did'st thou find place within the human heart?

Ludovico Ariosto, *Orlando Furioso* (1516)

Contents

Illustrations

Maps

Figures

Preface

I originally approached this topic from an interest in nomads. Reading up on China's relations with the Mongols in the summer of 1991, I was struck by the strategic dilemma facing the Chinese. The Chinese had to defend a thousand miles of frontier against an enemy with superior mobility, one who could choose the time and place of an attack almost at will. The Mongols lived in tents and traveled with their flocks, so the Chinese could not pin them down. Nor could the Chinese possibly hold every point along the frontier with sufficient strength. Arthur Waldron's *The Great Wall of China* analyzed the range of options open to the Chinese and showed that the decision to fortify the frontier in the 1500s was anything but a foregone conclusion.

My interest in the Mongols then took me to other places they had been, like Russia and Iran, and I was struck by the similarities and differences with the strategic situation in China. The Russian border defenses were similar in principle to those in China, albeit far less elaborate. On the other hand, there were no such defenses separating Iran from the steppe. Although China and Russia broke free of the Mongol empire in the 1300s and 1400s, respectively, Turks gained and maintained the upper hand throughout the Middle East and India. The Middle East and India might be taken as an illustration of what happened when the defenses failed, except there was no evidence of such defenses, and anyway they had failed in Russia and China without similar consequences. It was clear that the Middle East and India were hospitable to pastoral nomads in ways that China and Russia were not.

Finally, archeological evidence from the 1970s that firearms had first been invented in China, not in Europe, was just being brought to the attention of the English-reading world, thanks as usual to Joseph Needham's *Science and Civilisation in China*. I found that I already had an answer to a question that no one had given much thought to yet: Why was it the Europeans who perfected firearms when it was the Chinese who invented them? It occurred to me that the two areas where the Mongols had not taken me were western Europe and Japan, which were also the two places where firearms had been most prevalent. Conversely, those who routinely fought against nomads did not do much with firearms, even when they had knowledge of such weapons and the means to produce them. This insight was the basis for this book.

It is a commonplace that the steppe and the desert are like the ocean. My approach has been informed by studies of the Mediterranean that give due weight to geography: first and foremost by Fernand Braudel's *The Mediterranean*, but more proximately by John H. Pryor's *Geography, Technology, and War* and John Francis Guilmartin's *Gunpowder and Galleys*. Geography imposes constraints on human action, and especially on warfare, that are neither foreordained nor eternal. It is a geographical fact that the steppes of Mongolia receive limited rainfall, but it is also a geographical fact (and not an inevitable one) that people adapted to that environment in specific historical periods through pastoral nomadic lifestyles. It is also a geographical fact (and again, not an inevitable one) that what we call "China" was united under a single government throughout most of this period and what we call "Europe" was not. Though neither south China nor western Europe borders on the steppe, the implications are very different, because the resources of south China were mobilized to defend north China, whereas the resources of western Europe were not available to defend eastern Europe.

The influence of geography on warfare is nowhere more apparent than in logistics. If we say that the steppe and the desert are like oceans, it is not only because they seem flat and featureless. Armies entering the steppe were like ships putting out to sea. They carried their own provisions with them, and they had to return to the "shore" before those provisions ran out. In the days before railroads and trucks, land transportation was slow and expensive, and soldiers could not easily carry provisions for more than ten or twenty days. Needless to say, nomads did not wander through the steppe and desert with carefree abandon either. Their migrations from summer camp to winter camp and back each year were carefully timed and planned to take advantage of the grass and water along the way. However, nomads were at home under these conditions in ways that others were not. Steppe and desert nomads did not need to fight if they could avoid combat long enough for invaders to run out of supplies. Military historians have rediscovered logistics in recent years, but generals never had the luxury of forgetting them.

I do not argue that technology and geography alone account completely for all experience with firearms. What I do argue is that technology and geography account for the most variation with the fewest factors. There are still cases that deviate from what we would expect based on this hypothesis, but the deviations are fewer than they would be with any equally elegant explanation. Technology and geography provide the baseline of expectations by which the truly exceptional cases can be identified. For example, one would expect an advanced country with a long coastline to have a strong navy. It is not really surprising to find that England usually has had a strong navy, nor is it surprising that Madagascar has not (despite its long coastline) or that Switzerland has not (despite its advanced technology). This does not mean that *every* advanced country with a long coastline *always* has a strong navy: China let its navy decline after 1433, and Japan did not build a navy in the 1700s, and we might legitimately expect to find some cultural or political reasons why. Until we know what to expect, however, we will hardly know what to find surprising.

I do believe that rational explanations generally suffice to account for the use and nonuse of firearms in the period covered by this book. It goes without saying that history is full of irrational behavior, but to quote Marshall Hodgson: "However irrational human beings may be, in the long run their irrationalities are mostly random. It is their rational calculations that can be reinforced in continuing human groups and can show persisting orientation and development – even when they are calculations on misconceived presuppositions."[1] If Shah Ismail and his Qizilbash cavalry charged Ottoman musketeers protected by a line of wagons at Chaldiran in 1514 (see Chapter 5, the section "Azarbayjan"), that was a stupid decision, pure and simple. Military history is full of them. If Shah Ismail's successors continued to fight the Ottomans for more than a century with cavalry instead of infantry, that is a sign that something else was going on.

Consistent with this approach, I have little to say about different cultural constructs of war. The truly different examples come from small isolated societies like the Moriori of the Chatham Islands, a peaceful and friendly people enslaved by the Maoris in 1835.[2] Societies capable of producing firearms were all pretty much indistinguishable from the Maoris in this regard. None of them bore the slightest resemblance to the Moriori. Weaknesses stemming from idiosyncratic notions about the conduct of warfare were exposed and ruthlessly exploited by neighbors who did not share them. Isolated cases did exist – there were European generals during World War I, and maybe even during World War II, who refused to admit that cavalry was no longer the decisive branch of the ground forces. Such notions did not survive long because the people who held them did not survive long. The examples to the contrary most often cited turn out to be questionable (see Chapter 4, note 78 on the Mamluks), or worse, simply wrong (see Chapter 7, note 84 on the Japanese).

As for what Hodgson called "misconceived presuppositions," some striking ones are held by modern historians about early firearms. When David

Ayalon expresses surprise that a Muslim historian who died in 1469 never "so much as hinted that bow and lance were obsolete weapons,"[3] or when Ray Huang concludes that Chinese firearms must have been poorly manufactured if a Chinese general who died in 1588 "maintained that each company of musketeers must be accompanied by a company of soldiers carrying contact weapons,"[4] then there is clearly some misunderstanding about certain basic facts of military history even among historians of this caliber. In 1565, a century after the death of the Muslim historian and in the middle of the career of the Chinese general, a typical picture of a European battlefield (see Figure 3.1) still shows, among other things, (1) two bodies of lancers on horseback and (2) pikemen marching in formation in front of musketeers.

If we do not know what people knew, then we can hardly know what they thought. If people knew that matchlock muskets could not be loaded on horseback; if they knew that pistols had an effective range of less than six feet; if they knew that musketeers without pikemen would be cut to pieces by cavalry with swords; if they knew that Mongols rode horses and lived in tents and had no cities or castles; if they knew that infantry could not carry much more than ten days' rations or march much more than twelve miles in a day – then we need to know some of the same things if we hope to understand why they thought what they thought and why they did what they did.

This is not a comprehensive history of warfare across the world in the first six centuries of the existence of firearms. Such a history would require many volumes much larger than this one. This book is an attempt to call attention to one particular influence (the relationship of nomads to firearms) on one particular facet (the successes and failures with firearms) of that history. I have had to keep the focus as tight as possible in order to keep this book down to a readable length. Where I have used primary sources, limitations of space have kept me from going into them in any great detail, and I have been forced to summarize more often than I would like. Where I have quoted translations other than my own, I have changed the romanization of names as necessary to conform to the romanization used elsewhere in the book.

I owe thanks to more people than I can possibly mention by name, but I will do the best that I can.

I was fortunate to grow up in a town with a fine public school system and a fine public library, and I would like to thank all the people who made these possible. I was also fortunate to have many enthusiastic language teachers throughout my education, but I would especially like to thank my teacher of classical Chinese at Princeton University, Yuan Nai-ying, whose commitment and enthusiasm are known to generations of students. I had many great professors at Princeton, but I should give special thanks to Arthur Waldron.

In the Department of East Asian Languages and Civilizations at Harvard University I would particularly like to thank my advisors, Peter Bol in Chinese history and Harold Bolitho in Japanese history, to whom I am indebted for my professional training as a historian. While conducting research at Kyoto University, I was privileged to study with two outstanding scholars, Mano Eiji in Central Asian and Islamic studies and Sugiyama Masaaki in Mongol and Chinese history, who started me thinking about world history. I am indebted to Robert Hymes and Manouchehr Kasheff for making my year at Columbia University both pleasant and productive.

When I returned to Harvard to complete my dissertation and begin this project, I benefited from the guidance of Roy Mottahedeh as well as the support of the Academy Scholar program; I feel like the black sheep of the program, most of whose alumni have gone on to successful academic careers, so I would like to take this opportunity to record my gratitude to Ira Kukin and Henry Rosovsky. I am extremely grateful to Wheeler Thackston, who spent years patiently helping me read Persian, both while I was in graduate school and long after I had gone off to law school.

Over the years that I have been working on this book, I have received encouragement and comments and suggestions and help from a great many people. Gunder Frank gave both suggestions and encouragement at an early stage. John Woods was very kind in sharing with me his own unpublished research on the history of firearms in Iran and Central Asia, for which I am very grateful. David Graff shared some of his knowledge of military history with me, and Leo Shin gave me timely help with some of the citations.

A number of people read drafts of this work or sat patiently through long explanations of it. Special thanks are due to Peter Lorge, William McRae, Karl Gerth, Judy Chase, and the two anonymous readers for Cambridge University Press, who gave me valuable suggestions and encouragement. If I was too stubborn to take full advantage of all their comments I have only myself to blame, and the reader need hardly be told that responsibility for all remaining errors is completely my own.

I would also like to thank Gang Gong and Ryan Duty for their patience through countless drafts of the maps, and the staff at the Starr East Asian Library at Columbia University, the New York Public Library, the Princeton University Library, and Art Resource for their assistance with the illustrations.

Finally, and above all, I would like to thank my family.

Introduction

Why was it the Europeans who perfected firearms when it was the Chinese who invented them?

Boiled down to a single sentence, that is the question this book tries to answer. There was once a great deal of confusion and controversy surrounding the invention of firearms, but it is now generally accepted that firearms originated in China. Although there is no solid evidence for firearms in Europe before the 1300s, archeologists have discovered a gun in Manchuria dating from the 1200s, and an historian has identified a sculpture in Sichuan dating from the 1100s that appears to represent a figure with a firearm. Since all the other evidence also points to Chinese origins, it is safe to conclude that this was in fact the case.[1]

The earliest known formula for gunpowder can be found in a Chinese work dating probably from the 800s. The Chinese wasted little time in applying it to warfare, and they produced a variety of gunpowder weapons, including flamethrowers, rockets, bombs, and mines, before inventing firearms. "Firearms" (or "guns") for purposes of this book means gunpowder weapons that use the explosive force of the gunpowder to propel a projectile from a tube: cannons, muskets, and pistols are typical examples. Although there were many kinds of gunpowder weapons other than firearms, none ever rivaled firearms in importance.

Firearms remained in use in China throughout the following centuries. Meanwhile, gunpowder and firearms spread elsewhere very quickly. Gunpowder seems to have been widely known by the 1200s. The Europeans certainly had firearms by the first half of the 1300s. The Arabs obtained firearms in the 1300s too, and the Turks, Iranians, and Indians all got them no later than the 1400s, in each case directly or indirectly from the Europeans. The Koreans adopted firearms from the Chinese in the 1300s, but the Japanese did not acquire them until the 1500s, and then from the

Portuguese rather than from the Chinese. Firearms were known to other peoples, but few others manufactured them until fairly recent times.

Although firearms spread very far very quickly, three areas stand out for their success at producing and deploying firearms. Europe, of course, was one. The Ottoman empire was the second, although it might also be counted as a European power, geographically if not culturally. Japan was the third. The Japanese eagerly adopted firearms in the 1500s, even though they found no further use for them after Japan's unification in the 1600s.

When the Chinese came into contact with foreign firearms in the 1500s, they found those firearms to be far superior to their own – not only European firearms, in fact, but also Ottoman ones, and eventually even Japanese ones. One Chinese military manual, published in 1644, compared Chinese firearms to European and Ottoman muskets in the following terms:

> Firearms have been in use since the beginning of the dynasty, and field armies in battle formation have found them convenient and useful to carry along.... Since muskets have been transmitted to China, these weapons have lost their effectiveness.... In battle formation, aside from various cannon such as the three "generals," the breech-loading swivel gun, and the "hundred-league thunder," nothing has more range or power than the Ottoman musket. The next best is the European one.[2]

If the Europeans had been the only people to use firearms effectively, one might suspect that some unique aspect of European culture was responsible, but the Ottoman and Japanese experience complicates any speculation along these lines. It is not enough to identify some trait that was unique to Europe. There also has to be something that set Turkey apart from closely related societies in Egypt and Iran. There also has to be something that set Japan apart from closely related societies in Korea and China. Finally, these distinctions have to be linked to firearms in a way that could plausibly account for their use or neglect.

Once the question is posed, it becomes impossible to confine the answer to Europe and China alone. Europe was not the only latecomer, nor was it the only region where firearms were used effectively. Any answer to the question has to account not just for Europe and China but for the rest of the world as well.

So why was it the Europeans who perfected firearms when it was the Chinese who invented them?

As a preliminary matter, it should be clear that one prerequisite for firearms development was a certain level of technological sophistication, particularly in chemistry and metallurgy. It is no simple matter to make gunpowder pure enough to ignite and explode or gun barrels strong enough to withstand and direct that force. There were four regions of the world during these centuries that possessed the necessary technology for these purposes: Europe, the Middle East, India, and East Asia. Although not every area within these four regions boasted an equally high level of technology, each region did contain areas that did.[3]

It is often assumed that European technology was generally superior to that of the rest of the world. Although true enough for recent centuries, this assumption does not hold for the centuries when Europeans were actually gaining their superiority in firearms technology. The further back the assumption is pushed, the harder it is to reconcile with what we now know about the origins of firearms. If the Europeans had such a clear-cut technological superiority, why was it the Chinese who invented firearms in the first place? Technology may explain why the Europeans kept their lead, but not how they gained it.

Among those who recognize that Europe started behind and had to catch up, the most popular explanation seems to be political fragmentation. European powers were engaged in a continuous life-or-death struggle with each other, and this struggle impelled them to seek the best possible military technology. Unfortunately for this explanation, all the other areas that possessed similar levels of technology were also involved in more or less constant warfare, the principal exception being Japan after 1615. Although this does explain why the Japanese neglected firearms after 1615, it says nothing about other areas.[4]

The argument in this book picks up where the political fragmentation argument leaves off. Although nearly all the areas with the requisite technology experienced almost continual warfare during this period, that does not mean they all would have found firearms equally useful in those struggles. In particular, those areas that were most concerned with defending themselves against steppe and desert nomads had the least use for firearms. Early firearms were ineffective against steppe and desert nomads.

Of all the technologically advanced areas of the world, only western Europe and Japan did not face any threat from steppe or desert nomads, and it was those two areas where firearms developed most rapidly. Russia and the Ottoman empire faced this kind of threat on their eastern borders, though not on their western borders, and their development of firearms was slower. The Middle East, India, and China were preoccupied with the threat from the steppe or desert and tended to neglect firearms.[5]

It is easy to speak of Europe "starting behind" and "taking the lead," as if there were a worldwide race to develop firearms. However, there was no arms race either between the Europeans and the Chinese, or between the Indians and the Japanese. Neighbors like the Habsburgs and the Ottomans or the

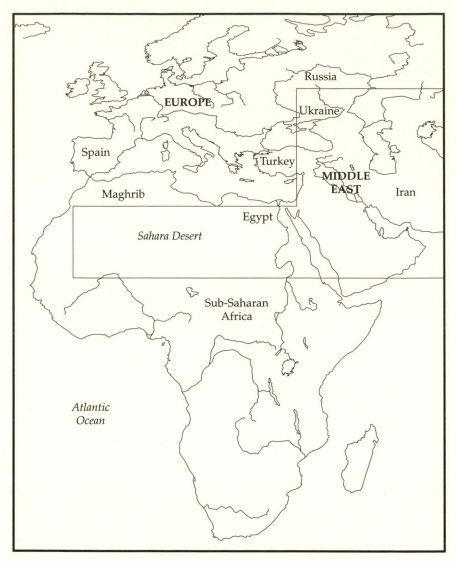

Map 1. "The Oikoumene" consists of the four regions marked in bold type – Europe, the Middle East, India, and East Asia – which possessed advanced technology at the time when firearms were invented. "The Arid Zone" is the outlined area – from Mongolia in the northeast to the Sahara Desert in the southwest – where there was generally too little rainfall to support agriculture.

Chinese and the Mongols each had their own separate rivalry, but the latter was not a race to get more and better firearms. Most places in the world had lost the firearms race long before they ever knew there was one.

Of course, no simple answer can account for all the complexity and variety in the historical record. Nor does there have to be one answer that will

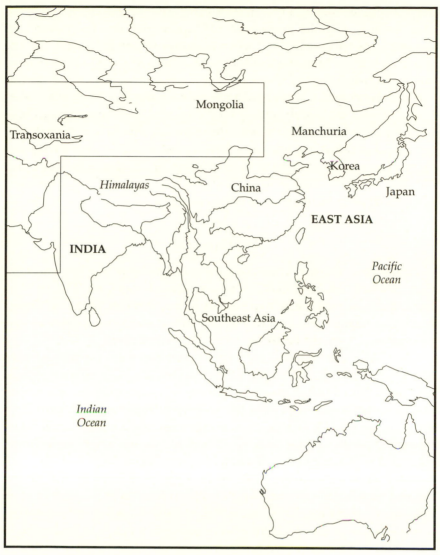

Map 1. (*continued*)

account for everything, because similar effects can have different causes.[6] However, the ineffectiveness of firearms against steppe and desert nomads goes a long way toward explaining why some areas of the world had more success than others in applying firearms technology. This book shows just how far this one argument brings us and what else is necessary to get us the rest of the way there.

The next section (The Oikoumene) deals with the issue of technology. The rest of this chapter discusses the interaction between nomads and their neighbors: how nomads lived on the steppe (The Steppe) and in the desert (The Desert); why the nomads of the steppe and the desert were not conquered by their richer and more populous neighbors (Logistics); and why people chose to fight nomads by some means (Cavalry) rather than by others (Firearms).

The other chapters of the book then trace the history of firearms as they spread around the world: starting where firearms were invented in China (Chapter 2), following them west as they were introduced in Europe (Chapter 3), and then tracking European firearms east again through Turkey and Egypt (Chapter 4) and Iran and India (Chapter 5) all the way back to China (Chapter 6) and beyond to Korea and Japan (Chapter 7). The conclusion (Chapter 8) takes the story up to the present day.

The Oikoumene

Certainly up to the year 1700 and even well after that, nearly all firearms were produced by inhabitants of four regions: Europe, the Middle East, India, and East Asia. These four regions formed a roughly crescent-shaped band from England to Japan (see map 1) that is sometimes known as "the Oikoumene," from the Greek for "the inhabited quarter."[7]

The Oikoumene was characterized by cities that were supported by the agricultural and pastoral surplus of the countryside. None of these regions was industrialized before 1700, and industry was responsible for only a small part of the economic output, but that industrial output set them apart from areas outside the Oikoumene, even though most of the inhabitants lived on farms and produced food. Not yet industrial but not simply agricultural, these civilizations might be referred to as "agrarianate."[8]

Large, dense populations were able to support specialists in writing and keeping records and accounts, which led to civilization in the sense of common literary traditions. In this sense there were perhaps four major civilizations in the Oikoumene when firearms were invented: Latin, Arabic, Sanskrit, and Chinese. That is to say, there were four established literary traditions that connected large numbers of people together and allowed the literate persons among them to exchange ideas across time and distance.

It is not entirely coincidental that we also find four major religions in the Oikoumene in this period: Christianity, Islam, Hinduism, and Buddhism. Each of these religions was linked to one of the literate traditions, although each one in its own way: Latin and Chinese had classical literatures that predated Christianity and Buddhism, for example, whereas Arabic and Sanskrit literature grew from the Qur'an and the Vedas. Except perhaps in China, religion probably shaped cultural identity more than did the associated literate tradition.

Speaking still in very general terms, it is also possible to identify each civilization and religion with one region of the Oikoumene in the 1100s. Europe was home to Latin and Christianity, as India was to Sanskrit and Hinduism – these regions are easy to label. The territory covered by Arabic and Islam was the most diverse, but its historical core was the land between the Nile and the Oxus Rivers, usually known as the Middle East. The territory covered by Chinese and Buddhism, including not only China but also Korea, Japan, and northern Vietnam, is generally known as East Asia.[9]

These were the four regions of the world in the 1100s with the technology needed for the production of firearms.[10]

Comparisons of technology between areas within the Oikoumene are more controversial. Theoretical science in the 1100s was probably more highly developed in Arabic civilization than anywhere else, as Arabic civilization drew upon and built upon both Greek and Indian science. Be that as it may, the marriage of science and technology so characteristic of the world today was a much later phenomenon. At least through the 1700s, if not later, technology advanced principally by trial and error, without much in the way of theoretical underpinnings.[10]

If Arabic civilization excelled in science, Chinese civilization excelled in mechanical technology. To the Muslims, who were in the best position to judge, the Greeks and the Indians were known for their philosophy, but the Chinese were famous for their artistry and their artisanry.[11] The Armenian monk Hetoum, writing just two decades before the first record of firearms in Europe, had the following to say about Chinese technology:

> And for very treuth, out of this realm of Cathay are brought many strange and meruelous thynges of subtyll labour and art ingenyous, wherby this peple well seme to be the moste subtell and inuentife of the world in arte and laboure of handes.[12]

To take the broadest possible view of things, it is safe to say that Europe lagged behind the other three civilizations in the Oikoumene in the year 1000 and had passed them all by the year 1800. The question of when exactly Europe did overtake each of the other three civilizations is highly contentious.[13] Without necessarily committing to a definite position on that issue, it is safe to say that the development of firearms was not determined by any general technological superiority on the part of Europe.

Very few people believe that Europeans possessed superior technology in the 1300s or 1400s, even those who believe that the roots of the Industrial Revolution can be traced back to those times. However, those two centuries are the most relevant time frame for the question at hand. European firearms already were quite clearly superior to those in any other part of the world, aside from the Ottoman empire, by the early 1500s (firearms not being introduced to Japan until 1542). Whatever happened had already happened by then.

What makes firearms so significant in the history of technology is not that they were symptomatic of some general European superiority, but rather that they were one of the very first items of technology in which Europeans did excel. Although Europe made tremendous progress in the 1300s and 1400s, very little of it represented anything that was unknown elsewhere. Europe was gaining ground on other regions, but it had not yet taken the lead. Optics (i.e., eyeglasses) and horology (i.e., clocks) are the two fields aside from gunnery where they were legitimately at the forefront in practical technology of universal application. This is all the more reason for giving close attention to firearms.[14]

Whatever the relative accomplishments of regions within the Oikoumene, they all enjoyed immense advantages over lands outside of it. At any given time after the rise of urban civilizations, some three fourths of the world's population resided within that arc from Europe through the Middle East and from India to East Asia. New ideas spread far more quickly within the Oikoumene than outside of it, firearms being a case in point. Isolated populations tend to be technologically backward precisely because they cannot benefit from other peoples' ideas. This disparity is highlighted in the initial contacts between peoples from inside and outside the Oikoumene – between Spaniards and Aztecs, for example.[15]

Sub-Saharan Africa lagged behind the Oikoumene in the necessary technology and perhaps in industrial organization as well. North and South America were even more isolated, and their metallurgical and chemical expertise was negligible, whatever their other accomplishments. The same goes for places like Australia and New Zealand. Even though some natives of these regions learned to use firearms effectively, they remained dependent on external sources of firearms and gunpowder.

Nevertheless, the development of firearms was a global phenomenon. It involved more than just the people of the Oikoumene. Even if the populations of Africa and the Americas did not produce firearms, they helped shape how firearms were used. This is all the more true for the nomads of the steppes and deserts bordering the Oikoumene.

The Steppe

Cutting through the middle of the Oikoumene is "the Arid Zone," stretching from the steppes of Mongolia to the deserts of North Africa.[16] The Arid Zone is shaped like a big backward Z (see map 1). From Mongolia, it extends west to the Ukraine, southeast into India, and west again all the way across North

Africa to the Atlantic Ocean. The northern half of the Arid Zone is largely steppe, an enormous expanse of rolling grassland broken up by a few large rivers and mountain ranges. The southern half is largely desert, including the largest desert of all, the Sahara. Both halves were inhabited by nomads.

When firearms were invented in the 1100s, none of the civilizations of the Oikoumene boasted stable unified empires. Latin Christendom never reunited after the fall of the Western Roman Empire. The Eastern Roman Empire had lost most of its territory, and Constantinople would be sacked by the Fourth Crusade in 1204. The Abbasid Caliphate had disintegrated into rival dynasties, with the caliph ruling little more than the city of Baghdad, if that. The Hindu kingdoms of northern India were worn down by two centuries of Turkish invaders, who would establish the Delhi sultanate in 1206. The Song dynasty lost north China to the Jurchens and was locked in a stalemate with them for the rest of the century. Japan was beginning its long slide from centralized aristocratic rule to decentralized warrior rule to all-out civil war.

By contrast, the nomads would reach the height of their power in the 1200s. The tribes of the steppe to the north of China were united in 1206 by a man named Temüjin, the son of a minor chieftain of the Mongol tribe. He took the title Chinggis Khan, popularly though inaccurately rendered as Genghis Khan. Chinggis Khan spent the remaining two decades of his life extending Mongol power in every direction, and his sons and grandsons continued his legacy. When Chinggis Khan's grandson Möngke became *khaghan* (emperor) in 1250, he inherited an empire that extended from north China and Korea across the steppe to Russia, and over the following decade he sent armies to the Middle East and south China.[17]

Although the Mongol empire itself failed to maintain centralized control past 1260, four branches of the family established successor *khanates* (kingdoms) that ruled over China, Transoxania, Iran, and Russia. Other areas within the Oikoumene like Turkey, Egypt, and northern India were ruled by Turkish dynasties of nomadic origin whose military power also rested on mounted archery. Except for western Europe (at the far western end), southern India (at the far southern end), and Japan (at the far eastern end), most of the Oikoumene came under the rule of nomads at some point over the course of the 1200s.

The Mongols were in many ways a product of their environment. The steppe was a harsh and forbidding land: "flat, empty, and desolate in every direction," according to one Chinese visitor in the early 1200s. There were few streams or rivers, and rainfall was irregular and light. The climate was frigid, the weather highly erratic; it sometimes snowed in the middle of the summer. Little grew there except the wild grass. The grass turned green in

May, grew thick in July, and withered by September. The seasonal rhythms of the grass affected the animals, which grew lean in the winters and fat in the summers.[18]

The Mongols relied on their flocks to convert the grass into food and raw materials. Without their animals they could not survive. The women looked after the oxen; the men, the horses and camels; and both sexes managed the sheep and goats. In the winter they camped down south, and in the summer they stayed up north. (Depending on the local topography, they might change altitude instead of latitude, migrating down into the plains or up into the mountains.) During the spring and autumn they traveled from one camp to the other, spending several months on the move to avoid overgrazing.

Because they were often on the move, the Mongols had no cities or even buildings. They lived in large tents, made of interwoven sticks covered with felt, which could reach thirty feet in diameter. When they struck camp, the tents were disassembled or else loaded on large wagons drawn by oxen or camels. The wagons and the flocks moved at no faster than a walking pace, covering just a few miles each day.

The Mongols spent much of their lives on horseback. "When I went back and forth on the steppe, I never saw a single person walking," wrote one Chinese emissary. Infants were tied with rope to a board, which was in turn tied behind the mother's saddle. At the age of three, they were tied to the saddle of their own horse. At the age of four or five they began to carry small bows and short arrows and to learn how to hunt.

Hunting was good training for warfare, not only for "the handling of the bow and the endurance of hardships," but also for the discipline and organization that characterized Mongol armies. For great hunts, the Mongols would send out scouts to locate the game, then send out more men to encircle it. They would spend one or two or even three months driving the game into a smaller and smaller area, taking care not to allow any animals to break through the ring, until it was time for the final slaughter.

The basic weapon for both hunting and warfare was the bow, and every man carried at least one, with several quivers of arrows. Some had swords, and some had lances, and the lances had hooks to drag other horsemen from their saddles. The men might be protected by armor, made from leather or iron or steel, but they generally did not use shields. Since the Mongols did not produce their own iron or steel, but acquired metal products through trade or plunder, their equipment varied in quality. Each man had a string of horses, and they all fought on horseback except under special circumstances.[19]

On campaign, the Mongols would not make a move without first sending out scouts in every direction. In battle, they used their speed and maneuverability to harass the enemy from long range with their bows. If this proved ineffective, they might feign flight to lure the enemy into an ambush. Sometimes they would withdraw from an area completely, then suddenly reappear after the enemy let down his guard. They would not close with the enemy until they were confident of victory.

Their harsh lifestyle made the Mongols incredibly tough. While away from the flocks, the warriors could subsist on dried milk and dried meat, drinking the blood of their horses and supplementing their rations by hunting, for long stretches of time, as long as there was grass and water for the horses. "I say to you with confidence," wrote William of Rubruck to Louis IX after visiting the Mongols in 1253, "if your peasants, I will not say Kings and knights, were willing to go as do the Kings of the Tartars and to be content with the same kind of food, they could take possession of the whole world."[20]

Survival on the steppe required cooperation, and the tribe was the basic building block of Mongol society. Each tribe migrated between pastures together, pitched its tents together, and herded its animals together. Tribes were united by common traditions and myths of common ancestry and were headed by a tribal chief who was chosen from the leading family in the tribe. Each tribe followed the same routes and used the same pastures year after year, subject to the vagaries of political rivalries and natural disasters.

Even if steppe nomads were entirely self-sufficient in the necessities of life, and it is not clear how often this was really the case, they needed agricultural goods to reduce their dependence on their flocks. Disease or weather could wipe out the resources of a tribe almost overnight. Moreover, those resources could not be increased beyond a certain point because pasturage limited the size of the flocks. Nomads could only diversify their risk and accumulate wealth by acquiring agricultural or industrial products through trade or warfare.

So tribes banded together into tribal confederations to bargain for more favorable trading conditions or to seize what they wanted by force. Successful leaders gained access to sources of agricultural or industrial products that in turn allowed them to grant or withhold patronage. Tribal confederations that failed to deliver the goods could collapse in spectacular fashion, but there was an evolving political tradition on the steppe that contributed to the formation of larger and more stable confederations over time.[21]

Even a successful tribal confederation like the one founded by Chinggis Khan must have been very small in absolute numbers. There were probably no more than two million people in all of Mongolia in 1206. Although the steppe could not support a large population, every man could serve as a soldier, because every man could ride a horse and use a bow, so the Mongols compensated for their small population with a very high mobilization rate. The women and children could manage the tents and the flocks on their own, if necessary, while the men were off at war.

When the nomads were not united, tribal rivalries must have significantly limited their mobility. One tribe could not travel through the pastures of another tribe without inviting attack. Nor could the warriors of one tribe strike deep into settled areas without leaving their own families and flocks vulnerable to raids from other tribes. Disunity made life much easier for their settled neighbors, who could play one tribe off against another.

When the nomads were united, however, their power increased exponentially. They were not tied down to the defense of any fixed positions. Only the capture or destruction of their flocks could force them to submit, and their flocks were far out on the open steppe where they were difficult to find. With the ability to choose the time and place they wished to fight, and to avoid battle under any but the most favorable circumstances, steppe nomads were very difficult to defeat.

The Desert

Desert nomads were different in important respects from their steppe cousins. Take the Bedouin of the Arabian Desert as an example.[22] Some Bedouin raised horses, sheep, cattle, and goats on the fringes of the desert, where there was some water and grass available for the flocks but where the land was unsuitable for agriculture. However, other Bedouin raised camels deep in the desert, where horses and sheep and cattle and goats cannot survive. The Tuaregs and other camel herders led a similar existence in the middle of the Sahara Desert.

Desert nomads were less self-sufficient than steppe nomads, since they relied entirely on just one animal for their livelihood. They were more likely to engage in trade for the items they could not produce themselves. They also tended to be fewer in number than steppe nomads, because the desert was even harsher than the steppe. They lived in smaller groups and had less experience in forming large stable tribal confederations. Generally speaking, they were less of a threat to their neighbors than steppe nomads were.[23]

Camels did not give desert nomads the same kind of advantage in combat as horses gave steppe nomads. It is possible to fight while mounted on a camel, but the rider is seated precariously high off the ground, and a camel will not charge like a horse. The Bedouin rode on camels, but generally speaking they fought on foot. When threatened, they would simply withdraw into the inaccessible regions of the deep desert, where it was impossible for cavalry on horses (never mind infantry) to follow.[24]

The Bedouin played little role in world history before the rise of Islam. They were responsible for one of the great feats of conquest in world history when they exploded out of the Arabian Peninsula to overrun everything between Spain and Transoxania in the 600s and 700s. However, they receded into obscurity again after the first couple of centuries of Islam, as the centers of power moved to cities like Cairo, Damascus, and Baghdad. Meanwhile, the caliphs lost control of most of the Arabian Peninsula outside of the holy cities.

The Tuaregs of the Sahara Desert were similar in this respect too. They had their moment in the 1000s, when they came out of the desert to conquer Morocco and found the Murabit dynasty. They even crossed the Straits of Gibraltar and saved the Muslims in Spain from defeat at the hands of the Christians. This dynasty lasted less than a century before it was overthrown. The Tuaregs raided the people on the margin of the desert in later centuries, but they did not conquer.

The camel herders of the deep desert shared with the Mongols the ability, when threatened, to withdraw far out of range of armies from agrarianate states. The Mongols and the Bedouin are both examples of what might be called "excluded nomads," nomads whose pastures lay outside of the bounds of civilization. The opposite of excluded nomads would be "enclosed nomads," whose pastures lay within the bounds of civilization, where they occupied land that was unsuitable for agriculture.[25]

If the Arid Zone is shaped like a big backward Z, then the top of the Z is steppe, home to excluded nomads like the Mongols. The line separating the steppe from the farmlands of Europe and China was fairly clear. The line might shift a little one way or another, and the border area itself could be fuzzy, but on one side there was enough rainfall to support agriculture, and on the other side there was not. Within China and Europe, the population was almost exclusively sedentary, and on the steppe, it was almost entirely nomadic.

The bottom of the Z is desert, particularly such large and inhospitable ones as the Arabian and Sahara Deserts, home to excluded nomads like the Bedouin and the Tuaregs. In this sense, the bottom of the Z is the mirror image of the top. However, these desert nomads did not play the same role in the history of firearms. Not only were camel herders not as dangerous as horse breeders, but the Red Sea separated the Bedouin from the Tuaregs, while the Mediterranean Sea prevented the Tuaregs from reaching areas of the Oikoumene outside of the Maghrib and Egypt.

The backward slash on the Z slices right through the heart of the agricultural regions of the Middle East. Except in a few small areas next to large bodies of water, like the southern coast of the Caspian Sea, there is little rainfall within this region. Most of the land, including mountains and plains and the fringes of the desert, was only suitable for pasturage, except where it could be irrigated. The nomads who inhabited this land were classic enclosed nomads.[26]

The largest cities in the Middle East were located along the major rivers, such as Cairo on the Nile and Baghdad on the Tigris, in places that had been the sites of cities and the centers of empires since ancient times. These islands of irrigated agriculture might support dense populations, but they were not very large. Even the largest cities were hardly more than a day's ride from mountains or plains or deserts. Because the land under cultivation was scattered throughout the areas devoted to pasturage, agricultural and pastoral communities lived side by side.[27]

Starting from the 900s, Turkish steppe nomads gradually migrated south and west into the Middle East – from the top of the Z to the backward slash, in other words. They settled particularly in areas like Anatolia, Azarbayjan, and Khurasan, where there was water and grass to support their flocks, sometimes displacing or assimilating the indigenous pastoralists, both sedentary and nomadic ones. They adapted to the demands of vertical migration (mountains in summer, valleys in winter) by using pack animals in place of wagons.[28]

The influx of Turks shifted the balance of power within Islamdom in favor of pastoral nomads, and specifically in favor of steppe nomads. This imbalance was confirmed by the Mongol conquests of the 1200s. From the 1000s up into the 1800s, practically every major Muslim dynasty as far west as North Africa and as far east as India was founded by Mongols or Turks. The Ayyubids in Egypt and Syria were Kurds, and the Safavids in Iran may or may not have been Iranians, but even they behaved in all relevant respects like Turks.

The Turks on the steppe could protect themselves at need by withdrawing from danger into inaccessible regions, but they gave up this option when they migrated off the steppe. This raises the question of how the Turks maintained their position in the Middle East for so long. How could they have avoided being overwhelmed by their sedentary neighbors? Three reasons in particular come to mind.

First, their control of livestock gave them the military advantages associated with the use of horses. Horses provided both speed and power on the battlefield.

Second, they could control the trade upon which the cities depended for their prosperity. The caravans that connected the cities into trading networks required beasts of burden, of which the nomads controlled the largest numbers, and they traveled far beyond the protection of the cities, where they had to rely on the protection or the forbearance of the nomadic tribes.

Third, cultivated lands were highly fragmented. Within the Middle East, there were few areas – Egypt, thanks to the Nile River, and Iraq, thanks to the Tigris and Euphrates Rivers, being the two outstanding examples – that could support large agricultural populations. It comes as no surprise that Cairo and Baghdad were always two of the largest cities in the region. Still, any ruler who wanted to expand beyond a single one of these islands of cultivated land would need to control the seas of uncultivated land around them. Only the nomads were capable of that.[29]

Where the survival of the dynasty rested on the allegiance of nomadic tribes, rulers necessarily had a different relationship to their cities. Nomadic rulers often camped outside their cities in preference to living within them. Some even pitched tents in the courtyards of their palaces rather than sleep indoors. Rulers were not indifferent to the loss of their cities, but the tribes could survive without the cities, whereas the dynasty could not survive without the tribes.

Thus, many cities in the Middle East had a strong citadel and weak walls. Rulers could not count on the loyalty of the inhabitants of the cities, although the inhabitants had little to gain from taking sides in political struggles, so the city walls were not always strongly defended. The citadel housed a small garrison whose loyalty was to the ruler and whose job was both to guard and to police the city.[30]

Conflicting loyalties of this sort led to the following exchange when the city elders of Damascus decided to surrender to besiegers in early 1401:

> [T]he viceroy of the Damascus citadel forbade them to do so, and threatened that if they did he would burn the city against them. They disregarded his words and said, "Rule over your citadel and we will rule over our city."[31]

The political and military dominance of the Turkish nomads gave rise to a sharp division of social roles, whereby Turks served as "men of the sword" and Iranians and Arabs as "men of the pen." The withdrawal of Iranians and Arabs from active participation in political and military affairs made the position of Turks all the more secure. Military forces were drawn largely from Turkish populations, and almost exclusively as either tribal forces or military slaves.[32]

So, although camel-herding desert nomads like the Bedouin and Tuaregs may not have been as dangerous as horse-breeding steppe nomads like the Mongols and Turks, the migration of Turks into the Middle East eventually brought Egypt, northern India, and even southern India within their reach – areas that otherwise were safely distant from the steppe.

Unfortunately for the inhabitants of the Oikoumene, their relationship with the steppe nomads was very one-sided. Although most of the Oikoumene was within easy striking distance for steppe nomads, it was not so easy for the people of the Oikoumene to strike back. The reason is simple: armies have to eat.

Logistics

People who do not produce their own food, whether workers or soldiers, can only survive where others produce enough food for them to eat. Large concentrations of soldiers will consume as much food as a small city – some armies during this period were probably as large as all but a handful of cities. Before the invention of railroads and trucks made it possible to transport food overland for long distances, cities and armies alike would draw on the agricultural output of the immediately surrounding countryside for most of their needs.

The total agricultural output within a given area would have been generally proportionate to population density. Unless an army would remain on garrison duty in the same place over a number of years, there did not have to be an agricultural *surplus* in the local economy. The soldiers could take what they needed and others would go hungry. There did have to be enough food to steal, though. A nineteenth-century Russian army commissary once reduced the problem to its simplest terms: an army could subsist entirely through foraging where population density exceeded ninety persons per square mile.[33]

The core areas of western Europe had a density of ninety persons per square mile, although places like Spain, Poland, and Russia undoubtedly fell short of that. High population densities were also found in the agricultural regions of China, although more so in the south than in the north, and in parts of India, particularly the coastal areas in the south and the Ganges River valley in the northeast. In the Middle East, where the Arid Zone intersected the Oikoumene, only the river valleys supported such dense populations.

Of course, population density does not tell the whole story. Food reserves were greatest immediately after the harvest, and smallest immediately before. An army could gather more food by spreading out over a wider area, but risked being surprised and defeated in detail. An army could also draw supplies from a wider area by moving from place to place, but it had to avoid staying in one area too long, passing through the same place twice, or entering territory another army had already passed through. Still, if there were no people, then there was no food.

Whether at rest or on the move, a large army could not survive long outside of agricultural lands. Nothing destroys an army faster than hunger, except thirst, and thirst is also an issue on the steppe and especially in the desert. Leaving aside thirst for the moment, an army could only survive on the steppe or in the desert if it brought its own food. How long it could stay there depended on how much food it could carry. To get an idea of what this meant in practice, it might be helpful to look at some numbers.

A soldier requires a minimum of about 3 pounds of rations per day to maintain his strength and health. A soldier can carry about 80 pounds of equipment and supplies for an extended period, so ten days' rations is a reasonable maximum, assuming 50 pounds for arms and armor and other equipment. Infantry in large bodies can march about 12 miles a day, so infantry alone without supply wagons or packhorses might be able to cover 120 miles before running out of supplies.

A stall-fed packhorse might consume 10 pounds of grass and 10 pounds of grain (barley or oats) each day and carry a burden of 250 pounds. A stall-fed warhorse might carry a greater burden but would require a proportionately greater amount of fodder. Assuming that grass is readily available for grazing, a horse might consume as much grain as it can carry in twenty-five days. Of course, if a packhorse consumes its entire load then there is not much point in bringing it along.[34]

A cavalryman with 50 or 75 pounds of equipment might weigh nearly as much as a horse could reasonably carry. A second horse might carry ten days' food and fodder (250 pounds, with the rider and two horses consuming 23 pounds each day) plus serve as a spare mount in case the first horse was injured. Large bodies of cavalry could travel somewhere between 18 and 30 miles a day, depending on the likelihood of meeting the enemy and the degree of caution required, or between 180 and 300 miles on ten days' supplies.[35]

So, assuming that grass and water are readily available, an army could carry enough food and fodder for about ten days without much of a supply train at all. This is a rough estimate, but a reasonable one. In a heavily populated agricultural region, foraging would bring in food and fodder, so if the average amount gathered equaled the average amount consumed, there would in effect be ten days' reserve for emergencies. An army might campaign indefinitely under those conditions, at least until the countryside was stripped bare or until the arrival of winter put an end to campaigning.

On the steppe, such an army would starve after ten days. It would have to turn back after five.

In the desert, the assumption that grass and water are readily available no longer holds, and the range of such an army drops precipitously. For each day in the desert, an additional 10 pounds of fodder would have to be carried for each horse, plus 80 pounds of water per horse and 5 pounds of water per person. This is why armies could not travel through the desert except along rivers or for very short periods of time. Infantry would have to turn back after just two days in the desert; cavalry, after just a single day.

Supply trains provide no simple solution. The men and horses in the supply train have to eat too. Pack horses consume 10 pounds each day and carry 250 pounds of supplies, or twenty-five times their daily consumption. Porters who consume 3 pounds each day and carry 75 pounds of supplies would be equally efficient.[36] Supply wagons are better: the driver and two horses would consume 23 pounds each day but the wagon might hold 1,400 pounds of supplies, or sixty times their daily consumption, depending on the efficiency of the harness and other factors. Supply wagons were restricted to relatively flat terrain, however. Ships and boats were far more efficient than even supply wagons, but they were even more restricted in where they could operate.

Imagine a platoon of thirty infantrymen marching out onto the steppe with one large supply wagon. After ten days, they exhaust their rations and turn to the supply wagon for more. They will find that the driver and the horses have consumed 230 pounds of the load, and that another 230 pounds have to be set aside for the driver and horses on the return trip. The remaining 940 pounds is just enough for each of the thirty infantrymen to fill his knapsack with the 30 pounds he can carry, and that in turn will last him just long enough to march back to where he started from.

Increasing the number of wagons runs quickly into the law of diminishing returns. One wagon will double the range of thirty infantrymen from 120 miles to 240 miles, or rather 200 miles with one day of rest in six for the horses. (Horses become permanently incapacitated without periodic rest.) To double it again to 400 miles requires not two wagons but actually *six* – one wagon for every five infantrymen, already the maximum likely to be found in practice.[37] The number of wagons will reach *thirty* – one wagon, one driver, and two horses for every infantryman – before the range doubles again.

So if there is one wagon for every five infantrymen, and enough grass and water along the march, then infantry can make a 400-mile round trip (i.e., 200 miles in each direction). Take away the grass and water, and its range drops to one-fifth of that. Naturally, these numbers are only rough estimates, but they suggest the order of magnitude. To put them in perspective, Russian armies faced a 600-mile round trip from Kiev to the Crimea and back, and Chinese armies faced a 1,600-mile round trip from Beijing to Outer Mongolia and back.

In practice, there were a couple ways to project force deep into the steppe. The first was to establish supply depots on the steppe where stockpiles might be built up. Such depots had to be protected, and their garrisons consumed supplies, but there would have to have been some source of water nearby anyway, so some limited agriculture might have been possible. The Chinese had such a depot at Kaiping, some 150 miles north of Beijing. Supply wagons could be sent out in relays from the depot to meet the armies at specified rendezvous points, as the Chinese did during the 1410 and 1414 campaigns in

Outer Mongolia. On the other hand, if they missed the rendezvous point, as they did in 1410, the consequences could be dire. Furthermore, maintaining such depots was very expensive.[38]

The second was to employ steppe auxiliaries. The Russians made use of Cossacks, and the Chinese went to great lengths to attract Mongols. Such auxiliaries contributed more than just soldiers, as important as those soldiers undoubtedly were. They also contributed animals. Marco Polo commented that Mongol horses "will subsist entirely on the grass of the plains, so that there is no need to carry store of barley or straw or oats."[39] The effective range of agrarianate armies shoots way up if the horses that transport their grain do not eat 10 pounds of it each day. Pasture-fed horses come close to providing friction-free transportation on the steppe. Herds of cattle or sheep could also provide "meat on the hoof" at little extra cost. However, auxiliaries could be expensive too, and it was not easy to police the auxiliaries or to ensure their obedience.

Nomads had their own problems, to be sure. Still, they were at home on the steppe. So long as they could keep their flocks out of harm's way, they could afford to avoid combat until invaders ran out of supplies and returned home. Agrarianate states could only attack them at great cost and sacrifice, and short-term gains seldom translated into long-term advantages. The steppe could not be occupied by an army that was not itself composed of nomads because there was no way such an army could feed itself. Meanwhile, the nomads profited from their raids on settled lands, and nothing prevented the nomads from occupying settled lands.

Being subject to attack at any time by cavalry and being unable to strike back with infantry, the people of the Oikoumene faced a difficult dilemma. They could adopt a passive defense with infantry, pursue an active defense with cavalry, or go over to the offense with cavalry. The passive defense was the least effective, but the other options required fielding cavalry that could hold its own with that of the steppe and desert nomads.

Cavalry

The invention of the chariot sometime in the second millennium B.C. first gave the inhabitants of the steppe the speed and mobility that would be their greatest weapon. The infantry of the Oikoumene were helpless against them. Charioteers overran centers of civilization from Egypt to Mesopotamia to India to China, roughly the same areas that marked the maximum range of the steppe nomads in later periods. Eventually, the peoples within these areas had no choice but to take up chariots to protect themselves.[40]

Chariots began to give way to cavalry between the eleventh and ninth centuries B.C. Cavalry was cheaper to maintain, not requiring a chariot or driver, and it could traverse terrain that was too rough for chariots. Horse-riding steppe nomads moved into the Middle East in subsequent centuries: the Medes destroyed Nineveh in 606 B.C., and the Persians conquered Babylon in 539 B.C. Those peoples who were not conquered by cavalry adopted it in self-defense. In China, the traditional date for the transition from chariots is 307 B.C., when King Wuling of Zhao announced his intention to teach the common people "barbarian dress and horse archery" – barbarian dress because it was more convenient for riding and shooting.[41]

The Parthians moved off the steppe into Iran and Iraq in the third century B.C., displacing the successors to Alexander the Great. The Parthians were renowned as mounted archers, and they gave their name to the "Parthian shot," a rearward shot by a fleeing mounted archer, one of the staples of steppe warfare. In 53 B.C., Parthian horse archers harassed and destroyed the Roman legions under Crassus in the desert at Carrhae, bringing a halt to Roman expansion eastward.

But Carrhae was also where the Romans got their first look at Parthian heavy cavalry. These men wore iron helmets and scale armor and carried spears; they rode powerful horses that could support the weight of armor for both their riders and themselves. The heavy cavalry could finish off the enemy after the horse archers had softened up their ranks. This style of heavy cavalry was passed on to the Sassanids, the successors to the Parthians in Iran in the third century A.D., and from them to the Eastern Roman (or Byzantine) empire in the fourth century.

Between the fourth and sixth centuries, the Roman infantry legions gradually declined as the Byzantine empire came under attack by nomads from the north, the east, and the south. Meanwhile, both Sassanid and Byzantine heavy cavalry started to carry bows and arrows in addition to spears and swords. These armored horsemen could withstand the arrows of the light cavalry of the steppe nomads, return fire with their own bows, and seize the decisive moment to charge and put the enemy to flight.[42]

The knight of western Europe was one offshoot of this line of evolution, but he did not have to fight the fast-moving light cavalry of the steppe nomads, so he could wear heavier armor and dispense with the bow. Between battles, the knight did not move as part of a body of cavalry, but instead traveled with a small group of servants, some of them on foot. Everything possible was done to bring the knight into range to deliver the decisive charge without exhausting him or his horse: he rode a different horse to the battlefield and had a servant carry his armor and lance for him.[43]

The *mamluks* of Egypt at the time of the Crusades were heavily armed and highly trained, both with the lance and with the bow, but their original mission was to fight nomadic light cavalry. They were expected to meet high standards on the archery field and outshoot the nomads from horseback at long range on the battlefield. If the nomads tried to close the range, they became vulnerable to a sudden charge by the *mamluks*, whose armor and weapons gave them the advantage in hand-to-hand fighting.[44]

At the other end of the Oikoumene, the northern and southern dynasties of fourth-century China organized their armies around heavily armored men, carrying lances and swords and riding heavily armored horses, equipped to prevail over infantry (and each other) in hand-to-hand fighting. After China was reunified in 589, and steppe nomads again became the primary concern, this heavy cavalry was modified to deal with the light cavalry of the Turks. The men still wore some armor, but horse armor was abandoned, and more men carried bows.[45]

For fighting within densely settled agricultural areas, where mobility conferred less of an advantage, cavalry tended to carry the heaviest arms and armor possible. In fourth-century China, this was equally true for the northern dynasties, ruled by steppe nomads, and the southern dynasties, ruled by Chinese emperors. On the other hand, European knights lightened their equipment and modified their tactics when they left Europe to fight on the Crusades, even incorporating some mounted archers (the so-called Turcopoles) in their ranks.[46]

To generalize, steppe nomads fought as light cavalry and agrarianate soldiers as heavy cavalry. Light cavalry rode smaller horses, carried lighter equipment, and skirmished at long range; heavy cavalry rode larger horses, carried heavier equipment, and fought hand to hand. The previous descriptions of both steppe nomads and agrarianate cavalry should not be taken to mean that the one fought *exclusively* as light cavalry and the other fought *exclusively* as heavy cavalry. However, the tendency was very strong.

Light and heavy cavalry were ranges of options and not fixed types, so inevitably there was some blurring of the lines in practice. For example, if the knights of Europe and the horsemen of fourth-century China were heavy cavalry, then the *mamluks* of Egypt might be better described as medium-heavy cavalry. Conversely, if the apparently unarmored Chinese or Mongol horse archer in Figure 2.1 represents light cavalry, then the Turkish horsemen with their shields and helmets in Figure 5.1 might be better described as medium-light cavalry.[47]

Still, when all is said and done, there was a clear choice to be made between fielding more heavy cavalry and fielding more light cavalry, and the choice had less to do with cultural traditions than with ecological constraints and economic trade-offs. There are many examples of nomads who conquered agrarianate kingdoms and chose heavy cavalry. Grain was cheap, so they bred larger horses; iron was cheap, so they took to wearing armor. The

Parthians in Iran, the Arabs in Spain, the Turks in India, and the Mongols in China, among others, made this choice.[48]

For steppe nomads, horses are cheap and men are expensive. Pastoral nomads need horses for herding the flocks on which they depend for survival, so horses are a necessary part of the production of wealth – they do not compete with people for resources. Herding and hunting train them for use as cavalry mounts. On the other hand, it takes so much land to support one animal and so many animals to support one person that population density on the steppe is very low and population size is generally small.

For agrarianate civilizations, men are cheap and horses are expensive. Draught horses are useless as cavalry mounts, and riding horses are a luxury item. The same land that supplies one horse with fodder can provide several people with food, and additional people can produce goods through industry even without further inputs of arable land. The opportunity cost of raising a horse that can double as a cavalry mount is very high in farming areas and near zero on the steppe.

Nomads graze their horses, so their horses tend to be smaller. The size of the horse is constrained by the amount of time it would have to spend grazing during the winter in order to survive. If the horse grows too large it will need more food than it can easily find. Steppe ponies need little attention, so nomads can raise large herds with little effort, allowing them to change mounts frequently and travel long distances without exhausting their horses.

Agrarianate civilizations can economize on land by growing more intensive fodder crops and bringing the fodder to their horses. Stall-fed horses will grow larger if fed regularly, but they become dependent on the extra fodder. Their need for extra fodder limits their range by tying them to baggage trains or supply depots. Settled populations have too few horses to supply their cavalry with many spare mounts, so their horses cannot be ridden too long or too hard either.

Small horses cannot bear the weight of a heavily armored horseman. Nomads have no industry to produce armor anyway, at least not of metal. They do make excellent recurved composite bows from horn and sinew, and they get plenty of practice hunting with them. Because they lack armor and cannot easily replace losses, they avoid taking unnecessary risks, skirmishing with their bows until they discover a weakness, and only closing when they sense vulnerability.[49]

Large horses may be strong enough to carry armor of their own in addition to the weight of a heavily armed and armored rider. Agrarianate civilizations can produce all the armor and weapons their cavalry can use. Their cavalry can replace losses more easily, and usually is better protected, so it seeks out opportunities for hand-to-hand combat. Stronger horses put more force behind a sword or a lance, and the cavalry charge is as natural to their cavalry as the feigned retreat is to the nomads'.

Whatever the strengths and weaknesses of light versus heavy cavalry, only cavalry had the mobility to patrol the border, respond to alarms, reinforce sectors under attack, head off nomads before they broke through the border defenses, and pursue them as they retreated back onto the steppe. Infantry could not react as quickly. Since the nomads were likely to refuse combat and retreat into the steppe if the odds were not in their favor, they had to be trapped and forced into battle. Infantry could hold fixed positions at passes or fords to try to hem them in, but only cavalry could run them down and force them to fight.

So long as nomads avoided combat with infantry, it made little difference whether or not the infantry carried firearms.[50] Unfortunately, early firearms did little to help cavalry either, because early firearms could not be used on horseback. Early firearms were exclusively infantry weapons.

Firearms

Modern firearms are truly amazing. The standard-issue U.S. Army rifle, the M-16, fires over 10 rounds of 5.56mm ammunition *per second* on full automatic, with an effective range of over 600 yards. The M-61, a six-barreled Gatling gun, fires a mind-boggling 100 rounds of 20mm ammunition *per second*. The MK-19 fires 40mm high explosive armor-piercing grenades out to an effective range of nearly a mile and still manages a rate of fire of six rounds *per second*. The M109A6 Paladin self-propelled howitzer shoots 155mm shells out to a range of over eighteen miles with the help of an inertial positioning and navigation system linked to its computerized automatic fire control system. With weapons like these as the implicit frame of reference, it is no wonder if the deliberate neglect of firearms in the past appears inexplicable.

Early firearms were nothing at all like that.

Fifteenth-century cannon were unwieldy, unreliable, inaccurate, and all but immobile. It could take hours to load and fire a single shot, which may not have been a bad thing for the gunners, who risked being blown up each time they applied the match. Cannon were unlikely to hit anything much smaller than a city wall, but they were pretty much limited to shooting at stationary targets anyway, since it took so long to drag them into position. Large cannon weighed thousands of pounds and required dozens of horses to haul them around. Sometimes it was easier to transport the raw metal, build a furnace just outside a besieged city, cast the cannon on the spot where they would be used, and later melt them down again for future use elsewhere. Clearly, such weapons were limited to use as siege artillery, or else on ships, where weight was less of an issue. However, cannon did have one big advantage over catapults: the cannonball traveled on a flatter trajectory than a projectile thrown from a catapult and so imparted more force to a vertical target like a wall.

Fifteenth-century muskets shared some of the same drawbacks. Although a skilled archer could shoot six or more arrows in a minute, a musket took at least that long to get off a single shot. The musket was less accurate than a bow as well, so its effective range was shorter, and it could not be reloaded on horseback, whereas horse archers could ride and shoot at the same time. The musket could penetrate thicker armor, but its greatest advantage over the bow was that it was easy to learn: it took a week of simple training to produce a musketeer, but years of constant practice to produce an archer.[51] As the Chinese work from 1644 quoted earlier put it:

> The bow and arrow are only able to hit the mark and kill the enemy if one has both skill and strength. The gun contains skill and strength itself, completely independent of the person. The stock and the sight supply the skill, and the long barrel and the pure powder supply the strength. Just get someone to wield the gun and you know that the skill and strength are present.[52]

The point is not just that early firearms were primitive, but that they were primitive in ways that made them marginally useful for certain purposes and completely useless for others. Specifically, early cannon were marginally useful for siege warfare, early muskets were marginally useful for infantry warfare, and both were completely useless for cavalry warfare. Given what was said about cannon already, it should be obvious why they were restricted to siege warfare. However, it may be worthwhile to explain in more detail why muskets were restricted to infantry warfare.

What I call a musket in this book actually refers to two slightly different weapons. The "arquebus" came into use in the late 1400s, the "musket" in the early 1500s. Although the musket was heavier and more powerful – it was usually fired from a Y-shaped rest – they were otherwise very similar. Eventually the two weapons became indistinguishable, the musket having lost its Y-shaped rest, and they were known indiscriminately as muskets. Anyway, up to around 1700, most muskets shared two traits in common: they were matchlocks and they were smoothbores.[53]

The lock was the mechanism that ignited the gunpowder. In the case of a matchlock, the lock mechanism held a two- or three-foot length of smoldering rope, the "match." Pulling the trigger lowered the match into the priming pan, on the outside of the barrel, and ignited the priming powder. The priming powder in turn ignited the gunpowder inside the barrel that propelled the bullet. The lock was one of the three essential parts of the gun – lock, stock, and barrel.

The matchlock was sturdy but awkward. The match had to be detached while the gun was being loaded to avoid accidentally igniting the gunpowder. The match was kept lit at both ends, in case one end went out, so one end would be held between the pinkie and ring fingers of the left hand, and the other end between the ring and middle fingers of the same hand. Soldiers followed elaborate procedures to keep the match always as far from the gunpowder as possible.[54]

Specifically, after firing his musket, a soldier had to (1) hold the gun up with his left hand, (2) remove the match from the lock with his right hand, (3) put the end of the match back in his left hand, (4) blow any sparks out of the priming pan, (5) put priming powder in the pan, (6) shut the pan, (7) shake any powder off the lid of the pan, (8) blow any remaining powder off the lid of the pan, (9) pick up the gun in both hands, (10) transfer the gun to his left side, (11) open a flask with his right hand, (12) insert the powder and bullet into the muzzle, (13) draw the ramrod out of the stock, (14) adjust his grip on the ramrod, (15) ram home the bullet and powder, (16) pull out the ramrod, (17) adjust his grip on the ramrod, (18) return the ramrod to the stock, (19) hold the gun up with his left hand, (20) grasp the gun with his right hand, (21) transfer the gun to his right side, (22) take one end of the match in his right hand, (23) blow on the match, (24) insert the match in the lock, (25) adjust the match in the lock, (26) blow on the match again, and (27) level the gun, before he could finally (28) pull the trigger again.

These twenty-eight steps are taken from *The Exercise of Armes for Calivres, Muskettes, and Pikes*, a drill manual published by Jacob de Gheyn in the Netherlands in 1607.[55] The point of a drill manual was to make this complicated procedure as mechanical as possible. Soldiers were drilled until the procedure became second nature. Nevertheless, it was very hard to run through the entire procedure in less than a minute.

All the while, the soldier was engaged in a dangerous juggling act. One moment he was holding the gun and both ends of the lit match with one hand while pouring gunpowder into the muzzle with the other. The next moment he was holding the gun on the other side of his body and blowing on the match to keep it lit while trying to keep any sparks from falling onto the priming pan. Nearly every step required both hands.

Now imagine trying to run through those twenty-eight steps – shifting the gun from one side to the other, detaching and reattaching the match, pouring gunpowder into the muzzle – while bouncing up and down on a galloping horse, in the equivalent of a twenty or thirty mile per hour wind, without holding the reins. That is why, for all intents and purposes, it was impossible to load a matchlock on horseback.[56]

In addition to being a matchlock, the musket was also a smoothbore, meaning that there were no grooves inside the gun barrel. A rifle has grooves that impart a predictable spin to the bullet, greatly increasing its accuracy. Although a smoothbore has no grooves, it also imparts a spin to the bullet, but the spin is basically random, so the effect is to send the bullet off randomly. Accuracy is a function of where the gun is aimed and whether the bullet lands on the spot where the gun is aimed, but the shooter can only control where the gun is aimed. If the bullet could stray 5 feet off target, as it might if shot from a smoothbore musket at 200 feet, then good marksmanship is irrelevant. The question instead becomes "How many other targets are within 5 feet of where the gun is pointed?" If the gun is fired into a crowd, the bullet could easily hit someone; if the target is an individual, it will almost always miss. That is why muskets were best against large bodies of infantry packed together in tight formations.[57]

This all goes to show why cannon and muskets were largely restricted to siege warfare and infantry warfare. However, siege operations and infantry formations were not characteristic of warfare everywhere. Steppe and desert nomads had no cities or castles whose walls would be vulnerable to cannon, and their fast-moving cavalry armies could not be pinned down by infantry. Of course, better firearms – lighter, handier, more accurate ones – would eventually shift the balance of power in favor of those agrarianate and industrial states that could produce them. Those who came up with better firearms gained an advantage not only over each other but also over the steppe and desert nomads. Nevertheless, the limitations of early firearms affected not only the incentive to use them but also the incentive to improve them.

The analogy between the development of technology and the evolution of organisms is inexact, but instructive. Although evolution is blind, it is usually hard to predict just how a piece of technology will prove most useful and to guide its development in that direction. In the vast majority of cases, technology advances through trial and error. Slow cumulative improvement is the norm.[58] Critics of Darwin pointed to complex organs like eyes to refute the theory of evolution: How could something so complicated evolve through blind chance? Supporters of Darwin responded by pointing to some survival benefit for the organism at each intermediate stage. The survival benefit at any intermediate stage need not be the same as the benefit at the final stage, but there has to be one.[59]

The same point can be made for technology like firearms. The longer the lead time before the technology starts to pay off, the greater the initial investment required and the less likely that it will be made. There has to be some intermediate or short-term payoff. In places like Europe and Japan, firearms could be put to good use right away. Each small incremental improvement made the weapons that much more effective against infantry formations, castle walls, or ships. This was enough incentive to drive innovation. In places like Iran or China, the immediate incentives were too weak and the distant ones too remote. In the meanwhile, the intermediate steps in that development offered no significant additional security against the threat from nomads.

The nomads would finally lose their military edge thanks in no small part to the development of firearms, but it was by no means obvious at the beginning that that would happen. Maybe the inventors of firearms in the 1100s dreamt of the day when a soldier on horseback could shoot a firearm with the same range, accuracy, reliability, and rate of fire as a bow, but rifles only matched bows in terms of range, accuracy, and reliability in the 1700s, and not in terms of rate of fire until the 1800s. Maybe those inventors dreamt of flying machines that could obliterate cities too – from their perspective, these were not much further off in the future than breech-loading repeating rifles. This is not to say that people never pursue distant goals, only that they seldom pursue them with the same intensity they do closer ones.

It was no more than a coincidence that firearms were invented at the same time that nomads reached the height of their power, because the early firearms were almost useless against them. What I argue here is in fact almost the reverse: that nomads discouraged the development of firearms in the areas that they ruled or threatened. It is not that nomads deliberately discouraged firearms, that they feared them and tried to keep them out of the hands of their subjects or their enemies: the Mongols were very keen at adopting new weapons,[60] and they had no reason to fear firearms in particular. But the people who wanted to fight nomads found firearms of little help.

The balance shifted decisively once firearms became as handy and as accurate as even the best bows. The 1700s and 1800s saw the agrarianate and then the industrial civilizations extend their power over the steppes at the expense of the nomads – a development that benefited America and Russia more than anyone else and helped make world powers of both of them. The telegraph and the railroad completed the conquest of the steppes by nullifying the superior mobility of the nomads, their only remaining advantage over the infantry armies of agrarianate and industrial states.

This book is the story of the first stage in this dynamic, before the balance had shifted to the agrarianate civilizations, when nomads still ruled the steppes and cast a long shadow over neighboring lands.

2

China to 1500

China might broadly be divided into two regions based on its two major river systems: the Yellow River valley in the north and the Yangzi River valley in the south. The ancient political and cultural centers were concentrated in the north, but over the centuries the population and the economy shifted to the south. By 1250, the population of south China probably exceeded that of north China, and the largest (and richest) cities in the world were located in the south, starting with the city of Hangzhou with a population of more than one million.[1]

Thanks to the monsoon winds that blow off the ocean from the southeast in the summertime, south China has enough water for intensive rice agriculture. The climate becomes drier and the rainfall more erratic as one moves north. North China is characterized by extensive cultivation of wheat, barley, millet, and sorghum. Farther north still, on the Mongolian steppe, there is insufficient rain to support agriculture, and the land is better suited for grazing livestock.[2]

Since China was unified under the first Qin emperor in 221 B.C., periods of unity alternated with periods of disunity. The first period of unity lasted from 221 B.C. to A.D. 220, the same time that the Roman republic and empire ruled much of Europe. The second lasted from 589 to 756, the same time that Islam was spreading over the lands between Spain and Transoxania. The third lasted from 960 to 1127. Political unity became the norm in Chinese history only after the Mongols imposed it again in 1276.

Periods of unity in China were linked to periods of unity on the steppe to the north of China. For example, the unification of China in 221 B.C. was followed by the unification of the steppe under the Xiongnu, whereas the unification of China in 589 was preceded by the unification of the steppe under the Turks. On the other hand, disunity within China was typically

28

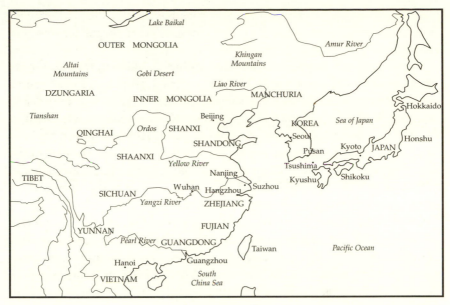

Map 2. East Asia

accompanied by the rise of powerful non-Chinese dynasties in the border-lands of Inner Mongolia and Manchuria. Such dynasties often ruled parts of both China and the steppe, keeping the steppe nomads divided and relegating Chinese dynasties to the south.[3]

In the late 1100s, the latter pattern prevailed. The Jurchen Jin dynasty ruled Manchuria and north China, the Chinese Song dynasty ruled south China, and the steppe was divided. The Jurchens were a Manchurian people, not nomads themselves but still relatively savvy at steppe politics. Neverthe-less, the Jurchens were unable to prevent Chinggis Khan from uniting the Mongols in 1206. However, the unification of the Mongols did not prompt the unification of China under a Chinese dynasty. Instead, the Mongols broke with the past by conquering first north China in 1234 and then south China in 1276. The Mongol Yuan dynasty became the first non-Chinese dynasty to rule all of China.

Even after the Ming dynasty brought China back under Chinese rule in 1368, Mongol-Chinese relations were profoundly affected by the expe-rience of the Mongol conquest. Ming officials subscribed wholeheartedly to the most exaggerated stereotypes of nomad behavior and motivation. They frequently likened the Mongols to wild animals with insatiable ap-petites, who could neither be reasoned with nor satisfied. Mongols were "dogs and sheep," "fierce and wild"; there was "no difference between them and birds and beasts," they were "people on the outside, but wild animals at heart."[4] For their part, the Mongols never forgot their former glory.[5]

The Chinese classics in the dominant Confucian-Mencian tradition stress the attraction of the virtuous ruler. Less civilized peoples are expected to admire the virtue of the ruler and submit voluntarily to his rule in order to share in the blessings thereof. This ideology was particularly influential in shaping government policy toward the population in times of unrest. Military force was seen as a last resort and an admission of failure on the part of the ruler. However, few if any Ming officials believed that the Mongols could be swayed by virtue, and the rhetorical dehumanization of the Mongols was partly a reaction to their baffling intransigence.

On the other hand, the transformative power of Chinese civilization was felt throughout the eastern end of the Oikoumene. The culture and institutions of the Tang dynasty were superimposed on Korean and Japanese society with unpredictable but fruitful results. The Koreans wrote largely in classical Chinese; the Japanese, sometimes in classical Chinese but usually in Japanese with a mixture of Chinese characters and phonetic symbols derived from Chinese characters. Buddhism and Confucianism became integral features of Korean and Japanese culture.

Chinese material civilization had an influence far beyond the eastern end of the Oikoumene. In historical times, at least up through the 1200s, more technology of universal application appeared first in China than anywhere else. The Chinese genius for invention was not confined to peaceful pursuits either. It is particularly noteworthy that the Chinese invented the crossbow and the trebuchet, missile weapons suitable for infantry and siege warfare and predecessors in terms of function to muskets and cannon.[6]

There is a myth that the Chinese were not interested in weapons, that they discovered gunpowder but only used it for firecrackers. Nothing could be further from the truth. The Chinese experimented with all kinds of gunpowder weapons, from flamethrowers and rockets to bombs and landmines. When they eventually discovered how to adjust the formula to create more of an explosive effect than an incendiary one, and how to control that explosive effect to propel a projectile from a tube, the first firearms were born.

The Invention of Firearms

Gunpowder is one of the earliest technologies for storing, transporting, and applying energy. The sword relies on the strength of the arm wielding it. The lance is driven by the power of the horse beneath it. The bow stores energy gradually and releases it quickly, but it only stores energy temporarily. The same goes for the crossbow and the trebuchet. Mills could harness wind and water power but not store it; dams could store water power but not transport it. Wood and coal stored energy but released it as heat, which could not be used to perform work before the invention of the steam engine. If the shift from muscular to chemical power is one of the hallmarks of modern life, then gunpowder is one of the first "modern" inventions.

Up through the second half of the 1800s, gunpowder meant "black powder," a mixture of saltpeter, sulfur, and charcoal. Saltpeter is the critical ingredient for dating the discovery of gunpowder. Saltpeter was produced in ancient times, but not necessarily, and only then by chance, in its pure form. A Chinese alchemical text from 492 noted that saltpeter gave off a purple flame when ignited, providing for the first time a practical and reliable means of distinguishing it from other inorganic salts. This made it possible to evaluate and compare purification techniques. By contrast, the earliest Arabic and Latin descriptions of the purification of saltpeter do not appear until the 1200s.[7]

The discovery of gunpowder was the product of further centuries of alchemical experimentation. The first reference to gunpowder is probably a passage in the *Zhenyuan miaodao yaolüe*, a Daoist text that is tentatively dated to the mid-800s. The earliest surviving formulas for gunpowder can be found in the *Wujing zongyao*, a military work from around 1040. The three formulas in that work contain at most around 50 percent saltpeter, not enough to create an explosion but enough to be highly incendiary. The optimal formula for explosive gunpowder contains about 75 percent saltpeter, 15 percent sulfur, and 10 percent charcoal. Experimenting with different levels of saltpeter content eventually produced bombs, grenades, and mines, and fire-arrows got a new lease on life thanks to new incendiary compounds.[8]

Control the direction of an incendiary device and the result is a flame-thrower. (Reverse the direction of the flame and the result is a rocket.[9]) The earliest evidence of a gunpowder weapon anywhere in the world, even earlier than the formulas in the *Wujing zongyao*, is probably the illustration of a flamethrower on a tenth-century painted silk banner from northwest China. There is literary evidence that Chinese soldiers used fire-lances, which were spears with a flamethrower attached next to the spearhead, against the Jurchens at the siege of De'an in 1132, but the fire-lance was certainly much older.

The fire-lance was the direct ancestor of the firearm in two important ways. First, small projectiles were sometimes placed in the barrel so that they would fly out together with the flames. Most of the explosive force of the gunpowder would have been expended on the flames, but the idea of channeling more of that force into propelling a projectile would have followed in due course. Second, the original paper or bamboo barrels came to be replaced by metal barrels. A metal barrel is able to withstand more pressure, allowing a more explosive (less incendiary) charge to be used, allowing still more force to be channeled into propulsion. A fire-lance with a metal barrel and just one projectile is very close to a true firearm.

The earliest true firearms may well date from as early as the first half of the 1100s. The evidence comes from sculptures in a Buddhist cave temple in Sichuan. The figures are supernatural, but the weapons they carry are recognizable, such as swords, spears, and, in one case, a bomb with a lit fuse. One sculpture shows a demon holding a vase-shaped bombard with flames and a cannonball coming out of it. This shape is very typical for early cannon, including the earliest firearm depicted in Europe, which dates from 1326. The earliest inscription in the cave dates from 1128, but even the later inscriptions all date from the 1100s, so this sculpture precedes the earliest European depiction of a firearm by at least 125 years, and perhaps by as much as 200 years.[10]

The earliest firearm surviving today is a bronze gun that was discovered by archeologists in Manchuria in 1970. It consists of a barrel 6.9 inches long and 1 inch in diameter, a chamber for the gunpowder 2.6 inches in diameter, and a trumpet-shaped socket for the handle. It would have been mounted on a long wooden handle; without the handle it is 13.4 inches long and weighs 7.8 pounds. This gun was buried together with bronze artifacts in the style of the Jurchen Jin dynasty, which came to an end in 1234, and it was found near the site of battles that were fought in 1287 and 1288, where gunpowder weapons are known to have been used. From this evidence, it can be dated with some confidence as no later than the year 1288, almost forty years before the earliest evidence of firearms in Europe.[11]

If the threat from steppe nomads inhibited the development of firearms, why were firearms invented in China in the first place? China suffered from long periods of disunity during which there was some immediate use for infantry and siege weapons. Whenever different regions within China were fighting each other, even when some of those regions were controlled by steppe nomads, the geographic conditions were much like those in Europe. Rival powers fought for control of walled cities and the surrounding farmlands, just as they did in Europe.

The crossbow and the trebuchet were both invented before the unification of China in 221 B.C. The rise of heavy cavalry in fourth-century China coincided with one long period of disunity, from 220 to 589. The discovery of gunpowder in the 800s coincided with another such period, from 756 to 960. The invention of firearms in the 1100s coincided with a third such period, from 1127 to 1276. In the case of gunpowder, the timing may have been fortuitous, but its immediate application to weaponry was not, nor was the subsequent invention of firearms.

It was the Mongols who ended the third of these long periods of disunity by conquering first north China in 1234 and then south China in 1276. They ruled over all of China for less than a century before the dynasty they founded, the Yuan dynasty, began to collapse. The fighting that accompanied the fall of the Yuan and the rise of the Ming provided one more opportunity, albeit only a brief one, for infantry weapons like firearms.

The Rise of the Ming

The Yellow River overflowed its banks in 1344 and shifted its course to the south, causing great suffering and destruction.[12] China was swept by banditry and rebellion. The chief minister mobilized large numbers of peasants for construction work, risking even greater discontent in the short run to try to repair the damage quickly, but he was dismissed from power just when success seemed within his grasp. The country rose up again in revolt, and the Mongols never regained control.

The rebels were known as the Red Turbans. (Chinese men wore their hair in a topknot, which they covered with a piece of cloth – customarily translated as "turban" in this context.) The Red Turbans espoused a form of millenarian Buddhism, known as White Lotus, mixed with elements of Manichaeism, a dualistic religion related to Zoroastrianism that had reached China from Iran. They broke the Mongol grip over China and shattered the empire into fragments but were unable to put the pieces back together themselves.

Three powerful rebel regimes coalesced along the Yangzi River in the south: the Wu in the east (at Suzhou), the Ming in the center (at Nanjing), and the Han in the west (at Wuhan). There were also five smaller regimes farther south, including one along the southeast coast ruled by a salt smuggler turned pirate. The north remained under the nominal control of the Mongol emperor, but in reality it was divided among a number of Mongol warlords.

The eventual victor was the chief general of the Ming regime, a fascinating character named Zhu Yuanzhang. His entire family had died in the famines and epidemics following the floods of 1344. He himself had wandered the countryside as a monk, beggar, and maybe soldier for some eight years before joining one of the Red Turban movements. Within a decade he had become its *de facto* leader.[13]

Warfare in the south was very different from warfare in the north. The major cities up and down the Yangzi River and along its navigable tributaries were the primary strategic objectives. These walled cities controlled the surrounding countryside (the source of recruits and supplies) as well as the navigable rivers (the network for transportation and communication). Fleets of oar-driven ships patrolled the rivers and transported armies quickly up and down them. Ships were used directly in assaults on cities along the riverbanks – soldiers scaled city walls from the decks of their ships, which had high sterns designed to allow just that. Ships also supplied besieging armies and blockaded besieged cities.[14]

Firearms fit well into this style of warfare. Although the firearms of this period were still quite primitive, they were produced and used on an impressive scale. Dozens of cast-iron cannon have been excavated from the territories of the Wu regime, all dating from these decades in the middle of the 1300s. Firearms are mentioned prominently in both naval and siege warfare. The author of the *Huolong shenqi zhenfa*, a treatise on firearms and other gunpowder weapons, even goes so far as to claim that the firearms he presented to Zhu Yuanzhang allowed him to unify China, a claim that may not be entirely fanciful.[15]

The decisive battle in the rise of the Ming was fought on Lake Boyang in 1363. The lake is about a hundred miles from north to south; the Yangzi River flows by its northern end, and the city of Nanchang lies on its southern shore. The Han fleet was on the lake blockading Nanchang when Zhu Yuanzhang sent the Ming fleet in after it. He ordered his commanders: "When you approach the enemy boats, first fire the firearms, then the bows and crossbows, and when you reach their boats, then [board and] attack them with hand-to-hand weapons."[16] The battle stretched over four days and ended in a decisive Ming victory, though thanks more to fire ships than to firearms.[17]

After absorbing the territory of the Han, the Ming regime was twice as big as the Wu, the other rebel regime in the Yangzi River valley. The Ming armies methodically reduced the Wu fortifications at Huzhou and Hangzhou in 1366 before besieging the Wu capital at Suzhou in 1367. Fire-arrows, rockets, and cannon were all employed in taking the city, which fell before the end of the year. Zhu Yuanzhang then dispatched armies to the south to deal with the smaller rebel regimes there and to the north to deal with the remnants of the Yuan dynasty in Beijing. The Yuan court and the Mongol warlords withdrew to Inner Mongolia, leaving Beijing to the new dynasty.[18]

The unification of China under the Ming dynasty in 1368 had far-reaching consequences. South China is shielded from the steppe by north China, just as western Europe is shielded from the steppe by eastern Europe, so warfare in south China might have developed independently of influence from the steppe, as was the case in western Europe. When China was divided between rival powers, this was in fact ths case, as demonstrated by the warfare in the Yangzi River valley in the 1350s and 1360s.

However, when China was unified, the economic and technological resources of south China were devoted to the defense of north China. South China's own defense needs were relatively slight. To the extent that the government could mobilize the resources of south China to defend north China, those resources were poured into steppe warfare; otherwise, they were diverted into peaceful pursuits. In either case, they were not invested in firearms production or development.

"China" as a geographical concept is a product of history, politics, and culture, just as "Europe" is. The unification of China in 1368, a political development, ensured that the influence of steppe warfare would be felt throughout China, even in south China. Consequently, it makes sense to say that "China was adjacent to the steppe," even though the equivalent statement for Europe would be meaningless. The rise of the Ming prevented south China from becoming like western Europe.

After 1368, the theater of war shifted from the rivers and valleys of south China to the dusty plains of north China and the steppe and desert of Mongolia. The kind of warfare described earlier, with ships battling for control of rivers and infantry besieging walled cities, largely disappeared from China after 1368. How firearms might have developed in China if ships and infantry had continued to dominate warfare can only be imagined. Instead, once the Ming armies had expelled the Mongols and unified all of China, the Ming dynasty had to face the demands of an entirely different style of warfare.

The Ming Military

Like the rest of the Ming state, the Ming military bore its founder's imprint. Zhu Yuanzhang kept some of the more anomalous features of Mongol administration, including the registration of each household according to the kind of service it was supposed to perform for the dynasty. Most households were simply registered as "commoner," which gave them no special duties beyond paying taxes, but the next largest group was "military," meaning that they served as soldiers. Military families were exempted from some taxes but were expected to support themselves by cultivating state-owned land. Military colonies were established along the frontier both to reclaim land for agriculture and to support garrisons where they were needed most.

The basic unit in the Ming army was the brigade, a unit of around 5,600 men responsible for supervising soldiers on garrison duty. Each brigade was divided into five battalions and each battalion into ten companies. Each company was to have forty men armed with spears, thirty with bows, twenty with swords, and ten with firearms. Not only was service in the military hereditary, but so were the ranks within the brigades and battalions and companies.[19]

Brigades were grouped into provincial-level regional military commissions that were in turn subordinated to the five chief military commissions in the capital; posts at these levels were not hereditary but instead were filled by officers who were promoted up from the brigades or were recruited through other channels.

Specialized training was conducted in the so-called training divisions. Three of these were established near Beijing in the early 1400s and counterparts were also set up near Nanjing. Troops from the brigades were rotated through these divisions for training on a regular basis. One of these training divisions was the Firearms Division, which instructed soldiers in the use of firearms; the other two taught tactics and reconnaissance.[20]

Brigades were designed for garrison duty. When it was necessary to put an army into the field, units were detached from brigades and placed under the operational command of different officers. Supreme command of a field army was often entrusted to a civil official or a eunuch (eunuchs being personal agents of the emperor). These arrangements were designed to prevent generals from gathering enough troops under their command to stage a coup. However, the constant threat of attack from the Mongols eventually forced the Ming to establish defense commands along the northern and northwestern borders, each of which might be thought of as the nucleus of a permanent field army.[21]

The Ming dynasty tried to compensate for its weakness at cavalry warfare by welcoming Mongols who were willing to fight for it. Throughout the late 1300s and well into the 1400s, a steady trickle of Mongols left the steppe to enter Ming service. The government provided them with animals, land, housing, furniture, clothes, and food to help them settle. Practically all of the Mongols who entered China were given military ranks and salaries and assigned to military units, often under their own officers, typically around Beijing or along the northern frontier.[22]

Figure 2.1 shows the kind of soldier that the Chinese needed and the Mongols provided. Galloping at speeds of up to thirty miles per hour, shooting half a dozen arrows a minute in any direction (including backward, as in the illustration), the mounted archer was the ultimate weapon system in flat and open terrain. The soldier in the illustration is drawing a recurved composite bow, a weapon identified with steppe nomads but also shared by Chinese archers. He is dressed in Chinese robes (note the absence of even a helmet), so he could be a Chinese or a Mongol in Chinese service.[23]

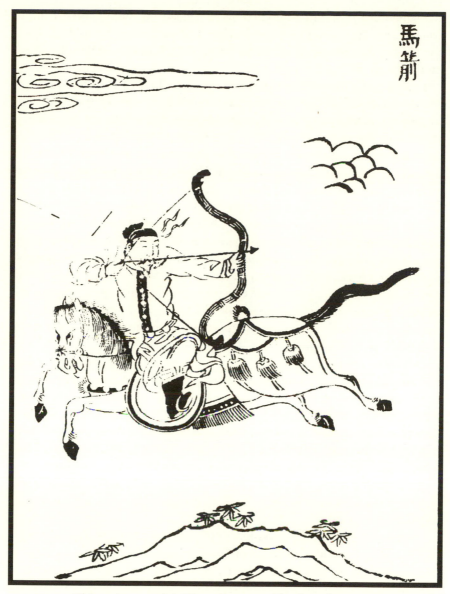

FIGURE 2.1. Chinese horse archer. Zheng Ruozeng, *Chouhai tubian* 13/58a (p. 1308).

The military establishment was quite large – numbering 16,489 officers and 1,198,442 men in 1392 – though hardly disproportionate for a total population of somewhere between sixty-five million and eighty-five million people. There were problems almost from the beginning with managing, feeding, and supplying this manpower. The army was supposed to be self-supporting, but large numbers were needed on the northern frontier, where farming was not very productive. Just supplying the soldiers along the frontier put a heavy strain on the Ming budget, never mind campaigning on the steppe.[24]

One might look at these numbers (which ballooned over the course of the dynasty) and at China's immense wealth and suppose that the Ming dynasty could overpower any of its neighbors by its sheer size.[25] The Chinese themselves sometimes wondered how they could be bullied by such small numbers of nomads. In the words of a famous memorial from the second century B.C., known to generations of Chinese officials: "Those wielding authority should be ashamed that something as big as the empire could be troubled by something as small as the population of one county."[26]

There were probably fewer men in Mongolia than there were soldiers in China, but nearly all Mongol men were soldiers in some sense. If the population of Mongolia was around two million, and if one in four Mongols was an adult male, the number of warriors could have been as many as half a million, all of them mounted. Considering how difficult it was for the Chinese to concentrate their forces on the northern frontier and what an advantage the Mongols' horses and lifestyle represented, the Mongol threat was nothing to take lightly.[27]

Whatever their advantage in numbers, the Ming armies did enjoy a definite advantage in equipment. Much of the production of military equipment in the capital was in the hands of eunuchs. Eunuchs controlled the Palace Armory, which produced a wide variety of armor and weapons; the Saddlery Service, which produced saddles, bridles, and whips – later renamed as or replaced by the Armor Service; and the Sewing Service, which produced uniforms. There were two special offices that handled firearms: the Gunpowder Office, which was attached to the Palace Armory, and the Wanggong Depot (later renamed the Anmin Depot), which produced both firearms and gunpowder.

On the other hand, the civil officials of the Ministry of Works controlled the Weapons Bureau. The Weapons Bureau manufactured a wide array of military equipment too, everything from helmets and mail to swords and spearheads to Vietnamese bows and black lacquer arrows. Even the bowstrings came in two varieties, waxed and unwaxed, like dental floss. The Weapons Bureau was also responsible for making firearms – the eunuchs did not have a monopoly on those either. Between the Weapons Bureau and the various eunuch agencies, the elite units of the imperial guard at least could have been completely outfitted from government sources.[28]

The *Huolong shenqi zhenfa* is the only work on firearms still surviving from fifteenth-century China. The author describes some thirty-eight different weapons, including eleven land weapons, eight naval weapons, four types of mines, three weapons for defending camps, three weapons for attacking camps, five weapons for defending cities, and four weapons for attacking cities. The profusion of naval and siege weapons reflects the experience of warfare in the south in the mid-1300s. Only the eleven land weapons might have been of use in the north, and most of these were ill-suited for mobile warfare.[29]

Of the eleven land weapons, the only one that might have been used at long range that was not itself immobile was the solo-flying divine-fire arrow, actually a kind of gun firing an arrow 26.7 inches in length. This gun looks very similar to the earliest firearm, the one dating from 1288 found in Manchuria. The illustration shows a powder chamber in the middle, the barrel on one side, and a socket for the stock on the other side. This is the description:

> Use fine bronze to cast the tapered part. The body is 40 inches long, and it holds one arrow. Use 0.39 ounces of propulsive powder; when it ignites, the arrow will go. It is like a fiery snake. It can hit 500 to 700 yards away, and is a match for several men. It is used together with the fire-lance.[30]

The most common Chinese gun in the early decades of the 1400s was the "heaven" model, very similar to the solo-flying divine-fire arrow gun, and a number of specimens have been recovered by archeologists. There are slight differences in the recorded caliber, length, and weight of the different specimens, even within the same year, but they all average about 0.6 inches in caliber, 14.2 inches in length, and 4.8 pounds in weight. In appearance, they are still similar to the earliest firearm from 1288 or to the "hand cannon" in use in Europe. The chamber for the powder and shot is in the middle, with the barrel of the gun on one side and a socket on the other side. Each weapon was inscribed with the month and year of manufacture and a unique serial number, so we know that some 100,000 guns of this model were produced by 1436.[31]

Outside of the capital, the production of military equipment was highly decentralized. Each of the thousand-plus counties in the empire was given a list of items to submit as part of its tax burden and a list of places to deliver them. Each government office or military unit drew on dozens of counties for all its different supplies. Furthermore, soldiers of the brigades produced some of their own equipment. For example, in 1451 each brigade was ordered to produce 160 sets of equipment per year, and each independent battalion 40 sets. Each set consisted of helmet, armor, sword, bow, bowstring, thirty-five arrows, and a knapsack, plus a long spear and round shield for every two sets. Soldiers who were unfit for combat were put to work making equipment.[32]

Horses were one critical item of military supply whose production could not be concentrated in the capital. Much more is known about the supply of horses to the Ming armies than the supply of firearms, perhaps because firearms were kept secret, but perhaps because horses were simply more important. To quote the Yongle emperor: "In ancient times, the official in charge of military administration was known as the 'Overseer of Horses.' When asked about the wealth of a ruler, they answered by counting the horses. This shows that horses are the most important thing to a country."[33] The Ming dynasty supplied its armies with horses from four different sources: the tea-horse trade, the government breeding program, the private breeding program, and the border horse markets.

The tea-horse trade was under the control of the horse-trading offices. The horse-trading offices were given a monopoly over the export of tea to Tibet, which they used to purchase horses from Tibetans. The tea-horse trade flourished up to the mid-1400s. This system was dislocated by the Mongol invasion of 1449, and although it resumed around 1470, trade was disrupted again in the early 1500s and again in the late 1500s as Mongols fought Tibetans for grazing land on the plateaus of Qinghai.

The government breeding program was managed by the pasturage offices. Four of these were established across the northern border in 1406, but the one near Beijing was abolished in 1420, and the one in western Shaanxi was abolished in 1439. The others operated at far below their authorized levels because Mongol raids drastically limited the available pasturage.

The private breeding program was supervised by the Court of the Imperial Stud. Some families were registered as horse-breeding households in the same way that other families were registered as military households. Each horse-breeding household was required to maintain or to help maintain a herd of a certain size. However, powerful families encroached on the pasturage of the horse-breeding households, and the households skimped on fodder to save money, so the health and strength of the horses suffered.

Although the quality was not very high, the private breeding program did supply most of the army's horses: 25,000 a year by the 1500s, against maybe 5,000 a year from the tea-horse trade and maybe 3,000 a year from the government breeding program.[34] Finally, the Ming could also get horses from the Mongols. Early in the dynasty they must have captured horses from defeated Mongol armies, and they would have obtained more when Mongols left the steppe to enter Ming service. The Ming could also buy horses from the Mongols at border markets. Ironically, the more they bought horses, the less they needed them, because the more goods the Mongols received through trade, the less incentive they had to raid. Unfortunately, the Ming often closed the border markets to punish the Mongols, unwittingly aggravating the very problem that was causing the raids in the first place. The Ming made the same mistake with the smugglers and pirates along China's southeastern seaboard, and it was only late in the dynasty that the court grasped this relationship.[35]

The chronic shortage of horses, particularly horses suited for use as cavalry mounts but also horses for pulling supply wagons, sharply limited the offensive capabilities of the Ming army.

The Hongwu Campaigns

There is a myth that the Chinese hid behind the Great Wall for two thousand years to isolate themselves from the outside world. This myth arose after border defenses that were built in the 1500s and 1600s were misidentified with walls that had been built in the third century B.C. When Zhu Yuanzhang ascended the throne as the first emperor of the Ming dynasty and chose the reign name "Hongwu," in 1368, it was not even clear where exactly China ended and the steppe began. No walls had been built between China proper and Inner Mongolia since the early 600s, more than seven centuries earlier. ("China proper" is the usual term for the core areas of China where agriculture was the way of life.) It was an open question how far north the Ming dynasty could extend its rule and how it would defend the territory it claimed.[36]

The Ming armies stayed busy in north China for two years after the capture of Beijing, particularly in the northwest. Shanxi was pacified in 1368, and Shaanxi in 1369 and 1370, at least formally. Both these areas had traditionally been part of China proper – Shaanxi had been the site of the capitals of most of the major dynasties up to the 900s. Ming armies also campaigned in Inner Mongolia, the frontier area where farmlands gave way gradually to steppe, north of China proper but south of the Gobi Desert. The Ming armies captured Shangdu, roughly 150 miles north of Beijing, in 1369. Shangdu had been the Yuan summer capital, just as Beijing had been the Yuan winter capital. In the following year they captured Yingchang, another thirty miles north of Shangdu, where the Yuan emperor had taken refuge.[37]

Not content with securing Inner Mongolia, the Hongwu emperor prepared several armies to cross the Gobi Desert and strike at the heart of Outer Mongolia in 1372. The central army set out in the first month of 1372 and defeated the Mongols at the Tula River in the third month, but was in turn decisively defeated by the Mongols in the fifth month. No details have come down to us about the battle, but the Chinese suffered heavy losses. The eastern army penetrated the same region in the sixth month, but only after splitting off from its supply train and pressing forward with just twenty days' rations. It too ran into trouble. It pushed the Mongols back to the Orhon River but was surrounded in turn by swarms of Mongol cavalry. The Chinese commander had his horse shot out from under him, and the Ming troops only escaped because their show of bravado made the Mongols smell a trap. The survivors made their way back to China by the eleventh month.[38]

The Hongwu emperor must have been attracted to some degree by the prospect of extending his rule over all of the former territory of the Mongol emperors, in China and Mongolia alike. Anything less would have been an admission that his rule was less universal than theirs. Nevertheless, the defeats of 1372 must have persuaded him to abandon any ambitions he might have had along those lines. In his *Ancestral Injunctions*, which he first drafted in 1373 and later revised (the version we have today) in 1381, he warned his heirs to be on guard against the barbarians to the north and northwest but not to seek military glory.[39]

The border did not necessarily remain quiet after 1372; skirmishes and battles broke out whenever the Mongols raided. Still, the Ming did not launch another major expedition to the north for fifteen years. The 1387 expedition was aimed not at Outer Mongolia but at Manchuria, where the Uriyangkhai Mongols were defying Ming authority in the Liao River valley. The Ming army set out in the first month and scored a quick victory in the second month, when the Ming light cavalry rode through a blizzard to catch one party of Mongols napping. After constructing four fortresses and a command center on the Manchurian border in the third month, the army continued east. The target of the campaign surrendered to this show of force in the sixth month, so the main objective was accomplished, but otherwise the Chinese did not fare too well. One Ming detachment was ambushed and its commander killed on the way out in the sixth month, and the rearguard was ambushed and its commander killed on the way back in the following month.[40]

The next year saw a more ambitious campaign, back into Outer Mongolia. A Ming army of 150,000 headed for Lake Buyur in eastern Mongolia, almost 600 miles north of Beijing, close to the Khingan Mountains separating Mongolia from Manchuria. The heir to the Yuan emperors was reported to be there. The army suffered greatly from thirst while crossing the Gobi Desert in the third month, but it found the Mongols camped at the lake in the fourth month. The Mongols, slowed down by their flocks and baggage, elected to stand and fight, but the force they sent to oppose the Ming army was defeated. While the Mongol emperor escaped, over 77,000 people and 47,000 horses were captured.[41]

There is little if any mention of firearms on the campaigns in the north. What mention of firearms one finds from the Hongwu emperor's reign generally comes from campaigns in the south. It took some time for the Ming dynasty to round out its borders in the south, as it did in the north. Sichuan was brought under control in 1371, and Yunnan was finally conquered in 1382, though hardly entirely pacified. In fighting that prefigured in some ways the battles in Vietnam in the early 1400s, Ming cannon routed war elephants in Yunnan in the late 1380s.[42]

The Hongwu emperor's eldest son died young, so the Hongwu emperor designated his eldest son's eldest son as the heir to the throne. This young man succeeded to the throne in Nanjing after the death of his grandfather in 1398, but he had the misfortune of having an ambitious and experienced uncle residing in Beijing. This uncle decided to take the throne for himself, with the backing of most of the veteran border troops and also of the Uriyangkhai Mongols. Starting from Beijing, it took the uncle four years to defeat his nephew, capture Nanjing, and take the throne as the Yongle emperor.

The Yongle Campaigns

The Yongle emperor was ambitious, energetic, and ruthless. During the twenty-two years of his reign, from 1402 to 1424, China went through a burst of expansionist activity, with armies sent to annex Vietnam and fleets dispatched to cruise the Indian Ocean. However, the Yongle emperor's chief focus was always on the Mongols, and he led five campaigns against them in person.[43]

This focus on Mongolia became almost inevitable when the Yongle emperor moved the capital to the north, to the site of his former appanage at Beijing. Beijing was well situated for overseeing further expansion north, but it was also very close to Inner Mongolia and Manchuria, and it forced the Ming emperors and their officials to pay much closer attention to the security of the border. Furthermore, the move entailed transplanting large numbers of economically unproductive officials, servants, and soldiers to an area little better than self-sufficient to begin with. Feeding the capital required massive shipments of grain up the Grand Canal from the Yangzi River valley each year and made it all the more difficult for supplies to be gathered for campaigns against the Mongols. Moving the capital was itself a logistical nightmare that took place in three stages over the course of two decades and was only completed in 1421.[44]

Paradoxically, as the Yongle emperor was moving his capital from Nanjing to Beijing, he was also reducing the Ming presence on the edge of the steppe. In the last decade of his rule, the Hongwu emperor had established eight outposts in Inner Mongolia and Manchuria to guard the main approaches to Beijing. The Yongle emperor abandoned four of these in 1403, almost as soon as he had secured his rule over China, and he later abandoned most of the others. Perhaps eight outposts in two rings consumed too many supplies for essentially defensive purposes. For offensive purposes, the only outpost he really needed was Shangdu (renamed Kaiping) in Inner Mongolia, which could serve as a staging point for armies heading north into Outer Mongolia. Reducing garrisons freed up both men and supplies for armies in the field.[45]

The Mongols of the late 1300s were divided into three large groups. The Oirats or Western Mongols inhabited the lands between the Altai and Tianshan ranges far to the northwest. The Tatars or Eastern Mongols inhabited the Orhon and Kerulen River valleys in the central and eastern parts of Outer Mongolia. The Uriyangkhai inhabited the valley of the Liao River in western Manchuria. Together, these made up three of the four areas north of China with the combination of grass and water that made them ideal for raising livestock but also suitable for limited agriculture as well. The fourth was the Ordos, which became a battleground in the late 1400s.[46]

The Oirats and Tatars fought each other for control of the steppe, giving the Chinese a chance to play them off against each other. The Yongle emperor initially sided with the Oirats. When the Tatars killed a Ming envoy, he sent a punitive expedition after them in 1409. In the eighth month, the expedition was defeated and destroyed at the Kerulen River. The Tatars feigned retreat to lead the Chinese on, and the Chinese commander ignored the warnings of his officers; he pursued the Tatars at the head of the light cavalry, only to be cut off and surrounded. The vanguard was wiped out, and the main army was destroyed trying to save it.[47]

In the second month of 1410, the Yongle emperor set out on the first of his five campaigns, to punish the Tatars for the defeat of the previous year. Some 30,000 wagons transported 15,600 tons of grain with the army. In the fifth month, the army crossed the Kerulen River and defeated the Tatars at the Onon River – the emperor split off from the main army with a force of light cavalry carrying twenty days' rations to catch them. The Ming army then pursued them east into the Khingan Mountains in the following month. The Yongle emperor lured the Tatars out of the mountains, then charged them at the head of his cavalry, scattering them. However, the supply train from Kaiping missed its rendezvous with the army on the return and the men suffered greatly before being resupplied. The army returned to Beijing in the seventh month under orders not to forage.[48]

The defeat of the Tatars had tipped the balance on the steppe too far in favor of the Oirats, and the Yongle emperor soon decided it was time to teach them a lesson. In the third month of 1414, he set out on his second campaign. The vanguard reached the Tula River in the sixth month and skirmished with an Oirat force. A few days later, they were suddenly confronted by the main Oirat army on the hilltops surrounding the valley. According to a Chinese eyewitness, the guns frightened the Oirats, who abandoned their spare horses and fled. When they regrouped later in the day, the Chinese sprang a trap on them with concealed guns. When the Chinese encountered the Oirats yet again several days later, the Oirats avoided battle, "fearing that the guns had arrived again," according to this Chinese observer. The army returned to Beijing in the eighth month, again short of supplies and under strict orders not to forage.[49]

After the defeat of the Oirats, the Tatars began to raid the borders again, and this time they persuaded the Uriyangkhai to ally with them. In the third month of 1422, the Yongle emperor set out on his third Mongolian campaign. The army was supported by 117,000 wagons, with 235,000 men and 340,000 donkeys, carrying some 28,900 tons of supplies. As the army approached the Tatar camp at the foot of the Khingan Mountains in Inner Mongolia, the Tatars abandoned their baggage and fled into Outer Mongolia. The Yongle emperor then took 20,000 infantry and cavalry to deal with the Uriyangkhai in Manchuria. After a series of victories over them, the armies returned to China proper in the ninth month.[50]

The fourth campaign was launched in the seventh month of 1423, almost on the spur of the moment, in response to a report that the Tatars were preparing to raid the border. There seems to have been little preparation. An army of as many as 300,000 marched around Inner Mongolia for a couple months ready for battle – "the emperor ordered the generals to deploy formations outside of each of their camps, with guns in front and cavalry units behind" – until news arrived that the Tatars had been defeated by the Oirats. The army then withdrew to Beijing in the eleventh month without having contacted them at all.[51]

The fifth campaign was similarly anticlimactic. The army set out in the fourth month of 1424 in response to reports that the Tatars were once again massing to raid Inner Mongolia. The heavy supply wagons were slowed down by the summer rains. After marching for two months, the vanguard reached the rumored location of the Tatar camp, far in the north where Outer Mongolia meets the Khingan Mountains. The emperor ordered the men to be prepared: "If the enemy arrives, first hit them with the firearms, then follow up with the long bows and strong crossbows." They searched the entire area and found nothing. Troops were sent out on reconnaissance but returned when they ran short of supplies, and the army headed south that same month. "In this vast and boundless desert," complained the emperor, "it is like looking for a grain in the ocean." He died of illness in the seventh month before reaching Beijing.[52]

It was not that the firearms performed poorly when they were used. In the 1410 campaign, "[the Emperor] ordered Liu Sheng, the Far-Conquering

Earl, to lead the way with the guns, and when the guns fired the sound shook for several leagues, and each arrow pierced two people, and then hit the neighboring horse, and killed them all."⁵³ (Note that the guns were still firing arrows.) In the 1414 campaign, "the Emperor ordered Liu Sheng, the Far-Conquering Marquis [he had been promoted], and others to fire the guns and cannon, and they killed several hundred bandits [Mongols]." When the Mongols continued to hold their ground, "the Commissioner-in-chief Zhu Zhong, the Commander Lü Xing, and others advanced and pressed the caitiffs [Mongols], continuously firing the guns and cannon, and the robbers [Mongols] who died were countless."⁵⁴ If anything, the Chinese sources seem to exaggerate. If this generation of Mongols was unfamiliar with firearms, it is possible that they were scared off by the impressive noise; it is doubtful that they were slaughtered *en masse* by crude arrow-firing guns.

However, it was extraordinarily difficult to get the infantry with the firearms to where they were needed. It took the better part of three months to march to Outer Mongolia, and the same amount of time to return, and the men had to be supplied overland in both directions, with little prospect of gathering provisions along the way. The earlier campaigns must have relied heavily on Mongol auxiliaries of the type mentioned earlier and on large numbers of horses acquired from them or raised in Inner Mongolia. If the horses were fed grass instead of a mixture of grass and grain, some of the logistical limitations pertaining to grain-fed horses may have been circumvented.

It comes as no surprise that only the first (in 1410) and second (in 1414) of the emperor's five campaigns penetrated the heart of Outer Mongolia. The third and fourth campaigns (in 1422 and 1423 respectively) were restricted to Inner Mongolia and Manchuria, and the fifth campaign (in 1424) hugged the border between Manchuria and Outer Mongolia without striking out into the steppe. Similarly, it comes as no surprise that only the first two of the emperor's five campaigns succeeded in forcing the Mongols to fight. As long as the Ming armies remained close to China proper, in Inner Mongolia and Manchuria, the Tatars and Oirats could avoid them by withdrawing deep into the steppe. Only the Uriyangkhai Mongols in western Manchuria were close enough to be battered into submission.

In the later campaigns, the Ming army seems to have been increasingly weighed down by its baggage trains and infantry columns. Large, slow-moving forces were unable to bring the Mongols to battle, and they suffered from other drawbacks as well. It was extremely expensive to collect so many men and so much supplies, and extremely risky to commit them all on a campaign in Outer Mongolia, since they would have little hope of retreating back to safety in the event of a major defeat. The risk was not worth the reward, because isolated campaigns (as in 1410 and 1414) could only punish the Mongols but not establish reliable ongoing control over them.

The Yongle emperor led five campaigns in person and made those campaigns a top priority of his reign. He built up the number of horses available to the army from 37,993 horses in 1403 to 234,855 horses in 1413 and 1,585,322 horses in 1423.[55] If any of the Ming emperors could have conquered Mongolia, he would have been the one to do it. He had the military experience. He had persuaded the Uriyangkhai Mongols to support his usurpation of the throne. He had all the resources of China behind him. It was even rumored among both Chinese and Mongols that his biological mother had been a Mongol. But if his goal was to conquer and rule over Mongolia, it is remarkable how far short he fell of it.

By comparison, Vietnam must have seemed an easy target.

Vietnam

The northern part of Vietnam was just another part of the Chinese empire in ancient times, much like Korea. The local inhabitants spoke their own language and had their own customs, but that was once true of many places that today are part of China. The Vietnamese preserved their separate identity because they broke free of the Chinese empire during a period of disunity in the 900s. That was not the end of the story, as the new kingdom of Dai Viet had to fight first the Chinese Song dynasty and then the Mongol Yuan dynasty to preserve its independence. Although much smaller and weaker, Dai Viet was distant from the main centers of Chinese and Mongol power, and heat and malaria also helped to protect it.[56]

The first Ming emperor included Dai Viet in his *Ancestral Injunctions* on the list of countries never to be invaded, but after a usurper took the throne of Dai Viet, the Yongle emperor decided to intervene to restore the old dynasty. He first sent a Chinese force as an escort for a Vietnamese pretender, but the Chinese escort was ambushed and the pretender captured and killed. Enraged, the Yongle emperor then dispatched an army of over 200,000 to Vietnam in late 1406. The Vietnamese army was overwhelmed. Rather than restore the old dynasty, the Yongle emperor decided in 1407 to set the clock back five centuries and annex the territory of Dai Viet. It took about eight years to establish order in the face of Vietnamese resistance; the Chinese had to keep a large army of occupation in place and ship massive amounts of rice from China each year to supply it.[57]

The Chinese tried to establish civil administration in Vietnam, but resistance was too strong. After a brief hiatus from 1414 to 1417, the

Vietnamese took up arms again in 1418. The first rebels were defeated but slipped away into the mountains. Another rebellion broke out the following month and the same thing happened: "[the Vietnamese leader] fled with his men, but the mountains and forests were deep and obstructed, and pestilential miasma took its toll, and the government troops searched without finding them, so they withdrew and sent someone with a proclamation." This was the pattern for the next year as well: the Chinese would defeat the Vietnamese in battles, but the Vietnamese would disappear into the jungles.[58]

The Yongle emperor sent reinforcements for a major offensive in 1420. The Chinese troops won a major battle in the first month of 1421 when they "charged into the bandit ranks, shot the elephant riders [with arrows], then followed up by attacking with firearms, [so] the elephants ran away and the bandits were routed." (Was it the noise that scared the elephants?) There was a lull in 1422 as the weakened Vietnamese forces recuperated, but soon their fortunes would take a turn for the better.[59]

The death of the Yongle emperor in 1424 was the turning point. His son and successor only reigned for one year. The Vietnamese seized the initiative and began to score some victories over the Chinese armies. When the Yongle emperor's grandson, the Xuande emperor, ascended the throne in 1425, he began to consider setting up a Vietnamese puppet and withdrawing from Vietnam. Meanwhile, Chinese armies were ambushed whenever they dared to venture outside the fortified towns, and even behind the walls of the towns they were not entirely safe, although they used their firearms to some effect on defense.[60]

The end came in the ninth month of 1427, when a huge Chinese relief army was dispatched to Vietnam. The Chinese commander Liu Sheng, mentioned earlier as the commander of the firearms on the 1410 and 1414 campaigns in Mongolia, was ambushed and killed even before he could cross the border, and his army was routed. Liu Sheng was criticized posthumously as "brave but lacking strategy." The remaining Chinese garrisons withdrew from Vietnam.[61]

Although the fighting in Vietnam did involve infantry, unlike the fighting in Mongolia, guerrilla tactics counteracted Chinese firepower. Early firearms were generally ineffective against targets that could spread out or take cover, because they could not hit individual targets except at point-blank range. Europeans would later run into the same problem in North America and in Africa. Enemy infantry had to be forced into tight formations to give the firearms targets they could hit.

The easiest way to keep enemy infantry in tight formations was to overrun them with cavalry if they spread out. However, that did not work in forests and jungles, where cavalry could not operate. Tight infantry formations could push their way through scattered snipers operating behind trees and rocks, but they would suffer higher casualties than they inflicted in the process, and in guerrilla warfare the aim was not necessarily to capture terrain. This was the dilemma that the Chinese faced in Vietnam.[62]

However, the Vietnamese style of warfare posed no threat to China. Guerrilla warfare is primarily defensive in nature, as guerrillas have to rely on the cooperation of the local population for supplies and intelligence. Although both Mongols and Vietnamese were able in their own way to baffle the Chinese, only the Mongols could turn the tables on the Chinese. The Chinese could walk away from Vietnam whenever they wanted. Ultimately, of course, that is exactly what they did. Unfortunately, they did not have the luxury of dealing with the Mongols in the same way.

The South Seas

Cannon design was a trade-off between size and mobility. Improved alloys eventually provided greater size with less weight, but in the early days of firearms, even fairly small and weak cannon were extremely heavy. Any cannon large enough to be effective was typically heavy enough to be immobile.

There were two situations where weight was not a serious drawback: siege warfare, which is largely static, and naval warfare, because weight does not impair mobility at sea to the same degree as on land. Generally speaking, siege warfare and naval warfare provided the best opportunities for the use of cannon.

The Chinese hardly ever encountered siege warfare after 1367. The Mongols had no cities for the Chinese to besiege, and the Mongols did not besiege Chinese cities either. However, naval warfare also declined in frequency after 1367. Not only did the unification of China spell the end of fighting on the rivers but, for unrelated reasons, the rise of the Ming interrupted the growth of Chinese seapower as well.

The origins of Chinese seapower can be traced back to the 900s. Where maritime trade between China and Islamdom had previously been in the hands of Arab and Persian merchants and sailors, Chinese junks began to dominate the trade from China as far west as the southern tip of India. Fueling this trade was a heavy demand for Chinese products overseas, particularly tea, silk, and porcelain.[63]

Naval power was not neglected either. The Song dynasty built a powerful fleet to patrol the Huai and Yangzi Rivers and the East China Sea. The Mongols used Korean and Chinese ships to launch invasions as far away as Japan and Java. The Mongols also sent ships through the Indian Ocean on a regular basis to maintain contacts with the Mongol *khanate* in Iran. Marco

Polo returned from China on one such voyage, which delivered a bride to the Mongol *khan* of Iran.[64]

The first emperor of the Ming dynasty initiated a sharp break with this practice. It is not entirely clear why he chose to do so, although his background may have given him anti-mercantile biases. Anyway, he prohibited all privately conducted foreign trade in 1371, and the prohibition was reiterated a number of times during his reign: in 1381, 1390, 1394, and 1397. The tributary system became the only legal outlet for foreign trade.[65]

Under the tributary system, each foreign ruler who accepted a ritually subordinate relationship to the Chinese emperor was permitted to send delegations of specified sizes at specified intervals to China. Each delegation would present gifts to the emperor and receive even more valuable gifts in return; members of the delegation were also allowed to do some trading on the side. The tributary system had had a long tradition in China, but the prohibition on maritime activity was new.

Although the Yongle emperor did not specifically permit foreign trade, he did not explicitly ratify the prohibition either. Perhaps as an alternative, he greatly expanded the reach of the tributary system. Aside from bringing the Japanese back into the system for the first time in centuries, he established a Chinese diplomatic and military presence in the "South Seas" (the Chinese name for Southeast Asia and the Indian Ocean) that attracted tribute from a host of distant lands.[66]

At the heart of this policy were six expeditions dispatched to the South Seas by the Yongle emperor in 1405, 1407, 1409, 1413, 1417, and 1421. These expeditions were massive in size: they averaged fifty to sixty large ships, a couple of hundred smaller ones, and about 27,000 men. The relevant comparison is not the three ships that Columbus commanded in 1492 or the four ships that Vasco da Gama led in 1497 but rather the Spanish Armada of 1588, which was roughly the same size. Each expedition lasted about two years, and all but one of the expeditions were commanded by a Muslim eunuch named Zheng He.[67]

The largest of these ships were the nine-masted treasure ships. Not only were the treasure ships bigger than the largest European or Indian ships, but also they featured technology like watertight bulkheads, sternpost rudders, and compasses, all of which originated in China. Little is known about their armament, but Chinese ships did carry bronze cannon at this time, as evidenced by the wreck of a small two-masted patrol vessel discovered in Shandong together with its anchor (inscribed 1372) and cannon (inscribed 1377).[68]

Unlike the Portuguese sailing to India around the Cape of Good Hope, the Chinese did not have to carry supplies for the entire voyage. Instead, they could count on resupplying their fleets at the port cities that lay along their route. Also unlike the Portuguese, the Chinese already knew where they were going and how to get there. The Chinese could send 27,000 soldiers and sailors into the South Seas as far as Arabia or Africa with a fair degree of confidence that they would survive the journey. With such overwhelming naval and land forces at their disposal, the Chinese could have intervened at will in the internal affairs of the small states they visited.

To a certain extent they did. On a stele erected by Zheng He himself, he described his mission in the following terms:

> Upon arriving at foreign countries, capture those barbarian kings who resist civilization and are disrespectful, and exterminate those bandit soldiers that indulge in violence and plunder. The ocean routes will be safe thanks to this, and foreigners will rely on them to secure their livelihood.[69]

The Chinese recognized Melaka as an independent state and warned the king of Thailand not to meddle with it. They destroyed a Chinese pirate fleet operating out of Palembang on Sumatra in 1407, bringing the pirate chief back to Nanjing for execution and granting an official title to his rival. They intervened in Sri Lanka in 1411, bringing the ruler back to China for judgment, although he was released and allowed to return home later. They attacked and captured the occupant of the throne of Semudera on Sumatra in 1415, and brought him to Nanjing for execution as well. No doubt there were occasions where a show of force helped to secure supplies or permission to anchor.

Nevertheless, the Chinese did not seek to establish colonies overseas, even when they anchored in places with large Chinese populations, like Sumatra and Java. They turned Melaka into a kind of protectorate and built a fortified warehouse there, but that was about it. They sought instead to impress people with the wealth and power of the Chinese emperor. To this end, Chinese ships visited dozens of lands, many of them repeatedly, as far as the eastern coast of Africa.

Like the occupation of Vietnam, the voyages to the South Seas began and ended with the reign of the Yongle emperor. The brief reign of his son was too short to have much of an impact either way, but naval activities wound down during the reign of the Yongle emperor's grandson, the Xuande emperor. The Xuande emperor sent out the fleet one last time in 1431, but after the fleet returned to China in 1433, it never set out again.

The aggressive foreign policy in Mongolia, Vietnam, and the South Seas, together with the expense of moving the capital to Beijing, imposed a terrific strain on the budget. If the Ming dynasty had followed in the footsteps of the Song and Yuan dynasties by promoting and taxing private trade, then the voyages might have paid for themselves in increased customs revenues, but as a way of raising China's diplomatic profile overseas, the costs greatly outweighed the benefits.

Once the move to Beijing was complete and the Xuande emperor had withdrawn from Vietnam, the competition for resources was narrowed to Mongolia and the South Seas. Between these two, there was no question which was the more important, especially as Beijing was hardly a hundred miles from the edge of the steppe in Inner Mongolia. The Mongols had to take precedence.[70]

Three centuries of Chinese seapower came to an end in 1433, and with it any chance that the Chinese might have developed better cannon for use at sea. Cannon were useless against the Mongols, and they would not be used against ships and ports in the South Seas. If there was any lingering doubt where the strategic interests of the Ming dynasty lay, however, that question was soon put to rest.

Tumu

Both the invasion of Vietnam and the expeditions to the Indian Ocean were short-lived. The Ming initiated them and the Ming could terminate them – neither was vital to the security of the empire. The northern frontier was different. Like it or not, every Ming emperor had to face the threat from the Mongols. The northern frontier was the most enduring influence on the Ming military as well as the greatest drain on the Ming budget.

The Xuande emperor was the last Ming emperor (except for the strange case of the Zhengde emperor, described in chapter 6) who knew how to fight. While his father was living in Nanjing, he himself was accompanying his grandfather, the Yongle emperor, on campaigns in Mongolia. Although personally brave – he even patrolled the border with his men – he was too prudent to risk a major expedition into Outer Mongolia. This prudence was also reflected in his decisions to withdraw from Vietnam and refrain from sending more voyages to the South Seas.[71]

His son came to the throne as a young boy in 1435. By 1449 he was still a young man of just twenty-one, accustomed to following the suggestions of his chief eunuch, Wang Zhen. The emperor allowed himself to be persuaded by the eunuch to lead a military expedition in person against the Mongols. The original plan called for the army to proceed through the inner ring of Chinese fortifications at Juyong Pass three days north of Beijing, march west to the city of Datong, and from there strike out into the steppe.

The march from Beijing to Datong in the seventh month of 1449 covered about 200 miles and took about two weeks. The Chinese army is said to have numbered half a million. By the time the army reached Datong, Wang Zhen was already having second thoughts about the wisdom of his plan. The Oirat leader Esen had recently destroyed a large force from the Datong garrison not far from the city, and the imperial army passed by thousands of corpses that had been lying unburied for two weeks. Wang Zhen decided to declare victory and go home.

The army now retraced its path back toward the safety of the Juyong Pass. Only a few days' march from the Ming fortifications at the pass, the rearguard was massacred by the Oirats. Another detachment of cavalry (thirty, forty, or fifty thousand, depending on the source) was organized to cover the rear of the army – it too was slaughtered. The main body proceeded onward for one more day before it was surrounded by the Oirats at Tumu. The camp had no water, and the army was cut off from a nearby stream. On the following day, Esen attacked the thirsty and demoralized Chinese army and destroyed it utterly. Wang Zhen was killed, by which side it is not clear; the emperor was captured alive.

Apparently, the Mongols were no longer bothered by the sound of Chinese guns.

The whole affair was a complete fiasco from beginning to end, but it shows how little margin for error existed in these operations. The army was actually operating within the outer ring of the Chinese border defenses. It had just left the fortified town of Xuanfu three days earlier and was only two days away from the fortified town of Huailai when the rearguard was destroyed. The army was only seven or eight miles short of Huailai when it was surrounded on the following day. This was anything but the trackless wastes of the Mongolian steppe.[72]

The Oirats pressed on to Beijing, but they had no means of carrying out a siege, and they withdrew after a week. The officials who had remained in the capital put a brother of the emperor on the throne and refused to deal. Esen released the "old" emperor a year later, now age twenty-two, without any conditions. Esen's failure to exploit the situation damaged his prestige; he was killed by rivals in 1455, and Oirat power on the steppe soon collapsed. The Oirats withdrew to the west and the Tatars were again ascendant.[73]

Meanwhile, the old emperor was placed under house arrest in Beijing. His brother remained on the throne and did a very credible job of defending the empire, but the presence of the old emperor undermined the unity of the court. The old emperor regained the throne after a coup in 1457. His brother had been very ill at the time, and he died shortly thereafter, perhaps of natural causes, perhaps not. The officials who had defended the capital in 1449 were executed, and a memorial was built to the eunuch Wang Zhen.[74]

Ming border defenses were in disarray after the defeat at Tumu, and the abandonment of the defensive outposts by the Yongle emperor now came back to haunt them. The Chinese outpost in the Ordos region west of Beijing having been withdrawn, Tatar groups gradually filtered into the vacuum that was left behind. The Ordos was one of the four areas north of China mentioned earlier, where the combination of grass and water particularly favored stockbreeding but also might have supported agriculture. It was also the one closest to China proper, so close that Mongols in the Ordos enjoyed the benefits of interior lines and could strike at almost any point along the entire northern border.

Two strategies were debated at the Ming court in the late 1460s and early 1470s. The more aggressive officials advocated driving the Mongols out of the Ordos and moving Chinese settlers in to plant crops to supply the garrisons that would be needed to defend it. The more cautious ones advocated fortifying the eastern and southern edges of the Ordos, where the steppe and desert met the hills and mountains of Shanxi and Shaanxi.

Several estimates agreed that something like 150,000 men would be needed for an offensive to succeed. Shanxi and Shaanxi were hilly, poor, thinly populated areas where mustering an army would impose a heavy burden on the inhabitants. In addition, the army would have to operate in the Ordos for an extended period of time without any local supplies to draw upon at all. To supply such an offensive would require an estimated 35,000 tons (or 50,000 wagonloads) of supplies.[75]

The difficulty with supplies was exacerbated by a shortage of horses. The horse-raising areas of Inner Mongolia had been abandoned in the aftermath of Tumu, crippling the government breeding program. The private breeding program was in shambles, the tea-horse trade had been disrupted, and the border markets were closed. Offensive action was impossible without horses for cavalry troopers and for supply wagons. Furthermore, the Mongols in China who supplied some of the best cavalrymen for the Ming armies were viewed as a potential fifth column, and many were transferred *away* from the northern frontier.[76]

The Ming court turned to the less expensive alternative of building defenses to the south of the Ordos instead. The resulting line was almost 700 miles long from east to west, with forts, towers, and signal-beacon platforms scattered along its length. The eastern and western ends of the line both rested on the Yellow River, closing off the Ordos region within the large northward loop of the river. This construction was not a "repair" of some preexisting "Great Wall": these were the first walls built in this region in nearly eight centuries. The line was built up and supported by other lines that were added over the following decades.[77]

We pick up the story again in chapter 6, but this is a good place to pause, for two reasons. First, the military balance between the Ming dynasty and its neighbors had shifted after Tumu, permanently as it turned out. Ming offensive reach had contracted drastically. Where once the Hongwu and Yongle emperors could challenge the Mongols in the heart of Outer Mongolia, now their successors could not muster the means to retake even the Ordos. It is no exaggeration to say that Tumu had thrown the dynasty on the defensive for good. The Great Wall was just one symbol of that.[78]

Second, the Chinese had already lost their lead in firearms technology by the end of the 1400s. When European and Ottoman firearms arrived in China in the early 1500s, the Chinese discovered that their own weapons were markedly inferior to the foreign ones. How the Chinese reacted is a story for chapter 6. First we have to see how the Europeans and the Ottomans gained that lead.

3

Europe

Europe is roughly comparable in size and diversity to India or China. Europe has no strikingly obvious eastern boundary – the Ural Mountains are about the same height as the Appalachians, and the Don River was traditionally taken as Europe's eastern boundary instead – and it gradually merges into the steppe. Few thirteenth-century Europeans would even have heard of the word "Europe" (although this would change by the 1600s), and it might be equally appropriate for the purposes of this book to refer to it as Christendom instead.[1]

Pastoral nomads did not establish themselves any farther west than Hungary, the last outpost of the great steppe belt that stretches all the way from Mongolia. Transhumance (the seasonal migration of livestock) was common throughout southern Europe, in the familiar figure of the shepherd and his flocks, but the shepherds were no more nomads than were the cowboys who drove herds of cattle from Texas to Kansas every year – they were marginal members of agricultural societies. Their families, if they had any, lived in villages or towns.[2]

Nevertheless, the horse was enormously symbolic for European culture. In the words of one knight, writing around the year 1250, "No animal is more noble than the horse, since it is by horses that princes, magnates and knights are separated from lesser people, and because a lord cannot fittingly be seen among private citizens except through the mediation of a horse."[3] Paintings and statues of monarchs on horses were ubiquitous. When European monarchs had their images struck on medals, the reverse typically showed the monarch on horseback. Thoroughbred horses were princely gifts that were exchanged between rulers on ceremonial occasions.[4]

By the 1000s, Latin Christendom no longer suffered from the depredations of Vikings and Magyars and Muslims; instead, Latin Christendom itself expanded aggressively in all directions. There was both an external and an internal component to this expansion. On the one hand, the Vikings, Slavs, and Magyars were all converted to Christianity, and the ultimately unsuccessful Crusades in the Holy Land were offset by successful ones in the Iberian Peninsula. On the other hand, population growth also stimulated the clearing and cultivation of vacant spaces within western Europe, and the land began to fill up with cities and towns and farms, not to mention castles.[5]

From the First Crusade in 1096 to the fall of the last crusader stronghold in 1291, Latin Christendom had firsthand contact with Greek and Arabic civilization. A wave of advanced technology reached Europe in the 1100s, most of it Chinese in origin, including the sternpost rudder and the compass, both essential to the later voyages of exploration. Sicily and Spain, once under Muslim rule, now produced Latin translations of Arabic works, including secondhand translations of Greek texts. Although still lagging behind other parts of the Oikoumene, Latin Christendom was poised to make up a lot of ground over the next few centuries.[6]

By contrast, Greek Christendom bore the brunt of the Muslim advance from the 1000s on. The battle of Manzikert in 1071 marked the end of Byzantine rule over most of Anatolia and the beginning of the end of Byzantine existence. Without much territory remaining to supply manpower for its armies, the Byzantine empire relied on the walls of Constantinople for its survival. Although Orthodox Christianity spread to Russia in the 1000s,

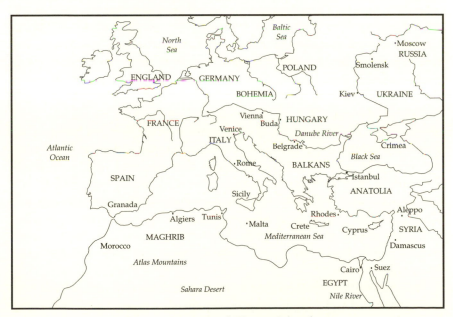

Map 3. Europe and Western Islamdom

Russia was conquered by the Mongols in the 1200s, and it was ruled indirectly by the Mongols of the Golden Horde, who themselves converted to Islam, until the late 1400s.

The Introduction of Firearms

The Mongols were probably responsible for bringing gunpowder and firearms to Europe. Chinggis Khan organized a unit of Chinese catapult specialists in 1214, and these men formed part of the first Mongol army to invade Transoxania in 1219. This was not too early for true firearms, and it was nearly two centuries after catapult-thrown gunpowder bombs had been added to the Chinese arsenal. Chinese siege equipment saw action in Transoxania in 1220 and in the north Caucasus in 1239–40. Shortly after the latter campaign, the Mongols also invaded Poland and Hungary, but they turned back in 1241 after the death of the *khaghan*. The invasion scare of 1241 raised questions throughout Europe about the identity and motives of the Mongols.[7]

William of Rubruck was a Franciscan friar who traveled to the court of the Mongol *khaghan* Möngke between 1253 and 1255. Although his account of his journey did not circulate widely in Europe, one person who took a keen interest in his experience was Roger Bacon, a fellow Franciscan. Whether by coincidence or not, the earliest European reference to gunpowder is found in Bacon's *Epistola de secretis operibus artiis et naturae* from 1267. The earliest formulas suitable for firearms appeared soon afterward, in the *Liber ignium ad comburendos hostes* attributed to "Marcus Graecus," in a part thought to date from the last quarter of the 1200s. Since saltpeter was not identified in Europe until the 1200s, earlier formulas are unlikely to be uncovered.[8]

The four formulas in the *Liber ignium* have saltpeter ranging from 66.5 percent to 75 percent, right in the optimal range for firearms. There is no record in Europe of the centuries of experimentation either with gunpowder recipes or with gunpowder weapons that occurred in China. While the Chinese tried all kinds of chemicals in all kinds of proportions, the Europeans started off with the right chemicals in the right proportions. While the Chinese produced a variety of flamethrowers, rockets, bombs, and mines before they hit upon firearms, the Europeans started out with firearms. Early European "hand cannon" even look a lot like the 1288 Chinese gun.[9]

The information trickling into Europe would have drawn attention to Chinese military technology. Chapter 1 quoted a passage by the Armenian monk Hetoum from around the year 1307, shortly before the first appearance of firearms in Europe. Although this work does not mention firearms by name, it does go on to say this about China:

> The men of this countrey ar no stronge warryours nor valyant in armes, but they be moche subtyll and ingenyous; by mean wherof, often tymes they haue disconfyted and ouercome their ennymes by their engyns, and they haue dyuers sortes and maners of armours and engyns of warre whiche other nacions haue not.[10]

The earliest records of firearms in Europe date from 1326. Not only is there an illustration of a primitive cannon in an English manuscript from that year, but also, in the same year, two of the magistrates of Florence were given responsibility for obtaining firearms and ammunition for the defense of the city. Of course, the actual introduction of firearms must have taken place somewhat earlier.[11]

The introduction of firearms coincided with a more prominent role for infantry. Battles like Courtrai (1302), Bannockburn (1314), and Morgarten (1315) showed that infantry could defeat knights on horseback in favorable terrain. Swiss pikemen at Laupen (1339) proved that disciplined infantry could challenge cavalry on any terrain, and English archers (supported by dismounted knights) drove the point home in the Hundred Years' War. The rise of infantry was independent of firearms; however, early firearms were actually of little use on the battlefield.[12]

It seems that firearms were first used in Europe at the siege of Cividale in northeastern Italy in 1331. The first city walls to be breached by cannon were possibly those of Saint-Saveur-le-Vicomte in France in 1374. Individual handheld firearms were still rare at this point, multiple-barreled weapons mounted on wagons being more common. These cumbersome weapons were unsuitable for offensive action, and they probably had more of a psychological than a physical impact on the battlefield, through the sound and smoke they produced.[13]

Firearms came with a sinister and even satanic aura. Firearms were "an instrument sent from hell," according to Petrarch. They were a "diabolical instrument," according to John Mirfield; their discovery was due "not to human but to devilish agency," said Francesco di Giorgio. When the hero of *Orlando Furioso* threw the first gun into the ocean, he exclaimed "O cursed, abominable engine, which malign Beelzebub put together in the Tartarean depth, who intended to ruin the world through you, I reassign you to the hell from which you came." Francesco Guicciardini referred to firearms as "diabolical rather than human"; Erasmus called them "the engines of hell." As late as 1667, John Milton made firearms the surprise weapons of the infernal forces of Satan in *Paradise Lost*.[14]

These remarks may conceal a germ of truth. The Mongols were sometimes referred to as Tatars, after the name of a related and originally more prominent group of steppe nomads. The latter name was corrupted into "Tartar" by Europeans, apparently due to its similarity to the Latin word for hell, Tartarus. Since it was probably the Mongols who brought firearms to Europe, it is easy to see how confusion could arise. The association of sulfur with hell was also misleading. Eventually, myth attributed the invention of firearms to a fictional German monk, Berthold Schwarz, a necromancer and alchemist who had dealings with the devil, and their true origins were largely forgotten.[15]

Despite the satanic overtones, and despite a general contempt for missile weapons that was also peculiar to Europe, firearms spread quickly. The principal bottleneck was the expense of gunpowder. With a few exceptions, Europe lacked the natural saltpeter deposits that China and India enjoyed. However, the institution of saltpeter "plantations" within Europe helped lower the price of saltpeter by one-half or even two-thirds between the 1380s and the 1420s. The resulting increase in the supply of gunpowder then permitted the use of larger weapons firing heavier projectiles and expending more powder.[16]

The early 1400s saw the appearance of large, wrought-iron, stone-firing cannon known generically as bombards. The English conquest of Normandy between 1415 and 1422 demonstrated such bombards being used to good advantage in siege warfare. The French struck back with their own siege cannon, retaking Normandy and Guienne from the English between 1449 and 1451. The Spanish used cannon to batter Granada into submission, completing the "Reconquista" in 1492. Meanwhile, military architects were busily experimenting with ways to upgrade old fortifications to cope with the new pounding that they were taking.[17]

Firearms took longer to find their place on the battlefield. The early firearms were all but immobile, so they could only be used in defense of static positions. A Czech religious sect known as the Hussites won battle after battle in the 1430s and 1440s by combining firearms with wagons. They would circle their wagons to form a laager and use their firearms from within it. Wagons compensated for two of the main weaknesses of firearms. They protected the firearms from cavalry and infantry during battles and they transported the firearms between battles. Still, Hussite battle tactics simply confirm the general rule: fifteenth-century firearms were best employed against or behind fortifications.[18]

Truly portable firearms with worthwhile range and power, capable of being carried and fired by individual soldiers, had to await refinements in gunpowder. If the three ingredients of saltpeter, sulfur, and charcoal are ground up and mixed together dry, the result is what is called "serpentine gunpowder." At some point in the first half of the 1400s, Europeans discovered that gunpowder became more powerful if it was mixed with a liquid, allowed to dry in cakes, and then crumbled up into a fine but not too fine powder. The resulting product is known as "corned gunpowder." Corned gunpowder was too powerful to use in cannon at first, and serpentine powder continued in use for some time thereafter, but corned powder helped make muskets possible.[19]

The direct predecessors to the musket were the "hook guns" mounted on the walls of some German cities in the early 1400s. The late 1400s saw the appearance of handheld firearms ("arquebuses") that could be carried into battle, followed by heavier versions ("muskets") in the early 1500s that were fired from Y-shaped supports. Arquebuses and muskets were both shoulder arms; pistols did not appear until the mid-1500s. Armor was rated as pistol-proof or arquebuses-proof, depending on its thickness and strength, but there was no musket-proof armor. As the musket became more prevalent, soldiers dispensed with most of their useless armor. This in turn made the heavier musket redundant as well, although it was the term "musket" that continued to be used down into the 1800s.[20]

By the late 1400s, then, about a century and a half after their first introduction in Europe, firearms had begun to make their mark on the conduct of both sieges and battles, and also on the relationship between sieges and battles.

Sieges and Battles

Lasting control of territory was only possible through possession of fortifications. Armies had no enduring presence. An army was like a missile: it was very expensive, and it could only be used once. Once it was launched at the target, it might hit or it might miss, but either way it would blow up. (A seventeenth-century army could lose 50 percent or even 75 percent of its strength before it ever reached its objective.[21]) If the campaign did not end with the capture of a fortified city or other strongpoint, there was probably little of lasting value to show for it, no matter how many battles were won.[22]

Battles between armies in the field were actually rather rare. Even a small garrison might tie up a large army for an entire campaign season, if the garrison were protected by sturdy walls. The garrison eventually would be starved into submission, but the besieging army could easily run out of supplies first, because a stationary army would quickly exhaust local food reserves. Under these conditions, it made sense to wait until an enemy army began a siege, assemble a relief army while the siege was in progress, and then fall upon the weary and starving besiegers before the garrison surrendered. There was little need to keep an army permanently in the field.

Firearms upset the balance between offense and defense. More mobile versions of the cannon that had proven their worth in France in the mid-1400s entered Italy with a bang in 1494. Charles VIII of France swept down the length of the peninsula to Naples in a matter of weeks with an army of 18,000 and a horse-drawn siege train of 40 or more cannon. Fortresses that were expected to resist for months were taken in a matter of days. Strategic planning changed overnight. Everything now depended on stopping the enemy in battle before he reached the walls of the city.[23]

Sixteenth-century battles involved a complex interaction of different units and weapons. Infantry units contained both pikemen and musketeers. The pike was basically just a long spear, fourteen or even eighteen feet in length, unwieldy in one-on-one combat but matchless as part of a solid mass of unbroken infantry presenting a continuous front to the enemy. The musketeers had to move in and out of the pike formations, trying to get a clear shot while avoiding contact with enemy infantry or cavalry. The ratio of pikemen to musketeers was often 4:1 at the beginning of the 1500s but it approached 1:1 by the end.

Cavalry could make no impact on an unbroken infantry formation. Their own weapons (swords and pistols) were shorter than infantry weapons (pikes and muskets), and horses are too smart to charge into rows of sharp pointy objects. But if they could catch pikemen out of formation, or musketeers unprotected by pikemen, then a massacre would ensue. Cavalry lurked on the wings of the army, looking for a chance to turn on and outflank the enemy's infantry and artillery in the center.

Artillery could wreak havoc on tightly packed infantry formations. If the artillery could crack open opposing infantry formations, the cavalry could then finish them off. Artillery itself had to be protected against enemy infantry and cavalry, however. It was even slower than infantry – basically immobile in a tactical sense. When armies retreated, cannon were often abandoned to the enemy.

Pikemen, musketeers, cavalry, artillery – if any element was missing, the others became vulnerable. Without pikemen, the musketeers would be swept off the field and the artillery overrun. Without musketeers, the pikemen would be sitting ducks for enemy muskets. Without cavalry, the infantry would be surrounded and cut to pieces as soon as they lost formation. Without artillery, the infantry would be bombarded with impunity at long range. The matchlock-pike-cavalry-artillery model remained the norm until the invention of the bayonet collapsed the distinction between pikemen and musketeers in the 1700s.[24]

It goes without saying that the outcomes of battles depended on more than just the strengths and weaknesses of different weapons. Morale, leadership, fatigue, hunger, illness, fear, weather, terrain, reconnaissance, and luck all meant a great deal. Nevertheless, weapons were one of the few ways to get a systematic advantage. As Sir Roger Williams wrote in 1590, "True it is, braue men will shew themselves valiant with any kinde of weapons, all manner of waies; but the best sort of arming and mounting is the more profitable, & the more seruiceable."[25]

Skirmishes were much more common than battles, and an emphasis on battles exaggerates the effectiveness of firearms. Shooting a smoothbore matchlock musket at an individual target 75 or 100 yards away is a waste of powder. Where infantry could spread out without being ridden down by cavalry – whether in the jungles of Vietnam, the forests of North America, the savannahs of southern Africa, or even the woods and hills of Europe – smoothbore muskets lost much of their effectiveness.[26]

Figure 3.1 shows a detail from an imaginary battle and siege scene from a book published in 1565. The upper left-hand corner shows a body of pikemen (marked R) marching in formation with their pikes held vertically. In front of them is an officer on horseback. Behind them are musketeers marching in columns (marked S), also led by officers on horseback. The men with halberds are the equivalent of noncommissioned officers, charged with keeping the common soldiers in formation. The overall impression is of a closely ordered and crowded battlefield, although formations did not necessarily survive the stress of combat, as the melee in the upper right-hand corner suggests. The upper right-hand corner also shows two bodies of lancers (marked E and F). A body of dragoons is depicted at the bottom of the original engraving, but none of them appear within this detail.[27]

The siege takes place in the bottom half of the picture. The bottom left-hand corner shows the cannon park (marked P), together with siege implements like ladders and fascines (bundles of sticks) or gabions (baskets filled with dirt). A group of sappers (marked AA) carries standards bearing picks and shovels. The bottom right-hand corner shows the castle under siege (marked B), surrounded by siege cannon (marked G) protected by gabions. Infantry (marked C) sortie from the castle. Although the engraving dates from the mid-1500s, the castle seems to be rather old-fashioned, with rounded walls and high battlements, not the new style of fortification that was introduced in the early 1500s to withstand artillery.

When the French cannon made existing fortifications obsolete in the mid-1490s, there was a desperate search for a way to make cities safe again, so that the fates of kingdoms would not rest on the uncertain outcome of battle. No one knew quite what to do. Machiavelli described the basic dilemma:

"If the walls are built very high, they will be too much exposed to artillery; if they are built very low, they may be easily scaled."[28] Everyone knew that low walls could withstand artillery fire, but walls had been built high for a purpose: to keep enemy soldiers from climbing over them. The trick was to build them low but still do something to prevent an assault.

Firearms created the problem, and firearms supplied the solution. Low walls could be protected from assault if they were covered by interlocking fields of fire. Bastions were built that projected out from the walls so that the fire from the guns of the defenders would sweep down the lengths of the walls. Angular bastions provided the best coverage with the fewest blind spots, for reasons of geometry. The new style cohered in Italy around 1515 and crossed the Alps in the 1530s; it is commonly known by its French name, *trace italienne*, or "Italian design."[29]

For those who could afford to build it, the *trace italienne* basically restored the situation that had existed before siege cannon. Armies could again respond to sieges, instead of fighting battles to prevent them. Indecisive sieges multiplied and decisive battles disappeared. Because even the capture of a frontier fortress or fortified city was not enough to win a war, wars became long, expensive, and indecisive. Rulers repeatedly went bankrupt trying to wage them. Borders changed very little as a result of warfare in the 1600s and 1700s. The strategic stalemate was not broken until Napoleonic times, when mass mobilization changed the nature of warfare again.[30]

Siege warfare and infantry warfare were prerequisites for the spread of firearms in Europe. Whatever else one might say about it, the transformation of European armies between the 1300s and 1700s would not have occurred if European warfare had not been characterized by siege warfare and infantry warfare. Chapter 2 has already demonstrated that siege warfare and infantry warfare were not characteristic of warfare everywhere in this period. If they were in Europe, it was thanks to geography.[31]

Geography

Western Europe enjoys a temperate climate with adequate rainfall to support a large population within a fairly small area. Population was sparse in the Early Middle Ages, but by 1300 much of this area was covered by towns and

FIGURE 3.1. Sixteenth-century European battle and siege scene. Leonhardt Fronsperger, *Von Kayserlichem Malefitz und Schuldhändlen, Ordnung und Regiment*, insert preceding folio 54. Franckfurt am Mayn, 1565. Courtesy of the Stuart Collection, Rare Books Division, The New York Public Library, Astor, Lenox and Tilden Foundations.

farms. The Black Death struck Europe in 1347, and within a few years it had killed between a quarter and a half of the population, a staggering death toll. Furthermore, the plague returned with each new generation to carry off a new batch of victims. It was not until perhaps the 1500s that population returned to thirteenth-century levels. Still, although a good many villages were abandoned in the aftermath of the Black Death, and some marginally productive land was left uncultivated, Europe was not depopulated by the disease.[32] Europe remained a land of cities and towns and farms, a fact with two important consequences.

First, even fairly large bodies of slow-moving infantry could live off the land in many parts of Europe, reducing or obviating the need for organized sources of supply. There were very few governments before the 1800s that could organize effective supply lines (the Chinese and the Ottomans were probably the two best), and even these relied on obtaining some supplies locally, whether through purchase or pillage. Before railroads and trucks allowed large volumes of supplies to be moved overland, infantry warfare was generally limited to relatively populated areas. Europe was one of these areas.

Second, a victorious army could occupy the territory of a defeated one, and, depending on the organizational resources available to the victorious side, exploit it for either short-term (plunder) or long-term (taxation) gain. Wars could be fought to acquire territory, or to protect it.

Machiavelli was only noting the obvious in this passage from 1521, but the point is worth making:

> [A]n army in the field cannot possibly avoid an engagement if the enemy is absolutely determined to fight, unless it suddenly decamps, moves to a distance of 50 or 60 miles from the enemy, and always keeps retreating as the enemy advances. Fabius Maximus never refused to fight Hannibal, but did not choose to do so without an advantage; and Hannibal, considering the manner in which Fabius always took care to fortify himself, was too wise to force him to it; but if Fabius had been attacked, he would have been forced to fight him at any cost, or to have fled.[33]

An army cannot refuse battle indefinitely while holding its position. Since European generals were defending territory with cities and farms, they could not refuse battle indefinitely without abandoning them. Mobility could help an army choose the time and place of battle, but there were limits to what maneuvering could accomplish. Once an important city was threatened, the choices would narrow down to fighting in the open to prevent a siege, fighting from behind city walls while under siege, or fighting in the open to lift the siege. Because cities were the only prize worth fighting for, most battles in European history took place precisely under these conditions, when the only alternative was to let a city fall to the enemy without a fight.

On the steppe, where there were no fixed positions to defend, where flocks could often be moved out of danger, the nomads might refuse battle with impunity. As the Armenian monk Hetoum explained:

> The Tartas [i.e., Mongols] haue more vauntage than other men: for if they be in a felde togyder for to fyght agaynst theyr ennemys, if it please them thei shall fight; and if the batayle pleased nat them, theyr ennemis can nat fyght agaynst them nor come nygh them.[34]

The conditions of warfare were not the same everywhere in the world. Machiavelli for one recognized that geography made a difference. Although he knew little of history outside of Europe, the Roman experience with the Parthians taught him not to extrapolate from European conditions. In another passage from the same work he acknowledged:

> I either told you before, or meant to, that what I intended to say concerning the art of war should be limited to Europe. Therefore I think myself excused from accounting for the conduct of Asiatic nations. I cannot help observing, however, that the discipline of the Parthians was quite different from that of the Romans. The Parthians all fought on horseback in a loose and irregular manner, which, as a mode of combat, was unsteady and full of uncertainty; the Romans, one might say, fought chiefly as infantrymen in close and regular order – their success varied according to the nature of the countries in which they happened to fight. In enclosed places the Romans generally got the better, whereas the Parthians had the advantage in large open plains, and indeed the nature of the country they had to defend was very favorable to their manner of fighting; it was flat and open, a thousand miles from any seacoast, with so few rivers in it, that they might sometimes march two or three days without seeing any, and with very few towns and inhabitants.[35]

Infantry could be effective in Europe because it could force an engagement on an unwilling enemy. This did not mean that infantry *would be* effective, however. Cavalry had two basic advantages over infantry: mobility and power. Even if mobility was less important in the context of European warfare, power was still a crucial factor. It would do no good to march infantry up to an enemy city if they would just be overrun by enemy cavalry once they got there. So the balance of power between infantry and cavalry in Europe came down to a question of which would prevail in a slugfest. This in turn created a strong bias in European cavalry toward sacrificing mobility for power – for example, wearing heavier armor, carrying heavier weapons, and riding stronger but slower warhorses.

The balance of power between infantry and cavalry on the steppe was largely determined by mobility, rather than by power, simply because there was so much room to maneuver and there were no fixed objectives. This was no contest – cavalry was always superior to infantry on the steppe, at

least until the railroads arrived. Furthermore, there was a strong bias toward
light cavalry on the steppe, again because it was more mobile than heavy
cavalry. Nomads could be forced to fight when their camps and flocks were
threatened, just as Europeans could be forced to fight when their cities and
farms were threatened, but camps and flocks were themselves mobile, so
nomads could not easily be forced to fight *by infantry*.

Even western Europe was not always sheltered from steppe and desert nomads. The Arabs overran Spain and threatened France in the 700s, whereas
the Magyars raided Germany, France, and Italy in the 800s and 900s. However, the great expansion of the 1000s and 1100s pushed the frontiers back.
The last threat to western Europe from the steppe appeared shortly before
firearms arrived (it actually brought firearms with it, most likely). As mentioned earlier, the Mongols invaded eastern Europe in 1241, but news of the
death of the *khaghan* in Mongolia prompted them to abandon the invasion,
and it was never resumed. Eastern Europe remained exposed to attack from
steppe nomads, but western Europe never faced that danger again.[36]

Guns and Horses

It cannot be emphasized too strongly just how cumbersome and unwieldy
the early firearms were. This is an obvious point but a crucial one. For at
least the first few centuries of their existence, firearms could be used only
on foot, not on horseback. To put it another way, firearms were infantry
weapons, not cavalry weapons. There were of course a few exceptions to
this rule, but none of these exceptions vitiates the general principle, and
none of them affected the strategic choices open to people threatened by
nomads on horseback. Still, three of these exceptions are worth examining
in more detail.

The first of these exceptions was dragoons. Dragoons were basically
mounted infantry: they rode to the battlefield on horses but fought on foot
like infantry. The idea was an old one. Both archers and crossbowmen were
provided with horses whenever possible in fourteenth- and fifteenth-century
Europe, although they still fought on foot and not (like nomads) on horseback. Dragoons are mentioned in China at least as early as 1429. Probably
because dragoons could use the same weapons as musketeers, dragoons could
be found across the Oikoumene. From the second half of the 1500s, light
cavalry in Europe often carried muskets, which they would have used on
foot.[37]

Dragoons performed all kinds of duties: conducting raids, escorting supplies, scouting, and foraging, to name a few. They were backed up by cuirassiers (heavy cavalry) or lancers (medium cavalry), but they also supported

the cuirassiers and lancers in action, like musketeers supported pikemen. Dragoons remained in service in Europe into the 1800s, but in some armies they simply became medium cavalry, distinguished from hussars (light cavalry) more by the size of their horses and the cut of their uniform than by their weapons or tactics.[38]

Dragoons were versatile, but they were no answer for horse archers. When mounted they could not reload their muskets; when dismounted they would be left in the dust. As long as the army as a whole was slowed down by its artillery and supply train, dragoons provided little additional strategic mobility either.

The second of these exceptions was the pistol. The matchlock was never practical for use on horseback because the match had to be kept lit for the gun to be fired, so the pistol had to await the invention of the first matchless firing mechanism. That firing mechanism was the wheel lock. The wheel lock was a circular contraption powered by a spring that caused it to spin when released, creating sparks by the friction between the edge of the wheel and another surface. European expertise with watchmaking undoubtedly contributed to this invention. The wheel lock was very expensive, very delicate, and not easy to reload, but it could be wound up beforehand and kept ready to fire at a moment's notice.

The wheel lock pistol was introduced in the mid-1500s and used successfully in battle as early as 1552. German cavalry switched to the pistol and discarded the lance, although French cavalry clung to the lance for some time, looking down on firearms as "base and servile." The pistol was much easier to use than the lance because it could be fired in any direction, even from a standstill, whereas the lance had to be aligned with the momentum of the horse for maximum effect. The lance fell out of use in western Europe by the beginning of the 1600s, although it was used in eastern Europe into the 1800s by Polish uhlans, Russian Cossacks, and Prussian Bosniaken.

Because there was no burning match, a rider could keep a brace of pistols ready to fire, compensating for the difficulty of reloading them. However, the pistol had to be small and lightweight for a rider to carry more than one, so its effective range was only a few feet. Cavalry armed with pistols could not trade fire with infantry armed with muskets, nor could they avoid hand-to-hand combat with cavalry who preferred to use lances or swords. Cavalry experimented with a special maneuver designed to permit volley fire, known as the *caracole*, but soon abandoned it as impractical in favor of the old-fashioned cavalry charge.[39]

To put it another way, as odd as it may sound, pistols were a hand-to-hand weapon, not a ranged weapon.[40] They competed with lances, the original weapon of choice for heavy cavalry, and not with bows and arrows, the weapon *par excellence* of light cavalry. The same goes for the carbine, which was basically a cut-down musket, light enough to use on horseback but lacking the range and power of a full-scale musket. Pistols and carbines made heavy cavalry even more effective at close quarters, but agrarianate societies usually had the edge in heavy cavalry anyway. What they lacked was some answer to the recurved composite bow, which the pistol and the carbine did not provide.

The third of these exceptions was horse artillery. Horse artillery was a special kind of artillery that was designed to accompany cavalry. It used smaller and lighter cannon to save weight and special gun carriages to improve speed, as well as faster draught horses and specially trained crews. However, horse artillery did not appear until the 1700s. Firearms design was a balancing act between strength, cost, and weight, and it was quite an achievement to produce cannon that were strong, cheap, and light all at the same time. The level of achievement represented by horse artillery was beyond any power that did not already have considerable experience with less advanced firearms.

It is worth noting in passing how many horses were needed to pull cannon. In 1604, one writer suggested that 1,000 infantrymen should be accompanied by 1 cannon, and estimated that 200 horses would be needed to haul that cannon plus the wagonloads of powder and shot it would require. In 1708, Marlborough required 16,000 horses to move his siege train of 80 cannon and 20 mortars across the Belgian countryside to the French fortress at Lille. By the 1700s, when the number of cavalry had fallen to a fraction of the number of infantry, artillery may have employed as many horses as did cavalry in western European armies. Where cavalry was at a premium, on the edge of the steppe, it was difficult to justify using 200 horses for a single cannon.[41]

Firearms eventually contributed to the Russian and Chinese conquest of the steppe in the 1700s, but this technology was largely imported from western Europe, or else it grew out of technology that was. Eighteenth-century firearms would have been impossible without the advances of the preceding four centuries, and the advances of the preceding four centuries are inconceivable outside of a framework where firearms were widely used on a regular basis in infantry and siege (and naval) warfare.

Guns and Ships

Naval warfare provided an extra dimension where firearms could be deployed, particularly cannon. From the Baltic to the Black, Europe was surrounded by seas. Many countries had coastlines to defend. For some countries in some periods, such as England in the 1600s and 1700s, the number of cannon deployed at sea must have exceeded the number on land. The special requirements of naval gunnery (greater safety, for example) and the special advantages (less concern with weight) must have pushed technology in new directions.

The only specialized warships in fourteenth-century Europe were the galleys in the Mediterranean. Galleys had limited room to mount cannon, both because the rowers took up so much space and because their limited freeboard mitigated against using cannon in broadsides anyway. Even sixteenth-century galleys had just one large cannon and four smaller cannon mounted on the bow, plus a number of swivel guns. Nevertheless, galley fleets contained enough galleys to stimulate demand for bronze cannon, which remained expensive and scarce even into the 1500s.[42]

There was no distinction between warships and merchant ships in the Atlantic in the 1300s. Since sailing ships could only fight by grappling and boarding, any ship could be made ready for battle by the addition of "castles" fore and aft. Kings had ships, but not navies; royal ships could be rented to merchants to carry goods just as merchant ships could be rented by the king to carry soldiers. Firearms appeared on board ships by the end of the 1300s, but these were antipersonnel weapons like the swivel guns on galleys. Ship design and naval tactics changed little in the 1400s.[43]

The introduction of heavier cannon on sailing ships did lead to changes in design and tactics in the 1500s. Heavy cannon had to be placed closer to the waterline so as not to make ships capsize. Ships were fitted with gunports to allow cannon to be placed on a special gun deck below the main deck. Where the shortage of bronze cannon once limited heavy ordnance to a few guns mounted on the bow, the development of cheap but reliable cast-iron cannon in England in the 1540s made it feasible to arm sailing ships with two full broadsides. These developments eventually led to the line-of-battle tactics that dominated fleet battles through the 1600s and 1700s.

New ships known as galleons were designed with lower castles and narrower beams; although at a disadvantage in a boarding action with the older carracks, they could use their superior speed and maneuverability to avoid grappling and to bring their guns to bear. Technical improvements in hull construction and rigging design further improved sailing qualities and opened up new possibilities in naval tactics. Cannonfire could be concentrated on individual targets and crippled ships could be separated from their fleet and captured.[44]

Smoothbore cannon seldom sank a ship outright, but they could pummel a ship into submission by slicing up its rigging, raking its decks, and punching holes in its hull. In 1588, the Spanish still planned on firing their cannon just once as a prelude to boarding, but the English stood off and fired their cannon repeatedly. The Spanish lacked the maneuverability to close with the English, and the Armada was forced out of the English Channel into the North Sea, suffering most of its losses as its battered ships tried to return to Spain.[45]

These changes in design and tactics could not have taken place without the improvements in reliability and safety achieved on land. Early cannon were dangerous enough on land; it would have been foolhardy to use them in the confined spaces of the hull of a ship at sea if they were liable to explode. The force of an explosion would not be dissipated into the air – it would crush everyone below decks or blow a hole in the deck or the hull. Once heavy cannon could be used on ships, however, the experience gained there could also be applied on land. Experience came quickly since fleets carried many cannon. The Anglo-Dutch fleet that defeated the French at La Hogue in 1692 mounted 6,756 cannon, compared to the 58 cannon, 38 mortars, and 8 stone-throwing guns in Louis XIV's siege train in 1690 or to the 80 cannon and 20 mortars in Marlborough's siege train in 1708.[46]

The new fleets were more specialized. A galley fleet derived most of its fighting strength from the soldiers embarked on it; it was possible to run galleys up on a beach and convert the fleet into an army. The galleys themselves were hardly irreplaceable. A sailing fleet relied on its cannon for its fighting power; without horses to pull them or infantry to protect them, the cannon and their gun crews could not fend for themselves on land. Sailing ships (built strong to withstand cannonfire and bad weather), their crews (skilled sailors to navigate away from land and work the rigging), and their weapons (heavy bronze or iron cannon) represented a tremendous investment of capital that could not easily be replaced. Not only did separate organizations, navies distinct from armies, appear to manage these specialized assets, but destroying an enemy's sailing fleet now became a viable strategic objective.

The substitution of cannon for soldiers as the fighting strength of the sailing ship allowed the size of the crew to be cut while maintaining the fighting strength of the ship. The British navy of 1697, with 9,912 cannon, was manned by only 24,000 sailors, just 2.4 sailors per cannon. By contrast, armies averaged around 1,000 soldiers for every cannon. There were at best just enough men in a ship's crew to handle the rigging and fire half of the cannons, one broadside or the other. The consequent savings in the consumption of supplies increased the effective range of sailing ships. Not only could warships blockade or raid enemy coasts for extended periods, but merchantmen could carry cargoes over longer distances while still being able to defend themselves.[47]

Ultimately, the substitution of cannon for manpower on ships permitted European powers to extend their reach in the 1500s, at sea if not on land, into the Indian Ocean and beyond. The demand for cannon generated by the merchantmen and men-of-war in turn drove production and innovation of cannon beyond whatever the needs of siege warfare on land alone might have produced.

Guns and Bows

Cannon were indispensable for naval warfare and siege warfare, but where there were neither ships nor fortifications, the choice between guns and bows was not so easy.

There is no question that bows were once superior to guns in nearly every way imaginable on the battlefield. Even the best firearms in the 1300s were inaccurate, unwieldy, unreliable, and at times positively dangerous to their users. Bows, particularly better ones like the English longbow or the Mongol recurved composite bow, in the hands of experienced archers, were far more lethal. They were accurate at longer ranges, could shoot several arrows for every bullet, were light and easily portable, were much easier to maintain, and were quite safe to use. It is possible that firearms only developed as rapidly as they did because the dramatic sound and flash and smoke held out the promise of greater things to come.[48]

The English were still debating the relative merits of the longbow and the musket in the last decade of the 1500s. The leading proponent of the longbow was Sir John Smythe, a professional soldier with twenty years of experience in France, the Low Countries, and Hungary, who published his views in 1590. Much of Smythe's book is anecdotal, but at the heart of it is a comparison of firearms and bows in three specific respects. First, Smythe argued that bows had a higher rate of fire than firearms, so that archers could discharge four or five arrows before musketeers could shoot one bullet. Second, he argued that bows were much more reliable than firearms, because firearms were liable to overheat and crack, and because gunpowder could be spoiled by dampness. Third, and frankly very unpersuasively, Smythe claimed that arrows created more havoc than bullets, by terrifying and wounding as well as by killing.[49]

In 1594 a captain by the name of Humfrey Barwick published a rebuttal in which he specifically addressed these same three points. First, Barwick argued that rate of fire under battlefield conditions was not as important as it might appear. If the enemy was attacking with cavalry, one's troops would only have time to get off one shot, even if they had bows. If the enemy was advancing with infantry, then one's troops would have time to fire repeatedly, even if they had firearms. Second, Barwick argued that archers had to be in top physical condition to operate effectively. If firearms were more likely to malfunction than bows, archers were more liable to underperform than musketeers due to fatigue or hunger or illness. Third, Barwick denied that arrows were anywhere near as deadly as bullets, and he dismissed the claims that arrows could wound and harass the enemy as being of little consequence.[50]

In the hands of an experienced archer, rate of fire and accuracy clearly favored the bow. The Turkish *mamluks* of Egypt could get off a second and third arrow before their first arrow hit a target 75 yards away, and experienced archers can generally keep up a pace of six to eight well-aimed shots per minute until they tire.[51] By contrast, sixteenth-century infantrymen with matchlocks might manage one shot every several minutes, with misfires up to half the time.[52] The Turkish *mamluks* were also expected to hit a 38-inch circle at a range of 75 yards with five out of five arrows, and a good archer might hit a target the size of a man on horseback one out of four times at a range of 280 yards.[53] By contrast, eighteenth-century muskets shooting at a target 50 paces wide (i.e., 33 yards!) from a distance of 100 paces (i.e., 67 yards) only scored hits 46 percent of the time. A smoothbore musket had no chance of hitting a man-sized target at more than 80 yards.[54]

Still, Barwick's contention that more familiarity with firearms would make them more reliable as well as more effective was amply born out in the long run. I hardly wish to argue that bows were more effective than firearms *for Europeans* in the 1590s, but only that the disadvantages pointed out by Smythe – low rate of fire and high rate of malfunction – were real and were serious. Less obvious but more relevant here are the limitations on the acknowledged advantages of firearms. The two greatest advantages to firearms would not have been equally valuable to all peoples in all places.

One point in favor of firearms, that bullets could pierce armor better than arrows, had little value in fighting nomads. Nomads generally did not wear heavy armor. Either they could not obtain it or it was too heavy for their horses. Europeans and Japanese spent almost all their time fighting each other, so they were most likely to be shooting at armored targets. The Russians and the Ottomans had to fight both armored and unarmored soldiers, but the Mamluks and the Chinese were most concerned with nomads, so they were least concerned with the ability of their weapons to pierce armor. The nomads themselves had to fight both armored and unarmored soldiers, because they fought both agrarianate powers and other nomads, but of course they had other reasons for not adopting firearms.[55]

The other point in favor of firearms, that they were easy to learn, did not really apply outside of agrarianate societies. In nomadic societies, boys learned to handle a bow as part of their everyday life. No special training was required, so there was no advantage to shifting to a weapon that was easier to learn. Simplicity was only an advantage in societies where new recruits had to be trained in the use of their weapons. Furthermore, simplicity mattered most where large numbers of new recruits could be armed with firearms. If there were other constraints on the number of men who could be deployed, such as the availability of horses, then it still made more sense to arm them with bows, to the extent that training archers was cheaper than breeding horses.[56]

Reliance on pikemen and musketeers eventually changed the way that armies were recruited and trained. Recruiting and training soldiers was not the obvious approach in every place at every time. Some styles of warfare demanded so many years of practice that they could only be learned as a way of life. The longbow may have been a more effective weapon than the musket, but the longbow required enormous amounts of practice, limiting the pool of recruits to men who had grown up with the weapon. Firearms helped increase the pool of potential soldiers to all able-bodied men.

Since pikemen and musketeers could be recruited from unskilled peasants, armies grew rapidly in the 1600s, limited only by the capacity of rulers to feed and clothe and pay them. To take the example of the French: The projected peacetime strength of the army had never exceeded 20,000 before the Thirty Years' War, but it rose to over 100,000 before 1700. Similarly, the projected wartime strength of the army had never exceeded 80,000 before the Thirty Years' War, but it surpassed 400,000 before 1700. By either measure, the French army grew about five times as large in less than 100 years.[57]

Handling a musket was a comparatively simple matter, but musketeers, like pikemen, had to learn to work together in units. If everyone fired their muskets at once, the enemy could approach while they were all reloading. The Dutch pioneered the technique of volley fire in the 1590s, whereby each rank of musketeers fired in unison and then retired to reload. To make sure that they did not get in each other's way, and that they would finish reloading by the time their turn came up again, they had to practice and practice.[58]

Drill turned out to have side effects that were at least as important as permitting volley fire. When men are drilled together in units, they are more likely to stay together in battle, when confusion and danger would otherwise scatter them. They are more likely to obey orders under stress. At a time when it would be natural to turn and run, their first reaction would be to stand and fight. The idea of drill went back to the Romans, but without the immediate benefit of improving the rate of fire, the less obvious benefits of drill might not have been rediscovered.[59]

The increase in army size and the spread of drill helped transform European warfare yet again after 1700. How these developments fed into European military superiority in the 1700s and 1800s will be addressed in chapter 8. The point here is that these developments could never have taken place, certainly not in a recognizably similar way, if muskets had not come to replace bows in western Europe. The other point is that muskets might not have replaced bows so quickly in western Europe if not for the presence of a buffer zone between western Europe and the steppe: eastern Europe.

Eastern Europe

Eastern Europe bordered on the steppe and lived under the shadow of the steppe nomads. As western Europe leaned more heavily on infantry and firearms, Poland and Russia were caught between two very different styles of warfare, open to attack by infantry armies from the west and cavalry armies from the east. The conflicting demands of the two fronts, together with eastern Europe's relative backwardness, meant that firearms did not catch on as quickly in Poland and Russia as they did in western Europe.[60]

Polish armies of the 1300s and 1400s were composed largely of horsemen. A small standing army was created in the late 1400s, but its main task was to defend the border on the steppe, so it was comprised almost entirely of cavalrymen, with only a few infantrymen to garrison fortifications. Cavalry remained the backbone of Polish armies throughout the 1500s and 1600s as well. Infantry generally fought from behind wagons, as in Bohemia and Hungary, originally with crossbows and later with firearms. Only in the 1600s were substantial numbers of pikemen included, as the threat from the Swedes came to outweigh that from the Tatars.[61]

Russia entered the 1300s under the control of one of the Mongol successor *khanates*, the Golden Horde. The princes of Moscow submitted to the Mongols and manipulated Mongol rule to their own advantage, gradually extending their power and influence over the other Russian princes. The Mongol conquest was the catalyst for a shift in the political center of gravity from Kiev to Moscow, although it took centuries for this process to be completed.[62]

Prince Dmitrii of Moscow fought and (maybe[63]) defeated the Mongols at Kulikovo in 1380, and the Golden Horde began to self-destruct in the early 1400s. Still, it was not until 1480 or later that Ivan III ("the Great") renounced Russian submission to the Mongols. He also reorganized the army around the system of "servitors" and tripled the size of his realm.[64] Most of that expansion was to the north, however, not to the south. Down to the mid-1500s, Russian settlements were largely confined to the forest zone in the north; the forest-steppe and steppe lands to the south were dominated by the nomads.

The collapse of the Golden Horde did not end Russian troubles with the steppe nomads. The Golden Horde was succeeded by four semisedentary *khanates* (Crimea, Kazan, Astrakhan, and Siberia) and one fully nomadic horde (the Nogai). The Crimean Tatars took control of the lucrative slave trade, selling Russian captives to Genovese merchants in Black Sea ports for resale elsewhere, especially Italy, Spain, and North Africa.

The sedentarized Tatars still fought like steppe nomads. The Crimean Tatars, for example, were armed with bows and supplied with remounts; each man generally had several horses. They struck quickly, to gain the element of surprise, pillaging the population and carrying off slaves before the defense could react. They avoided combat except to defend their encampments or their booty and did not get tied down in sieges. It is said that they were frightened by firearms when they first encountered them, but lost that fear when they realized how ineffective they were.[65]

The Russians developed a complicated defensive system to counter this threat. Fortified lines of logs, earthworks, and trenches protected the frontier. These lines were garrisoned by the local servitors and reinforced each summer by large contingents of servitor cavalrymen who were called up in two shifts. Guard posts were set up well south of the frontier at intervals of six to eight miles, linked by a regular system of patrols, to provide early warning of raiders. The Cossacks also helped shield the frontier from Tatar raids, although the Cossacks themselves were something of a mixed blessing.[66]

The "servitors" were members of the landholding elite organized in an elaborate hierarchy of ranks that dated from the late 1400s. Service began at age fifteen and typically lasted for life; it defined in many ways the expectations and the experiences of the males of that social class. Their duties depended on their rank and their region, but one of the most important was guarding the frontier as part of the system described earlier. These servitors were required to bring their own weapons and mounts and spend several months of each year on duty.[67]

In terms of weapons and equipment, the Russian servitor cavalrymen were little different from their steppe counterparts. Giles Fletcher, an Englishman in Russia in the late 1500s, painted this picture of them: "The common horseman hath nothing else but his bow in his case under his right arm and his quiver and sword hanging on the left side, except some few that bear a case of dags or a javelin or short staff along their horse side."[68] They even rode their horses in the Mongol style, with short stirrups that allowed them to stand clear of the saddle.[69]

The result was an army that looked quite different from western European ones. In the early 1500s, an Austrian observer commented on the Russian emphasis on mobility:

[I]n battle they never used artillery and infantry. Whatever they did, whether
they were attacking, pursuing, or fleeing from the enemy, they did it quickly.
Therefore neither artillery nor infantry could keep up with them.[70]

Firearms are first mentioned in Russia in the 1380s, although if we accept
the hypothesis that firearms were brought across the steppe by the Mongols,
they must have been known even earlier than that. Different passages in
the chronicles suggest both gunpowder weapons imported from the east and
cannon reimported from the west. In the second half of the 1400s, craftsmen
from western Europe were brought to Russia to cast bronze cannon. The
earliest surviving example dates from 1485.[71]

Russia produced its own iron, but neither copper nor tin was mined, so
raw materials for bronze cannon were imported through Novgorod. Saltpeter was plentiful – indeed, it was an export item in this period – so the raw
materials for gunpowder were readily available. The techniques for producing firearms and for producing gunpowder all came from abroad, however.
Russia was not known in this period for its advanced technology, nor is it
known to have made any particular contribution to firearms technology.[72]

Despite these difficulties, the Russians had built up an impressive arsenal
of bronze cannon by the 1500s. As Giles Fletcher noted in 1591, these cannon
were useful against the Poles, but the Russians often left them behind when
they went to fight the Tatars:

Of pieces for the field they carry no great store when they war against the Tatar;
but when they deal with the Pole (of whose forces they make more account) they
go better furnished with all kind of munition and other necessary provisions.
It is thought that no prince of Christendom hath better store of munition than
the Russe emperor.[73]

Meanwhile, muskets were just making their appearance. Only in 1550
did Ivan IV ("the Terrible") organize special units of musketeers known as
strel'tsy. These units were incorporated into the servitor system, as were
similar units of artillerymen, and like all servitor units these were hereditary.
They had little impact on battle tactics. They were used as a police force in
times of peace, and to defend or attack fortification in times of war.[74]

Like the Hussites, Poles, Hungarians, and Ottomans, the Russians relied
on wagon laagers instead of pikemen to protect their musketeers. Like the
Mamluks, Mughals, and Chinese, the Russians also used portable wooden
walls built just for that purpose. The musketeers and artillery would fight
from behind the walls. The combination of small numbers of *strel'tsy* musketeers supporting large numbers of servitor cavalry is reminiscent of nothing
more than the combination of janissary musketeers and *timariot* cavalry in
the Ottoman army, but it is broadly typical of many states on the edge of
the steppe.[75]

Ivan IV succeeded in conquering the *khanates* of Kazan and Astrakhan in the 1550s, but this success was due in large part to fortuitous geographical factors: the Russians could transport supplies and firearms quickly and easily down the Volga River. The Crimean Tatars were a tougher nut to crack, both because they were Ottoman vassals and because the Dniepr River was not navigable below the rapids. The Tatars showed they were still a force to be reckoned with, reaching the outskirts of Moscow in 1571 and again in 1591.[76]

However, the Poles soon eclipsed the threat from the Tatars, occupying Moscow between 1610 and 1612 during the "Time of Troubles." More wars with Poland followed in 1617–18 and 1632–4. Rivalry over the Ukraine embroiled Russia in another war with Poland in 1654, one that lasted thirteen years. The servitors were not up to the demands of such a long war, and peasants were drafted into the army for the first time. The peasant draftees were organized into new-style infantry regiments, with most of the officers being Europeans. By 1681, the new regiments (infantry and cavalry both) numbered 80,000 men, with infantry now in the majority.[77]

The reforms created an army better able to handle the Poles but no better (perhaps worse) at dealing with the Tatars, as experience would soon demonstrate. An alliance with Poland and Austria obligated Russia to send an army against Crimea as part of a coordinated effort against the Ottomans in 1687. The logistical challenges were strikingly similar to those facing the Chinese in their campaigns in Mongolia and the Ordos.

Russia mobilized some 112,000 men, nearly half of them infantry, and hundreds of cannon for the offensive. They had to cover 300 to 400 miles of open steppe to reach the Crimea itself; at a pace of 12 miles a day this might have taken a month each way. Grain for the men for three or four months would have weighed around 20,000 tons. The Russians transported half the grain by boat down the Dniepr as far as the rapids; soldiers carried some, and the rest was loaded onto 20,000 wagons. Some 100,000 horses were assembled to meet the needs of the cavalry, artillery, and supply wagons.[78]

The army set out in May. It traveled in a tight defensive formation, with the wagons in a compact mass in the center surrounded by the infantry, which were in turn preceded and flanked by cavalry and followed by the artillery. This unwieldy force only averaged eight miles a day when it moved, and it had to stop and break formation every fourth or fifth day to collect fodder for the horses. At this rate the trip would have taken almost two months in each direction, stretching the supplies to their limit.

Then, in the middle of June, the army discovered that the Tatars had set fire to the dry summer grass. This was a trick often used against the nomads, but it was just as effective against the Russians. The army could not collect enough fodder for the horses without scattering all over the steppe.

The wagons could not move without horses, and the infantry could not continue without the wagons. Consequently, the army turned back without either having reached the Crimea or having fought the Tatars at all. All the effort that had gone into stockpiling grain, building boats, and requisitioning wagons was wasted.[79]

The fiasco in 1687 was no fluke; another expedition in 1689 also had to turn back due to insufficient supplies. Infantry and artillery might have defeated the Tatars in battle, but they could not even reach the Crimea until Russian settlements had encroached far enough onto the steppe to bring them within striking range. Improved firearms did help protect those settlements as they spread south of the forest-steppe zone, but it was a painfully slow process.

Russia's long and vulnerable border with the steppe slowed the integration of firearms into its army in the 1400s and 1500s. The threat from the west induced reforms in the 1600s that changed the orientation of the Russian army. This new-style army was poorly adapted to steppe warfare. Once improvements in firearms reversed the balance of power between steppe and sown in the 1700s, however, Russia's geographical position offered spectacular opportunities for rapid expansion, similar to the opportunities enjoyed by the descendants of European settlers in the Americas.

The Americas

When the Italian doctor, mathematician, and gambler Girolamo Cardano sat down to write his autobiography in 1575, he identified four "extraordinary, though quite natural" changes in the world. Three of these were inventions: firearms were one, the compass another, printing a third. The fourth, and to Cardano the most noteworthy, was the discovery during his lifetime of the other two-thirds of the world.[80]

Contact between the Old and New Worlds resulted in the rapid destruction of the two largest empires of the New World, those of the Aztecs and the Incas, by a handful of Spanish adventurers. Firearms played only a minor role in this stunning turn of events. The native populations were devastated by diseases to which they had built up no immunity. (Some 40 percent of the population of central Mexico died of smallpox the year after Cortés arrived.) The Spanish found many allies among native communities that had been victims of the Aztecs and Incas. Finally, the Spanish possessed an array of weapons that the natives could not match. Take away any one of these three factors, and it is far from certain what the final result might have been, and horses and steel contributed as much as firearms to the Spanish edge in weaponry.[81]

The smallpox epidemic of 1520–21 was just the beginning. The Oik-oumene had more virulent diseases than the Americas, thanks to its greater population and more numerous domesticated animals, among other reasons. Smallpox, measles, and other diseases ravaged the native population of the Americas, reducing it by as much as 95 percent within a century. Catastrophic population losses far exceeding even the effects of the Black Death in Europe two centuries earlier precipitated in many cases the collapse of political and social structures and undermined the capacity and the will to resist. European settlers spread to the recently depopulated areas, particularly the temperate regions, bringing with them their domesticated animals and plants.[82]

The settlers who landed on the east coast of North America brought with them European weapons and tactics. What they found was that ranks of militiamen firing volleys from matchlocks were ineffective against warriors who spread out and took cover. With their experience as hunters, the natives knew how to use the terrain, and they were better marksmen than most farmers. Although this style of warfare was alien to the European military tradition, the settlers had no choice but to learn it, or to find native allies to fight for them.

Although the settlers never quite overcame their tactical disadvantages, they enjoyed strategic advantages that more than compensated. The natives were entirely dependent on them for firearms and for gunpowder. Guerrilla warfare was not suited for defending fixed points, so the natives had no way to protect their homes or crops. Conversely, the natives lacked the weapons and manpower to destroy settlements protected by firearms and forts, so the loss of territory could rarely be reversed.[83]

The natives best able to defend themselves turned out to be nomads living in difficult terrain, dispersed over large areas, who learned to tame and ride horses. Horses adapted quickly and well to life in the Americas, and before long there were herds of feral horses on the pampas of Argentina and the prairies of North America. The nomadic tribes that followed the buffalo herds across the prairies between the Mississippi River and the Rocky Mountains took to traveling and hunting on horseback. They also adopted styles of warfare reminiscent of warfare on the steppe.[84]

The Great Plains could have become America's Mongolia. It is true that there were probably less than 100,000 Plains Indians in the 1800s, not even one-tenth of the population of Mongolia, but the entire U.S. Army never numbered as many as 40,000 men except during the Civil War decade of the 1860s. The nomads had all the advantages of mobility. Grain-fed cavalry horses were just as dependent on supply wagons as the men who rode them. Warriors riding tough grass-fed ponies and switching mounts throughout the day could easily outrun them. The same dynamic was at work on the pampas of Argentina, where the natives even pushed back the frontier in the 1850s and 1860s.[85]

The crucial difference was industrial technology. By the time that the United States had absorbed the lands east of the Mississippi, the Industrial Revolution was well underway. The railroads and the telegraph provided transportation and communication. Barbed wire restricted the movement of the game on which the nomads depended. Repeating rifles with brass cartridges combined accuracy, portability, and killing power. Even with some firearms from traders, the natives never had a chance.

But repeating rifles with brass cartridges did not come out of nowhere. They came out of a long line of development that went back to people who fought with infantry armies and city walls, namely Europeans. The Sharps rifle and Spencer carbine were far more lethal than any bow ever made, but without centuries of experience with matchlock and flintlock smoothbore muskets, some of them probably inferior to many bows, the Sharps and Spencer might never have appeared.

Despite their late start, the Europeans were able to surpass the Chinese in firearms technology. If a late start was not necessarily a fatal handicap, then what about the people of the rest of the Oikoumene? Why did they fail to keep up or catch up with Europe? To answer this question, we have to look beyond China and Europe to consider other parts of the Oikoumene, beginning with the western and eastern halves of Islamdom.[86]

4

Western Islamdom

At the time of Muhammad's death in 632, the Muslim community was still confined to the Arabian Peninsula and concentrated in the two towns of Mecca and Medina. Within a hundred years, Islam had spread from there to encompass Spain, the Maghrib, Egypt, Palestine, Syria, Iraq, Iran, Transoxania, and northwestern India. Within this area there were initially few Muslims, but over time the majority of the population converted. This rapid expansion subjected the political organization of the Muslim community, the caliphate, to powerful centrifugal forces that it was not equipped to handle. By the 900s, the caliphate had for all practical purposes split into a number of independent sultanates, although the caliph remained a potent symbol of religious community.

Beginning in the 900s, Turkish tribes migrated south and west off the steppe into the settled regions of Islamdom. Thanks to the missionary work of Sufi mystics and others, these tribes had generally converted to Islam beforehand. Still, this migration had profound effects on Islamdom, especially in regions like Anatolia, Azarbayjan, Khurasan, and Afghanistan that were suited to nomadic pastoralism. The balance between settled and nomadic shifted toward the latter. Thanks to their military prowess, the Turks were able to found dynasties all throughout Islamdom, even in places farther removed from the steppe like Egypt and India.

The invasion of the Mongols in the 1200s was more traumatic. Not only had the invaders not been converted to Islam, but they also sacked Baghdad and killed the caliph in 1258. Deprived of its spiritual figurehead, Islam nonetheless continued to spread – both southward into Africa and eastward into India and Southeast Asia. In the 1300s, the Moroccan scholar Ibn Battuta could travel from Spain and west Africa to Syria and India, and even to Muslim communities in the great ports of Southeast Asia and south China, and find much that was familiar wherever he went. Islamic law was a unifying force in commercial transactions, as the Arabic language was in scholarship, and both goods and ideas flowed freely over great distances.[1]

Islamdom possessed advanced science and technology, particularly in mathematics and chemistry. Cast iron was produced centuries before it was in Europe, and fine steel was made by combining cast iron and wrought iron. The first formulas for gunpowder in Islamdom are found in an untitled and undated Arabic work that may be as early as the 900s or 1000s, perhaps only a century or two after the first record of gunpowder in China. The *Kitab al-furusiyya bi rasm al-jihad* by al-Hasan al-Rammah, who died in 1294, contains the first description in Arabic of the purification and crystallization of saltpeter as well as seventy formulas for different varieties of gunpowder. Significantly, saltpeter was known as "Chinese snow" in Arabic and as "Chinese salt" in Persian.[2]

al-Hasan al-Rammah not only includes a number of typically Chinese ingredients in his formulas but also describes a weapon like the fire-lance that might easily have originated in China. It is not clear whether firearms per se reached Islamdom directly from China or indirectly through Europe; because the earliest confirmed use of firearms in Islamdom took place in Egypt, they could have arrived by sea from either the east or the west. Firearms did come to the Maghrib from Spain and to Turkey from the Balkans, however.[3]

For the purposes of this book, I divide Islamdom into western and eastern halves roughly on a line drawn through the old capital of Baghdad. The eastern half is discussed in chapter 5. This division does not quite match the cultural division between the Arabic-speaking lands to the west and the Turkish- and Persian-speaking lands to the east, because Anatolia and the Balkans are included in the west. Rather, western Islamdom for these purposes generally includes the Ottoman empire and points west, whereas eastern Islamdom consists of Iran and points east. This division also coincides fairly well with two styles of warfare: one in the west characterized by heavy cavalry and infantry and one in the east marked by light cavalry.[4]

Turkey

Anatolia enjoys a mild climate and moderate rainfall that allow a flourishing agricultural economy. The Romans founded the city of Constantinople on the Bosphorus, the narrow straits between Anatolia and the Balkans, and after the loss of the western provinces it became the capital of the Eastern Roman (or Byzantine) empire.

The ancestors of the Ottomans were among those Turkish tribes that had migrated off the steppe into eastern Anatolia by the 1200s. Pressure from the Mongols pushed them farther west, where they encroached on Byzantine territory. Originally just one of many small Turkish principalities in western Anatolia, the Ottomans were the first to establish themselves on both sides of the straits, in 1352. Over the next half century, they expanded and consolidated their territory in both Anatolia and the Balkans.[5]

Meanwhile, firearms had arrived in the Balkans in 1351, when the Venetian Senate decided to send eight guns to the city of Zara to strengthen its defenses against the Hungarians. By 1378, cannon were being produced in Dubrovnik, and it seems they were used by the Serbs against the Ottomans at the battle of Kossovo in 1389. There is scattered evidence that the Ottomans themselves may have used firearms at Kossovo, at Constantinople in the unsuccessful siege of 1396–97, or at Ankara in 1402, but none of it is conclusive.[6]

Despite the disaster at Ankara in 1402, where Temür captured the Ottoman emperor and (according to some sources) displayed him in a cage, the dynasty recovered and prospered. The Ottomans apparently had acquired firearms by 1422, from whatever source, because they deployed cannon against Constantinople in that year. The city did not fall, but it was only a matter of time before it did. The Byzantine empire had been reduced to little more than Constantinople itself, and there were hardly enough men left to man the walls. When the high medieval walls began to crumble before the Ottoman bombardment in 1453, there were not enough defenders to plug the holes and the city fell.[7]

The second half of the 1400s saw the Ottoman empire spread as far east as the Euphrates and as far north as the Danube. Their expansion brought them into contact with new adversaries: Hungary and Austria to the north, Venice and Spain to the west, the Mamluks in Egypt to the south, and the Safavids in Iran to the east. Needless to say, the Ottomans could not afford to be at war with all of these adversaries at the same time. On the other hand, they were rarely at peace on all four of these fronts at the same time either. The Ottoman empire was almost always at war somewhere.[8]

The Ottomans and their rivals actively aided each others' enemies. Despite the rhetoric of crusade and *jihad*, and despite real enmity between the religions, such cooperation routinely crossed religious lines. The Ottomans had a long-standing alliance with the French, for example, aimed at their common enemy, the Habsburgs. Ottoman agents gathered intelligence on the Protestant Reformation as a possible counterweight to Habsburg power. The Ottoman pretender Cem was sheltered by the Mamluks of Egypt, the Knights of St. John, and finally the Pope.

Whether or not gunpowder was "disclosed to the Turks by the treachery of apostates and the selfish policy of rivals," as Gibbon famously stated, such rivalries did hasten the spread of firearms. The Venetians, Portuguese, and Russians all supplied firearms to Iran to check the Ottomans, whereas the Ottomans in turn sent gunners and firearms to the Uzbeks to pressure

Iran, and to Ethiopia, India, and Sumatra to foil the Portuguese. Diplomacy greatly encouraged the spread of firearms, especially from western to eastern Islamdom. Nevertheless, whether or not firearms took root in a given area remained, more than anything else, a question of local conditions.[9]

The Ottoman Military

The Ottoman land forces were drawn from several sources. The sultan had a standing army, quartered in the capital of Istanbul (formerly Constantinople), composed of the janissary infantry corps, six cavalry regiments, and the artillery corps. More infantry could be raised from the population at large. The sultan could also call upon the *timariots*, men who were given land revenue assignments in different parts of the empire in exchange for the obligation to serve as cavalry when called upon. Finally, he could call upon his allies – Crimean Tatars in the north, Kurds and Türkmens in the east – to provide auxiliaries.

The janissaries were selected from among the non-Muslim population of the empire as young boys. Islam forbids the enslavement of Muslims, so non-Muslim boys were taken; once these were instructed in Islam, their sons (as Muslims) were ineligible to succeed to their positions. As slaves, the janissaries lost some of their personal freedom, but in return, they often enjoyed great power and wealth. Not only was the standing army composed of slaves, but so was the staff of the palace, including administrators and officials. Enslavement made it possible for the sultans to invest money and time on their training and education. It was more the expense of training and maintaining the janissaries than any difficulty in obtaining slaves that kept their numbers down.[10]

The janissary infantry was equipped with firearms but not with pikes. To protect themselves from cavalry, they lined up cannon or wagons and chained them together to form a barrier or laager, a trick they learned from the Hungarians in the early 1440s.[11] This task was considered important enough for a special "gun wagoner corps" to be organized among the janissaries, probably in the late 1400s, to handle it.[12] The infantry would hold the center with its muskets and cannon, while the cavalry would attack in the vanguard and on the flanks, using the wagon laager as a rallying point as necessary. Ottoman infantry thus had more firepower per man than (other) European infantry, at the cost of some tactical mobility.

Irregular infantry was recruited from workless and landless peasants. These troops either fought in front of the wagon laager as skirmishers or protected the rear. They were also used to garrison fortresses or to serve as marines in the fleet. Many of them had muskets. During peacetime they were a particularly unstable element within society, liable to turn to banditry or to support pretenders to the throne.[13]

The *timariots* were men who were given the right to collect and spend the land taxes from the peasants within a certain defined location. Each *timariot* was responsible for his own horse and weapons, and he might be required to bring one or more armed horsemen with him as well, depending on the amount of revenue assigned to him. The *timariots* fought as cavalry on the wings of the army.[14]

The Crimean Tatars became Ottoman vassals in 1475, and they supplied light cavalry to the Ottomans for scouting and raiding when they were not occupied with their own raids in Russia. The Kurdish and Türkmen auxiliaries also fought on horseback.[15]

The sultan's standing army in 1527 contained approximately 11,000 infantrymen, 5,000 cavalrymen, and 2,000 artillerymen, while the *timariots* added another estimated 90,000 men to the total. By 1609, the standing army had increased fourfold to 47,000 infantry, 21,000 cavalry, and 8,000 artillery, while the *timariots* had increased by perhaps another 50 percent. These numbers do not include the irregular infantry or the auxiliaries. Not all these soldiers could be mobilized for a single campaign, of course. Given various logistical and administrative constraints, no single field army would have exceeded perhaps 70,000 men in the early 1600s.[16]

The Ottomans carefully organized transportation and supply to bring these soldiers to the front and to meet their needs in the field. Supply depots were established along the main transportation arteries, especially along the Danube on the northern front. Draft animals were either supplied from the imperial stables or hired from local contractors. Every effort was made to spare the population within the empire from the destructive effects of large troop movements, and Ottoman soldiers probably enjoyed better supply conditions than soldiers in any (other) European army during this period.[17]

The production of military supplies was also carefully organized. The Ottomans established gunpowder mills in a dozen cities across the empire. Saltpeter and charcoal were abundant, sulfur less so but still adequate. There was no particular shortage of iron, lead, or copper within the empire either, but tin (to mix with copper to make bronze cannon) was always scarce. Tin was imported from as far as the mines of Cornwall in southwest England, despite attempts by the Ottomans' neighbors to stop the trade. Bells and images from churches ransacked in the English Reformation also found their way to Ottoman buyers to be melted down and recast as weapons.[18]

The commoners (peasants or townspeople, Muslim or non-Muslim) were not allowed to bear weapons of any kind, including firearms. All weapons

were to be stored in arsenals and only released for use by the order of the sultan. Searches were conducted periodically to confiscate weapons in the hands of the population. However, this policy was impossible to enforce. The irregular infantry mentioned earlier bought their own weapons and kept them when they were demobilized, for example. Too many people had experience with firearms for the government to monopolize them.[19]

The Ottoman navy had perhaps the largest shipyards in the world in the 1500s, with 160,000 men employed in the yards in Istanbul alone. The forests of Anatolia supplied timber in abundance, and everything else they needed could be found within the empire. In 1572, the year after the Ottomans lost over 200 galleys at Lepanto, they managed to build and outfit enough new galleys to replace them. Ultimately, the limit on the size of the fleet was not the capacity of the shipyards to build ships but the ability of the government to pay for the materials and crews and supplies needed to operate them.[20]

The Balkans

The capture of Constantinople in 1453 linked Ottoman territory in Anatolia and the Balkans and opened the way for further expansion to the north. The Ottomans brought most of Serbia, Albania, and Wallachia under their rule over the following decades, but the Hungarians defended Belgrade successfully in 1456, and Belgrade continued to shield Hungary for the remainder of the century. Selim "the Grim" was busy throughout the 1510s with the Safavids in Iran and the Mamluks in Egypt, but his successor, Süleyman "the Magnificent," turned Ottoman attention back north.

In 1521, the year after Süleyman came to the throne, the Ottoman army put Belgrade under siege. The political infighting in the Ottoman camp was only exceeded by the political paralysis in Hungary, and no army was mobilized to oppose the invasion or lift the siege. After two failed assaults, the city walls were breached by cannon and the city itself was captured. The remnants of the garrison retreated into the citadel. Despite the breaches opened by Ottoman cannon and mines, the garrison repulsed three assaults on the citadel, but no relief was in sight, and the defenders surrendered rather than continue a hopeless struggle.[21]

Figure 4.1 is from an Ottoman miniature depicting the fall of Belgrade. Note the fortifications bristling with cannon at the top, the Ottoman siege

---

FIGURE 4.1. Ottoman army at the siege of Belgrade, 1521. Lokman, *The military campaigns of Süleyman the Magnificent*. Hünername manuscript. Istanbul, 1588. Courtesy of the Topkapi Palace Museum.

cannon in the middle of the picture, and the janissaries with their muskets on the bottom left. The Ottoman camp is at the bottom. This painting celebrates Ottoman prowess at a very technical form of warfare. There are no horses or cavalrymen in sight.

The Ottomans then followed up with an invasion of Hungary itself in 1526. The Hungarian army confronted the Ottomans at Mohács, halfway between Belgrade and Buda. The Hungarians pounced on and routed the Ottoman left as it was pitching its tents, but the Ottoman center had had time to set up its cannon and wagons, and the musketry of the janissaries decimated the Hungarian ranks. Ottoman numerical superiority then made itself felt. The Hungarian army was destroyed, the king and most of the nobles were killed, and Buda surrendered without a fight.[22]

Figure 4.2 is a detail from another Ottoman miniature from the same source, this one commemorating the battle of Mohács. Süleyman is the extra-large figure in the center. The most powerful impression from this miniature (or at least this detail) is from the ranks of Ottoman cavalry, but note the row of cannon directly in front of Süleyman, and the janissaries with muskets behind the cannon and also above and to the left. This is the famous wagon laager that no Ottoman army was complete without. Note too that the gunner appears, from his clothes, to be European.

Süleyman led another campaign north from Istanbul in 1529. Buda was occupied again, and the army pushed on to Vienna early in the autumn. The city walls were not of the newest design, and the Ottomans set to work with 300 cannon and a series of mines. The garrison fought back with aggressive sorties and beat back several assaults. After less than three weeks in front of the walls, the Ottoman army had to retire due to the lateness of the season and the shortness of supplies. The snows came early that year, and the army suffered greatly on the retreat.[23]

Süleyman finally annexed Hungary in 1541. The Ottomans took over existing castles, built new fortifications of wooden beams, and pounded earth throughout the occupied territory, with a chain of fortresses along the frontier, another group of fortresses around the capital of Buda, and a string of fortresses guarding the supply route up the Danube River. These fortifications were garrisoned by janissaries, locally paid garrison troops, and local *timariots*.[24]

Meanwhile, the sliver of Hungary now under Habsburg control also bristled with fortifications. A number of major fortresses were built under the direction of Italian military architects in the *trace italienne* style from the 1540s on. Older fortifications were integrated into the new defense system or torn down to deny them to the enemy. These defenses were manned not

FIGURE 4.2. Ottoman army at the Battle of Mohács, 1526. Lokman, *The military campaigns of Süleyman the Magnificent*. Courtesy of the Topkapi Palace Museum.

only by local Hungarian recruits but also by mercenaries recruited by the authorities in Vienna.[25]

These mercenaries brought with them up-to-date weapons and tactics from across Europe. Recruitment commissions from the decades before and after 1600 show a high proportion of firearms among the infantry. Musketeers outnumber pikemen in all 33 battalions on record, and in Walloon and French battalions the ratios were 5:1 or 10:1. All cavalrymen carried a sword and some combination of firearms: two pistols for heavy and medium cavalry, two pistols and a wheel lock carbine for mounted musketeers, and a pistol and a wheel lock musket for dragoons.[26]

Sporadic fighting continued despite a formal truce signed in 1547. Süleyman led one last campaign north in 1566, at the age of seventy-two, but he passed away in the middle of it and the effort was abandoned. A peace treaty was signed in 1568, and the 1570s and 1580s were more quiet, but war broke out again in 1591. Like wars in most parts of Europe, the Fifteen Years' War (1591–1606) was fought for and around fortresses, and it ended in a stalemate, with neither side able to gain much territory. Significantly, the Ottomans did capture four of the Habsburg *trace italienne* fortresses during the course of the war.[27]

The only major field battle of the Fifteen Years' War took place at Mezőkeresztes in 1596, after the Habsburg army arrived too late to relieve the fortress of Eger. The two armies were separated by a swamp, and the Habsburgs were ensconced in their own wagon laager, so two days were spent in tentative skirmishing. An Ottoman foray on the third day was repulsed by the guns of the Habsburg wagon laager, and the repulse turned into a rout as panic spread through the Ottoman army. However, the Habsburg soldiers fell to plundering the Ottoman camp, and the unexpected arrival of a body of Ottoman cavalry put them to flight, leaving the Ottomans in possession of the field.[28]

The Habsburgs were familiar with the wagon laager from the Czechs and Hungarians. The Habsburg commander on the Hungarian front in the mid-1560s even proposed that special wagons be built for the purpose. Each wagon would carry half a dozen "double arquebuses," heavy muskets like those mounted on city walls. The wagon laager would also be equipped with light cannon known as "falconets." Chains would link the falconets and presumably the wagons together. Whether or not such special wagons were ever actually built, the Habsburgs did form wagon laagers in some battles, such as Mezőkeresztes.[29]

The protection of the wagon laager allowed every janissary to carry a musket, but the number of janissaries could not be expanded quickly. As the Fifteen Years' War dragged on, the Ottomans supplemented them with companies of 50 to 100 volunteers, many of whom brought their own muskets. Each company was given a standard when it was mobilized, and it was supposed to demobilize when the standard was taken away, although things were never that simple.[30]

European soldiers who fought the Ottomans in the 1500s and 1600s singled out the Ottoman cavalry as their greatest challenge. European cavalry were typically outnumbered by their Ottoman counterparts. Their pistols and carbines lacked the range of the Turkish bows, so they had to close with the Ottoman cavalry to be effective. In typical steppe fashion, the Ottoman cavalry in turn would pretend to flee to draw them away from the protection of their infantry.[31]

The Ottoman wagon laagers held up well against the European pikes, and the Ottomans could cope with the *trace italienne* as well. There is no evidence of decline before the second siege of Vienna in 1683, although the turning point came shortly thereafter, when Austrian infantry abandoned the matchlock and the pike in favor of the flintlock and the bayonet. Like Spain, the other great imperial power of the 1500s and 1600s, the Ottomans remained at best a second-rank power throughout the 1700s and 1800s, but their attitude toward firearms was not responsible.[32]

The Mediterranean

The Ottomans were both a land and a sea power – no other Muslim dynasty in this period had such a powerful navy. From 1352 the Ottomans controlled territory on both sides of the Bosphorus, and they needed a fleet to maintain communications between their possessions in Anatolia and the Balkans. The capture of Constantinople in 1453 gave them first-class naval resources and control over the Black Sea – Aegean Sea trade route. The conquest of Egypt in 1517 and the subsequent acquisition of Tunisia and Algeria gave them a long coastline to defend and maritime lines of communication to maintain.[33]

Prevailing winds and currents channeled Mediterranean shipping into a few well-defined routes. The islands that lay along these routes – particularly Cyprus, Rhodes, Crete, and Malta – were prime Ottoman targets. Because the cruising range of galleys was sharply limited by the water consumption of the men who rowed them, control of naval bases on these islands determined whose shipping was protected against piracy, or whose privateers were tolerated in an area, or whose fleet could take shelter in fortified ports.[34]

Ottoman naval records from the late 1400s show a full complement of firearms mounted on galleys and galiots. A galley had one cannon and four culverins (light cannon) mounted at the bow, plus eight swivel guns known as *prangi*. Their armament was comparable to that found on Spanish or Venetian galleys of the same period. A galiot – a small galley favored by corsairs – had one cannon and two culverins in the bow, plus four swivel guns. Ottoman marines were armed with muskets and bows.[35]

The long war with Venice from 1463 to 1479 ended with Ottoman control over most of the islands in the Aegean Sea. The Ottomans then turned their attention to Rhodes. The first siege of Rhodes ended in failure in 1481, and the Ottomans did not return for over forty years, until the summer of 1522. The second siege faired better. The Ottomans used artillery and mines to open gaps in the walls, but repeated assaults failed to exploit the breaches, and the city still held out into the fifth month of the siege. However, with no relief in sight – Venetian neutrality ensured that none would arrive – the Knights of St. John surrendered on favorable terms and were allowed to leave the island at the end of the year.[36]

Another forty years passed after the siege of Rhodes before another major island was attacked. This time the target was the island of Malta in the central Mediterranean, which ironically had been given to the Knights of St. John in 1530, shortly after they had left Rhodes. The siege of Malta lasted for three and a half months in the summer of 1565. The Ottomans captured one of the smaller fortresses, but while the Ottoman artillery breached the walls of the two larger fortresses, their garrisons repulsed every assault. This time, a relief force arrived early in the autumn, and the besiegers withdrew in disorder.[37]

The Venetian garrisons on Cyprus were not so fortunate when an Ottoman army landed on the island in the summer of 1570. Nicosia fell after three weeks; although the fortifications were *trace italienne*, they were still breached with cannon and mines, and the small garrison was overwhelmed. The arrival of winter spared the port of Famagusta until the following year. Three and a half months of cannonfire, mining, and assaults over the summer of 1571 left that garrison too weak to resist, and they were slaughtered after being tricked into surrender.[38]

The combined Spanish–Italian fleet that had been gathered to save Famagusta was still assembling in Sicily when the city fell. The fleet headed east anyway and met the main Ottoman fleet at Lepanto on the coast of Albania in the fall of 1571. Six galleasses (large hybrid sailing galleys) and some 220 galleys, with 20,000 soldiers, defeated the Ottoman fleet of perhaps 270 galleys and 16,000 soldiers. It was an infantry battle at sea, and the Spanish and Italian soldiers prevailed in large part because they had heavier armor and more firearms. Only about 40 of the Ottoman galleys escaped destruction or capture.[39]

The Ottoman naval yards worked overtime to replace the losses, and the Venetians were dismayed to find a large Ottoman fleet blocking their way the following year. The archers who were lost at Lepanto were replaced by musketeers from among the irregular volunteers mentioned earlier. Lepanto did not loosen the Ottoman grip on the eastern Mediterranean. After the fall of Cyprus, which Lepanto did nothing to prevent, the Ottomans controlled the entire coast from Albania around to Tunisia, with the exception of Crete. The Ottomans recaptured Tunis from the Spanish in 1574, just three years after Lepanto, and finally took Crete from Venice in 1669.[40]

The aftermath of Lepanto shows why fleet battles rarely occurred separate from sieges. The destruction of an enemy galley fleet conferred no permanent advantage. Limiting the range of enemy galleys by denying them bases was another matter. After the fall of Cyprus, Christian galleys could not penetrate far into the eastern Mediterranean, and Christian merchants could not operate there without Ottoman permission, Lepanto notwithstanding. The possession of fortified ports conferred control over the sea much as the possession of walled cities conferred control over land. Earlier Ottoman naval victories at Prevesa (1538) and Jirba (1560) caused no territory to change hands either, and neither of them can be said to have had any decisive effect.

Defeat in battle meant the loss of the "sunk costs" – the physical and human capital invested in the fleet. In the case of a galley fleet, these were less significant than maintenance costs – feeding and paying the large crews that they required, including both rowers and soldiers. The same might not hold for a sailing fleet, which embodied more physical capital (cannon) and human capital (sailors) but were not as expensive to operate (smaller crews). The destruction of an enemy sailing fleet could be a legitimate strategic objective.

Galleys originally stimulated demand for cannon, but the sharp rise in the cost of finding and feeding galley crews over the 1500s limited the number of galleys that could be operated. Once sturdy northern merchant ships began to appear in the Mediterranean armed with cheap cast-iron cannon, the days of the galley were numbered. If a single galley or a squadron of galleys could not overpower a single merchantman, then they could not control the sea lanes in any meaningful sense. Mediterranean powers began to switch over to sailing ships late in the 1600s.[41]

The Ottomans did send ships to the Indian Ocean after their conquest of Egypt gave them interests to defend in that region. As guardians of the holy cities of Mecca and Medina, a job formerly enjoyed by the Mamluks, the Ottomans had a particular duty to safeguard the Red Sea. However, the Ottomans never sustained a major effort in the Indian Ocean, and the Red Sea could be defended by galleys, so the Ottomans were not compelled to experiment with sailing ships in that direction.[42]

Ottoman Success

As far as firearms are concerned, the Ottomans were a clear success story. Given that they were descended from steppe nomads very similar to the Mongols, they adapted to both siege warfare and naval warfare remarkably well. Of course, the Mongols themselves also adapted to siege warfare and naval warfare without serious difficulty, so maybe it is not so remarkable after all. Both Mongols and Ottomans were happy to exploit the talents of the people they conquered.

Ottoman horsemen may have disdained firearms themselves. Having been told that the Safavids were afraid of firearms, one Ottoman commander armed a squadron of 200 cavalrymen with muskets before setting out on a campaign:

> But they had scarcely completed half the journey before the usefulness of the muskets began to be impaired. Every day some part would be broken or lost, and there were few who could repair them. Thus the majority of the muskets had become quite useless, and the men wished they had never brought the weapons. Also they offended the sense of cleanliness, on which the Turks set so much store; they were seen going about with their hands all begrimed with soot, their uniforms dirty, and their clumsy powder-boxes and coaches hanging down, so that they became a laughingstock to their comrades, who jeeringly called them apothecaries.[43]

However, this attitude did not stop the Ottomans from arming their infantry, fortresses, and ships with guns, nor did it necessarily put their cavalry at a disadvantage against European cavalry. The bow was still the only long-range cavalry weapon available. Furthermore, Ottoman cavalry did start carrying pistols in the 1600s, to supplement the sabre for fighting at close quarters.

The source for this story is a letter written by the Habsburg ambassador in Istanbul in 1560. The same letter also tells the story of a Dalmatian horseman in the Ottoman service who brought back news of an Ottoman defeat. When he was questioned by the council of ministers, it came out that more than 2,500 Ottoman soldiers had been defeated by no more than 500 Christian dragoons, and the ministers expressed their anger that the messenger was not ashamed by it.

> The messenger, thereupon, by no means unabashed, replied, "I do not think you understand the matter aright; did I not tell you that our men were overcome by the might of muskets? It was the fire that routed us, not the valour of our foes. Very different, by my faith, would have been the issue of the fight, if they had faced us with genuine courage; instead of that, they summoned fire to their aid. It was the might of fire that overcame us, we admit it – fire, one of the elements, nay the fiercest of them. How can any mortal strength contend with it? Does not everything yield to the fury of the elements?"[44]

One historian has cited this story as evidence for cultural opposition to firearms, omitting the reaction of the audience: "When the Dalmatian uttered these high-flown sentiments, scarcely any one present, in spite of the sad tidings, could refrain from laughing."[45]

The Ottomans particularly excelled with cannon. It is sometimes suggested that the Ottomans were fixated on massive siege guns at the expense of mobile field artillery, but archival research has exposed this as a myth. It does not fit in with other evidence, such as the existence of a gun wagoner corps or the widespread use of swivel guns, and probably reflects latent impressions from the fall of Constantinople, when Ottoman siege artillery made an indelible impression on European minds.[46]

The choice of wagons instead of pikemen to protect the musketeers may suggest a more limited role for musketeers on the battlefield. There were presumably countervailing advantages in strategic mobility that compensated for the loss of tactical mobility inherent in this choice; the issue is discussed further in chapter 8. On the other hand, there is evidence to suggest that Ottoman muskets were more powerful than European ones, such as the testimony of the Chinese author quoted in chapter 1, among others.

This is not to say that the Ottomans were at the forefront of technological innovation. They were generally dependent upon Christian "renegades," like the European gunner shown in Figure 4.2, perhaps, for knowledge of the latest advances in military technology. On the other hand, most gunners in Venetian service in the late 1400s came from north of the Alps. At least half the gunners in Portuguese service east of the Cape of Good Hope after 1498 were Italians, Flemings, Germans, or other non-Portuguese. The Scots and the English both were still hiring French and Italian gunners in the early 1500s. By the 1500s, most Ottoman gunners were native born, and most of these were Muslims.[47]

Ottoman history (and the history of Islamdom as a whole) is permeated by the notion of decline, whether viewed as a failure to live up to the example of Muhammad or as a failure to keep up with northwestern Europe in the Industrial Revolution.[48] If the Ottomans did not keep up with some of the European powers in the 1700s and 1800s, the same is true of some of the other European powers. We tend to treat the Spanish as the unsuccessful members of a successful group ("Europeans") and the Ottomans as the successful members of an unsuccessful group ("Muslims"). This division, which is also reflected in the organization of the chapters of this book, distracts us from the similarity in their experiences.

Military innovation was by no means evenly distributed throughout Europe. Practical experience was nurtured in the "Schooles of Warre" – the Low Countries, Germany, and Hungary – the last of which also exposed the Ottomans to the same lessons. Weapons production migrated with other industries from the old centers of northern Italy and southern Germany to northern France, the Low Countries, and southern England. There seems to be an unconscious double standard at work here. When experts travel from Italy to England, it is taken as a sign of openness to new ideas; when they travel from Italy to Turkey, suddenly it is a crippling dependence on foreign technology.⁴⁹

The geography of Europe – and again I mean geography in its broader sense, including not only natural terrain but also the human geography of cities, towns, farms, and roads – encouraged the use of infantry and artillery in warfare. Naval warfare in the Mediterranean did the same. The Ottomans benefited from these conditions as much, or nearly as much, as any (other) European power. For whatever reasons, some European states – both large empires like the Habsburg and Ottoman ones and small principalities like those in Italy and Germany – fared poorly in the 1700s and 1800s. Medium-sized countries like England and France did particularly well. But placing the Ottomans in an entirely separate category on the basis of religion only obscures the dynamics involved.

The Ottomans remained a threat right up to the siege of Vienna in 1683. They successfully managed the transition from nomadic tribal cavalry to a balanced force of cavalry, infantry, artillery, and galleys that could more than hold its own with any (other) European power of the day. They also employed this force against their Muslim neighbors to the south and to the east, with varying degrees of success. Their conflicts with the Mamluks and the Safavids tested the strengths and weaknesses of this style of warfare outside of Europe.

Egypt

Egypt and Syria were ruled by a Kurdish dynasty, the Ayyubids, during the late 1100s and early 1200s. This was the dynasty founded by Salah al-Din, known in Europe as Saladin. Parts of Palestine were still controlled by the crusaders when the Mongols appeared on the scene in the mid-1200s. As the Mongols and crusaders tried to work out an alliance against their common enemy, the Ayyubids were overthrown by their own Turkish slave soldiers. These slave soldiers were known as *mamluks*, and the regime they set up came to be known as the Mamluk sultanate.⁵⁰

The new sultan immediately scored a decisive victory over the Mongols at 'Ayn Jalut ("the spring of Goliath") in Syria in 1260. This victory punctured the myth of Mongol invincibility and allowed the Mamluks to represent themselves as saviors of the Muslim community. The new sultan's murderer and successor followed this up by taking control of the holy cities of Mecca and Medina, and one of his successors captured the last crusader stronghold in 1291.⁵¹

By the beginning of the 1300s, the Mamluk sultanate had become the preeminent power in Islamdom. However, the Mamluks reached the limit of their expansion with these acquisitions. The road from Cairo to Aleppo was almost 700 miles. Ethiopia was 1,000 miles to the south as the crow flies, and Tunis was 1,300 miles to the west. Given the political structure of the regime, sultans could not afford to leave the capital for too long, to send off their own personal *mamluks*, or to entrust sizeable armies to potential rivals, except at considerable personal risk.[52]

The *mamluks* were part of the same tradition of military slavery as the janissaries, and there were many similarities and a few differences between the two groups. Like the janissaries, the *mamluks* were non-Muslims who were enslaved, trained as soldiers, and converted to Islam. Whereas the janissaries remained slaves until death, however, *mamluks* received their freedom when they completed their training. Because Muslims could not be enslaved, the sons of the *mamluks* were barred by Islamic law from becoming *mamluks* themselves, just as the sons of janissaries were barred from becoming janissaries. Whereas new janissaries were obtained from the non-Muslim population within the Ottoman empire, however, new *mamluks* were imported from Turkish and Circassian tribes outside Islamdom. Finally, whereas most janissaries fought on foot, *mamluks* fought exclusively on horseback.

Strong bonds were formed between a master and his *mamluks* and among the *mamluks* of a single master, and all the *mamluks* of a single master operated as a single unit. This system fostered both *esprit de corps* and serious political rivalry, with the disadvantages of the latter eventually outweighing the advantages of the former over the course of time. Each sultan relied ultimately on the support of his personal *mamluks*, just as they relied on him for their own power and influence. Upon coming to power, he had to strengthen his own unit while weakening those of his predecessor and his potential rivals.[53]

The Mamluk sultanate was extremely unusual for this period of history. The position of sultan was not passed down from generation to generation within a single family, as was true with the Ottomans, or for that matter with virtually every other regime discussed in this book. Rather, the senior *mamluks* competed among themselves, by fair means or foul, to succeed to the position of sultan. Only *mamluks* – former slaves – were eligible to serve as sultan, so the sons of *mamluks* and even the sons of sultans were ineligible. Attempts to bypass this rule were never successful for long.

The Mamluks are said to have possessed cannon as early as 1342, although this claim by a fifteenth-century writer has not been confirmed. The earliest contemporary testimony is that of al-Qalqashandi, who personally saw and described a cannon in Alexandria, probably either in 1365 or else between 1366 and 1368, and certainly no later than 1376. Since the Ottomans are not known to have had firearms before 1422, the

Mamluks must have obtained them from another source. Direct transmission from China cannot be ruled out, but it seems more likely that the first firearms arrived in Egypt from Europe. In any event, later generations of firearms, such as the musket, would have come directly or indirectly from Europe.[54]

Despite having obtained firearms earlier than the Ottomans, the Mamluks were unable to integrate them successfully into their armed forces, and they were defeated and conquered by the Ottomans in large part because of that failure.

The Mamluk Military

The Mamluk land forces were drawn from several sources. The sultan had a standing army, quartered in the capital of Cairo, composed of the royal *mamluks*. Each commander might also have his own *mamluks*. There was also a corps of freeborn (non-*mamluk*) cavalry drawn from refugees and from the sons of *mamluks*. Türkmen, Kurdish, and Bedouin tribes at times contributed auxiliaries, and the provinces had their own garrisons.

The royal *mamluks* included both those *mamluks* who had been bought and trained by the ruling sultan and those who had originally been in the service of others, whether earlier sultans or other commanders. The *mamluks* of the ruling sultan enjoyed the best training and weapons, but they often were the most recently acquired and had the least combat experience. Whatever their provenance, all the *mamluks*, royal and nonroyal, were trained and equipped to fight on horseback, and the preferred weapons were the lance and the bow. Well armored, the *mamluks* were medium-heavy cavalry specifically adapted to dealing with light cavalry.[55]

The freeborn cavalry formed a separate unit of their own. Some of its members were refugees from the Mongols, who arrived in large numbers during the early years of the sultanate, even including some Mongols who had gone into exile. Others were the sons of *mamluks*, who were ineligible to serve as *mamluks* themselves but who comprised the elite element within the freeborn cavalry. Precisely because they were not *mamluks*, the freeborn cavalry could not compete with *mamluks* in power or prestige, and they were hit hard by the decline in the military budget in the 1300s.[56]

The Mamluks could also draw upon tribal auxiliaries. Türkmen auxiliaries occupied northern Syria and southeastern Anatolia, where they formed a buffer between the Ottomans and the Mamluks. Kurdish auxiliaries also played a role in the same area during the early years. Bedouin were found throughout the territory of the sultanate, in Egypt and Arabia as well as in Syria and Palestine. The Bedouin contributed auxiliaries at times, but they also constituted a drain on military power by defying government authority.[57]

All the troops described previously fought on horseback; infantry occupied a much less prominent role within the Mamluk military. What infantry did exist was largely recruited and supported locally rather than centrally. In Syria, where most of the battles of the Mamluk period were fought, there were considerable numbers of such infantry. The rugged terrain in northern Syria and eastern Anatolia made them indispensable, but unfortunately little is known and little has been written about them.[58]

At peak effectiveness, the *mamluks* were unquestionably a match for nomadic cavalry, but it was very difficult to keep the *mamluks* operating at peak effectiveness. The nomads learned what they had to learn about fighting from everyday life. They lived on horseback, used their bows in hunting, and were hardened against suffering. Professional soldiers could only surpass them with a lot of conscious dedication and hard work. For elite soldiers like the *mamluks*, there were all sorts of distractions to keep them from putting in the time they needed at the archery fields or at the hippodrome.[59]

The Mamluk army gradually shrank over the 250-odd years of its existence. The total number of royal *mamluks* typically exceeded 10,000 in the 1300s but usually fell short of that number in the 1400s. The freeborn cavalry units declined in strength as well. If there were only about 24,000 horsemen in Egypt in the early 1300s, there would have been even fewer two centuries later, after the ravages of the Black Death and the contraction of the Egyptian economy.[60]

Egyptian weakness at sea both handicapped Mamluk expansion and limited the demand for cannon. Egypt was a thriving center for long-distance trade, but the chronic shortage of timber apparently hindered the growth of the merchant marine. Timber had to be imported from Turkey, India, and east Africa. Even entire ships were purchased from India. With few exceptions, Egyptian ships steered clear of Mediterranean warfare. Egyptian ships were more active in the Indian Ocean, but they proved no match for the Portuguese in the 1500s.[61]

Border Wars

Egypt was surrounded by deserts and oceans. Egypt was only accessible through Syria, which in turn could only be approached from Anatolia or Iraq. The coastal areas of Syria were relatively fertile, but there was still much more wasteland than in Europe, and distances between population centers were greater. A slow-moving army might easily run out of water, and infantry in particular was at a great disadvantage.[62]

After the fall of the last of the crusader states in 1291, the only external threat to the Mamluk sultanate came from one or another of a series of nomads in lands bordering on Syria: the Mongols (1256–1336), the Jalayirids (1336–1432), the Qaraquyunlu (1380–1468), and the Aqquyunlu (1378–1508). The Jalayirids were themselves Mongols, the Qaraquyunlu and Aqquyunlu both Türkmens, but all were basically variations on nomadic confederations, and all relied first and foremost on light cavalry.

Mamluk fortresses on the Euphrates guarded the approaches to Syria from the northeast, with cavalry mobilized from the barracks in Cairo to back them up. The Mamluks suffered defeats at the hands of the Mongols, who occupied Syria in the winter of 1299–1300, and Temür, who did so in the winter of 1400–1401, but in each case Egypt was spared and Syria was quickly retaken. Syria was an excellent buffer for Egypt.[63]

For their part, the Mamluks rarely took the offensive. The relative isolation of Egypt made it both easy to defend and hard to expand from. The Mamluks lacked the naval capacity to expand overseas. When they did intervene in the squabbles of the Türkmen tribes to their north, they relied principally on cavalry, but they also deployed cannon in sieges, for example against the Aqquyunlu at Ruha and Amid.[64]

In the late 1400s, Ottoman expansion into eastern Anatolia brought them into conflict with the Mamluks. The first Ottoman-Mamluk war in 1485 followed two decades of struggles over the Türkmen buffer states. The *mamluks* were sent from Cairo to Aleppo in late 1485, where they recruited Syrian infantrymen, and then they marched on Ramadan in early 1486, pausing on the way to cast cannon. The Mamluks placed the capital of Ramadan under siege with their cannon and catapults, and the city surrendered after the Mamluks scored a major victory over an Ottoman relief force.

In 1488, the Ottomans retook Ramadan with a combined land-sea expedition numbering 60,000 or more. The Mamluks again sent the main army from Egypt to Syria and again recruited local infantry to supplement it. Some of these infantrymen carried muskets in this campaign, the first time any Mamluk army is recorded as having used them. The Mamluks again besieged the capital of Ramadan, and the Mamluks again defeated a major Ottoman relief force, which abandoned its cannon and left the garrison to its fate.

The second Mamluk victory restored the inner line of buffer states, although the outer line remained in Ottoman hands. After some inconclusive maneuvering, a peace agreement was signed in 1491. The Mamluk treasury was exhausted. Still, the Mamluk forces had successfully defended their borders and had won both of the two major battles. There was no sign that the *mamluks* were outclassed by the janissaries or in imminent danger of total destruction. If the *mamluks* were complacent, it is easy to see why.[65]

In 1490, toward the end of the war, Sultan Qayit Bay dispatched a unit of musketeers with an expeditionary army against the Ottomans. This was the first unit of musketeers organized as part of the main army in Cairo. Its ranks were filled by sons of *mamluks* who otherwise might have served with the freeborn cavalry. One camel was issued to every two men: whether they walked or rode to battle, they clearly fought on foot. Apparently, however, this expeditionary army did not see any real fighting before it returned to base.[66]

A few years later, Sultan al-Nasir decided to train black slaves as musketeers. This did not sit well with the *mamluks*, who were outraged when the sultan allowed the black musketeers to march in parades and when he gave one of their number special honors. The *mamluks* despised musketeers, but they also despised blacks, and the two impulses are difficult to separate here. The *mamluks* attacked the black musketeers in 1498 and killed a number of them, after which the sultan promised to change his ways. Little more is heard about these black musketeers, so perhaps the unit was broken up, although black musketeers did participate in the ill-fated 1505 expedition to the Indian Ocean.[67]

The 1505 expedition was directed against the Portuguese, who had circumnavigated the Cape of Good Hope in 1497 and now threatened Muslim commerce in the Indian Ocean. The Mamluks shared this concern with the Muslim sultanate of Gujarat, the premier seapower in India at that time. However, despite a victory over the Portuguese in 1508, the combined Mamluk–Gujarati fleet was defeated and destroyed at Diu off the coast of Gujarat in 1509.

The Mamluks responded to the defeat at Diu by forming yet another unit of musketeers, in 1510. This unit was known in Arabic as "the fifth class." The fifth class was recruited from the sons of *mamluks*, certain foreigners like Türkmens and Iranians and Maghribis, and other groups of low social status, although black slaves are not mentioned. It was given the pejorative nickname "the motley force." There was already a shortage of money to pay the existing regiments, so the pay of the musketeers was very low, and on one occasion the *mamluks* even robbed them of it.[68]

Meanwhile, with their Gujarati allies out of the picture, the Mamluks cast around for others to help them against the Portuguese. They initially turned to the Venetians for assistance, but while the Venetians did appeal to the Pope on their behalf, they suggested that the Mamluks look to the

Ottomans for military aid. Despite the recent wars they had fought in south-eastern Anatolia, the Ottomans nevertheless did agree to cooperate with the Mamluks in the expedition against the Portuguese in 1515.

The Ottomans supplied most of the timber and firearms, and the commander was an Ottoman as well. Gunners, firearms, and gunpowder are mentioned repeatedly in the preparations for the expedition; the Mamluks seem to have devoted all their available firearms to it. However, by the time the combined Ottoman–Mamluk fleet was defending Jidda against the Portuguese in the Red Sea in 1517, war had already broken out again between the Ottomans and the Mamluks for control of the eastern Mediterranean.[69]

Marj Dabiq

The Ottoman expansion into eastern Anatolia brought them into conflict with the Safavid regime in Iran. This served to draw their attention away from the Mamluks for some time. Once Sultan Selim had scored a decisive victory against the Safavids at Chaldiran in 1514, he turned his attention back to the Mamluks and quickly defeated the last of the Türkmen buffer states.

Sultan al-Ghawri left Cairo in May of 1516 and arrived at Aleppo with his army in July. The army included both older *mamluks* whom he had inherited from earlier sultans as well as younger ones whom he had acquired during his own reign, and it was reinforced by local Syrian troops. Among the Syrian troops were 5,000 infantry, an example of the locally recruited infantry formations alluded to earlier, but nothing is said about how they were armed or deployed in battle.[70]

The Mamluk army met the Ottoman army at Marj Dabiq north of Aleppo in August. The *mamluks* first gained the upper hand but then faltered as the Ottomans rallied. The Mamluk sultan put the older *mamluks* in the front line in order to preserve the younger *mamluks*, and the older *mamluks* interpreted this gesture as permission not to stick around. The Mamluk viceroy of Aleppo also left the battlefield early, having made separate arrangements with the Ottoman sultan beforehand. Finally, when it must have seemed that nothing else could go wrong, the Mamluk sultan apparently died of natural causes, perhaps a heart attack, on the battlefield.[71]

Although nothing went right for the Mamluks on that day, the Ottoman firearms were apparently still the decisive factor. The *mamluks* themselves preferred this explanation over others because it preserved their reputation (at least in their own minds) as masters of horsemanship. Some of these explanations are reminiscent of nothing so much as the speech of the Dalmatian soldier to the Ottoman ministers mentioned earlier. For example:

None of us would have run away from attacks with the lance or from sword blows, for we know these people [the Ottomans]. They are not better horsemen than we are, and they are not braver than we are, that we should fear them. The only thing which does harm to us is these firearms and these bullets and these cannon which, if you fired at mountains with them, would wipe out the mountains.[72]

With the death of the sultan at Marj Dabiq, the viceroy in Cairo was persuaded to become the new sultan. His reluctance may not have been feigned; the situation was very bad. A new army was assembled to stop the Ottoman army when it reached Egypt. This time, the preparations indicate what kind of lesson the Mamluks had learned from Marj Dabiq. In the month after Marj Dabiq, priority was given to the production of muskets and wooden shields – wooden shields being used together with wagons to protect the gunners. About three months after Marj Dabiq, it is recorded that the sultan inspected thirty-odd wagons carrying musketeers and an unspecified number of camel bearing wooden shields.[73]

About one month after the inspection, and just two weeks before the Ottomans reached Egypt, the new army was almost ready:

> The sultan brought out the royal armory that he was dispatching along with the army, and he seated himself in the field, and the wooden wagons that were made for the expeditionary force were pulled along in front of him. Their number was 100 wagons, and in Ottoman they call them *araba*, and a pair of oxen pulls each of them, and in them were bronze cannon that shoot lead balls. The sultan got down from his seat and mounted, and in his hand was a staff, and he began to arrange the wagons as they went by in the field. Then after the wagons came 200 camels carrying shields, about 1,500 shields, and carrying also gunpowder, lead, iron, and wooden spears, and in front of the wagons were four drums and four fifes, and in front of them were about 200 gunners, comprised of Türkmens and Maghribis.[74]

The Maghribis – people from the western parts of North Africa, including Morocco, Algeria, and Tunisia, and perhaps refugees from Granada in Spain as well – may have been chosen for this kind of duty because of their low status as foreigners in the Mamluk realm.[75] On the other hand, they may have been recruited because they knew how to handle firearms from their experience fighting the Spanish. As mentioned earlier, Türkmens and Maghribis had been included in the "fifth class" musketeer regiment organized in 1510.

The Mamluk army took up positions outside of Cairo. According to a contemporary chronicler, the Mamluks were prepared for a different kind of battle than Marj Dabiq:

> Sultan Tuman Bay, after he proceeded to al-Raydaniya and set up the camp there, fortified the camp with cannons and guns, and lined up shields there,

and constructed wooden screens for them, and dug a trench from al-Jabal al-Ahmar to the depression of al-Matariya, and he sent word ahead concerning that. The Sultan placed about a thousand camels behind the cannon, and on them were sacks in which there was fodder, and on their humps were great white and red flags that waved in the air, and he assembled a great number of oxen for the purpose of pulling the wagons. He supposed that the battle would be protracted between himself and the Ottomans, or even that a siege would last a long time. However, the matter turned out differently from that.[76]

The Mamluk front faced northeast, with its left flank resting on the Nile River and its right on the small mountain of al-Jabal al-Ahmar. With hindsight, it appears that the Mamluks had overcompensated for the failure of their cavalry at Marj Dabiq by digging into fixed positions. Perhaps they had little cavalry remaining after Marj Dabiq. Anyway, part of the Ottoman army looped around the Mamluk entrenchments and turned their right flank while the remainder engaged the Mamluk front. "The noise of their musketry was deafening, and their attack furious." The Mamluks launched a desperate assault on the Ottoman center in hopes of killing Selim, but they came up empty – while they killed the grand vezir, Selim himself was off leading the flanking forces. The Mamluks were routed. The Mamluk sultan made himself scarce, and the Ottomans occupied Cairo.[77]

Mamluk Failure

If the Ottomans were a clear success in the use of firearms, the Mamluks were a clear failure. The success of the Ottomans rules out the most facile explanations for the failure of the Mamluks, that Islam or slave soldiers were somehow incompatible with the use of firearms. However, there are two plausible explanations for the failure of the Mamluks, either of which is probably sufficient to account for it.

The first explanation is that the Mamluks were infatuated with horsemanship and could not understand or accept that some mechanical contrivance might change the face of warfare and make infantry more effective than cavalry. To the extent that they understood what was going on, they nevertheless refused to have anything to do with it. They continued to fight in the way that they had always fought, and they were willing to go down to defeat rather than compromise a value that was at the core of their identity. Since their privileged place in society was predicated on their military prowess, they could not admit that mounted archery was no longer supreme without seriously undercutting their own legitimacy.[78]

The second explanation is that the Mamluks had developed a military system to cope with a different kind of threat. The Mamluks won tremendous prestige by defeating the Mongols at ʿAyn Jalut in 1260. The victory ratified both their coup against the Ayyubids and their subsequent claims to be leaders of the Muslim community and protectors of the two holy cities. Even more to the point for our purposes here, the victory validated the Mamluk military system. Small numbers of heavily armed and highly trained *mamluks* were able to stand up to larger numbers of lightly armed horse archers and defeat them; they were also able to stand up to the heavy cavalry of the crusaders. The *mamluks* seemed to have all the answers.

For more than two centuries, right up to the 1480s, the external threat to the Mamluks varied in intensity but not in quality. After the fall of the Mongol regime in Iran in 1336, the lands on the borders of Mamluk-controlled Syria were variously contested by the Jalayirids, the Qaraquyunlu, and the Aqquyunlu. The nomadic challenge peaked when Temür sacked Damascus in the winter of 1400–1401, but he soon turned his attention in other directions, and the Mamluks were spared. Temür and the others all relied on horse archers for their main striking power, and the Mamluks continued to use the same tried-and-true methods that had worked previously against the Mongols.

By contrast, the Mamluks had little occasion to fight Europeans between the fall of the last crusader stronghold in 1291 and the arrival of the Portuguese in the Indian Ocean after 1497. The rise of the Ottomans actually helped to shield the Mamluks from firearms by pushing the frontier between Islamdom and Christendom away from Egypt, toward the Balkans and the Maghrib. Only when Ottoman expansion reached the borders of Syria did the Mamluks have to face infantry armed with firearms, and even then the *mamluks* defeated the janissaries twice.

No one would deny that the *mamluks* venerated horsemanship or that their claim to legitimacy rested on their purportedly indispensable military role. Negotiating the transition to a different sense of identity and a different form of legitimacy would have been quite a challenge, and it is no surprise that they never undertook it willingly. On the other hand, they were never in the position where they had to try it, willing or not, at least not until the eve of the Ottoman conquest. Sultan Tuman Bay's efforts to save Cairo from the Ottomans in 1517 suggest that they would have tried, but the Ottomans would not give them the time they needed.

The Maghrib

To the Arabs, everything west of Egypt and Libya was the Maghrib – the "west." The Maghrib was closely linked to the rest of the Mediterranean world, both in Roman and in Islamic times. The coastal plains north of the Atlas Mountains enjoy a mild climate with adequate rainfall, suitable for agriculture. Sandwiched between the Mediterranean Sea to the north and the Sahara Desert to the south, the Maghrib was a medium-sized oasis where goods were transferred from camel caravans to merchant ships and vice versa.[79]

The Arabs overran the Maghrib in the first century of Islam, during the 600s. The Arabs also linked up with the indigenous Berbers in the Maghrib to conquer Spain in the following century. The history of the Maghrib in the following centuries was characterized by close ties with Spain and recurrent invasions from the desert and mountains. In the 1000s, Tuaregs came out of the Sahara Desert to conquer Morocco, after which they came to the rescue of the Muslims of Spain. In the 1100s, they were supplanted by a rival dynasty of Berbers from the Atlas Mountains that also took over southern Spain. The 1200s saw the rise of more Berber dynasties and a further influx of Arab tribes to the Maghrib.

In the late 1300s, the Tunisian scholar Ibn Khaldun described the nomads of the Maghrib in terms reminiscent of steppe nomads like the Mongols:

> They are people of plunder and pillage. They take whatever they can without fighting and running any danger, then they withdraw to their place of refuge in the desert. They do not go on campaign or into battle unless to defend themselves. Every stronghold or thing that is difficult for them they leave alone in favor of something less difficult, they do not embark upon it.[80]

The Maghrib may not seem a promising candidate for the spread of firearms, but there were two countervailing influences at work. First, the Muslims of Granada were engaged in a long and bitter struggle, fortress by fortress, to stem the advance of the Christians in Spain. Some of the earliest reports of gunpowder weapons in Islamdom come from Granada. After the reconquest of Spain was completed by Ferdinand and Isabella in 1492, an event in which cannon played no small part, Muslim exiles brought this experience with them to the Maghrib.[81]

Second, port cities like Algiers and Tunis were in a much stronger position vis-à-vis nomads than were oasis cities like Samarqand or Bukhara. Nomads could never cut them off completely from their trade routes. On the contrary, the port cities controlled the bottlenecks between the caravan trade and the sea routes. Their rulers could sit tight behind their walls and invest in weapons to use from behind walls or on board ships. Naval powers like the Habsburgs and Ottomans could also hope to capture them from the sea and hold onto them profitably without undertaking the Herculean task of subduing their hinterlands.

After the fall of Granada in 1492, the Maghrib was drawn into the Habsburg-Ottoman rivalry, and the focus of warfare shifted from the desert to the coast. The Ottomans had the advantage of recruiting allies from among their fellow Muslims. Khayr al-Din Barbarossa was a Tunisian native who entered Ottoman service in 1519; he captured the Spanish forts at Algiers and Tunis with their help, and the naval resources of Algeria and Tunisia went to strengthen the Ottoman fleet, which Barbarossa himself commanded after 1534.

The coast of the Maghrib became the site of a number of major battles, including the capture of Tunis (again) by the Spanish in 1535, the disastrous Spanish expeditions to Algiers in 1541 and Jirba in 1560, and the recapture of Tunis by the Ottomans in 1574, three years after Lepanto. The combination of naval and siege warfare favored the use of firearms, and the involvement of the Habsburgs and Ottomans ensured a steady supply of them.[82]

Farther yet to the west, Morocco was under relentless pressure from the Portuguese, who took advantage of their superior firepower to capture and hold a number of ports. Too far west to look to the Ottomans for protection, Moroccans began to use firearms themselves at an early date. The Portuguese captured a cannon when they took the Moroccan city of Sabta (Ceuta) in 1415, and Sultan Abu Sa'id used fire-lances, catapults, and cannon when he tried to retake the city in 1419. The cannon and their gunners may have been from Granada, still under Muslim rule at this point, which had an interest in keeping Morocco in friendly hands.

Portuguese power in Morocco had peaked by 1515, and the contest for Morocco turned into an internal struggle between the Wattasid dynasty and the Sa'adian movement. The Sa'adians are not even known to have possessed firearms before 1524, but their muskets won them a major victory over the Wattasids only a dozen years later, in 1536. Meanwhile, the 1530s also saw the appearance of a domestic Moroccan firearms industry.

As the king of Portugal noted in 1541, "We must recognize that warfare in Morocco has changed. The enemy is now very adept in the arts of war and siegecraft, due in part to the aid of many Turks and renegades, numerous artillery weapons, and the important materials of war." However, it took a crushing defeat at the hands of the Moroccans in 1578 (including the death of the Portuguese king and the subsequent incorporation of Portugal into the Habsburg empire from 1580 to 1640) before the Portuguese finally abandoned their designs on Morocco.[83]

Sub-Saharan Africa

The Mediterranean Sea connected North Africa to Europe and the Middle East, but the Sahara Desert tended to isolate the rest of Africa from the Oikoumene. The Sahara Desert was a formidable barrier to interaction, peaceful or otherwise. Caravans crisscrossed the desert north and south, carrying gold, ivory, and slaves north and bringing horses and manufactured goods south, but the volume of traffic was fairly low. Military conflict across the desert was likewise rare, and warfare in sub-Saharan Africa developed according to its own logic.[84]

Cavalry warfare flourished immediately south of the Sahara Desert. A broad band of arid grasslands (the sahel) extends from the Atlantic coast in the west to the Ethiopian highlands in the east. The terrain is ideal for cavalry warfare. The climate is rather warm for breeding horses, and local breeds were not very powerful, but warhorses were imported from north of the desert. Firearms did not take root here easily, the conquest of Songhay by a force of Moroccan dragoons in 1591 notwithstanding.

To the south of the sahel, a belt of wooded grasslands (the savannah) marks the northern range of the tsetse fly. Trypanosomiasis, or sleeping sickness, is deadly to domestic livestock, so horses cannot survive long, even where there is open land to graze them. Nevertheless, the savannah is also fine cavalry country, and horses were brought in from the north despite forbiddingly high death rates. The Portuguese even exported some horses to this region by sea. Firearms had only a limited impact here too.[85]

Firearms came to the forest zone below the northern savannah by sea. The Portuguese sailed to west Africa in the 1400s in search of gold, ivory, and slaves. Once the demand for slaves to feed the plantations in the Americas started to mount, European countries competed with each other to sell guns for slaves. Only here did firearms take root. Firearms were easily adapted to the infantry tactics of the forest zone and became very common.[86]

South of the forests, Portuguese efforts to introduce cavalry failed as their horses quickly succumbed to the tsetse fly. Instead, European infantry met African infantry on the open savannah inland. African infantry fought in open order, although sometimes they were backed up by heavy infantry in close formation, and without cavalry to force them into close formation, the impact of the Portuguese muskets and cannon was diluted.

The Portuguese adapted by recruiting light infantry from their African allies. Portuguese soldiers guarded the baggage and provided the heavy infantry core around which the rest of the army maneuvered, much like the wagon laager in Ottoman warfare. The light infantry played the same role that cavalry played elsewhere, screening the heavy infantry and maneuvering for advantage. The light units bore the brunt of the fighting; if the light units were defeated, the heavy units would be surrounded and overwhelmed.[87]

On the other side of the continent, the eastern coast was connected to the Middle East and India by trade routes across the Indian Ocean. There were religious ties as well; Muslim merchants settled in the port cities, and local converts to Islam made the pilgrimage to Mecca. Firearms could not have been completely unfamiliar even before the Europeans arrived, and the Portuguese and Ottomans helped put firearms in the hands of local powers in the early 1500s, although there is little sign of firearms spreading inland.[88]

European settlement in large numbers only succeeded in the temperate regions of southern Africa beyond the southern range of the tsetse fly. The Portuguese set up a colony in Mozambique, and the Dutch in South Africa, but Dutch settlers (the Boers) were later supplanted by the English. Cavalry and firearms gave European settlers a military advantage that helped secure their presence, but without disease on their side the white settlers remained a minority. Disease worked against European imperialism in Africa, unlike in the New World.

Firearms did not give Europeans an advantage over Africans sufficient to overcome disadvantages of distance, numbers, and disease. Instead, large numbers of firearms (though often obsolete models) were introduced to sub-Saharan Africa through the gun-slave trade. However, Africans seldom if ever manufactured firearms on their own, even if local craftsmen could repair some firearms and produce some ammunition for them. Perhaps the technological and industrial base was lacking. Perhaps the availability of cheap imports discouraged production. In any event, Africans remained dependent on imports and eventually paid the price.[89]

5

Eastern Islamdom

Eastern Islamdom comprises all those lands to the east of the Ottoman empire, including Iran and points farther east. As explained in chapter 4, the division between Western and Eastern Islamdom seems to have been the dividing line between two styles of warfare throughout this period, and perhaps in earlier periods as well.

The heavy cavalry of the Mamluks in Egypt could not cope with the janissary musketeers of the Ottomans. By contrast, the light cavalry of the Safavids in Iran was able to hold its own against them. This light cavalry was none other than the familiar mounted archers of the steppe nomads operating in a slightly more arid environment of mixed deserts and grasslands surrounding small oases of agrarianate civilization. In other words, these were the Turkish desert nomads described earlier in chapter 1.

In Iran, a military ruling class of Turkish pastoral nomads was imposed over the Iranian settled population. In northern India, a similar ruling class was imposed over the Indian settled population. Given that the Ottomans and Mamluks were themselves Turks, virtually all of Islamdom (aside from newly converted areas in central Africa or Southeast Asia) was ruled by Turks by the time that firearms arrived.

Nevertheless, despite the similarity in their cultural background, each regime adapted to the land over which it ruled. The Ottomans (in Turkey) and Mughals (in India), who ruled over densely populated agricultural lands, came to rely more heavily on infantry armed with muskets and cannon. The Mamluks (in Egypt), who were cut off from the steppe, became a narrow urban military elite with heavy cavalry as its primary force. The Safavids (in Iran) stayed closest to the pastoral nomadic model with the greatest emphasis on light cavalry – even though they were the one royal family whose Turkish origins were doubtful.

Iran

Iran is a high arid plateau between the Caspian Sea and the Indian Ocean. Its western border is defined by the Zagros Mountains, which separate the plateau from the Tigris and Euphrates River valleys that comprise the heart of Iraq. These mountains, together with the Alborz Mountains running east–west between the plateau and the Caspian Sea, cut off much of the rain that might otherwise have reached the interior.[1]

Historically, the land inhabited by Persian-speaking and Persian-writing agricultural and urban populations included much more than the Iranian plateau or the present boundaries of the country of Iran. Cities like Samarqand and Bukhara in Transoxania, or Herat and Balkh in Afghanistan, were as much a part of Persian culture as Isfahan or Shiraz. However, those same areas to the northeast of the Iranian plateau also had the best grass-lands that were the most attractive to steppe nomads like the Turks, who started to migrate southwest off the steppe in the 900s.

The Mongols conquered Transoxania in the 1220s and Iran in the 1250s. These two areas were ruled by two different branches of the family of Chinggis Khan as two different *khanates*. The mid-1300s in Iran and Transoxania alike were marked by political chaos, and when Mongol rule was reconstituted in Transoxania in the second half of the century, the

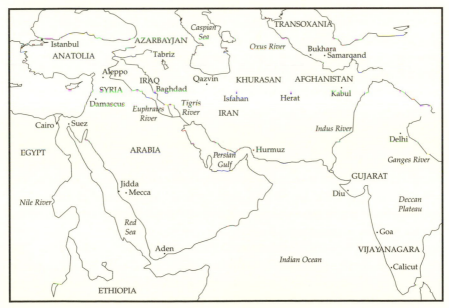

Map 4. Eastern Islamdom

Mongol *khan* was just a figurehead. The new power behind the throne was
Temür, better known in English as Tamerlane, a Turk and a descendant of
Chinggis Khan on his mother's side.

Temür's career as a conqueror was not far behind that of Chinggis Khan,
and he picked up where the Mongols left off, visiting destruction on most
of the lands within reach of his capital in Samarqand. Temür was adept at
incorporating diverse elements into his army, just as the Mongols had been,
but the main force in his army consisted of light cavalry, and there is no
real evidence that his army made use of firearms. Instead, we might say that
it was Temür who maintained nomadic power throughout the Middle East
after the collapse of the Mongol empire.[2]

Temür's descendants reigned in Transoxania and Afghanistan down to
the end of the 1400s. They were remarkable more than anything else for
their patronage of literature and the arts. Temür never succeeded in consolidating his control over the nomadic tribes of western Iran and eastern
Anatolia, and after his death the Türkmen tribal confederations known as
the Aqquyunlu ("those with white sheep") and Qaraquyunlu ("those with
black sheep") continued to struggle for power in the region down to the
mid-1400s.

The Aqquyunlu finally emerged victorious over the Qaraquyunlu in 1467.
The Aqquyunlu ruler, Uzun Hasan, promptly moved his own capital to the
Qaraquyunlu capital at Tabriz in Azarbayjan and established control over the
western half of Iran. The Aqquyunlu now appeared strong enough to serve
as a possible counterweight to the Ottomans, who had shocked Europe by
capturing Constantinople in 1453, and negotiations with Venice began to
pick up pace.[3]

The Ottomans had deployed firearms against the Aqquyunlu as early as
1461, when they used siege artillery to capture two Aqquyunlu fortresses.
Uzun Hasan now requested cannon, muskets, and gunners from the
Venetians in 1472 prior to his offensive against the Ottomans. His armies
captured many cannon from the Ottomans in the early stages of that campaign. In the following year, Aqquyunlu cavalry surprised and defeated the
Ottoman cavalry crossing the Euphrates but was itself routed in the decisive
battle at Bashkent, when Ottoman cannon and muskets opened fire from the
shelter of their wagon laager.[4]

The Venetian connection and the Ottoman experience soon told. The
Aqquyunlu also began to use firearms in field battles, as in the 1478 battle
between two claimants to the throne, when Yaʿqub defeated Sultan Khalil
(despite the latter's cannon and muskets). By the mid-1480s, the Aqquyunlu
had their own royal artillery corps. This artillery was deployed with effect by
Yaʿqub against the Georgians in 1485, leading to the capture of three cities,

and again in 1488–89, when Tiflis was captured. However, the Aqquyunlu experiment with firearms was cut short by the Safavids, who eliminated the Aqquyunlu as an independent power by 1508.[5]

The Safavid family rose to prominence as spiritual leaders of a religious order in Azarbayjan in the 1300s. In the second half of the 1400s, the order began to mobilize its wealth and prestige to attain military and political power. In 1501, the head of the family (a grandson of the Aqquyunlu ruler Uzun Hasan) was crowned Shah Isma'il at the age of fourteen in the city of Tabriz, in the heart of Azarbayjan, formerly used as a capital by the Mongols, Qaraquyunlu, and Aqquyunlu.[6]

The ethnic origin of the Safavid family is unknown. They may have been Iranians or Turks, or even of Kurdish or Arabic origin, but their appeal was religious rather than ethnic or tribal. Devotion to the Safavid order was widespread among the Türkmen tribes of Azarbayjan and Anatolia. Safavid followers wore a distinctive red turban and were known as Qizilbash, or "red-heads." The Safavid order was both Sufi and Shiite in orientation, and it is thanks to the Safavids that Iran is a Shiite country today.

Religious overtones aside, in most other respects theirs was a typical Turkish dynasty. As late as the 1660s and 1670s, a Frenchman at the Safavid court could still write: "Turkish is the language of the armies and of the court; one speaks nothing but Turkish there, as much among the women as among the men, throughout in the *seraglios* of the great; this comes about because the court is originally of the country of this language, descended from the Türkmens, of whom Turkish is their native tongue."[7]

The Safavid Military

Since the Safavid shahs had no tribe of their own to call on, the only troops under their direct control in the early years were their personal bodyguards, known by the old Mongol title of "quiver-bearer." When they went to battle, they took up position in the center of the line, surrounded by their quiver-bearers. The Qizilbash fought under the direct command of their tribal leaders, with each tribe taking part in the order of battle as a unit. Each tribe was assigned a position in one of the two wings, either left or right, depending on its prestige and power. The Qizilbash made up the bulk of the army, and it goes without saying that they fought on horseback. Like the Ottomans, the Safavids also made use of auxiliaries, particularly Kurds and Lurs, who fought for plunder and frequently changed sides.[8]

Figure 5.1 is a miniature from a 1589–90 manuscript of the great Persian epic, the *Shahnama* of Firdawsi. The battle is fictional, but there is some historical value in the details. All the soldiers are mounted. Most of them are

FIGURE 5.1. Persian battle scene: "Giv battles Piran." Firdawsi, *Shahnama* 185a.
Princeton Collection of Islamic Manuscripts, Third Series, no. 310. A.H. 998/A.D.
1589–90. Manuscripts Division, Department of Rare Books and Special Collections,
Princeton University Library. Courtesy of the Princeton University Library.

wearing helmets, but there is no sign of heavy body armor, and the use of shields suggests light armor, if any. A couple horses are armored, but most are not. Some of the men are using lances, others are wielding swords, and still others are shooting arrows, but every single man without exception seems to have a bow and a quiver of arrows. This is an artist's rendering of a kind of medium-light cavalry typical of steppe or desert nomads in the Middle East.

The earliest recorded use of firearms by the Safavids dates back to 1488, when Isma'il's father used cannon against the fortress of Gulistan. Isma'il himself bombarded the city of Yazd with "stones, cannonballs, and musket shot" in 1504, and he besieged the fortress of Jizra "with musket and mortar" in 1506. Two years after the great Ottoman victory over the Safavids at Chaldiran in 1514, the Safavids had manufactured 2,000 muskets with the help of Ottoman deserters, and they had also produced 40 copies of an Ottoman cannon recovered from a river bed. Isma'il's successor Tahmasp used Ottoman wagon-laager tactics against the Uzbeks at the battle of Jam in 1528.

The Safavids used their diplomatic connections to obtain firearms from abroad. Isma'il requested firearms from the Venetians, who had previously supplied the Aqquyunlu with weapons. Tahmasp may or may not have accepted some Portuguese firearms, but his son later obtained firearms from Russia by the hundreds in the 1580s. Still, little is said in the sources about Safavid use of firearms in the 1500s, even though the same sources mention Ottoman firearms frequently enough. It was not until 'Abbas reformed the army in the late 1500s that firearms were integrated into the Safavid army.[9]

'Abbas added several new units to the Safavid army at the end of the 1500s: the *ghulam* corps, the musketeer corps, and the artillery corps. The *ghulams* were slaves, comparable to the janissaries or the *mamluks* whom we have seen already in Turkey and Egypt; they were purchased from among the Circassians, the Georgians, and the Armenians, all non-Muslims of course. The musketeers on the other hand were freeborn Iranians. Initially, the *ghulams* were cavalry and the musketeers infantry, but the former also carried muskets and the latter were later provided with horses. In other words, both the *ghulams* and the musketeers became dragoons. There is no sign of infantry.[10]

Figure 5.2 is a hunting scene from the *Shahnama*. As mentioned earlier, the manuscript dates from 1589–90, or just several years after 'Abbas took the throne. This miniature shows hunters using bows, lassos, and even swords. One man on the left has a falcon on his hand. All these hunters are on horseback, and all of them have bows and quivers. Tellingly, the only ones on foot are the two men with matchlock muskets on the left – more proof that muskets were not used on horseback. Each of these hunters has a pouch

FIGURE 5.2. Persian hunting scene: "Bahram Gur hunts onager." Firdawsi, *Shahnama* 344b. Courtesy of the Princeton University Library.

on his belt, presumably for ammunition (recall the Ottoman dragoons who were jeeringly called "apothecaries"). The lower of the two is holding the match in his hand and blowing on it.[11]

Safavid armies never rivaled Ottoman ones in size. During the reign of Isma'il, the quiver-bearers numbered between 1,000 and 3,000, and the Safavid army as a whole could probably field no more than 20,000 men. In the mid-1500s, the quiver-bearers numbered around 5,000 men, but the army as a whole seems no larger than before. In the early 1600s, after the reforms of 'Abbas, there were between 10,000 and 15,000 *ghulams*, some 12,000 musketeers, and another 12,000 artillerymen, for a standing army of no more than 40,000, in addition to 10,000 or 20,000 Qizilbash cavalry and the usual auxiliaries. Since the Ottoman armies were also increasing in size through this period, however, the Safavid armies routinely faced superior numbers.[12]

To make matters worse, the Safavids faced both the Ottomans to the west and the Uzbeks to the east. These two enemies presented very different challenges: the Ottomans possessed a standing army equipped with firearms as advanced as any in the world, whereas the Uzbeks were tribal cavalry every bit as dangerous as the Mongols. Like the Russians, the Safavids needed an army that could fight in two very different environments, but whereas the Russian army was recruited from an agricultural society, the Safavid army grew out of the pastoral element of a mixed society.

Azarbayjan

Azarbayjan today is the name of a small country on the western shore of the Caspian Sea, one of the former Soviet Socialist Republics. In the past it was more generally the name of a large region to the southwest of the Caspian, including much of northwestern Iran. Azarbayjan shared with Khurasan the dubious distinction of having some of the finest grazing lands in the region, and it was a magnet for pastoral nomads from the steppes. When the Mongols conquered Iran in 1250s, they established their capital in Azarbayjan and distributed their followers among summer and winter camps in Anatolia, Azarbayjan, and Khurasan.[13]

The Safavids came into conflict with the Ottomans almost as soon as they disposed of the Aqquyunlu. Both empires were expanding rapidly. The Ottomans were staunch Sunnis, and they were worried about the effects of Shiite propaganda on the Türkmen tribes of eastern Anatolia. Sultan Selim led an army of 70,000 or more (including 12,000 janissaries) east in the summer of 1514 to deal with the Safavids, and Shah Isma'il confronted him with perhaps 20,000 men near Chaldiran in Azarbayjan.[14]

The senior Qizilbash commander on the left wing, who was familiar with Ottoman tactics, urged Isma'il to attack the Ottoman army before it could form its wagon laager. The senior Qizilbash commander on the right wing, who was a nephew of Isma'il, proposed instead that they wait until the Ottoman army had finished deploying. Isma'il had never lost a battle, and he considered himself divinely inspired, not to mention invincible. He waited until the Ottomans set up their guns and charged them head-on.[15]

By all accounts, the battle was won by Ottoman firepower. The Safavid cavalry charge almost carried the day, but the janissaries in the middle of the Ottoman line held their ground, and their fire was too much for the Safavid cavalry to withstand. After heavy losses on both sides, it was the Safavids who had to retreat. Chaldiran was a decisive battle in Safavid history: Safavid expansion came to a screeching halt, and Isma'il never again led an army in the field.

Many historians have cited Chaldiran as proof of the superiority of firearms, but as always the crucial question is context. Where did the battle take place and why? Chaldiran was proof, if proof was needed, that cavalry could not charge head-on at fortified musketeers and gunners with much chance of success. So what? There were many other strategic and tactical options open to cavalry, and the Safavids learned from their mistakes.

The Ottomans did not go on to conquer the Safavids after the battle of Chaldiran the way they would three years later with the Mamluks after the battle of Marj Dabiq. Part of the problem was logistics. The Safavids turned western Azarbayjan into a veritable no-man's-land. The Ottoman army pressed onward after the battle and occupied the Safavid capital of Tabriz, but after eight days it withdrew again for the winter. An Ottoman informer who passed through the area in the following summer reported that "These regions are empty, there is no one at all."[16]

Tahmasp never risked his army in a pitched battle with the Ottomans. Instead, he continued the "scorched earth" tactics, depriving Ottoman armies of forage and fodder while harassing their lines of supply with his cavalry. As the Habsburg ambassador in Istanbul wrote in 1560, "It is the custom of the inhabitants [of Iran], when their land is invaded, to lay waste and burn everything, and so force the enemy to retire through lack of food."[17] Hampered by difficult terrain, severe winters, and long supply lines, the Ottomans could not keep their army in the field more than two years at a stretch before it had to withdraw.

In 1534, the Ottomans seized Tabriz and Baghdad, but the Safavids retook Tabriz after the Ottoman army returned to Istanbul the following year. In 1548, the Ottomans again occupied Tabriz for a few days, but they withdrew from Iran the following year without anything to show for it. In 1554, an

Ottoman expedition again failed to make any permanent gains, and the two sides finally signed a peace treaty in 1555. Meanwhile, Tahmasp finally moved his capital eastward to Qazvin in 1555, and the capital was moved still farther away to Isfahan in 1597.[18]

Tahmasp was succeeded by a weak and incompetent ruler, and Ottoman aggression was renewed, culminating in the fall of Tabriz for the fourth time in 1585. Under constant pressure from the Uzbeks, who were allied with the Ottomans, the Safavids were unable to take effective countermeasures. 'Abbas seized the throne in 1587 and concluded a costly and humiliating peace with the Ottomans, buying time to reform the army (as described earlier) and deal with the Uzbek threat in the east.[19]

In 1603, 'Abbas decided the time was ripe to take on the Ottomans. A surprise attack on Tabriz caught the Ottoman commander and most of the garrison outside the city, and the remaining troops holed up in the citadel. The Ottoman commander, with 5,000 men, engaged the Safavid army of around 6,000 that was blocking his way back to the city. The Ottomans formed their wagon laager, as they had at Chaldiran, and manned it with musketeers and artillery, but they were routed by the Safavid cavalry anyway.[20]

With no further relief in sight, the citadel then surrendered, and 'Abbas had it torn down. The destruction of the citadel suggests that 'Abbas was prepared to abandon Tabriz again rather than defend it. The people of the city certainly suspected as much, because two years later 'Abbas was forced to rebuild the citadel to reassure them.[21]

'Abbas next moved against a trio of Ottoman forts at Erivan in Armenia. Not only were these fortifications particularly strong, but the Safavids were particularly weak at siege warfare. In the words of Iskandar Beg Munshi, a contemporary chronicler at the Safavid court:

> In the conspicuously fortunate and world-conquering reign of the Safavid sultans it was rare that the Qizilbash armies would take a fortress by force and violence from the Ottomans, and among the multitude it was widely believed that to [try to] take a fortress from the Ottomans was an absurd matter.[22]

The conduct of this siege highlights the changes that had occurred in the Safavid army under 'Abbas. The Safavids deployed musketeers and artillery against the forts in significant numbers and recruited 12,000 men from the local area to dig trenches to put them in position. After a siege that lasted all winter and into the summer of 1604, the walls were breached and the forts stormed.[23]

The Ottomans launched a major counteroffensive late that same year. The Safavids countered by laying waste to the lands along the Ottoman line of march and harassing their foragers, forcing the Ottomans to retire into winter quarters. The Ottomans resumed their campaign the following year, in the autumn of 1605, and again the Safavids adopted scorched earth tactics. According to Iskandar Beg Munshi, who was present with the Safavid army, 'Abbas planned to harass the Ottoman army during its march to Tabriz, but not to risk a battle to keep it from entering the city.

> After entering the city, if they should become engaged in besieging the citadel he would obstruct their retreat route and at a later date, when the weather had grown cold and the season of snow had arrived and supplies in their camp had become scarce, he would send the victorious troops from within and without . . . for the crucial blow.[24]

However, the Ottomans fell upon one of the Safavid detachments near Sufiyan and forced the main Safavid army to come to their aid. In the ensuing battle, the Safavids maneuvered the Ottomans out of position and broke their ranks with a decisive charge by the Qizilbash cavalry. 'Abbas hesitated to assault the Ottoman camp, which was fortified with the usual wagons, chains, and guns, but the Ottomans were already so demoralized by the setback that they retreated in confusion. This victory allowed 'Abbas to recover all the territory that had been lost during the previous reign. The only Safavid territory still in Ottoman hands was Baghdad.[25]

After years of inconclusive clashes and fruitless negotiations, 'Abbas took advantage of internal discord in Baghdad to recapture the city in 1623. When the Ottomans moved to place the city under siege toward the end of 1625, 'Abbas reinforced the garrison with musketeers and artillery and led a relief army to the rescue. The Ottoman siege army fortified its camp and set up its cannons and muskets behind the ramparts. Rather than assault the Ottoman position, 'Abbas used his army to cut their supply lines, and the Ottoman army eventually collapsed from hunger and sickness, abandoning its heavy equipment in the retreat.[26]

The Safavids did not hold Baghdad for long. 'Abbas was succeeded by the ineffectual Safi, and the Ottomans again sacked Tabriz and threatened Baghdad in the 1630s. The Ottomans finally recaptured Baghdad in 1638 when Safi failed to come to its relief. The Safavids signed a peace treaty in 1639 that confirmed Ottoman possession of Baghdad, and it remained in Ottoman hands thereafter. This treaty marked the end of serious fighting between the Ottomans and Safavids.

Khurasan

Khurasan is the name for the large region centered on what today is the intersection of Iran, Afghanistan, and Turkmenistan, including hilly country in the south and flat plains in the north. Like Azarbayjan, it contained good grazing grounds and was a natural home for pastoral nomads. Thanks in part to the caravans that linked the Mediterranean regions to China and India, this area also had a number of great cities, including Nishapur in modern Iran, Herat in modern Afghanistan, and Marv in modern Turkmenistan. Khurasan flourished under Temür's successors in the 1400s.

In the first decade of the 1500s, while Isma'il was defeating the Aqquyunlu and consolidating his rule in northwestern Iran, the descendants of Temür were being overrun by the Uzbeks. The Uzbeks were a confederation of Turkish steppe nomads whose leader claimed descent from the eldest son of Chinggis Khan. The Uzbeks still fought in the traditional fashion during the 1500s, much in the same way as the Mongols had. In 1500 they captured Samarqand; it was retaken by the Timurid prince Babur, but the Uzbeks quickly recaptured it in 1501 and established their control over Transoxania.

The Safavids had their own designs on the rich cities of Transoxania, and Isma'il led his first campaign against the Uzbeks in 1510. The Uzbek army skirmished with the Safavid forces before taking refuge in the city of Marv. Isma'il was not eager for a long siege, so he lured the Uzbeks out of the city by feigning a retreat and then fell upon them when they pursued. The Uzbek army was routed and the Uzbek ruler killed, and Isma'il added Marv and also Herat to his growing empire.

The Safavids helped Babur retake Samarqand in 1511, but Samarqand again fell to the Uzbeks, this time for good, in 1512. The Uzbeks also took Herat and Mashhad, forcing Isma'il to intervene personally in 1513; they refused to meet him in battle, so the border was restored to the *status quo ante* before he returned west to meet the Ottomans at Chaldiran. The Uzbeks were not content to leave things as they were, however. They attacked Herat in 1524 and Mashhad in 1526, and in 1528 they again placed the city of Herat under siege.[27]

Isma'il's successor Tahmasp led an army to relieve Herat. In the ensuing battle at Jam, the Safavids adopted Ottoman tactics, deploying wagons full of culverins and swivel guns in front of their army. The Uzbek cavalry broke both wings of the Safavid army but would not approach the gunners and musketeers in the center. Tahmasp then ordered his men to cease fire. Once the thick cloud of smoke from the guns had cleared away, the soldiers rallied around the standard of the shah, and his quiver-bearers and others launched a counterattack that carried the day. Although the wagon laager prevented a rout, the counterattack was the work of the Safavid cavalry. It was the combination of the wagon laager and the cavalry that gained the victory.[28]

The Uzbeks did not quit even then. They invaded again in 1529, 1532, and 1536. The Uzbeks maintained an active second front against the Safavids, preventing the Safavids from concentrating against the Ottomans, whereas of course the Ottoman threat prevented the Safavids from dealing freely with the Uzbeks. The pressure from the Uzbeks only eased after the death of the Uzbek ruler 'Ubayd Allah Khan in 1540.

After a long lull in hostilities, the Safavids found themselves again squeezed from both sides in the 1580s. Two years after the Ottomans captured Tabriz in the west, the Uzbeks besieged Herat in the east, in 1587. Although the Uzbeks deployed mortars against the city, the siege dragged on for almost a year, until hunger weakened the garrison enough to permit an assault to succeed in 1588. The citadel fell immediately thereafter, perhaps because its supplies were exhausted as well.[29]

As mentioned earlier, 'Abbas signed a humiliating peace with the Ottomans to buy time to deal with the Uzbeks. After nearly ten years of preparation, 'Abbas finally led his new army east in 1598. The Uzbek detachment in Nishapur fled at the approach of the Safavid army without offering any resistance. Concerned with the possibility of a lengthy siege at Herat, 'Abbas decided to try the same ruse that had worked for Isma'il at Marv in 1510.

The Safavid vanguard of some 6,000, operating far in advance of the main body, began to withdraw from the vicinity of Herat, drawing the Uzbek army of 12,000 out into the open. Meanwhile, 'Abbas led several thousand of his fastest cavalry from the main body to link up with the vanguard. Outnumbered and exhausted, the Safavid cavalry just managed to pull off the victory. Herat fell immediately after; Safavid supporters surrounded the citadel, but the Uzbek garrison cut its way out and made its escape.[30]

Contrast this victory with the debacle at Balkh in northern Afghanistan four years later, in the spring and summer of 1602. On this occasion, it is said that 'Abbas mobilized an army of 50,000 men, including 10,000 musketeers and 300 cannon. Due to the extreme heat and the size of the supply train, the army moved very slowly, and there was a shortage of water and an outbreak of dysentery along the way. By the time the army arrived at Balkh, it was in no condition for a battle or for a siege, and it suffered heavily on its retreat back to Iran.[31]

The Uzbeks had mortars at Herat in 1587 and muskets and cannon of their own at Balkh in 1602. Firearms probably arrived in Transoxania in the 1400s: Ottoman muskets reached China not long after 1500 along this route, and Babur picked them up somewhere before arriving in India in 1525. The Ottomans cultivated relations with the Uzbeks and sent them firearms on occasion, just to cause the Safavids some grief. Firearms did not fit into Uzbek-style mounted warfare, but like the Safavids, they began to deploy firearms in siege warfare, Herat and Balkh being cases in point.[32]

The Safavids faced other nomads on their eastern border who fought like the Uzbeks and were even slower to take up firearms themselves. Although the Safavids did clash briefly with the Mughals over Qandahar, the distance between the cores of their respective empires and the desolate nature of the territory that lay between them limited that conflict. Overall, their experience on their eastern border did not encourage the Safavids to make greater use of firearms.[33]

Safavid Success or Failure?

The Ottomans were clearly successful at using firearms, and the Mamluks just as clearly unsuccessful, but the Safavids are a more difficult case.

On the one hand, the Safavids did not make significant use of firearms until the 1600s, more than a century after they first came to know of them, and this despite having the further advantage (if it may be called such) of close contact with a power that did, namely the Ottomans.

On the other hand, the Safavids defended themselves rather successfully without much help from firearms throughout most of the 1500s. Given all the other advantages enjoyed by the Ottomans, including a larger population and a more efficient administration, it is unlikely that the Safavids could have recruited and equipped enough soldiers to go toe-to-toe with the Ottomans in any event.

The Ottomans accepted the logistical trade-off that came with the decision to use muskets and cannon in large numbers. This trade-off, more than anything else, determined the strategic dynamic on the Safavid-Ottoman front. The Safavids avoided the Ottoman strength, which was their firepower, and targeted their weakness, which was their logistics.

For all intents and purposes, Ottoman firepower ensured that they could capture any Safavid city that they could reach, at least during the 1500s. Whether they could hold onto what they captured was again a problem of logistics. The Ottoman garrison had to be large enough to hold out until relief arrived, but not so large that it could not be supplied for the most part from the local economy.

It is perhaps no coincidence that the Ottomans held onto Baghdad, the center of the most fertile region in that part of the world aside from the Nile valley, while they frequently sacked but just as frequently abandoned Tabriz, located in the heart of the grasslands of Azarbayjan. Nor is it entirely coincidental that the eastern borders of the Ottoman empire closely matched the easternmost expansion of the Roman empire, whose legions were baffled by the elusive Parthian cavalry.

In the 1500s, the Safavid regime had many characteristics of a nomadic confederation, including a remarkable resilience in the face of defeat. They could survive the repeated occupation of Tabriz and the ultimate loss of

Baghdad because their base of support lay elsewhere. The contrasting fates
of the Mamluks and the Safavids are instructive. The Mamluks were an
urban slave elite with no nomadic tribal following to fall back upon once
Cairo was occupied.[34]

The military reforms of 'Abbas should be understood in the context of
efforts by his three immediate predecessors (the three successors to Isma'il,
in other words) to dampen the fanaticism of the Qizilbash and extend the
base of support for the dynasty to a wider range of the population. The
new military units, particularly the slave corps, were arguably more loyal
to the person of the shah, being less concerned about the ideology of the
movement. In the process, the Safavid regime came to resemble a nomadic
confederation less and less.[35]

Nevertheless, even when the Safavids formed musketeer and artillery
corps, the effect on their battlefield tactics was less than one might imagine.
For one thing, the Safavids still avoided pitched battles with Ottoman armies.
The Safavids learned early to stay clear of the Ottoman wagon laagers, and
there is no indication of the Safavid musketeers and artillery being brought
to bear against them. Safavid dragoons sometimes appear as skirmishers,
but field artillery is hardly mentioned at all, and the decisive action is still
the cavalry charge.

There were greater changes in siege warfare, both on offense and on
defense. Isma'il had employed a mixed bag of tricks for taking fortresses,
either making threats or giving promises, storming the ramparts or luring
the defenders outside, filling the moat or diverting the water supply, under-
mining the walls with mines or breaching them with cannon, as the situation
demanded.[36] A hundred years later, the Safavids could use cannon to reduce
fortresses that would once have been out of their reach, as they did at Erivan
in 1603–4. On defense, they could resist Ottoman firepower long enough
for a relief force to arrive, as they did at Baghdad in 1625–26.

Still, it seems that fewer cities in Iran had walls in the late 1600s than
in the late 1400s, when firearms first appeared in the area. Both deliberate policy and benign neglect probably played a part. If the Safavids were
not going to stand and fight against the Ottomans, why would they build
fortifications that could only be used against them? The destruction of the
citadel of Tabriz in 1603 is an example of this trend as deliberate policy,
although there the action had to be reversed for political reasons. In areas
of the country not threatened by the Ottomans, strong walls would only
encourage separatist tendencies. Walls were most useful against the Uzbeks,
as at Herat.[37]

On the Safavid–Uzbek front, firearms saw even less use. Cavalry was
better adapted to the environment than infantry, and the Uzbeks tended to

withdraw rather than get bottled up in citadels. Cities changed hands after the armies were defeated in the field, as at Marv in 1510 and at Herat in 1598, both occasions when the Safavids used the hoary feigned withdrawal trick. In the west, the Safavids were the weaker force that avoided direct battle with the Ottomans; in the east, the Safavids were the stronger force that could not force battle upon the Uzbeks. Either way, firearms contributed little to Safavid security.

One European contemporary who lived for some years in the Ottoman empire ascribed the neglect of firearms among the Safavids to some odd contradictory combination of pride and scruples:

> The people of Persia are afrayde of Artillery beyond measure, and yet sometimes they haue not beene afraide with suddaine assaultes to assaile their enimies trenches, and lodginges in their Campes. And although they be so timorous and fearefull of that Engine, and yet know of what moment it is in a battel; yet haue they not hitherto receiued the use thereof, being rather obstinate in their blind ambitious conceite, that it is a sinne and shame to exercise so cruell a weapon against mankind, then ignorant how to make it, or destitute of matter to cast it.[38]

However, most European observers agreed that the real objection was speed: cannon would have slowed down the swift Safavid cavalry. Muskets were less of an issue because the musketeers were actually dragoons.[39]

No doubt the Qizilbash horsemen looked down (literally and figuratively) on infantry with firearms, just as Ottoman horsemen did, and Mamluk horsemen did, and French horsemen did. But what does that tell us? Apparently, we are supposed to believe that if it had not been for their "blind ambitious conceit," the Safavids would have manufactured more firearms, armed more infantry with them – and played right into the hands of the Ottomans.

Safavid Iran was much smaller and weaker than the Ottoman empire; it lacked the population and the resources to slug it out with the Ottomans. It succeeded in remaining independent because it did not allow itself to get drawn into the kind of war that only the Ottomans could win. Its reliance on cavalry instead of on firearms was the secret to its survival.[40]

India

For China and Europe, the line between steppe and sown roughly corresponded to the line between other and self. That is, pastoralists did not comprise separate tribes or societies within China or Europe, but interacted with the Chinese or Europeans from outside. Pastures and farms could be found side by side within both China and Europe, but the pastures were used by farmers, not by nomadic tribes, to graze animals.

For most of the Middle East, on the other hand, the relationship was rather different. Large areas suitable for pasturage but marginal for agriculture were found within the Middle East and did support pastoral tribes. The line between pasturage and farmland did not correspond to the line between other and self, but rather to an internal division of society.

The northwestern frontier of the Indian subcontinent was open to invasion from Afghanistan. Successive invasions originated in this quarter, beginning with the Aryans in the second millennium B.C. Like both China and Europe, India was only vulnerable to nomads from one direction – it was protected against invasion from other directions by the Himalayas and the sea.

However, India also had an internal frontier between pastoralists and farmers. Northwestern India is quite arid and forms a natural extension of the steppes and deserts of the Arid Zone, as does the Deccan Plateau in the interior, which is sheltered from the summer monsoon by the coastal mountains. Much of the population was concentrated on the peripheries, whether in the Ganges River valley in the northeast or along the coasts.[41]

The indigenous pastoralists were perhaps not quite as dangerous as the Mongols and Turks, if only because horses do not thrive in India. The hot moist climate is very different from the cool dry climate of the steppes where horses evolved. The more arid regions in the center and northwest are not as bad for these purposes, insofar as they are not actual desert, but they do not compare to Mongolia or the Ukraine. India was never known for its cavalry, either heavy or light.[42]

Long-range nomadic pastoralism within India was relatively uncommon. Many herders moved within closely circumscribed areas and were associated with fixed settlements. Even when the Turks entered India, they underwent partial sedentarization. Still, India offered abundant pastoral resources to maintain the herds that underpinned cavalry armies, even if imported horses were far superior to native horses as cavalry mounts. This was quite different from, say, the case in China.[43]

The jungle did provide India with an alternative to the warhorse, namely the war elephant. Elephants could carry as many as a dozen fighting men on wooden platforms on their backs, and each one might be escorted by several hundred foot soldiers and horsemen. In battle, they were used to break enemy ranks; at other times, they were used for transportation and construction work. Less mobile than warhorses, elephants were also more vulnerable to firearms, and they fought a long losing battle against both these military technologies over the centuries of the Turkish invasions.[44]

Geographically, India is an intermediate case, not as sheltered from the steppe and desert as western Europe or Japan, not as exposed as north China or the Middle East. Northeastern India had a large and well-armed peasant population that could serve as a reservoir of manpower for rulers or, if the rulers failed to coopt them, for potential challengers. This area was larger than any equivalent area in the Middle East, even Egypt or Iraq, yet it was still open to cavalry armies from within India, whether from the northwest or from the interior.[45]

Historically, Turks conquered and ruled much or most of India during the centuries before and after the invention of firearms. The age of Turkish rule in India can be divided into two periods, the Afghan period from the 1200s to the 1500s and the Mughal period from the 1500s to the 1800s. Firearms arrived in India during the Afghan period and began to change the conduct of warfare during the Mughal period.

The Afghans

In 711, the same year that they invaded Spain, the Arabs also reached the Indus River in what is today Pakistan. The Arabs were too far from home and too few in number to take on the Hindu kingdoms of the heavily populated Ganges River valley in the northeast, and they made no further inroads. This task was left for the Turks from Afghanistan with their warhorses and mounted archers three centuries later.

Starting in the beginning of the 1000s, Turks from Afghanistan raided northern India for two centuries and gradually made permanent conquests. Little is known about how these wars were fought, but the Turkish cavalry did not fight in ranks that would have been vulnerable to elephants. The Turkish armies did have swarms of horse archers and also a core of heavily armed and armored *mamluks* who could deliver decisive cavalry charges.[46]

It was one of these *mamluks* who founded the first sultanate in Delhi by declaring his independence from his master and sultan in Afghanistan in 1206 – the same year that Chinggis Khan became ruler of the Mongols. Delhi was conveniently located in the intermediate zone between the arid northwest and the humid northeast, well situated to draw reinforcements from the former and exert control over the latter.[47]

A succession of Muslim dynasties, known collectively as the Delhi sultanate, ruled northern India down to 1398, and in much diminished form down to 1526. The first of these (1206–90) is sometimes called the dynasty of the Slave Kings because three of the eleven sultans began their careers as *mamluks*, but for the most part succession passed within families, unlike in Egypt.[48]

The Turkish conquest of northern India did not mean an end to invasions from the northwest; it did not prevent Temür from sacking Delhi in 1398, for example. What it did mean though was the opening of the Deccan

Plateau in central India to Turkish influence. A Turkish officer of obscure origins took advantage of a power vacuum there to set up the Bahmani sultanate in 1347. The rule of the Bahmani sultans lasted more or less down to 1528.

Meanwhile, in southern India, the population was spreading from the fertile river valleys and coastal regions to the arid upland plateaus in the center of the peninsula. Pressure from the Bahmani sultans of the Deccan contributed to the rise of the powerful Hindu kingdom of Vijayanagara in the mid-1300s. For over three centuries, from the mid-1300s to the mid-1600s, four successive dynasties ruled the greater part of southern India from their capital on the plateau. Vijayanagara halted Muslim expansion by borrowing Turkish techniques of mounted warfare and by attracting Turkish horsemen into its own forces.[49]

Both the Bahmani sultans and the "lords of the horse" (as the Vijayanagara kings were sometimes called) depended on horses imported from Arabia and Iran. Vijayanagara kings even paid for horses that died en route, to encourage merchants to continue importing them. Horses were embarked at Aden and Hurmuz for a number of Indian ports, but especially Goa – Marco Polo commented on this trade as early as the 1200s. Control of Goa and Hurmuz would later give the Portuguese leverage over Hindu and Muslim rulers in southern and central India. Note that it was access to horses, not to firearms, that conferred this leverage.[50]

If things had turned out differently, southern India might have been isolated from the influence of the steppe and desert nomads by northern India in the same way that western Europe was isolated from that influence by eastern Europe. One can only imagine what might have happened then. Instead, the only major power in southern India was locked in a struggle for survival with the Turks in the arid interior of the peninsula when gunpowder and firearms first arrived.

Gunpowder arrived in India perhaps as early as the mid-1200s, when the Mongols could have introduced it, but in any event no later than the mid-1300s, when a contemporary source mentions fireworks displays in Delhi. Fireworks are also attested in contemporary sources for Vijayanagara in the first half of the 1400s. The ingredients in a formula for gunpowder recorded in the early 1500s suggest that gunpowder came directly from China rather than indirectly from Europe.[51]

In India, gunpowder was originally employed in rockets, which were a natural outgrowth of the application of gunpowder to fireworks, albeit one that was largely ineffective as a weapon.[52] Firearms first appeared in the 1400s. None of the histories that mention firearms were compiled earlier than the 1590s, and the earlier works on which these later histories were based have not survived, but there seems to be enough evidence to accept the account of their use in 1456 as reliable. A painting from the reign of Sikandar Lodi (r.1489–1517) showing a cannon is the earliest contemporary Indian evidence.[53]

The Portuguese already found firearms in considerable numbers along the coast in the first decade of the 1500s. The port of Diu in Gujarat was protected by "a very strong boom across the harbor, furnished with heavy artillery and many gunners always present." The port of Dabhol in Bijapur also had "a fortress with artillery for its defense." The port of Goa had "large and small pieces of artillery" in its fortifications. The port of Calicut in Malabar had "stockades fortified with artillery." Cannanore had "a great many musketeers."[54]

These weapons must have been brought from the Middle East. According to one Portuguese writer, the greater part of the Muslims of Gujarat were foreigners, either Turks or Mamluks or Arabs or Iranians or Khurasanis or Türkmens. There were hundreds of Ottomans in the Deccan. Turks, Arabs, and Iranians flocked to Goa in the 1400s. Even the Hindu kings of Vijayanagara had Muslim soldiers, "with many bombs and spears and fire-missiles." Significantly, firearms terminology in south Indian languages generally came from Turkish.[55]

The production of cannon seem to have remained the province of Turks and Europeans into the 1600s or even the 1700s. Local craftsmen were capable of forging wrought-iron musket barrels, but their blast furnaces could not produce the temperatures for casting iron, and even techniques for casting bronze were no better than adequate. Such technological limitations may have accounted for some of India's failure to make better use of firearms.[56]

The Mughals

Turks again invaded northern India from Afghanistan in the early 1500s. The leader of this invasion was Babur, who was forced out of Samarqand by the Uzbeks in 1512. Thwarted in his own homeland, Babur founded the Mughal dynasty (1526–1857) in India – "Mughal" being derived from the Persian word for Mongol. Babur was descended from Chinggis Khan through his great-great-great grandfather, Temür, who had sacked Delhi in 1398.

When Babur invaded India in 1525, he brought with him a full complement of firearms: cannons, culverins, swivel guns, mortars, and matchlock muskets.[57] Where he got them is a bit of a mystery. Firearms were still scarce in Transoxania and Afghanistan.[58] However, the identity of one of Babur's two master gunners, Mustafa Rumi (i.e., Mustafa "the Ottoman"), provides one hint. Babur's own description of his battle tactics provides another.

Babur's victory at Panipat in 1526 led to the capture of Delhi. In preparation for the battle, wrote Babur:

> I ordered the whole army, in accordance with rank, to bring carts, which numbered about seven hundred altogether. Master Ali-Quli [his other master gunner] was told to tie them together with ox-harness ropes instead of chains, after the Ottoman manner, keeping a distance of six to seven large shields between every two carts. The matchlockmen could then stand behind the fortification to fire their guns.[59]

His victory at Khanua in 1527 then secured his southwestern flank. Before the battle, not only did he line up the wagons ("in the Ottoman fashion") and connect them with chains, but he had men dig trenches where the wagons did not reach, and set up wooden tripods connected with ox-harness ropes. The cannon and muskets in the wagon laager at the center of Babur's army again contributed mightily toward the victory, with the musketeers even leaving the shelter of the wagons at the height of the battle, "as ordered," and advancing on the enemy, "causing their names to figure prominently among the lions of the jungle of courage and the chivalrous heroes of battle."[60]

After Panipat and Khanua, Babur was free to move southeast from Delhi down the Ganges River valley. Firearms and boats stand out in his account of this campaign. Crossing the Ganges in front of an Afghan army in 1528, he stationed Ali-Quli with a mortar at the point where a bridge would be built across the river, sent Mustafa downstream with cannons and culverins, and deployed matchlockmen upstream, all to provide covering fire. In a similar situation in 1529, crossing the Ganges against a Bengali army, the gunners provided covering fire while Babur's soldiers crossed the river by boat, and they sank four boats with shots from the swivel guns.[61]

Babur took an active personal interest in his gunners and their weapons. He went to inspect eight new mortars that Ali-Quli was casting, and when none of them turned out successful, he gave Ali-Quli a ceremonial robe to cheer him up. When Ali-Quli finally did cast a giant mortar, Babur gave him a belt and dagger, a ceremonial robe, and a horse. (Unfortunately, the mortar later burst, killing eight people.) Babur gave a dagger to the son of Ali-Quli to honor him, and he took care to deploy Ali-Quli and Mustafa at different positions in the line of battle because he knew that they did not get along well together.[62]

The Mughals lost control of India after the death of Babur in 1530, but Babur's son Humayun recaptured Delhi in 1555, and Humayun's son Akbar finally consolidated Mughal power in India. The last major field battle involving the main Mughal army was fought at Panipat (again) in 1556; Mughal victories there and at lesser encounters at Tukaroi in 1575 and Haldighati in 1576 dissuaded others from challenging them in the field. These victories established the supremacy of the Mughal military system.[63]

The combination of a wagon laager with artillery and muskets holding the center and horse archers attacking from the flanks dominated the battlefield at least through the 1600s. The wagons gave the cavalry stability, while the cavalry gave the wagons offensive punch, as the Safavid victory over the Uzbeks at the battle of Jam in 1528 clearly demonstrared. Both firearms and warhorses were essential, and as long as the Mughals controlled the supply of warhorses and the men who grew up riding them, it was difficult for rivals to duplicate their success.

The introduction of cannon to India did not spark a redesign of fortresses comparable to the *trace italienne* in Europe. Heavy cannon could be transported easily by water up and down the Ganges River valley, but the Mughals had a firm grip on the area, and no one wanted to face a Mughal relief army in the field. Once the Mughals moved out of the Ganges River valley onto the Deccan Plateau, dragging heavy siege artillery overland increased costs enormously, and there were few worthwhile targets. The Mughals proved they could reduce any existing fortifications when they captured Chitor in 1568, but it was not always worth the effort. Bribes were cheaper and faster, and better for all concerned.[64]

Like nomads before them who invaded and occupied agricultural lands, the Mughals gradually fielded a higher proportion of heavy cavalry – still armed with bows and sabres, but now with heavy armor for riders and horses alike. Their wagons and artillery and infantry slowed them down further. On top of that, the Mughal emperors traveled and campaigned with their courts, which slowed them to a crawl. The Mughals became vulnerable to the hit-and-run tactics of light cavalry in the 1600s, not only from the Turkish Rohillas of Afghanistan to their north but also from the Hindu Marathas of the Deccan Plateau to their south.[65]

The Mughals were like the Ottomans in many ways, and not only because they employed Ottoman weapons, tactics, and even personnel. However, the Mughals were never tested against European powers, and they had little in the way of naval power either, so one hesitates to put them on a par with the Ottomans. Still, the Mughals struck the right balance between firearms and cavalry in the 1500s and 1600s, and it would be odd to suggest that they "should" have done more with firearms.

To the extent that the collapse of the Mughal empire in the 1700s can be attributed to military causes, it was the failure to cope with the light cavalry of the Rohillas and Marathas that brought it about, not any failure to keep up with European firearms. The Mughal experience suggests that it was difficult to conquer the Ganges River valley without firearms, but difficult to defend it without cavalry. The Mughals pulled off this balancing act for nearly two centuries before they fell off the high wire.

The Portuguese

Europeans first appeared off the coast of India in 1498, after the Portuguese discovered the route around the Cape of Good Hope.[66] Instead of the fabled Christian king Prester John, they found Turks and Arabs and Iranians there ahead of them. The first Portuguese to land in Calicut was taken to meet two Spanish-speaking Tunisians, who asked him "What brought you here?"[67] What had brought the Portuguese there was spices, but it quickly became apparent that they had nothing anyone wanted, except bullion from the New World, to exchange for those spices.[68] Fortunately for the Portuguese, what they did have were cannon.

Operating at such a great distance from their home country, Portuguese ships relied on superior firepower to offset superior numbers. The king gave the following instructions to the Portuguese fleet bound for the Indian Ocean in 1500: "You are not to come to close quarters with them if you can avoid it, but only with your artillery are you to compel them to strike sail ... so that this war may be waged with greater safety, and so that less loss may result to the people of your ships."[69] The five caravels and three other ships that pummeled the fleet of Calicut off the Malabar coast in 1501 were well equipped for the task:

> Each of the caravels carried thirty men, and four heavy guns below, and above six falconnets, and ten swivel-guns placed on the quarter deck and in the bows, and two of the falconnets fired astern; the ships carried six guns below on the deck, and two smaller ones on the poop, and eight falconnets above and several swivel-guns, and before the mast two smaller pieces which fired forwards; the ships of burden were much more equipped with artillery.[70]

The Portuguese advantage was not commercial but military. The Portuguese had better ships – they were more sturdy and more maneuverable in addition to being better armed – but they were not necessarily more economical. They generated income by enforcing restrictions on trade and raising costs for competitors. Thus, all traffic in spices was monopolized by the Portuguese crown. Trade between specified ports was also monopolized, and rights to exploit these monopolies were sold to the highest bidders. Merchants who bought licenses allowing them to trade on other routes had to pay Portuguese customs duties; at times they were also forced to sail in Portuguese-organized convoys.[71]

The Portuguese very methodically went about securing the bases they needed to enforce these restrictions. In 1510, they captured the port of Goa on the western coast of India and set up their headquarters there. In 1511, they took the city of Melaka, which controlled the entrance into the Indian Ocean from the South China Sea. In 1513, they attacked the city of Aden, at the entrance from the Red Sea, but failed to capture it. In 1515, they took the port of Hurmuz, which controlled the entrance from the Persian Gulf. With a temporary monopoly over the route around the Cape of Good Hope, they had sewn up three of the four entrances to the Indian Ocean.

The organized use of violence for economic ends on this scale was new to the Indian Ocean. Pirates were ubiquitous, but piracy did not give rise to navies.[72] Building warships to escort merchantmen and patrol sea lanes was generally less efficient than arming the merchantmen themselves. Traders either shipped their goods on vessels large enough to resist attack or spread their cargoes across many smaller vessels as a form of insurance, trading uncertain risk of large losses for more likely but more manageable risk of smaller losses. If larger ships were too scarce and smaller ones too poor to make piracy very profitable, an equilibrium might be reached where pirate ships were large enough to knock off the smaller prey but small enough to turn a profit at it.

Monopoly profits helped subsidize Portuguese fleets. Since even the largest merchantmen were defenseless against their cannon, size alone was no longer adequate protection. Merchants presumably went for the other extreme and built smaller and cheaper ships instead. The only other options were to pay protection money or to ship goods on Portuguese vessels. Although Indian merchants could have built larger and sturdier ships capable of carrying cannon, such ships could only pay for themselves on voyages between the largest ports, and as long as there was no competing fleet to break Portuguese control of the seas, individual merchant ships could not run those routes in the teeth of the Portuguese fleets.[73]

The principal seapower in India at the beginning of the 1500s was the Muslim sultanate of Gujarat. A combined Mamluk-Gujarati fleet defeated a Portuguese fleet in 1508, but it was destroyed in turn by the Portuguese fleet at Diu in 1509. The Portuguese were determined to gain control over Diu, and they finally did so in 1536, after most of Gujarat had been overrun by the Mughals. Gujarat quickly shook off the Mughal yoke, but it failed to retake Diu, and in the meanwhile, succession struggles deprived Gujarat of the unity and strong central control that could have made a fleet possible. Gujarat was eventually annexed by the Mughal empire in the 1570s, as was Bengal, giving the Mughals outlets to the sea on both sides of the Indian peninsula. However, the Mughals remained a land-oriented empire without much interest in developing a navy.[74]

Meanwhile, the Ottomans had taken over Egypt in 1517, together with the Red Sea fleet that they had helped the Mamluks to build. This fleet repulsed the Portuguese foray into the Red Sea in 1517, but its galleys were not suited for operations on the open ocean, and Egypt was still just as unsatisfactory as a base for naval operations as it had ever been. The Ottomans did capture Aden at the mouth of the Red Sea in 1538, but combined operations with the Gujaratis against the Portuguese base at Diu later that same year ended in failure. Ottoman expeditions against the Portuguese base at Hurmuz in 1551–54 were an even bigger fiasco, with the Ottoman galleys first bottled up in the Persian Gulf and then scuttled on the Indian coast. The Ottoman galleys that operated along the eastern coast of Africa in 1585 and 1588 were destroyed by a Portuguese fleet in 1589.[75]

Unable to challenge the Portuguese on the open ocean, the Ottomans extended aid to Muslim powers instead. In east Africa, the Ottomans sent firearms to Muslims in Ethiopia in 1527, and the year after the Portuguese upped the ante with 400 musketeers for the Christian king in 1541, the Ottomans responded with 900 musketeers and 10 pieces of artillery. Babur's gunner Mustafa was mentioned earlier, but another Ottoman gunner named Mustafa, also known as Mustafa Rumi Khan, brought troops and cannon to help defend Diu in Gujarat against the Portuguese in 1531. Khaja Safar and his son, Muharram Rumi Khan, apparently Albanians, were both killed trying to recapture Diu from the Portuguese in 1546. At the eastern end of the Indian Ocean, 300 Ottoman soldiers were dispatched to the Sultanate of Aceh on Sumatra in the 1530s in exchange for four shiploads of pepper.[76]

Ottoman support for Muslim rulers never jeopardized Portuguese control of the Indian Ocean. On the other hand, the Portuguese never expanded far inland. The weapons and manpower available to them were insufficient for the task. At sea, European cannon were better than anything found on local ships. On land, European muskets and pistols were also superior to local weapons under many circumstances, but not nearly enough so to offset European numerical inferiority until the Industrial Revolution.[77] The Portuguese reliance on a handful of naval bases, unavoidable as it was, left them vulnerable to setbacks. The capture of Hurmuz by the Safavids (with English assistance[78]) in 1622 and then the loss of Melaka to the Dutch in 1641 broke the Portuguese grip over the Indian Ocean. However, control of the seas merely shifted to other European powers.

Southeast Asia

East of the Indian Ocean lies the region known as Southeast Asia. The climate is tropical and the land heavily forested, but much of the area is accessible by water. Indian influence was strong, and Hinduism and Buddhism both came

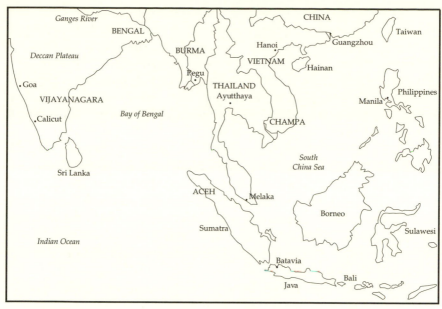

Map 5. Southeast Asia

to this region in early times. Chinese influence was felt as well, particularly in Vietnam, but the Chinese only began to migrate to the region in large numbers in the 1400s. Islam also began to replace Hinduism and Buddhism in the archipelago, though not on the mainland, around that time.[79]

Five hundred years ago, the region was still for the most part sparsely populated. Wars were fought to capture people rather than to control territory. Aggressors would not risk casualties by pushing an assault that might net fewer captives, and defenders would not sacrifice lives to hold land that was available elsewhere. Warfare was characterized by skirmishing and raiding, reminiscent of warfare in other sparsely populated areas of the world, particularly in the forests of Africa and North America.[80]

Elephants were used in warfare, but horses were scarce. Ma Duanlin relates the following story about a shipwrecked Chinese official:

> In 1171, there was a Fujianese who was crossing the sea to administer Jiyang Military Prefecture [on the southern coast of Hainan island] who was shipwrecked in Champa. He saw that that country and Cambodia rode elephants in battle without achieving decisive victory. So he persuaded the king to fight on horseback and taught him about mounted archery. That king was greatly pleased and prepared a boat to send him to Jiyang, and he sent a large sum of money with him to buy horses and obtained several dozen. They used them to fight, and won.[81]

The climate was even worse for horses than the climate of India, and the sources for good warhorses even farther away, so this episode had no lasting impact. On the other hand, the region was ripe for the introduction of firearms. Bronze and iron had been worked from very early times, even if the availability of spices and other unique natural resources to trade for Chinese and Indian goods generally kept the level of manufacturing low. Primitive cannon were useless for skirmishes in the jungle, but they were just right for harbor defenses and sailing ships.[82]

Considering that Chinese ships armed with gunpowder weapons, including cannon, visited the region regularly from the 1200s to the 1400s, it is not surprising that there were firearms before the Portuguese arrived. When the Portuguese captured Melaka in 1511, they also captured several thousand guns. One large cannon came from Calicut in India, but the Portuguese believed that most of them had come from Pegu in Burma and Ayutthaya in Thailand, where Indians and Chinese, respectively, had helped to establish foundries.[83]

Since firearms were already known, European firearms spread quickly. The Portuguese used firearms as a diplomatic tool, giving them away to curry favor with local rulers, despite their own reluctance to arm potential rivals and despite papal bans on selling weapons to infidels. Where they were not willing, the Dutch and the English were: when the King of Makassar (on the southern tip of Sulawesi) tried to buy bronze cannon from the Portuguese at Macau, he pointed out that the Dutch would supply him if they would not. The Jesuits also capitalized on the eagerness of local rulers to acquire cannon.[84]

In any event, there was no way to prevent European soldiers from deserting and offering their services to the highest bidder. Their ships and their guns made them uniquely valuable as auxiliaries. For example, Portuguese mercenaries helped Lower Burma (on the coast) to conquer Upper Burma (in the interior) in the 1550s, and then to establish a short-lived empire that controlled the entire Indian Ocean coast of Burma and Thailand. Many rulers maintained a small body of foreign musketeers, not all of them Europeans either.[85]

On the mainland, a few native armies adopted muskets on a large scale. The ratio of firearms to other weapons in Burma reached 1:3 or 1:2 in the mid-1500s, comparable to that in Europe. The Thais also used firearms on a large scale. Portuguese noted in the early 1500s that the king of Vietnam "has countless musketeers, and small bombards," and that "a great deal of powder is used in his country." When central Vietnam split off from northern Vietnam around 1627, its rulers turned to firearms to compensate for their numerical inferiority.[86]

Warfare was still characterized by skirmishing and raiding more than sieges and set-piece battles, so the most popular firearms were lightweight and mobile ones: muskets and swivel guns. The influx of these powerful new weapons initially gave a boost to political centralization in many parts of the region. However, as Dutch and English traders moved into the region, muskets became cheaper and more widespread, and the trend toward centralization reversed itself. Makassar began manufacturing muskets in the 1620s. Mataram was making muskets in the 1650s. By the 1700s, beautiful muskets were being produced by populations in Sumatra, Bali, and Sulawesi free of centralized control.[87]

Portuguese ships elicited two responses, both seemingly perverse, but both explicable in light of changing circumstances. First, the Malays actually stopped building large junks and switched to smaller and cheaper vessels in the 1500s. The disappearance of the large junk after the arrival of the Portuguese tends to confirm what was suggested about ships in the Indian Ocean, that smaller and cheaper ships were preferable to larger and stronger ones, either because they could outrun Portuguese carracks or because they spread the risk of loss and served as a kind of insurance.

Second, the Malays copied Portuguese galleys rather than Portuguese carracks. We know that the Portuguese used galleys in the Persian Gulf, along the coast of India, in Southeast Asia, and off the coast of China. It seems probable that the Portuguese constructed galleys in Goa and Melaka and elsewhere based on familiar designs, using them for local defense and amphibious operations, and reserving carracks and carvels for long-distance trade. Although the Malays had their own oar-driven vessels, Portuguese galleys must have better suited than indigenous designs for mounting cannon.

Galleys were more efficient than sailing ships when cannon were scarce, at least in shallow coastal waters. They became obsolete when merchant ships started carrying enough cheap cast-iron cannon that galleys could no longer defeat them, and when arming warships with cannon became cheaper than manning galleys. This process did not even get underway in the Mediterranean until the second half of the 1500s, over half a century after the Portuguese arrived in India, and it probably took longer to complete in Southeast Asia.[88]

Ultimately, control of the seas implied control of the region, at least in the negative sense of preventing its unification under any rival. (This is reminiscent of the dynamic described in the section "The Desert" in Chapter 1.) None of the centralizing local powers of the archipelago in the 1500s expanded beyond its own island before the centralizing trend reversed itself in the 1600s. Aceh made its last and greatest effort to take Melaka in 1629, only to lose its entire army and fleet in the process.[89] Twelve years later, it was the Dutch who evicted the Portuguese from Melaka instead. Dutch command of the seas allowed them to extend their control across the archipelago without exerting direct control on every single island.

Meanwhile, long before the competition for the spice trade had run its course, the Portuguese had already pressed on to make direct contact with China and Japan. The Portuguese brought advanced European firearms to China early in the 1500s that turned out to be much better than anything the Chinese had produced themselves, altering the course of firearms development in China permanently (chapter 6). The Portuguese were also responsible for the introduction of firearms to Japan in the 1540s, an event with tremendous consequences for that country's history as well (chapter 7). Surprisingly, despite China's long experience with firearms, it was the Japanese who made the better use of them. The next two chapters explain why.

6

China from 1500

Firearms spread from China to Europe at some point around the year 1300, and from there to the Ottoman empire around the year 1400. By the year 1500, greatly improved weapons were making their way back toward China. The reverse movement of firearms technology was a momentous event not only for military history: it foreshadowed a reversal in the direction of technology transfer across the Oikoumene. These firearms were the first in a long line of inventions to make their way from Europe to China.

There is some evidence that the Chinese may have encountered Ottoman firearms even before European ones. Certainly, the Chinese were aware of differences between Ottoman and European muskets.[1] The differences were fairly subtle, differences of degree rather than kind, because Ottoman and European firearms belonged to the same tradition, as did Japanese firearms, which were an offshoot of European ones. References to "foreign firearms" in this chapter should be understood to include all these firearms and not merely European ones.

Ottoman firearms reached the Chinese along two routes, by land and by sea. The land route was a series of caravan routes connecting the cities of Transoxania with those of China known as the "Silk Road," so called because valuable, lightweight, imperishable, unbreakable silk was one of the mainstays of the trade. The sea route of course passed through the Indian Ocean. The Ottomans themselves did not have a presence in the Indian Ocean until they conquered Egypt in 1517, but there was no shortage of possible intermediaries. Chinese records indicate that Ottoman emissaries visited Beijing in 1524.[2]

Portuguese contacts with China are better documented. When the king of Portugal dispatched the first expedition to Melaka in 1508, he ordered them to "ask after the Çhijns and from what part they come ... and if they are wealthy merchants, and if they are weak men or warriors, and if they have arms or artillery." When they arrived at Melaka, they found Chinese ships in port there. The Portuguese first reached the coast of China in 1514, and an ambassador was sent in 1517, guided by Chinese pilots taken on at Melaka. The Portuguese spent several years trying to establish formal relations with China, but Melaka had been part of the Chinese tributary system, and the Chinese had found out about the Portuguese attack, making them suspicious. The embassy was formally rejected in 1521.[3]

Chinese sources from the 1500s and 1600s are full of comments on the superior quality of foreign firearms, and foreign observers likewise commented on the inferior quality of Chinese ones.[4] It was clear to all that the Chinese were far behind. Equally significant is the Chinese reaction to this discovery. The Chinese did not turn their backs on foreign firearms technology – they quickly recognized its worth and began to learn from it.

Foreign Firearms

In 1519, while the Portuguese awaited the outcome of their embassy, they erected buildings and stockades a few miles down the coast from Guangzhou, at Tunmen. "They relied on their firearms to maintain themselves," says one Chinese account; "each discharge of a gun made a sound like thunder."[5] The Chinese were not pleased. To make matters worse, rumors spread that the Portuguese were cannibals and that they had come to China to buy small children to eat. Relations were tense.[6]

The story of how the Chinese first acquired Portuguese firearms technology is reported in a Chinese source as follows:

> He Ru, the police chief of Baisha in Dongguan county, had been to the Portuguese ship before because he had been assigned to collect the customs duty. He had seen Chinese people, Yang San and Dai Ming, who had lived in that country [actually Southeast Asia] for many years and knew all about their methods for building ships, casting guns, and making gunpowder. [Wang] Hong ordered He Ru to send someone to them secretly, using the sale of alcohol and rice as a pretext, to talk with Yang San covertly, order them to defect, and give them great rewards. They happily agreed, and arranged for He Ru to secretly row a small boat to bring them to the shore.[7]

No date is given for this episode, but it must have occurred before the fighting broke out. The hostilities began after the death of the Chinese emperor in 1521. The Portuguese trading at Tunmen and Guangzhou were told to leave the country. When they refused, the ones ashore in Guangzhou were imprisoned and their ships were attacked. Chinese forces also blockaded Tunmen. The Portuguese ships at Tunmen beat off the Chinese attack and escaped back to Melaka. The following year, 1522, another Portuguese squadron set sail for China, determined to reopen trade, again meeting determined Chinese resistance. One of the Portuguese vessels was blown up when a shot from a Chinese cannon hit a powder keg, and another was boarded and captured. The Portuguese had to abandon their base at Tunmen.[8]

Even if He Ru and Wang Hong had learned the secrets of Portuguese firearms before the fighting, it is questionable whether the Chinese could have manufactured these weapons in time to use them against the Portuguese. However, the Chinese would also learn from the weapons captured in the fighting. Wang Hong presented twenty cannon to the court after the battle in 1522, and He Ru was promoted to a post near Nanjing and given responsibility for producing these weapons there. It seems that he was promoted in 1523 and that the first cannon were completed in 1524. These cannon were the breech-loading swivel gun known to the Chinese as the *folangji*.[9]

There was considerable confusion among the Chinese whether *folangji* was supposed to be the name of a people (i.e., the Portuguese) or the name of a weapon (i.e., the swivel gun). In fact, the Chinese word represents two different words with two different etymologies. The term *folangji* as the name of a weapon is related to the *prangi* carried on Ottoman galleys and the *farangi* used by Babur in India, both of which were also breech-loading swivel guns; it can be traced back to the Italian word *braga*, meaning "pants" or "breeches." The word *folangji* as an ethnonym is unrelated and probably goes back to the Franks.[10]

The swivel gun had a breech shaped like a beer mug. The gunner would take the breech by the handle and insert it into the body of the swivel gun with the opening forward. The gunpowder and the projectiles were loaded in the breech before the breech was inserted, and if a number of breeches were prepared beforehand (Qi Jiguang recommended a ratio of nine breeches per gun) it was possible to maintain a high rate of fire for a brief period. The swivel gun could be loaded with one large cannonball (round shot) or many small ones (grapeshot). Grapeshot was deadly against troops at short range and greatly favored by the Chinese.[11]

Ironically, the breech-loader originated in Europe as a cheap substitute for the muzzle-loader. Because muzzle-loading cannon were cast in one piece, they could withstand greater pressures without bursting, which meant they could fire a larger cannonball with more force. However, bronze was several times more expensive than iron, and the Europeans lacked the skill to produce cast-iron cannon. The only alternative was wrought iron. Wrought-iron cannons were built up like wooden barrels, with long strips of wrought iron held in place by circular bands, but there was no way to close off the end of this kind of barrel, so the breech was forged as a separate block and fit into place.[12]

The Chinese had no trouble making cannons from cast iron, even in the 1300s, so they made solid one-piece muzzle-loaders from the beginning. This may explain why the Chinese did not develop breech-loaders on their own, although the Chinese actually had more use for light breech-loading antipersonnel weapons than for heavy muzzle-loading siege cannon. When the Europeans learned how to make solid cast-iron cannon in the mid-1500s, the less powerful breech-loaders fell out of favor, even while breech-loaders were replacing muzzle-loaders in China.

The other new weapon to make its way to China was the musket. The musket was known as the "bird-gun" or "bird-beak-gun" in Chinese, either because the musket was accurate enough for hunting birds or, more likely, because the action of the matchlock resembled a pecking bird. Qi Jiguang wrote that the musket was obtained from Japanese pirates in 1548, but this at best could only be the date when muskets attracted official attention. It is well known that muskets were introduced to Japan in 1542 by Portuguese passengers on a Chinese pirate ship that was blown off course on its way from Thailand to China, so Chinese pirates undoubtedly knew about them already. Since both Chinese and Japanese were very active in Southeast Asia, there is something more than a little artificial about trying to date the exact moment that muskets or swivel guns became known to "the Chinese" or "the Japanese." Anyway, there is also some evidence that the musket had already reached China along the Silk Road, as mentioned earlier. Whether muskets came as trade goods or as weapons of the caravan guards, the Chinese might have encountered Turkish muskets as early as the 1510s.[13]

The text that introduces the exploits of Wang Hong and He Ru prefaces the story with a description of Portuguese guns and a remark that "[Portuguese] methods of making gunpowder are different from Chinese ones." The story itself says that the two Chinese on board "knew all about [Portuguese] methods for building ships, casting guns, *and making gunpowder.*"[14] This can only be a reference to corning gunpowder, the technique of moistening gunpowder to form cakes and then crumbling it into small grains. Inexperience with corned powder might explain the disappointing results of the earliest tests with the swivel gun: "At the time, because the pirate-conquering intendant submitted one, *together with its gunpowder formula*, this device was tested on the parade grounds, but it could only reach 100 paces."[15] The phrase "together with its gunpowder formula" shows the Chinese were aware that special gunpowder formulas were associated with the new weapons. Clearly, corned gunpowder must have been introduced together with swivel guns and muskets, or else the new weapons would not have worked at all.

The earliest known Chinese instructions for producing corned powder appear in a work by the famous sixteenth-century general Qi Jiguang. Qi Jiguang fought against the pirates in the southeast in the first part of his career and in later years commanded the troops in the Beijing sector on the northern frontier.[16] He was a strong advocate of thorough training, and he wrote two books to spread his ideas: the *Jixiao xinshu* (1560, revised 1584), based on conditions in the southeast, and the *Lianbing shiji* (1571), addressed to conditions in the north. The earliest Chinese instructions for making corned powder can be found in the 1560 edition of the *Jixiao xinshu*.[17] Qi Jiguang's ideas were quite influential, and not only in China. The Korean official Yu Song-nyong quoted him frequently during the Japanese invasions of Korea between 1592 and 1598, and both of his books were later adopted for training purposes in Korea. Even the Japanese read him with interest: the *Jixiao xinshu* was reprinted in Japan in 1798 and the *Lianbing shiji* in 1844.[18]

New Chinese Firearms

The Chinese did not simply copy foreign firearms; they also began to modify their own firearms based on what they had learned. For example, the "invincible generalissimo" was originally a massive muzzle-loading cannon produced in the mid-1400s. It needed dozens of men to handle it, and it took a very long time to load and aim. By the mid-1500s, the "invincible generalissimo" had become a smaller breech-loading cannon. It was mounted on a two-wheeled cart that could be handled by three or four men, and the breech could be replaced by a single man (Qi Jiguang recommended a ratio of three breeches per gun). A number of other Chinese cannon were also redesigned as breech-loaders.[19]

The Chinese also began to modify foreign designs. Figure 6.1 is an illustration from a military manual published in 1598, the *Shenqi pu* by Zhao Shizhen, showing one of the simpler modifications, the "combination-mechanism gun." This is basically a regular musket with a special lock mechanism. The fine grains of the priming powder were susceptible to being scattered by wind or dampened by moisture. The lock mechanism on the combination-mechanism gun had two arms, one to hold the burning match and the other to cover the priming pan. When the trigger was pulled, the cover would be lifted as the match was lowered. On the windy plains of Mongolia or the wind-swept decks of a ship, the cover would keep the priming powder safe and dry until the moment it was ignited.[20]

While Chinese authors frequently extol the accuracy of the musket, at the same time it is apparent that they were never quite satisfied with it. The

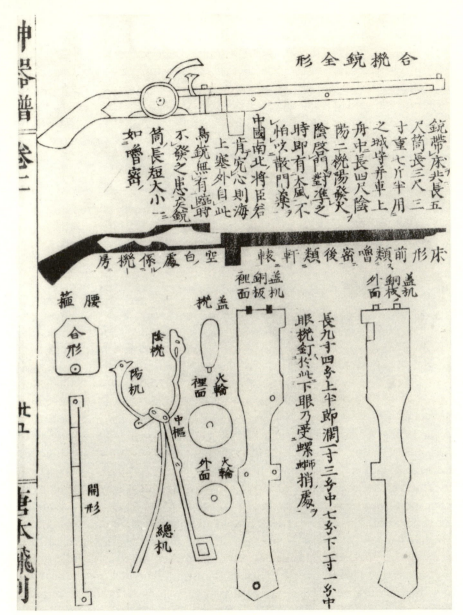

FIGURE 6.1. Chinese combination-mechanism gun. Zhao Shizhen, *Shenqi pu* 2/35a. From the 1808 Japanese edition. Courtesy of the C.V. Starr East Asian Library, Columbia University.

biggest drawback was its relatively slow rate of fire. Europeans dealt with this problem by the implementation of drill and volley fire. Although Chinese military theorists had an appreciation for the virtues of training, and Chinese had practiced volley fire for ages, the Chinese did not produce European-style bodies of drilled infantrymen firing in volleys. Instead, sixteenth-century China experienced a burst of creativity set off by the introduction of swivel guns and muskets and directed at reducing the weight of the swivel gun or increasing the rate of fire of the musket.

For example, the technology of the swivel gun was applied directly to the musket to make what was known as the "child-mother gun." The child-mother gun was basically a musket with a replaceable breech like a swivel gun. The breech was called the "child gun," whereas the gun itself was called the "mother gun." A description of the gun in a seventeenth-century military manual also shows a bayonet that fits into the muzzle of the gun.

The most innovative design may have been a kind of primitive machine gun known as the "continuous bullet gun." Several different charges of gunpowder were individually wrapped in thick paper and loaded into the barrel of the gun. A feeder was installed on top of the barrel just in front of where the foremost charge of gunpowder would be. The fuses would be lit so that the charges would go off in sequence, and a fresh bullet would fall into place as each succeeding charge was about to go off.

Another weapon designed for multiple shots was the so-called ten-eyed gun. This gun must have been inspired by the bamboo, and it looked just like a length of bamboo.[21] The soldier gripped the weapon in the middle, and there were five segments on each side, each segment with a separate touchhole and containing its own paper cartridge with gunpowder and bullet. After firing five shots from one end of the gun, the soldier could reverse it and get off another five shots from the other end.

Multiple-barreled weapons also proliferated, with 3-, 4-, 5-, 7-, 8-, 10-, and 36-barreled weapons described in the sources.[22]

Zhao Shizhen for one believed that the difference between the north and the south was responsible for the profusion in types of firearms. Many writers comment that certain firearms should be used in the north, whereas others should be used in the south. The north–south distinction extended also to wagons, which Qi Jiguang strongly advocated for use in the north but admitted were unsuitable for the south. It goes without saying that cavalry was more effective in the north and boats more effective in the south. There were even gunpowder formulas that differed for north and south, since the south tended to be more humid.[23]

In some cases, the reasoning is apparent, as with the "three-eyed gun," where Zhao Shizhen says the cavalry version should be used in the north and the infantry version in the south. If one takes Zhao Shizhen's list as a whole – he divides ten-odd firearms into ones appropriate to the north, appropriate to the south, and appropriate to either – it becomes much more difficult to discover the rationale. Furthermore, different authors do not necessarily agree on which firearms were better where. Zhao Shizhen thought that muskets were suitable for either area, but He Rubin, author of the *Binglu*, believed muskets belonged in the south and the three-eyed gun in the north. However, the key seems to be rate of fire.[24]

Recall what Humphrey Barwick said in 1594 about the higher rate of fire of bows as opposed to muskets. If the enemy had cavalry, there was only time to get one arrow off, and if he had infantry, there was time to fire several musket shots. Rate of fire is an elastic concept. A musket required perhaps one minute to reload. If we assume for the sake of argument that the three barrels of the three-eyed gun altogether required nine minutes to reload, then the musket would be three times as fast if the target were in range for nine minutes (nine shots to three), but only one-third as fast if the target were in range for only one minute (one shot to three).[25]

In the 1500s, Chinese were in the position of fighting pure infantry in the south (pirates disembarked from ships) and pure cavalry in the north (the Mongols). The south is full of streams and hills and forests, with many strong defensive positions. Infantry units in strong defensive positions are more likely to remain in contact and exchange fire over a protracted period of time. The north lacked that kind of defensive cover. If the Mongols charged, there was no time to get off more than one volley with muskets, even for trained infantry. In the north, multiple-barreled weapons provided the most firepower in the least period of time, since all the barrels could be fired at once.[26]

Rate of fire was a central concern, but it was only one of several. There were enough other considerations to confuse the picture. The disagreements over weapons and the continued experimentation seem to betray a certain amount of underlying dissatisfaction with foreign firearms. As impressive as they found the musket, it did not meet all of their needs, and they could not adopt it as the standard infantry firearm to the exclusion of all others, as in Europe. There was no simple solution, so there was no easy agreement among writers, and Chinese continued to experiment with different kinds of weapons.

The Chinese never solved the problem of reloading firearms on horseback. Figure 6.2 is another illustration from the *Shenqi pu* by Zhao Shizhen, showing a man on horseback using a "winged-tiger gun." The caption on top reads "Picture of the winged-tiger gun discharged on horseback"; the caption on the bottom reads "Picture of fighting after discharging." The

FIGURE 6.2. Chinese winged-tiger gun. Zhao Shizhen, *Shenqi pu* 2/25b. Courtesy of the C.V. Starr East Asian Library, Columbia University.

cavalryman can fire the gun and then draw his sword and use the gun as a shield. There would have been no way to reload, and even if there had been, there would have been no time to reload, given the short effective range of the gun.

The winged-tiger gun was a triple-barreled carbine that came in infantry and cavalry versions – basically an improved version of the three-eyed gun. One version (not specified, but presumably the cavalry one) weighed a little over 6.5 pounds and had barrels that were about 17 inches long, making it hardly a third of the weight or length of a full-scale musket. It came with a cover for the priming powder, although the cover did not release automatically as with the combination-mechanism gun. The infantry version could penetrate armor at a range of about 90 to 105 yards; the cavalry version had an effective range of only half that.[27]

Zhao Shizhen explained why the winged-tiger gun was developed:

> Muskets are effective on wagons, on boats, and on foot. Recently a gun has been created that is fired on horseback. Firing a musket relies entirely on the priming powder. [Some may say:] "When the horse gallops, which is how northerners are used to riding, if the priming powder is not spilled and scattered then it will be blown away by the wind, and then how will it fire?" This is the talk [of someone who] does not know a lot about firearms. If it is a three-eyed gun or one of the newly manufactured winged-tiger guns, it can first be used as a gun and then after having been fired then it can serve as a (hand-to-hand) weapon. As for hitting the target and killing the enemy [though], I don't know [about that].[28]

The Chinese used muskets "on wagons, on boats, and on foot," but they did not use them on horseback. Muskets were not cavalry weapons. When a firearm appeared that could be used on horseback, it was ineffective except at close range, as was also the case in Europe. The winged-tiger gun might substitute for the lance, as the pistol did in Europe, but it would not solve the problem of engaging the enemy at long range. Zhao Shizhen apparently did not harbor any illusions about its accuracy. Nor was it expected that the rider would be able to reload the winged-tiger gun on horseback. Like the other new Chinese firearms, the winged-tiger gun still fell short of what was needed.

Institutional Change

It is not enough to invent new weapons; they also must be produced in sufficient quantities and put in the hands of the soldiers who will use them.

The institutional framework through which the Ming government extracted goods and services from the population was transformed in the

1500s. The complicated and convoluted system of hereditary household registration categories had broken down even before the end of the 1400s, although it remained on the books for most of the dynasty. Over time, the obligations owed the government under the hereditary categories were converted into payments of silver. Government offices took this silver and went out and bought the supplies they needed on the market. This practice was to some extent recognized and standardized in the 1500s under the rubric of the "single-whip system."[29]

The brigades and battalions of hereditary soldiers described in chapter 2 had fallen drastically understrength by 1500 as soldiers deserted and families died out. Few units had as much as one-fifth of their paper strength. Volunteers had to be recruited in their place. For example, when Qi Jiguang needed men to fight the pirates on the southeast seaboard in 1559, he turned to Yiwu county in Zhejiang, where local clan militias had gained experience fighting salt smugglers and wildcat miners the year before. Military service became a favored career option for the young men of Yiwu, and by the mid-1570s, some 50,000 of the 80,000 men in the county deemed capable of military service were actually serving outside of Yiwu.[30]

Another example of the growing use of the market was the supply of grain to the army. In the early years of the dynasty, the government had given each soldier and his family a basic monthly allowance of grain, and soldiers were given extra rations when they were mobilized. Even in the early 1400s, however, there were times when soldiers were given paper money instead of grain. After paper money lost its value due to inflation, various commodities like cloth and silk were substituted for it until the government settled on silver. For a time in the early 1500s rations were issued entirely in silver, but in the end it proved better to issue part in grain again (perhaps to hedge against price swings), typically three months' worth each year.[31]

Yet another example was the supply of horses to the army. The government breeding program had been a failure. The private breeding program also had its share of difficulties; in particular, many of the registered horse-breeding households had found it cheaper to pay the stipulated fines than to raise the required horses. In the late 1500s, the government basically ratified this practice and converted the obligation to raise horses into an obligation to pay cash. These taxes went into a fund that was used to buy horses as needed.[32]

Given the changes in the way that the government collected taxes, recruited soldiers, raised supplies, and acquired horses, it would not be surprising if it also turned to private sources for its procurement of weapons. There was no general prohibition against the ownership of weapons in Ming China except for "prohibited military arms," a category that included armor, firearms, and banners but not such things as swords, spears, or bows. The prohibition on banners but not swords suggests that the concern was not danger to life and limb so much as danger to the government from privately organized military units.[33]

Chinese firearms production was sometimes centralized, sometimes not. During the reign of the Hongwu emperor, in the late 1300s, production was transferred from the imperial mint to the brigades and battalions spread across the empire. This trend was reversed under the Yongle emperor, in the early 1400s, when production was shifted back to the capital. During the aftermath of the Tumu debacle in the mid-1400s, there was again some decentralization, and there was some further decentralization at the end of the 1400s.[34]

There was certainly criticism of government secrecy. An anonymous author of a military manual from the 1500s had the following to say:

> As for firearms, in ancient times there were only fire-arrows and fire-bombs. Only in our dynasty can it be said they are complete, because we continuously obtain them from the various barbarians in the south and sometimes make them our own way. I believe that the techniques of the Firearms Division should not be kept secret like before. We should have the local districts disseminate them broadly, although private production and private possession should be strictly forbidden.[35]

However, it is questionable whether the official policy of strict secrecy still had much vitality. By the mid-1500s at the latest, information about the production of firearms and gunpowder was publicly available. Military manuals were published and disseminated to wide audiences, like the military manual by Qi Jiguang that contained the formula for corned powder in 1560. Such military manuals contained annotated diagrams of disassembled firearms and general notes about their production, probably because officers needed to order, inspect, and pay for the weapons that they procured for their men. It seems likely that officers used this information to order weapons from local craftsmen.[36]

Figure 6.1 illustrates the degree of detail contained in some military manuals, in this case the *Shenqi pu* by Zhao Shizhen from 1598. The bottom half of the illustration shows the different parts of the mechanism, each labeled with its name for easy identification. For example, the lower right-hand corner shows "the outside of the bronze plate of the lock cover." In the middle on the bottom is "the inside of the bronze plate of the lock cover." Between them, the caption that runs up and down reads: "It is 11.8 inches long. The top half is 1.6 inches wide; the middle is 1 inch wide; the bottom is 1.1 inches wide. The lock is attached to the middle hole. The lower holes are where the screws are attached." The three oval and circular objects are labeled, from top to bottom, "lock cover," "fire wheel inner face," and "fire wheel outer face." The X-shaped object in the bottom left consists of the *"yin* mechanism" (upper-right arm), *"yang* mechanism" (upper-left arm), "pivot," and "trigger."[37]

This level of detail might have been useful in inspecting or disassembling weapons, but the exact dimensions would have been of interest only to the craftsmen hired to make the parts. One writer from the mid-1500s, Tang Shunzhi, gives two estimates for the cost of manufacturing a musket. Each of the estimates specifies the exact cost in silver of each material and of each step in the production of the musket: 0.20 *taels* for 20 *catties* of Fujian iron, 0.18 *taels* for 6 worker-days of hammering out the iron into a sheet, 0.19 *taels* for 6 worker-days of forging the iron into a tube (the extra 0.01 *tael* is for the worker who holds the pincers), 0.21 *taels* for 7 worker-days to bore out the barrel, and so on, down to 0.01 *tael* for the bamboo ramrod (not including the metal tip). These figures are taken from the lower estimate of 2.31 *taels* (approximately 3 ounces of silver); the higher estimate comes out to 3.83 *taels* (approximately 5 ounces of silver). Not only do these figures tell us that a completed musket represented several months' wages for a skilled worker, but also they suggest that military commanders would not purchase the weapons ready-made but would pay for the materials and labor in cash.[38]

There is other circumstantial evidence that firearms were being produced outside of the Palace Armory and the Weapons Bureau. Firearms appear in places and circumstances where it seems unlikely that they were sent from Beijing. For example, Xingguo county in Jiangxi in south China had been required to raise 552 volunteers in the early 1560s and was ordered to send 300 of them off to the army. The magistrate of Xingguo requested permission to take the other 252 men and train 100 of them in the use of muskets, 20 of them in the use of swivel guns, and the remaining 132 of them in other weapons, so that they would be available for emergencies. Why train 120 men in firearms? Because the county had 100 muskets and 20 swivel guns on hand it had been ordered to produce that would otherwise go unused.[39]

In short, it is reasonable to conclude that government restrictions did slow firearms development to some extent in the late 1300s and through the 1400s. China entered the 1500s with inferior firearms, and those restrictions were probably one contributing factor. In the 1500s, most of those restrictions were effectively lifted. Technical knowledge of firearms was disseminated much more widely, and officials outside the capital were free to have firearms manufactured outside of government offices. As a reason for China's backwardness in firearms technology, the role of government restrictions would have been reduced if not eliminated by the 1500s.

Nevertheless, writing at the end of the war with Japan in 1598, Zhao Shizhen still felt that the quality of Chinese firearms was too low, especially compared to what he saw of foreign firearms. He believed that the problem was the absence of a profit motive in the production of firearms for the government:

> In matters for the public administration, craftsmen definitely are not willing to give their utmost care. Among the officials supervising the production, those who look out for themselves only demand frugality, and those who are not frugal embezzle. After a period of frugality or embezzlement it is then difficult to enforce the law. If there is not already some profit [incentive] given beforehand there is no fear of the bonds of the law afterwards.[40]

In other words, the craftsmen did not care how well the finished product worked. Ambitious officials would save money by cutting corners – the savings would make them look more efficient, and they did not care how well the finished product worked either. Greedy officials would simply embezzle the funds. However, allowing officers to have firearms made to specifications did not necessarily solve these problems. Indeed, it is not really clear whether Zhao Shizhen is talking about government workshops or simply government contracts here. No system of procurement would be free of these evils, and there is no reason to think that European practice was any better.

The one true difference between China and Europe in the 1500s would have been the comparative freedom to sell guns for nonmilitary use on the private market in Europe. This was apparently still impossible in China. To what extent the private market for nonmilitary firearms drove technological innovation in Europe is open to question.[41]

Japanese Pirates

The expeditions to the Indian Ocean were discontinued after 1433 and the prohibitions on overseas voyages remained in effect, but foreign trade continued apace. Large numbers of Chinese migrated from the coastal regions of Fujian and Guangdong during the Ming dynasty to what are now Thailand, Malaysia, Indonesia, Vietnam, and the Philippines. There were more Chinese in Manila than Spaniards; more Chinese in Batavia than Dutchmen. These overseas Chinese communities linked the Chinese market back home to the regional and world markets. There was so much money to be made in this trade that prohibition was futile; smugglers operated openly with the connivance of local officials. Silver from the Americas and from Japan paid for Chinese goods and also made possible the institutional reforms discussed earlier.[42]

The Chinese diaspora fostered trade because shared cultural norms facilitated transactions, but the profits at stake also attracted outsiders who were more ready to resort to violence. Japanese pirates, once kept in check by Chinese diplomatic pressure on the Japanese government, now had a free hand as the *shogun* lost power to regional warlords over the course of the 1400s. Meanwhile, denied permission to trade legally in China, the Portuguese were drawn into this network of smugglers and pirates. Smugglers set up a base in the Shuangyu islands off of Zhejiang in 1526 that became one of the principal hubs of trade in the western Pacific. By 1540 there were some 1,200 Portuguese and 3,000 other Christians in residence there, in addition to Chinese, Japanese, Okinawans, and others.

The ineffectual prohibition on foreign trade, the resurgence of Japanese piracy, and the arrival of the Portuguese all contributed to a crisis on the southeast seaboard of China in the mid-1500s. The Chinese coastal defenses had deteriorated since the early days of the dynasty, and pirates plundered towns along the coast with impunity. Pirates even took over garrison posts along the coast and used them as bases for their own operations. Some smaller walled cities were plundered from time to time and even larger ones like Hangzhou were threatened. These outlaws have always been known as "Japanese pirates," but contemporaries recognized that most of these so-called Japanese pirates were not Japanese at all, but Chinese. They were basically smugglers who had responded to armed suppression with armed resistance.[43]

The Chinese no longer built anything like the great treasure ships, but they did have a wide range of ships suitable for coastal defense, ranging in size from large war-junks to small scouting boats. The Fujian ship was a large, two-masted, ocean-going junk with a crew of up to 100. Its armament included one large cannon, six large swivel guns, three mortars, ten muskets, sixty flamethrowers, twenty grenades, 100 "fire-bricks," and 100 smoke bombs, among other things. Guangdong ships were somewhat larger than Fujian ones, and being made of rose chestnut instead of pine or fir they were far stronger, but Fujian ships were cheaper and easier to maintain. Guangdong ships are shown with sweeps – long oars – which the Fujian ones do not have.[44]

The Chinese understood the basic principle behind Portuguese tactics at sea: "They place four or five [cannon] on each side below the gunwales of their ocean-going ships and secretly fire them from within the ship's cabin. If another ship approaches them, one cannonball will smash its planks, water will enter and the ship will founder."[45] Still, like the Malays, the Chinese seem to have been more intrigued by Portuguese galleys than by Portuguese ships. One work from the mid-1500s describes the galleys as follows: "Each ship has 200 men rowing, with many oars and numerous men. Even without a wind they can move rapidly. When all the cannon fire, the cannonballs fall like rain. Whatever they move toward cannot oppose them. They are called centipede ships."[46] The Chinese built their own centipede boats in imitation of the Portuguese ones.[47]

Chinese officials vigorously debated the pros and cons of naval counter-measures. The boldest measure would have been to launch a fleet to attack the pirate bases in Japan, but the only official to raise the idea dismissed it as too hazardous. Most proposals involved intercepting the pirate ships at sea. There is a string of islands off the eastern coast of China that ships from Japan would use as landmarks on their way to Chinese ports. One plan was to keep a fleet on hand to attack the pirates before they could anchor at the outer islands. Another plan was to garrison the outer islands to prevent the Japanese from anchoring there. Yet another plan was to post patrols at the outer islands but to concentrate the defenses on other islands, much closer to the shore, that were well situated to cover the important Chinese ports. Some officials did not believe that patrols at sea could intercept the pirates and advocated defense of the shoreline instead.[48]

If the Chinese did not launch a blue water navy in the 1500s to deal with the pirates, it was not because the Chinese were somehow uncomfortable with the idea of a navy per se. Chapter 5 suggested that navies were not an efficient response to piracy. The pirates in question here were more like amphibious bandits than pirates anyway. To the extent that they had crossed that fuzzy line between armed smuggling and outright banditry, their targets were for the most part villages, towns, and cities rather than ships. Furthermore, a naval solution was unattainable without the cooperation of the coastal population. The very people needed to build a fleet were the ones most alienated by government policy. The Ming government could not have built or manned a fleet without the involvement of the inhabitants of the southeast coast, but if the government had had their support then the fleet would have been unnecessary in the first place.

So the Ming government deployed more land forces instead. The Ming equivalent of "special forces" were first brought to the scene. Some were ethnic minorities, like the "wolf soldiers" from Guangxi in the southwest, who were too fierce to be allowed to enter cities, or tribesmen from Huguang in central China, whose hooked spears were the only match for Japanese swords. Others were Chinese with special fighting skills, like miners, boxers, Shandong cudgellers, Xuzhou and Baoding archers, monks from the Shaolin Temple, and coastal inhabitants of Fuzhou and Zhangzhou in Fujian, many of whom had been pirates themselves and knew their tricks. The recruitment of Mongols discussed in chapter 2 was just one of many examples of the use of ethnic and social groups with special military skills. All these troops were thrown into the fray, but the results were disappointing.[49]

The crisis peaked in 1556, when three separate groups of pirates, each said to be "several thousand" in strength, landed at different points along the coast in the same month. Even these turned out to be only diversionary attacks clearing the way for the main force of "more than ten thousand." Most of the government troops were pinned down in garrisons along the coast, and the mobile reserves were too weak to be risked in direct combat with pirates. Pirates rampaged through Zhejiang and defeated government troops but failed to capture any walled cities, despite using cannon, due in part to dissension and jealousy among the pirate leaders. Only by skillfully pitting one against the other (holding out the possibility of surrender with a full pardon to the most cooperative) was the government commander able to defeat them.[50]

After their rebuff in Zhejiang in 1556, the pirates shifted their attention southward, to Fujian and Guangdong. Chinese coastal defenses stiffened as Chinese commanders reorganized and revitalized the local forces. A key figure in this process was Qi Jiguang, who recruited his troops from Yiwu county in Zhejiang, as described earlier. Qi Jiguang understood the importance of discipline and training. He trained his men to fight as units in squads of twelve with a collection of simple contact weapons. They fought on foot, but firearms were not heavily emphasized, although other commanders like Yu Dayou placed more reliance on them. Qi Jiguang and others won a number of victories over the pirates in the early 1560s.[51]

A change in policy now removed much of the incentive for the local population to collaborate with the pirates. When the Jiajing emperor finally died after a long reign of forty-five years, his successor was quickly persuaded to lift the prohibition on seafaring the following year, in 1567. The only exceptions were trade with Japan and exports of saltpeter, sulfur, copper, and iron (raw materials for gunpowder and firearms, in other words). Trade with other areas was now freely permitted with the payment of customs duties. The Portuguese were allowed to settle in Macau, near Guangzhou, and trade with China as well. Even the Japanese could participate in the trade indirectly at places like Manila.[52]

No longer able to count on local support, the remaining pirates shifted their activities offshore. One group of 4,000 pirates attacked the Spanish colony at Manila in 1574 but failed to capture it. Others set up bases on Taiwan, which was still inhabited largely by aborigines in the 1500s. The Dutch set up a base of their own on the island in 1624, and the Spanish followed in 1626, but after the fall of the Ming dynasty in 1644, a Ming loyalist named Zheng Chenggong (better known as Koxinga) took it from the

Dutch in 1661. Zheng Chenggong and then his son and grandson controlled Taiwan and the surrounding waters until the Manchus took over the island in 1683.[53]

The strategic dilemma along the southeast coast was oddly similar to that along the northern border in certain respects, so much so that officials who submitted memorials on naval policy sometimes borrowed examples from steppe warfare.[54] Both the north and the southeast were classic frontiers, in the sense that their inhabitants were skilled at mediating between the two sides of the frontier but were correspondingly difficult to control.[55]

However, there was a crucial difference between the Mongols and the pirates that went beyond their mutual desire to see the Ming dynasty liberalize its policies toward trade. The Mongols had ruled China for almost a century (a little longer in the north, a little shorter in the south) before the rise of the Ming. Neither the Mongols nor the Chinese could ever forget that. No one ever imagined the pirates conquering China. The pirates simply did not pose the same kind of threat to the dynasty as the Mongols.

The Great Wall

All the while that the Ming dynasty was struggling with piracy along the southeastern seaboard, its attention remained fixed on the north. The flurry of wall-building activity in the late 1400s was initially a temporary solution to a specific threat. The defensive lines sealed off the Ordos from the south, but the Ming did not fortify the rest of the frontier at that time, and those walls soon began to erode.

Meanwhile, the strategic situation took a turn for the worse as the Mongols recovered from their earlier internecine wars. In 1488, a Mongol leader named Batu Möngke proclaimed himself Dayan Khan, or "khan of the great Yuan," harkening back to the Yuan imperial legacy. Unlike Esen, the victor at Tumu in 1449, Dayan Khan was actually a descendant of Chinggis Khan, so he did not need to rule through a puppet. Dayan Khan succeeded in establishing control over most of Mongolia, including Inner Mongolia and the Ordos.

Dayan Khan's chief rival had been an Oirat leader with the Muslim name of Ibrahim. Ibrahim was driven off the steppe and onto the high plateau southwest of the Ordos and northeast of Tibet known as Qinghai (in Chinese) or Kökönor (in Mongolian) around 1509. For over two decades this group of Mongols was a thorn in the side of the Chinese, raiding the western borders as far south as Sichuan. Their presence disrupted the tea-horse trade with the Tibetans that had been a key source of horses for the Chinese.[56]

The early years of this crisis coincided with the reign of the Zhengde emperor, who ascended the throne in 1506. The Zhengde emperor was the last Ming emperor to take an active personal interest in military affairs. His personality is an enigma, in part because the official record of his reign twists and distorts the facts to mock and belittle him. Some of his actions can be seen as attempts to revive the martial spirit of the Ming military. He supervised military drills in person and revived the practice of rotating frontier troops through the capital for training. He toured the frontier despite the frantic pleas of his civil officials, who feared having another emperor captured by the Mongols, and in 1517, he commanded the Ming cavalry in one of its rare victories over an equally matched force of Mongols.

In other respects, his actions were simply reckless, foolish, or pointless. On one occasion he was so badly mauled while hunting tigers that he could not appear in court audiences for a month. On another occasion he burned down his palace by storing gunpowder in the courtyards during the lantern festival. Other actions called his sanity into question. He appointed himself general under an assumed name and issued himself orders to lead troops, which admittedly sounds more than a little schizophrenic. The civil officials claimed that he was drunk all day long. He surrounded himself with soldiers and ignored or bypassed his civil officials, but he did not have the talent or disposition to institutionalize the changes he desired, so his individual efforts had no lasting effects.[57]

The Ming had allowed the Mongols trade and tribute privileges in the late 1400s, probably because they had no choice, but when the Jiajing emperor took the throne in 1522, he was dead set against allowing this to continue. This was the same emperor who stuck to the policy of not allowing maritime trade in the southeast. He may have felt it to be an affront to his dignity that the Mongols could demand trade privileges by force. To be sure, as long as the Mongols could force the Chinese to trade, then the Chinese could hardly use the threat of an embargo to keep them in line. In that case, trade might only have strengthened the Mongols by giving them manufactured products and food reserves they otherwise would have lacked. Some officials certainly argued this way.

Dayan Khan died around 1532 and was succeeded (after a struggle) by a grandson who took the title Altan Khan, or "golden khan." Altan Khan could not understand why he was not allowed the same trade privileges his grandfather had enjoyed. He attacked the border year after year in the late 1540s from his camps in the Ordos. A major debate over the Ordos once again split the Ming court between offensive and defensive factions. The offensive faction occupied the moral high ground in the Ming court, but it was wildly unrealistic about Ming capabilities. Little had changed; the proposals for offensive action were still vulnerable to the same criticism as they had been in the 1460s.

The northwest was still too poor to support a major campaign. All the soldiers would have to have been brought in from the outside, and equipped and supplied from the outside, even before the campaign began. If somehow the Ordos were cleared of Mongols, a doubtful proposition considering how the terrain favored cavalry warfare, the area would have to have been repopulated by Chinese settlers to create an economic base to support garrisons and fortifications. If Shanxi and Shaanxi were too poor to support major forces, what were the prospects that the completely uncultivated and more distant Ordos would be able to?[58]

While the debate raged in the capital, the defenses between the Ordos and the capital had been built up to the point where they could withstand direct Mongol attacks, but here is where the strategic mobility of the nomads came into play. In 1550, Altan Khan led his army around those defenses and approached the capital from the less heavily guarded northeast. The Mongols spent three days pillaging and looting the suburbs of Beijing itself before withdrawing back to the steppe. The capital garrison hid behind its walls and did not dare to challenge them.[59]

Ultimately, the easiest policy to carry out was the defensive one. The border had to be defended before it could be built up, which meant in practice that more walls would be built. Some people must have wondered if the day for offensive action would ever arrive, since the previous eighty years had not brought it any closer. The problem was not that the dynasty was somehow irreversibly in "decline" – south China was booming in the 1500s, the cities in the Yangzi River valley were flourishing, the economy was becoming more commercialized than ever before – but the northwest was not sharing much in the prosperity, and the government lacked the means to divert that wealth to uses like fighting the Mongols.

So more and more sections of the frontier were fortified, and at huge cost. It was only at this time, after 1550, that something resembling the popular notion of the "Great Wall of China" took shape. Today, only a few short sections of the Great Wall north of Beijing have been restored, and unfortunately, the popular notion has been formed by what tourists and photographers have found there. Those heavily fortified strongpoints guarding the strategic passes into the capital region are very impressive, but they are not typical of most of the Ming frontier lines.

Despite the many misleading accounts that have been given of it, the Great Wall was not a thousand-mile-long castle that sealed off the border and kept the Mongols from entering China. The frontier was just too long for that.

In the words of one Ming official: "The three borders [in the north extend for] several hundred leagues. If one wanted to defend every single point, one could use up all the soldiers in the empire and still not do it. One can only select the important and critical points that are the routes whereby the Tatar caitiffs enter to pillage and cut them off."[60]

What we think of today as the Great Wall was more like an early warning system for detecting Mongol raids. Forts were spaced out along the border that were strong enough to resist direct Mongol attacks, and these served as command and control centers. A fort might have several hundred to several thousand men as a garrison. Smaller towers were interspersed between forts at intervals of between a sixth and a third of a mile, but these held at most a few dozen men and could not always resist direct attacks by themselves. Signal-beacon platforms manned by a handful of soldiers radiated out from the forts and provided warning of approaching forces.[61]

If Mongols tried to break through this line of defense, they could be expected to concentrate on areas between forts, not on the forts themselves. A stone or earthen wall might slow them down but that alone would not stop them. The soldiers in the signal-beacon platforms and towers were too few to oppose them in the field. If a signal could be transmitted back to a nearby fort, however, and a sufficiently large force could be sent to the area quickly enough, at least a small Mongol raiding party might be turned back before it could penetrate the interior. A major invasion force would be another matter entirely, of course.

This is also how the border defenses operated in the first century B.C., when the Han dynasty faced a steppe that was unified under the Xiongnu. Signal beacon platforms manned by five soldiers were located at intervals of one or two miles, feeding information back to slightly larger strongholds, which in turn would pass the message on to the main fort. The infantrymen manning the platforms and strongholds were not equipped to meet the Xiongnu in the field; that was the job of the cavalry stationed at the main fort. Ming practice a millennium and a half later was a similar response to similar conditions.[62]

This arrangement explains why firearms remained of little practical benefit to the Chinese even on defense. As long as the forts had strong walls and sufficient supplies, their garrisons could defend themselves easily enough; the Mongols had no guns to break down the walls, and no real reason to attack them directly anyway. Siege warfare negated the nomads' advantage in mobility, so they very seldom maintained a siege for long. The defenders were better off with guns than without them, but guns added little to Ming security on the whole.

When Mongols tried to bypass the forts, the key was to respond quickly and in force. Horses were needed for these purposes. Infantry might arrive on the scene too late, after the Mongols had penetrated the defenses. If the Mongols were inside the defense lines, infantry would find it hard to chase them down; if they were still outside the defense lines, infantry could not pursue them back onto the steppe either. Given that Mongols avoided fighting except when the odds were greatly in their favor, only cavalry had much hope of engaging them on favorable terms.

Of course, it did the Chinese no good to catch the Mongols if they could not defeat them when they did. In the second half of the 1500s, Ming morale had sunk so low that even large numbers of Chinese soldiers would run from small numbers of Mongols. Something had to be done so that Chinese armies could at least hold their own on their home ground.

Wagons

Chariots had been the mainstay of ancient Chinese warfare up until the introduction of cavalry. Every educated Chinese was familiar with this fact from the classics. Although chariots may have originated on the fringes of the steppe, the barbarian origin of cavalry was clear in the historical texts, as was its relatively late introduction (307 B.C. according to the traditional account). Given the basic assumption that the institutions of the classical period were models for imitation, and that subsequent history represented a falling off from those lofty heights, it is understandable that some might suggest reviving the chariot, which had the twin virtues of being both Chinese and very old.

The same Chinese character is used for both chariot and wagon (it basically means "vehicle"), so the conceptual leap from one to the other is easy to make. The wagon by itself was a negligible addition to military strength, but the discovery of firearms began to change that. Firearms transformed wagons from passive obstacles to fighting platforms, while wagons gave firearms some of the protection they were lacking.[63] Wagons had been used for carrying supplies in the early Ming, but proposals to use them in combat began to appear in the mid-1400s.[64]

One leading proponent of wagons was Qi Jiguang, a hero of the fighting against the pirates in the southeast who was transferred to take command of the Beijing sector border defenses in 1568. His ideas were set forth in the second of his two major works, the *Lianbing shiji*, in 1571. Wagons were part of the tactics he developed to suit the new environment in the north. It is worth going into his proposals in some detail to understand how firearms fit into the picture and what the new units were supposed to accomplish.

The *Lianbing shiji* contemplated the organization of four types of brigades: infantry brigades of 2,699 men, cavalry brigades of 2,988 men, wagon brigades of 3,109 men, and transportation brigades of 1,660 men. Unlike the garrison brigades of the early Ming dynasty, which had existed primarily for administrative and organizational purposes, these brigades were fighting units.

The basic infantry unit was the squad of twelve men. Squads came in two types: a musketeer squad with a squad leader, ten men with muskets, and an orderly, or a killer squad with a squad leader, ten men with various contact weapons, and an orderly. Three squads of the same type made one platoon of 37 men, and three platoons of the same type made one company of 112 men; a musketeer company therefore contained ninety muskets. Four companies formed one battalion of 449 men, and two battalions formed one regiment of 899 men, evenly divided between musketeer and killer companies. Three regiments formed one brigade of 2,699 men (including 323 officers, 2,160 soldiers, and 216 orderlies) with 1,080 muskets and 216 bows.[65]

The basic cavalry unit was also a squad of 12 men. Each cavalry squad had a squad leader, ten men with a mixture of weapons (two muskets, two firelances, two tridents, two spears, and two maces – some of the men also carried bows), and an orderly. Cavalry was organized into squads, platoons, companies, battalions, regiments, and brigades along the same lines as infantry, except that a cavalry brigade in the field was reinforced from 2,699 to a total of 2,988 men, with 1,152 bows, 432 muskets, and sixty "crouching tiger" cannon. The cavalry seems to have been mounted infantry (i.e., dragoons) rather than true cavalry, given the presence of so many muskets and cannon.[66]

Each wagon in a wagon brigade was manned by two squads of ten men each. The captain, the driver, two muleteers, and six gunners formed the first squad; they stayed with the wagon and operated the two swivel guns. A squad leader, four men with muskets, four men with contact weapons, and an orderly formed the second squad; they fought on and around the wagon. Two wagons made a platoon, two platoons a company, four companies a battalion, four battalions a regiment, and two regiments a brigade; each brigade thus included 128 of these wagons. In addition, another seventeen wagons were attached to the brigade, eight of them each with one "generalissimo"-style large cannon, the other nine with drums and fire-arrows and other supplies. Altogether the 3,109 men of the wagon brigade were equipped with 145 wagons, eight large cannon, 256 swivel guns, and 512 muskets.[67]

Figure 6.3 shows soldiers fighting behind wooden shields. The illustration is part of a series in Zhao Shizhen's *Shenqi pu* from 1598 depicting the equipment and tactics associated with wagon warfare. The walls are detached from wagons, and there are men holding the walls upright by handles; the walls also could be picked up and moved. The side facing the enemy is painted with a ferocious image of what appears to be a tiger with wings.

FIGURE 6.3. Chinese soldiers behind wagon walls. Zhao Shizhen, *Shenqi pu* 3/7b. Courtesy of the C.V. Starr East Asian Library, Columbia University.

In battle, the wagons and shields would be formed into a line or a square to make a kind of fort – a wagon laager. This is of course the same kind of wagon laager that was prevalent in eastern Europe, the Middle East, and India.

Most of the men in the illustration who are not carrying banners, beating drums, or holding up the walls seem to be using firearms. In the center of the picture there are four men loading muskets behind each musketeer who is firing. They appear to be in different stages of reloading. This part of the picture matches another illustration in the same source, "Picture of five men firing guns in rotation," down to the posture of the men. The men themselves did not switch positions; the ones behind reloaded the guns and passed them forward to the man at the wall. There are no pikemen, but there would probably have been squads of men with spears and swords for hand-to-hand fighting.[68]

Qi Jiguang was preparing to fight a defensive war. The relatively slow-moving infantry and wagon brigades could not hope to chase down the Mongols; even the cavalry brigades would have been ill-equipped to pursue the Mongols in a running battle. Where once the Mongol cavalry would have routed the Chinese forces, however, now the Chinese could at least stand up to them, he says, thanks to the wagons:

> [The wagons] can be used to surround and protect the infantry and cavalry. They can keep the ranks in order; they can serve as the walls of a camp; they can take the place of armor. When enemy cavalry swarms around, it has no way to pressure them; they are truly like walls with feet or horses without [need for] fodder. Still, everything depends on the firearms. If the firearms are lost, how can the wagons stand?[69]

His comments on the transportation brigade illustrate the logistical problems that faced the Chinese armies in a defensive war:

> The army marches and the supplies follow; this is the first principle of military affairs. In recent times, whenever the enemy invades, the government armies have no supply train. The enemy rides fat horses [the Mongols fattened their horses on the spring and summer grass and invaded in the summer or fall], so they can gallop fifty miles or more in one day. Our army's horses are already weak. When they arrive where there are walls and moats, the gates are shut [because Mongol forces are nearby too]. The rations are in the warehouses, the fodder is in the hay yards, and most of these are within the walls. Whenever they cannot get supplied, if they wait for the rations and fodder to be supplied, then they will necessarily fail to pursue the enemy. A large army on the move can be as many as twenty or thirty thousand men. . . . Distributing supplies cannot be completed in one or two days. If they wait until it is completed to pursue the enemy, the enemy will be up to a hundred miles away. The government armies can only pursue on an empty stomach, and after three days they will be extremely hungry and tired.[70]

Even more interesting are the limited claims that Qi Jiguang makes for his solution, the transportation brigades. Each brigade would carry enough food and fodder for three days for ten thousand men and horses. Assuming that he meant ten thousand men plus their horses, one transportation brigade could have supplied three other brigades plus itself for three days. An army with infantry and baggage train might cover twelve miles a day, so the transportation brigade would extend its range by only thirty-six miles. Clearly, what Qi Jiguang had in mind here was an army that could respond to Mongol incursions within Chinese territory, or perhaps intercept Mongol forces as they approached the border.[71]

The Chinese were far from taking the offense when Qi Jiguang was appointed in 1568. The Mongols had raided the border every year since looting the suburbs of Beijing in 1550, and the Ming armies had won only a single victory during that period. Not long after Qi Jiguang's appointment, however, a grandson of Altan Khan sought asylum in China. This event prompted a debate at court over border policy. The successful conclusion of the piracy problem through liberalization of trade provided an important precedent, and a vote among the high officials came out just in favor of trying the same approach with the Mongols. In 1571, Altan Khan was given the title of prince and permitted to submit tribute and engage in trade.[72]

By all accounts, the agreement to open the border markets was a great success. There were fewer incidents along the border and Chinese military expenditures dropped precipitously. However, Altan Khan did not control all the Mongols on the steppe, and those still loyal to the *khaghan* refused to cooperate, because the *khaghan* would not accept a Chinese title subordinating himself to the Ming emperor. Parts of the frontier were too far from the few permitted markets, and there raids continued. There was tension even among Altan Khan's followers, because the Mongol leaders monopolized the benefits from the restricted and highly regulated trade, whereas their followers had a better chance of sharing in booty from raids. Still, for the last dozen years of Altan Khan's life, the presence of his followers in Inner Mongolia shielded the central parts of the northern frontier from hostile nomads.[73]

After Altan Khan died in 1583, the northern frontier became less stable. Nevertheless, beginning from the 1590s, the most serious challenges to the Ming dynasty came not from the Mongols but from elsewhere: from the Japanese, from the Manchus, and from within.

The Fall of the Ming

The Ming military experienced a metamorphosis between the late 1300s and the late 1500s that left it barely recognizable. The Mongol auxiliaries were largely gone. The great cavalry armies and long supply trains that had campaigned in Mongolia were gone as well. The hereditary classifications that forced families into military service were gone. In their place were armies of infantry and wagons carrying European- and Ottoman-style muskets and cannon, supported by smaller amounts of cavalry, and deployed in support of elaborate and expensive border fortifications. These soldiers were recruited as volunteers and paid from the proceeds of a monetized taxation system.

Collecting taxes in silver could only have increased the supply of horses if it had reallocated productive resources, permitting some households to get out of the business of breeding horses and inducing other, more efficient ones to enter it. The problem facing Ming China was not so much an inefficient allocation of resources as an absolute shortage of pasturage for breeding horses. This may explain why two-thirds of the money that was collected from horse-breeding households in lieu of the delivery of horses actually went to other military uses instead.[74]

Much of the horse money must have gone toward personnel expenses. The collapse of the hereditary system and the substitution of paid volunteers put a huge strain on the Ming budget. Volunteers had to be paid market rates. What was not spent on soldiers was apparently spent on walls, which may also have entailed paying market rates for labor, or else on firearms. The economy was booming, but the bureaucracy was not strong enough, or else not flexible enough, to divert enough of that productivity to military uses.[75]

As "modern" as the late Ming army appears to have been, it is not at all clear that the change was an improvement. Quite the contrary. Compared to the early Ming army, it lacked offensive reach, and it ceded strategic initiative entirely to its principal opponents. Because there were not enough horses, stationing infantry in fortifications and equipping them with firearms was either the next best choice or perhaps just the least controversial one. The late Ming army grasped the opportunities presented by foreign firearms and silver to reconstitute itself along different lines, but for the Chinese it was really a step backward.[76]

Meanwhile, the Ming dynasty faced two new threats from the northeast. The first came from the Japanese invasions of Korea in the 1590s, which the Chinese helped the Koreans to repulse – these are discussed in chapter 7. The war with Japan distracted the Chinese from the second threat, the rise of the Manchus. The Manchus were descendants of the Jurchens, who had ruled north China between 1127 and 1234. In terms of lifestyle, they ran the gamut from farmers in settlements on the plains east of the Liao River to hunters in the forests farther northeast by the Amur River. Although the Manchus preferred to fight on horseback, they were not nomads; they had a healthy appreciation for fortifications that the Mongols did not share.[77]

The Chinese responded to a surprise attack from the Manchus in 1618 by organizing a punitive expedition for the following year. The Chinese mobilized perhaps half again as many soldiers as the Manchus, but they divided their forces into four separate columns. The wagons that were designed for use in Mongolia were hampered by the rivers and hills of Manchuria, and the first Chinese column met its defeat near Sarhu after crossing a river that its wagon brigade could not ford. The second Chinese column was disheartened by news of the defeat and fled upon contact with the Manchus on the following day. One of the other two columns was ambushed after it failed to get the order for a general withdrawal.[78]

After the disaster at Sarhu in 1619, the Chinese approached the Portuguese for help. Right around this time, the Portuguese were setting up a foundry at Macau, their enclave on the coast near Guangzhou, under the direction of the son of the chief gun-founder of Goa. They signed a contract with two Chinese in 1623 to cast iron cannon at Macau. The Portuguese also thought of bringing Chinese workers to Goa to produce cannon there, but it proved too expensive to bring the necessary raw materials from China to India. Macau therefore became the chief source of both bronze and iron cannon for the Portuguese outposts between Africa and Japan, with the Portuguese supplying the expertise for the bronze pieces and the Chinese for the iron ones, both following European designs.[79]

Perhaps because the foundry at Macau had not yet begun production, the Portuguese dredged up cannon from a Dutch ship that they sank off the coast of China in 1621 and gave them to the Chinese instead. The Chinese called these "red barbarian cannon" because they assumed they were made by the Dutch. The description of the Dutch in the dynastic history states: "What they rely on is only their great ships and large cannon. . . .When they are fired, they can pierce stone castles, and the vibrations [are felt] for several leagues. What people call 'red barbarian cannon' are made by them." In fact, the cannon were not Dutch either, but English. The two such cannon that still survive in Beijing bear English coats of arms.[80]

The Jesuits served as go-betweens, supported by a small number of influential Christian converts among the high officials at the court. The Portuguese first sent four cannon and four gunners from Macau, but the gunners were turned back at Guangzhou – the Chinese only took the cannon. Shortly thereafter, however, the Ministry of War requested that the Portuguese gunners be allowed through, and in 1624 seven of them arrived in north China. Before long they were sent back too. In 1630 a large contingent of soldiers, advisors, and equipment was dispatched from Macau, but again most of them were sent back. The Chinese needed Portuguese help but were suspicious of their motives.[81]

The Ming position in Manchuria collapsed after Sarhu, but the loss of Manchuria greatly shortened their defensive lines. The Manchus lacked the firepower to blast their way through Ming fortifications on a narrow front. The new cannon supplied by the Portuguese were well suited to the defense of static positions. When the Manchus assaulted Ningyuan, some ninety miles northeast of the Great Wall itself, in 1626, they were stopped by the firepower of a dozen heavy cannon, eleven of them red barbarian cannon. The Manchu ruler himself was wounded and died shortly thereafter. Impressed, the Ming court decided to cast more red barbarian cannon.[82]

Despite lingering distrust of Portuguese intentions, hardly unjustified under the circumstances, it was now politically feasible to train a unit in European firearms with Portuguese help. The new unit was apparently organized as a wagon brigade, with 240 battle wagons and 60 supply wagons, 196 cannon of different sizes, and 4,000 men with 1,200 muskets. Unfortunately, they saw their first action when some of their fellow soldiers in Shandong mutinied in 1631, and the unit was wiped out by the mutineers in 1632. A dozen Portuguese advisors were also killed. By the time the dust settled in 1633, the mutineers had escaped to Manchuria with the new weapons to join the Manchus.[83]

This mutiny was not an isolated incident. A drought in northwestern China in 1628 set the first one in motion, but the unrest soon spread to central China, between the Yellow and Yangzi Rivers, and remained there through the 1630s. There were both displaced peasants and deserters from the border garrisons among the various rebel groups. By 1642, the treasury was exhausted from nearly a decade and a half of rebellion, while the rebel bands had grown into mighty armies. The rebels now marched on the capital.[84]

The massive walls surrounding Beijing were a political monument rather than a military necessity. They had foiled Esen and his Mongol horsemen in 1449, but any thickness of wall would have done just as well. They failed to stop the rebels in 1644, but not because they were not thick enough. By the time the rebels reached Beijing, the empire was in complete shambles, and no taxes were coming in to pay the soldiers. There were no men to guard the walls. The emperor committed suicide when the capital fell.[85]

The Conquest of the Steppe

The fall of Beijing in 1644 prompted one of the Ming generals on the border to invite the Manchus into China to restore order. The combination of Manchu troops and veteran Chinese border guards was too much for the rebels, and the Manchus quickly occupied Beijing. Despite some opposition, the Manchus also extended their control over the rest of the empire and pro-claimed a new dynasty known as the Qing (1644–1911). Not only did the Qing dynasty rule China for over two and a half centuries, like the Ming dynasty had done, but it also succeeded where the Ming had failed, by bringing Mongolia under the control of an emperor in Beijing.

To be fair, we should note that the Manchus had been allied with their neighbors, the Eastern Mongols, even before they were invited into China. The Manchus found it easier than the Chinese to construct alliances with the Mongols, or else they were willing to go the extra mile to do so. The Manchus took their Buddhism from Tibet instead of China, for example, in part to attract and control the Mongols. In any event, the Manchus were able to use the resources of the steppe to conquer the steppe, and they never suffered from the same shortage of cavalry that plagued the late Ming.[86]

The Kangxi emperor and the Eastern Mongols launched four campaigns against the Western Mongols, or Dzungars, in the 1690s. The first campaign culminated in a battle less than 200 miles north of Beijing in 1690 that sent the Dzungars fleeing back to Dzungaria far to the west. The second campaign, in 1696, was designed to lure the Dzungars back east so that they could be dealt another blow. Three Manchu armies, each around 35,000 men strong, converged on the Kerulen and Tula Rivers in Outer Mongolia, where the central army drove the Dzungars into the waiting arms of the western army. The third and fourth campaigns in 1696 and 1697 were comparatively small affairs undertaken to follow up on the earlier victory.

The Dzungars recovered some of their strength in the early 1700s, and the Qianlong emperor set out to deal with them once and for all. Where the Kangxi campaigns had rivaled the Yongle campaigns of the early Ming in their logistical demands, the three Qianlong campaigns of 1754–55, 1755–57, and 1757–59 went far beyond them. Two separate supply lines were established, stretching more than a thousand miles into the far west. The cost of transporting grain that far overland was ten times the original purchase price. Under pressure from the west by the Russians at the same time, the Dzungars were defeated and had to submit. China never faced a serious threat from the steppe nomads again.[87]

The early Qing army combined the best features of the early and late Ming armies. The Qing could rely on a firm alliance with the Eastern Mongols against the Dzungars, whereas the Ming had had to settle for the neutrality or lukewarm support of the Uriyangkhai Mongols in fighting both the Tatars and the Oirats. The early Qing army was backed up by a first-class supply system with all the resources of what was still possibly the richest and most productive empire in the world. Finally, though perhaps least significantly, the Manchus also enjoyed access to European firearms through the Manchu emperors' Jesuit advisers. The Qing conquest of the steppe highlights just how difficult the Ming predicament had been. With all their advantages, the Qing conquest was still a very remarkable feat.

Looking back, it is not clear whether the Chinese "fell behind" in the late Ming or in the early Qing. The Europeans beat them to the first effective handheld firearm, the musket, in the late 1400s, but the musket was not the answer to Chinese prayers anyway. The fall of the Ming and the rise of the Qing suggest that Chinese security was better served by the kind of cavalry army that characterized the early Ming. The early Qing army was a step backward relative to the Europeans, but the European threat was still two centuries away.

Firearms alone were not the answer to the Ming dilemma, especially not the crude firearms available to them in the 1300s and 1400s. Given how little firearms contributed to any possible solution, it should not be surprising that so little was done with them. Allowing the private sale and ownership of firearms and getting more guns into the hands of peasants would not necessarily have prolonged the existence of the Ming dynasty, considering that it was overthrown by rebellions. Even if China had traded social stability for better firearms, it is not clear why the Chinese would have been better off, given that the solution to the problem of the steppe border had little to do with better firearms anyway, even after those did become available from European sources.

The same was not true elsewhere in the region, however. Korea and Japan faced very different strategic challenges and made use of firearms in very different ways.

7

Korea and Japan

To the east of China lies Korea, and to the east of Korea lies Japan. Although there were countless cultural differences among the three countries, they were all heirs to the classical civilization of Tang and pre-Tang China, and they had much more in common with each other than any of them had with anyone else. The Koreans obtained firearms from the Chinese in the 1300s, but they kept firearms secret from the Japanese for almost two centuries, until the Japanese acquired muskets from the Portuguese in 1542. This discrepancy set up a revealing comparison between Chinese, Korean, and Japanese adaptation to European technology when the Chinese intervened to protect the Koreans against the Japanese in the 1590s. Despite their much longer experience with firearms, the Chinese and Koreans found themselves outgunned by the Japanese.

Korea

Korea is a peninsula roughly the same size as the island of Great Britain. It shares a border with Manchuria to the north, and it is a short distance by sea to China and Japan. Like Vietnam, Korea had once been a part of the Chinese empire, but it broke off from the Chinese empire during the extended period of disunity between the third and sixth centuries, and it successfully resisted reintegration by the Sui and Tang dynasties, even though Korea itself was not unified until 671.[1]

The Chinese soon resigned themselves to the loss of Korea, and it remained independent under the rule of its own kings, who sent tribute to the Chinese on a regular basis. Korea became the most loyal of the Chinese tributary states and the one most influenced by Chinese culture. Its close contacts with China gave it access to much of Chinese technology. In some ways, the Koreans went beyond even the Chinese in their use of metal, which extended even to such everyday items as bowls and chopsticks. Korea, like Japan, was particularly rich in copper.[2]

Close contact with the Chinese probably meant that gunpowder weapons reached Korea early on. After the Jurchens attacked Korea from Manchuria in 1104, the Koreans organized a special unit armed with weapons known as "fire-emitters," which may have been gunpowder flamethrowers like those already in use in China. In 1135, a Korean army smashed a rebel fortress with catapults and set it on fire with "fireballs," one name for gunpowder bombs in China. Unfortunately, there is no hard evidence to prove that these were indeed gunpowder weapons.[3]

The Mongols invaded Korea repeatedly after 1231 and finally conquered it in 1259. Both China and Korea were under Mongol rule for about a century, during which time firearms technology should have been equally available to soldiers of both countries.[4] The 1288 firearm was discovered in Manchuria, not far from Korea. The earliest definite mention of firearms in Korea comes in 1356, as Mongol control over Korea (and China) was weakening:

> The Councilor Song Mun-gwan reviewed the northwestern defensive weapons; they fired a gun from Namgang and the arrow reached south of the Sunch'on temple and buried itself in the ground up to its feathers.[5]

In 1373, the Korean king asked the Ming emperor for guns and supplies (gunpowder, sulfur, saltpeter) to outfit a number of ships to take to the seas and pursue Japanese pirates. Some Chinese officials opposed the move, but the emperor approved it personally in 1374, and small amounts of saltpeter and sulfur were allocated for this purpose.

At around the same time, an enterprising Korean official named Ch'oe Mu-son was busily engaged in acquiring the secret of saltpeter extraction for Korea. Although some sources say he traveled to China to learn it, the better evidence is that he was taught by a Chinese craftsman in Korea named Li Yuan. Ch'oe Mu-son taught his own servants the procedure until he was able to convince the government to set up an independent Chief Firearms Directorate in 1377.

Not only did Korea now produce its own gunpowder, it also started producing some twenty different varieties of firearms and even stationing gunners (in small numbers) throughout the provinces. Gunpowder and firearms are credited with driving away the Japanese pirates in the 1370s and 1380s.[6]

These efforts were disrupted when the Koryo dynasty (918–1392) was overthrown by the Choson dynasty (1392–1910), but firearms development took off again in the first half of the 1400s. The Gunpowder Production Office was established in the Weapons Directorate in 1417. Firearms proved their worth against the Jurchens in the 1430s, and the Cannon Bureau and the Firearm Guard were both set up in 1445.

Meanwhile, techniques for firing multiple arrows were perfected, and stone cannonballs were introduced, soon to be followed by iron ones and even by experiments with explosive shells. New firearms were produced that were lighter, more reliable, used less powder, and had better range, and the existing arsenal was entirely replaced with new weapons in the mid-1400s. Saltpeter production was moved out of the capital to the provinces, sacrificing secrecy for greater production.

Then the pace slowed. From the mid-1400s to the mid-1500s, progress was much less impressive. There were improvements in casting techniques that enhanced the reliability of existing designs, and the domestic production of sulfur freed Korea from dependence on Japanese sources, so gunpowder shortages became a thing of the past. On the other hand, there were no particular technological breakthroughs.

Then, in 1545, Chinese sailors shipwrecked on the Korean island of Cheju divulged some information about firearms to the Koreans. The Korean arsenal was overhauled once again in the late 1550s and early 1560s, apparently to take advantage of this information. At least four types of cannon were produced for use at sea: the "heaven," "earth," "black," and "yellow" models. The firearms previously used on land were replaced by the "victory" model, a sort of Chinese-style hand cannon that came in three sizes (large, medium, and small). These were the guns with which the Koreans faced the Japanese invasion in 1592.[7]

Court records state that these Chinese taught the Koreans how to make firearms that shot cannonballs rather than arrows, but this could hardly be right – Ch'oe Mu-son himself already knew about cannonballs in the 1300s, and they were common enough in Korea in the 1400s, even if arrows were also in use as projectiles. The official story is so odd that one has to suspect some deliberate misinformation was being planted in the court records to mislead spies and preserve secrecy.[8]

Cannonballs were already known in Korea, but the timing would have been just about right for European firearms, particularly swivel guns. There is in fact still surviving today a breech from a swivel gun that was apparently cast in Korea as part of the overhaul of the Korean arsenal. The inscription gives the year 1563, the type of cannon to which the breech belonged (the "earth" model, one of the four types of naval cannon), the weight of the cannon (a little over 100 pounds), and the name of the craftsman (Pak Myong-jang).[9]

As noted in Chapter 6, the swivel gun was introduced to China around 1520. Even if the musket were introduced to China earlier than 1548, it is not too surprising that the Koreans might have learned about European cannon but not about European muskets in 1545, especially from ship-wrecked sailors. This in turn may help explain why the Korean navy and its cannon performed so splendidly in the war with the Japanese between 1592 and 1598, while the Korean army and its firearms were found so lacking.

The swivel gun is not the only reason why the Korean navy might have outperformed the Korean army. Korea has a short land border and a long coastline. It was sheltered from the Mongol threat by Chinese defenses in western Manchuria, so the only overland threat came from Jurchen tribes in eastern Manchuria, who were little more than a nuisance at this time. By the mid-1500s, Koreans probably had more experience fighting at sea than they did on land, and this gap was reflected in their use of firearms.

Korea had been a conduit for transmitting Chinese culture to Japan since ancient times, but the Koreans tried very hard to keep firearms out of the hands of the Japanese. When Yang Song-ji transcribed the *Ch'ongt'ong tungnok* ("Record of Firearms," 1448) from classical Chinese into the new Korean alphabet, his aim was not to make it easier for Koreans to read but to make it harder for Japanese! If the government was also concerned about keeping the secret from the population at large, it was obviously a lower priority.

Unfortunately for the Koreans, all their preventive measures could not prevent the Japanese from getting their hands on firearms through other channels. In fact, only five days after the news of the shipwrecked Chinese reached the Korean court in 1545, another report arrived saying that the Japanese now had acquired firearms too.[10]

Japan

Japan is made up of four large islands and numerous smaller ones. Without Hokkaido it is roughly the same size as Italy, and just about as rugged and mountainous. The distance from Kyushu to Korea is not much more than 100 miles, with the island of Tsushima halfway across it, whereas the distance from Kyushu to China is close to 400 miles, and that across the open ocean. Because Korea was weak, and China far away, Japan was seldom disturbed by foreign powers.

In the 600s, the Japanese borrowed more or less the entire complex of advanced civilization from China, including its writing system, its govern-ment institutions, and Buddhism, among other things. The Japanese also borrowed the Chinese practice of conscripting peasants to serve as infantry. However, this practice fell into disuse by the end of the 700s, for much the same reason that it disappeared in China: conscripted infantry could not match professional cavalry.[11]

When military force was needed, the aristocrats who controlled the government would call on small groups of mounted warriors. The ties of loyalty controlling these mounted warriors were more personal than institutional. Interestingly, these mounted warriors did not fight like heavy cavalry, probably because their horses were too small to bear the weight of heavy armor. Instead, they carried bows and fought like light cavalry. Indeed, one of the early terms for the warrior code was the "way of the bow and the horse."[12]

The shift to cavalry seems counterintuitive when one considers that Japan was a narrow and mountainous country. However, there was plenty of open space in northeastern Honshu, where the imperial state fought a series of wars in the 700s with indigenous peoples who fought on horseback with bows. The large infantry armies that were sent to conquer them proved so inefficient that conscription was actually cancelled during wartime, in 792. Small cavalry bands were better suited to tracking down a mobile enemy and required less logistical support as well.[13]

Even central and western Honshu were still largely empty during these centuries, with a few agricultural settlements carved out of the wilderness. The bottleneck was labor. Population in Japan was checked in early times by recurring bouts of epidemic diseases, and it did not break out of this cycle and begin to climb steadily until perhaps the 900s. The imperial capital of Kyoto was the only city of any significance. With plenty of room for maneuver, and little call for siege warfare, cavalry flourished.[14]

The founding in 1185 of the first *bakufu*, or "tent government" – a military government in Kamakura under the *shogun* that coexisted with the imperial court in Kyoto under the emperor – marked the rise of the mounted warriors into the highest levels of the ruling elite. The Kamakura *bakufu* eventually fell victim to domestic upheaval in 1333, being replaced by the Muromachi *bakufu* after a failed bid at reviving the emperor's power. However, it was becoming apparent that neither the *bakufu* nor the imperial court could control the warriors in the provinces.

The proprietors of the great estates in the countryside were members of the court and aristocracy in Kyoto. Their agents and officers lived on the estates in fortified houses. So-called evil bands of warriors and peasants began to disrupt this order in the 1200s, setting up mountain strongholds from where they could raid the lowlands. The following centuries saw a shift toward relatively inaccessible fortresses, including both mountain fortresses and fortified temples, many temples being located on mountaintops anyway.[15]

The devolution of political power in Japan had run its course by the 1400s. The Onin War of 1467–77 is traditionally taken as inaugurating the period of Japanese history known as the "Warring States," when effective control from the center disappeared and local warlords fought each other to build up their own domains. However, the three centuries from the 1300s through the 1500s were also a time of population growth and economic growth, despite the incessant warfare.[16]

The Onin War destroyed much of Kyoto as well as any lingering habits of obedience to the court and the aristocracy that resided there. Instead, new political entities formed around warrior bands in the countryside. As these bands grew in size, their castles began to attract artisans and merchants to supply their needs. Towns grew up "beneath the castles" much as they did in Europe under the same conditions. Walls could be extended to enclose the towns, turning castles in effect into citadels.[17]

Other than castle towns, the Warring States period also saw the growth of entrepôt towns and temple towns. Entrepôt towns were governed by merchant communities, temple towns by the militant religious sects that flourished in these troubled times. Entrepôt towns lacked the depth of resources to stand up to major warlords, but temple towns were much more difficult adversaries, because many of them were tied into networks of believers who might come to their aid.[18]

Finally, the Onin War also marked the appearance of large infantry formations in Japanese armies. The war was fought largely in the city of Kyoto, still the only major city in Japan despite the growth of the towns, and the exigencies of prolonged streetfighting prompted the mobilization of large numbers of footsoldiers, who gained a fearsome reputation for arson and destruction. Soon, infantry reappeared on battlefields elsewhere in Japan.[19]

The main infantry weapons were the pike and the bow. The pike had been introduced more than a century earlier, in the early 1300s, suggesting that there may have been some trained and disciplined infantry even then. The rise of infantry thus predated the introduction of firearms by anywhere from three-quarters of a century to as much as two centuries. Once firearms arrived, this pike-and-bow infantry found it easy to exchange its bows for muskets.[20]

The Japanese finally acquired firearms in 1542, two centuries after the Koreans did. They could not have been completely ignorant of gunpowder and firearms for those two centuries, considering how often such weapons were used against them. The Mongols may have used gunpowder weapons in their invasions of Japan in 1274 and 1281. The Koreans did use firearms against Japanese pirates beginning in the 1370s, as explained earlier, and the Chinese undoubtedly used them against Japanese pirates as well. Nevertheless, whether thanks to Korean security measures or some other reason, firearms were not introduced to Japan until the mid-1500s.[21]

When they were, their impact was immediate.

Tanegashima

The Chinese struggle against "Japanese" piracy was described in Chapter 6. Although most of those pirates were actually Chinese, Japanese were also among those involved. In an age when piracy, privateering, smuggling, and trading were barely distinguishable, the Japanese were heavily involved in all aspects of the regional network of trade. This regional network connected the southeastern coast of China to Japan and Southeast Asia and in turn to the global network of trade through the Spanish in Manila and the Portuguese in Melaka.

In 1542, a Chinese junk carrying three Portuguese on their way from Thailand to the smuggler base in the Shuangyu islands was blown off course and made landfall at Tanegashima, a small island off the southwestern tip of Kyushu. The Portuguese passengers demonstrated their firearms and sold two of them to the lord of the island for a considerable sum. He had his own craftsmen attempt to duplicate the weapons, and with some help from the Portuguese this was accomplished. This event has traditionally been taken as the first introduction of firearms to Japan.[22]

Given the deep involvement of both Portuguese and Japanese in the smuggling and trading network off the China coast, it is unlikely that 1542 was the first time that Japanese had seen European firearms and by no means certain that it was even the first time that such firearms had been brought to Japan. Certainly, advanced European firearms had been entering China for some time from the same trading and smuggling and piracy network. Nevertheless, the impact of firearms on warfare in Japan dates from after 1542.[23]

From Tanegashima, news spread rapidly through Japan. The name of the island became synonymous with the gun. It is said that a monk named Suginobo came to Tanegashima from Negoro temple in Kii province to learn the secret of firearms, and that a merchant named Tachibanaya Matasaburo also came from the city of Sakai for that purpose.

Negoro temple was an important center for mercenary training and arms production. The lord of Tanegashima gave one of the two original muskets purchased from the Portuguese, together with instructions for making gunpowder and firing the weapon, to the abbot of the temple. A smith from Sakai working at the temple successfully produced more firearms there; later he returned to Sakai and founded a family of hereditary gunsmiths.[24]

Sakai was the commercial center of Japan at the time. It was located in the center of Japan, near the imperial capital of Kyoto, on Osaka Bay. Possessing a certain degree of autonomy, governing its own internal affairs through a city council, it was an attractive location for arms merchants, who could sell to any buyer. Sakai quickly became the principal center of firearms production in Japan.[25]

Individual warlords also pursued firearms technology. Thanks to their geographical position, the warlords of Kyushu had the option of buying firearms from Tanegashima or importing them directly from the Europeans, and they appear to have done both. The Otomo of Bungo province also negotiated with the Portuguese to buy saltpeter from Macau. The earliest use of firearms in battle in Japan apparently dates from 1549, when the Shimazu of Satsuma province used them at Kurokawasaki in southern Kyushu.[26]

Christianity was an additional element in the equation. The Jesuits were eager to make converts in Japan, and they held out the prospect of increased trade with the Portuguese as an inducement for converting. Several prominent warlords, such as Shimazu Takahisa and Otomo Yoshishige, accepted Christianity at least in part to secure access to foreign goods, particularly firearms. Although their conversion may have been calculated, their support for missionaries resulted in many genuine conversions in Kyushu.[27]

The spread of firearms to central and eastern Honshu was connected not with warfare but with politics. Yoshishige sent one or several firearms to the *shogun* Ashikaga Yoshiteru in hopes of being appointed as constable of Hizen province in Kyushu. Although the *shogun* (like the emperor) was a powerless figurehead in the 1500s, an appointment by the *shogun* as a constable was apparently still of some symbolic importance. In 1553 Yoshiteru then sent one of the firearms he received to Yokose Utanosuke, the lord of Kanayama castle in eastern Japan, to strengthen his relationship with him.

In the Chugoku region of western Honshu, firearms are not mentioned until several years later. Documents from in and around 1557 speak of lead and saltpeter being collected for the production of bullets and gunpowder. Special units of gunners appear by 1562, and by 1567 there are frequent mentions of gunners being deployed by the Mori of Aki province. By the end of the decade it was possible for firearms to decide the outcome of battles.

In the Kanto region of eastern Honshu, firearms were also coming into use at this time. Takeda Shingen possessed firearms by 1555, although the number was still quite small. This was not exclusively his problem, as the other warlords in the east, like the Go-Hojo of Sagami province, suffered from the same shortage of firearms.[28]

Firearms spread quite rapidly throughout Japan. The availability of foreign sources and the existence of political ties between leaders in different parts of the country ensured that no single warlord would monopolize the new weapons. Rather than creating a new strategic stalemate, however, the introduction of firearms hastened the unification of Japan under a single ruler.

Nobunaga

Although the *shogun* was involved in the spread of firearms to central Honshu, the main beneficiaries were the so-called three unifiers: Oda Nobunaga,
Toyotomi Hideyoshi, and Tokugawa Ieyasu. All three came of age around
the time that firearms were spreading through Japan.

Nobunaga was born into the Kiyosu branch of the Oda family, minor
warlords in Owari province in central Honshu.[29] He applied himself to the
study of archery, gunnery, and other martial exercises as a young man in
the late 1540s and early 1550s. Nobunaga favored a particularly long pike,
between eighteen and twenty-one feet in length, that later became popular
across Japan. When Nobunaga set out to meet his father-in-law in 1553, not
long after the death of his own father, it is said that his bodyguard included
500 men with pikes and 500 men with bows and firearms.[30]

Nobunaga's men used firearms in combat on a number of occasions in the
mid- and late 1550s. His neighbors to the east, the powerful Imagawa family,
invaded Owari in 1554 and built a fort at Muraki. Nobunaga attacked the
fort, using firearms to keep up a continuous fire on part of the battlements
while the assault was made, and the fort was taken.[31] After a defeat at the
hands of his brother-in-law in 1556, Nobunaga and his rearguard held off
the pursuit while most of the army was ferried across a river, then used
firearms to keep the enemy horsemen from approaching while they escaped
on the last boat.[32]

Nobunaga's struggle with the Iwakura branch of his own family led to the
battle of Ukino in 1558 and to a dramatic confrontation between Hashimoto
Ippa, Nobunaga's gunnery instructor, and a famous archer named Hayashi
Yashichiro. The enemy was already in retreat when Ippa confronted
Yashichiro in single combat. Yashichiro wounded Ippa with an arrow, but
Ippa fired back and knocked him down, and Nobunaga's page finished him
off.[33] This victory set up an attack on the town of Iwakura the following
year, in 1559, when firearms were deployed in a prolonged (but eventually
successful) siege:

> We drove them into Iwakura and set fire to the town, rendering it defenseless.
> [Nobunaga] ordered sturdy "fascines two and three deep" on all four sides.
> The patrols were tightened, and for two or three months the army stuck close
> by, shooting fire-arrows and firearms into [the castle] and attacking in various
> ways.[34]

The capture of Iwakura brought all of Owari under Nobunaga's control,
but Owari was just one of Japan's seventy-odd provinces. Nobunaga survived
a scare when his 2,000 men defeated another Imagawa invasion force, this
one containing 45,000 men collected from the three provinces to the east

of Owari, at the battle of Okehazama in 1560. After this stunning victory, Nobunaga secured his eastern flank by allying with Ieyasu – then a warlord in the neighboring province of Mikawa and formerly a hostage in the household of Nobunaga's father – and began to expand northward. However, it took him until 1567 to wrest control of the neighboring province of Mino away from his brother-in-law's son.[35]

Nobunaga then swept through Omi province into Kyoto in 1568 as the champion of a claimant to the shogunate, Yoshiaki, whose elder brother Yoshiteru had been assassinated in 1565. This was a daring move for Nobunaga, because it pulled him away from his power base in Owari and Mino. Occupying Kyoto made Nobunaga a target for the warlords of the surrounding provinces. (He survived one assassination attempt when a bullet passed through his clothes.) On the other hand, it gave him access to the resources of the Kyoto region, including the city of Sakai, a key center of firearms production.[36]

References to firearms in Nobunaga's army begin to speak of definite numbers. When attacked by Asakura Yoshikage while campaigning in Omi in the sixth month of 1570, Nobunaga stripped 500 musketeers (and 30 archers) from different units to reinforce his rearguard and tried to lure Yoshikage's infantry within range to spring a trap on them. The ratio of musketeers to archers is instructive, but the fact that he could collect 500 musketeers only by drawing on different units is also suggestive: since Nobunaga had over 10,000 men with him at the battle of Anegawa six days later, the proportion of musketeers in his army apparently was still rather low.[37]

Further evidence of the proportion of firearms in Japanese armies comes three months after Nobunaga's victory at Anegawa. In the ninth month of 1570, the 20,000 troops that Nobunaga had recruited from Kii province for the siege of Osaka are said to have brought 3,000 firearms with them. Among these troops were men from the Negoro temple, mentioned earlier as one of the first places to show interest in the new weapons at Tanegashima. European armies had perhaps a third of their infantry armed with muskets by this time, but the proportion of firearms in Japanese armies was not inconsiderable.[38]

Osaka was the headquarters of the True Pure Land sect, a popular form of Buddhism with strongholds scattered across central Japan. Nobunaga's men collected grass to fill in the moat, dug entrenchments close to the walls, and built watchtowers around the city. Nobunaga used cannon to bombard the city – the account of the siege contains one of the earliest mentions of cannon in Japan – and the defenders replied with their own firearms. "Truly the enemy's firearms made the sky and the ground reverberate day and night," wrote one of his retainers. The siege was broken off after little more than a week when Nobunaga was threatened from another quarter, and Osaka and the True Pure Land sect would defy him for another ten years.[39]

The 1570s saw muskets and pikes come to dominate the battlefield and cannon begin to influence siege and naval warfare. Nobunaga spent the decade of the 1570s fending off challenges from all directions. He destroyed the powerful Tendai Buddhist temple of Enryakuji on Mount Hiei, on the outskirts of Kyoto, in 1571, and "sent many musketeers into the mountains and woods to hunt for monks who might still be hiding there." He quarreled with the *shogun* and drove him out of Kyoto in 1573, bringing the Muromachi *bakufu* to an inglorious end. He also wiped out the strongholds of the True Pure Land sect in the marshes of the Nagashima Delta in Ise province in 1574, bringing up several hundred ships that "came close to [the forts of] Otorii and Shinobase and smashed the walls and towers with their cannon."[40]

With the capital region hardly yet firmly under his control, Nobunaga was also under pressure from the Takeda family to the east. In the fifth month of 1575, Takeda Katsuyori placed Ieyasu's fort at Nagashino under siege, then challenged Ieyasu and Nobunaga's relief force as it approached. Nobunaga neatly dispatched a detachment around Katsuyori's army to relieve the fort, leaving Katsuyori in a bind, caught between Nobunaga's army and the still uncaptured fort. Katsuyori plowed straight ahead, but Nobunaga's men dug in and withstood attack after attack from the desperate and outnumbered Takeda forces, with most of the execution done by the muskets that Nobunaga deployed behind a long palisade.[41] There is a wonderful Japanese print illustrating the battle of Nagashino showing Nobunaga's musketeers mowing down the Takeda troops.[42]

Meanwhile, the True Pure Land forces in Osaka continued to hold out against Nobunaga. The Mori family of western Honshu sent ships to break Nobunaga's blockade of Osaka in 1576 and 1577. To counter them, Nobunaga built seven large ships armed with cannon and plated with iron. (The iron plating probably only covered part of the superstructure, to protect the gunners from enemy musketry.) The Jesuits, who kept close tabs on Japanese armaments, were surprised and impressed: "I was amazed that something like this could be made in Japan," wrote one of them; "[each ship] carries three pieces of heavy ordnance, and I have no idea where these could have come from. With the exception of a few small pieces, which [the Mori] had cast, we know for sure that there are no others in the whole of Japan." In the sixth month of 1578, Nobunaga's ships were attacked by an unknown number of smaller ones using arrows and muskets; the cannon on Nobunaga's ships kept the smaller enemy ships at bay and prevented them from approaching. In the eleventh month of the same year, Nobunaga's fleet met an enemy fleet said to number 600 boats, and again the cannon on Nobunaga's ships prevailed. Cut off from relief by sea, Osaka had no choice but to surrender to Nobunaga in 1580.[43]

The fall of Osaka gave Nobunaga control of most of central Honshu, and his forces were poised to expand both east and west when he was assassinated by an underling in 1582.

Unification

It fell to Nobunaga's successor, Toyotomi Hideyoshi, to complete the unification of Japan. Hideyoshi came from a small village in Owari province. The son of a farmer and soldier, he had risen from a position as a low-ranking officer in Nobunaga's army to become one of his leading generals. By striking quickly and decisively at the man responsible for Nobunaga's death, Hideyoshi put himself at the head of the coalition of Nobunaga's followers; after some further fighting, he defeated his rivals and brought the coalition firmly under his own personal control.[44]

Once Hideyoshi had secured his position as Nobunaga's successor, the unification of Japan was brought to a speedy conclusion. In 1585 he conquered Shikoku, occupied Etchu, and subdued the powerful Buddhist temples of Kii, including Negoro. His armies had grown so large that none of the remaining warlords could hope to resist him single-handedly. Hideyoshi mobilized over 200,000 troops to take Kyushu in 1586 and 1587, and a comparable number to reduce the Kanto region of eastern Honshu to submission in the final campaign in 1590. Many warlords chose to surrender rather than hold out against overwhelming odds, and Hideyoshi found himself at the head of something like a coalition government.

Hideyoshi adopted an innovative set of policies to stabilize society and forestall opposition. In 1588, he forbade farmers from possessing any weapons whatsoever, whether swords or spears or bows or firearms. Magistrates were dispatched to confiscate weapons in a series of "sword-hunts." Only soldiers were allowed to carry weapons, and in 1591, he forbade farmers and merchants from becoming soldiers. Hideyoshi also took a number of steps to ensure the loyalty of his allies: surveying their land, razing their castles, transferring them from one place to another, and taking hostages from their families. These policies would continue to serve as the foundation of the Japanese political order down to the mid-1800s.

It is generally accepted that firearms contributed greatly to the unification of Japan. True, Nobunaga and Hideyoshi had no monopoly on firearms, nor any decisive superiority in firearms, nor even necessarily any superiority in firearms at all. The integration of firearms into Japanese armies was not due to the individual genius of one or two men – the effectiveness of firearms was recognized by most if not all the major warlords.[45] However, this objection misses the point. By conferring an advantage on the larger warlords, firearms created a snowball effect that helped make unification possible.

When armies were composed of mounted warriors, large armies were difficult to hold together. The individual warriors had political ambitions that outweighed their loyalty to their superiors. When they were not plotting against their immediate superiors, they were supporting them in *their* plots against their ultimate superiors. This was the age of *gekokujo*, or "the lower overthrowing the higher." The samurai ethos of total loyalty was a later phenomenon, dating from the 1600s, 1700s, and 1800s, when Japan was at peace.[46]

When armies came to be composed of footsoldiers armed with pikes and firearms, the advantage went to the warlords who commanded larger populations and greater resources. Because anyone could be trained to wield a pike or fire a musket, large armies could be assembled by recruiting and training peasants. Insubordination became more difficult, as the organizational demands of supporting an army increased. Defeat was more decisive, as an army could not continue to resist for long after its source of supplies and ammunition was overrun. It was now possible for a single leader to grow at the expense of his rivals without becoming vulnerable to his own subordinates.

In Europe, this snowball effect was checked by fortifications. A single fortification could absorb the efforts of a major power for an entire campaigning season. The Japanese certainly had fortifications: Towns had walls; warlords had castles; bandits had strongholds. Battles and campaigns revolved around fortifications – the battle of Nagashino followed the siege of Nagashino castle, for example. The population took refuge in castles or forts whenever armies passed by.[47] Furthermore, cannon were still rare when unification was achieved. "They don't have them," the Portuguese Jesuit Luís Fróis could still write (slightly exaggerating) in 1585, "although they already use muskets."[48] Why then did all these fortifications not prevent unification?

One answer has to do with the motives of their garrisons. Japanese garrisons frequently fled, surrendered, or switched sides when threatened, or even before: Campaigns often *began* with fortresses switching sides and the former and new lords fighting to see if the switch would be permanent. The domains of the warlords were unlike independent countries in the sense that they had not built up identities strong enough to make changes of allegiance difficult. They were more like factions in a civil war instead. The one major exception was the True Pure Land sect, which was set apart by class differences and its own ideological commitment. Its followers often fought to the death because they could not count on being given quarter.[49]

It is also relevant that there were still very few major cities in Warring States Japan. Kyoto might have had 200,000 inhabitants in 1467 (before the devastation of the Onin War), but there were only three other cities with populations over 20,000 at that time, two of them being part of the Kyoto marketing network.[50] Much of the urban growth in the following century was concentrated in small towns. Land, peasants, and their crops were strategic objectives instead. According to Luís Fróis: "We fight to invest fortified places, cities and villages, and to grab their wealth; the Japanese do it to help themselves to wheat, rice, and barley."[51]

The countryside was dotted with small forts protecting the land, the peasants, and their crops. As long as there were many warlords, each with only a small army, one of these small forts could tie up an entire army. Nobunaga spent most of the 1550s unifying Owari province, and most of the 1560s wearing down resistance in neighboring Mino province, small hilltop fort by small hilltop fort. By the 1570s, the snowball effect mentioned earlier had resulted in fewer but much larger armies, and these small forts began to lose much of their strategic significance. What once required an entire army to accomplish now only tied up a detachment from a much larger army.

Truly grand castles began to appear in the 1580s, as warlords began to establish their headquarters in easily accessible locations from which they could gather information and send out orders. The prototype for this new kind of castle was Nobunaga's headquarters of Azuchi, built between 1576 and 1579. It was situated on a hill in the plains to the east of Lake Biwa, with soaring wooden buildings on top of a stone foundation. Azuchi was not designed with siege cannon in mind, but it was built to withstand a long siege, and it is not hard to imagine that the construction of more fortifications like Azuchi might have tied up larger armies and prompted the use of more cannon against them.

However, the impending showdown between cannon and castles was overtaken by political events. Just over two decades had elapsed between Nobunaga's move to Kyoto in 1568 and Hideyoshi's unification of Japan in 1590. Most of the major stone-foundation-wooden-superstructure castles like Azuchi were not yet built when unification was achieved: fifty of them were completed in the two decades from 1596 to 1614 alone, out of a total of no more than about eighty ever built. They were never asked to withstand siege artillery. Very few of them experienced any fighting at all. Neither castles nor cannon were really put to the test.[52]

If cannon remained rare in Warring States Japan, infantry and muskets were the mainstay of every army. The shift from cavalry to infantry happened well before the introduction of firearms, and it paved the way for the general and widespread acceptance of the musket. The belated acceptance of cannon may indicate a weaker demand for naval and siege weapons in Warring States Japan, or it may simply reflect their later introduction. Fortunately for the Koreans, the Japanese would be handicapped by their weakness in cannon when they shifted their sights overseas.

The First Invasion of Korea

With Japan now under his control, Hideyoshi turned his attention toward the mainland. In 1591 he began to make preparations to send an army to Korea. Untroubled by the lack of reliable information about conditions on the continent, Hideyoshi proposed to set the emperor of Japan on the throne of China, establish his own son as his advisor, put other sons in charge of Korea, and lead his armies on to the conquest of India.[53]

The first of more than 150,000 Japanese soldiers landed at Pusan on the southeastern tip of the Korean peninsula in the summer of 1592. Despite its walls and its garrison, Pusan fell on the following day. The Japanese muskets drove the defenders off the walls, and the Japanese quickly stormed the defenses.[54]

The Korean forces were ill-prepared to resist and the Japanese army swept them aside. Seoul fell after three weeks, and P'yongyang after two months, where the Japanese army halted. A detachment of 20,000 spent the next two months occupying the northeast. The Japanese began to organize their administration of the conquered territory.[55]

The tremendous success of the Japanese army was due in large part to its superior muskets. As a Korean official named Yu Song-nyong wrote later:

> In the 1592 invasion, everything was swept away. Within a fortnight or a month the cities and fortresses were lost, and everything in the eight directions had crumbled. Although it was [partly] due to there having been a century of peace and the people not being familiar with warfare that this happened, it was really because the Japanese had the use of muskets that could reach beyond several hundred paces, that always pierced what they struck, that came like the wind and the hail, and with which bows and arrows could not compare.[56]

If anything, the Japanese initially underestimated the importance of firearms to the campaign. The messages sent back to Japan from the front were insistent in their demands for more firearms. In a letter from the ninth month of 1592, one of the Kyushu lords wrote:

> Please arrange to send us guns and ammunition. There is absolutely no use for spears. It is vital that you arrange somehow to obtain a number of guns. Furthermore, you should certainly see to it that those persons departing [for

Korea] understand this situation. The arrangements for guns should receive your closest attention.[57]

The first effective resistance to the Japanese came from the Korean navy. The backbone of the fleet was a kind of sea-going galley known as a "turtle boat." The turtle boat had a curved roof (hence the name "turtle") studded with spikes to discourage boarding and carried twenty-four cannon. It was not armored, but it was enclosed in timber, which made it resistant to damage. The turtle boats could charge into the middle of larger Japanese fleets and fire their cannon at close range to maximum effect. Yi Sun-sin did not invent the turtle boat, contrary to popular belief, but he did lead a flotilla of them to four successive victories in 1592, endangering the Japanese lines of supply and communication. Hideyoshi conceded command of the ocean, and shortages of food and ammunition hampered the Japanese armies for much of the war.[58]

Meanwhile, having overrun most of the peninsula with surprising ease, the Japanese commanders found it surprisingly difficult to control. Outside of the immediate vicinity of the Japanese garrisons, Korean partisans continued to resist Japanese rule. Furthermore, the Chinese intervened on the side of the Koreans, their nominal vassals under the tributary system, much as they had intervened in Vietnam when the throne there had been usurped. A small force of just 3,000 Chinese soldiers was routed in the seventh month of 1592, but a larger force of some 40,000 crossed the Yalu River toward the end of the year and marched on P'yongyang together with 10,000 Korean soldiers.[59]

It must have been at least a century since a Chinese army had attacked a fortified city, but they acquitted themselves very well. The siege lasted for three days, with most of the fighting coming on the third day. The Chinese shot fire-arrows into the city and smashed through one of the city gates with cannon. P'yongyang had two walls – the inner and outer fortifications – and the Chinese assault carried the outer fortifications. However, the firepower of the Japanese muskets repulsed the assault on the inner fortifications:

> The Chinese soldiers fought harder and the Japanese could not withstand them; they retreated into the inner fortifications, slaughtering and burning. Large numbers died. The Chinese soldiers entered the [outer] fortifications and attacked the inner fortifications. The Japanese had made an earthen wall on top of the [inner] fortifications, in which they made many holes; it looked like a beehive. They fired bullets madly from the holes. Many of the Chinese soldiers were wounded. The Chinese commander worried about forcing the Japanese to fight to the death, and collected his troops outside the [outer] fortifications to give them an escape route. That night the Japanese crossed the river on the ice and fled.[60]

Encouraged by this victory, the combined Chinese–Korean army moved south against the main Japanese army at Seoul. The Japanese were too short on supplies to withstand a siege, so they elected to force the issue on the battlefield. The Japanese lured the Chinese vanguard into a trap north of Seoul; the Chinese had pressed forward without their cannon, and the Japanese inflicted heavy losses before the Chinese cannon could be brought up in support. Chinese morale plummeted, and the advance stalled. This defeat left a large Korean detachment stranded in an exposed position. The Japanese army turned on them next, but the Koreans dug in and fought back fiercely with their outmoded firearms and rockets. Stung by this unexpected resistance, the Japanese pulled back to Seoul. The Japanese abandoned everything north of Seoul, but even their hold on Seoul was precarious, because the Korean navy and Korean partisans made resupply almost impossible. Negotiations ensued.[61]

The Chinese agreed to a truce with the Japanese (the Koreans were not consulted) in the fourth month of 1593. Under its terms, the Japanese army withdrew south to Pusan, the Chinese army pulled out of Korea, and envoys met to negotiate a treaty. Differences in perspective between Hideyoshi and the Chinese court – each assumed as a matter of course that the other would perform a ritual submission – dragged out the talks through 1596. With the connivance of the envoys, the two sides ended up signing entirely different versions of a peace treaty.[62]

The Korean Response

Meanwhile, the Koreans were trying to digest the lessons of the first year of the war. The European-style musket had been first introduced to Korea in 1589, as far as we know, brought back from the island of Tsushima by a Korean emissary. Once the Koreans saw them in action, they hastened to produce their own.[63]

In the spring of 1594, while the negotiations with Japan were dragging on, Yu Song-nyong submitted a memorial concerning the supervisorate in charge of training soldiers in the use of muskets. Because muskets were time-consuming to make, they could only be produced very slowly, and there were not enough for training purposes:

> However, the musket is a very intricate instrument, and very difficult to produce. The *Jixiao xinshu* [written by Qi Jiguang in 1560] says one month for boring the barrel is optimal – that is, one musket takes the labor of one person for one month before it is ready for use. The difficulty and expense are like that. In recent days, the muskets used by the supervisorate have all been captured Japanese weapons. There are not many and they frequently burst, becoming fewer by the day.[64]

The supervisorate tried to produce its own muskets, but it lacked both materials and labor, and since muskets were needed at the front line, the trainees took their muskets with them after completing their training. Yu Song-nyong recommended training more craftsmen and setting them up in suitable locations under qualified supervisors to produce more muskets.[65]

In the winter of the same year, 1594, Yu Song-nyong submitted a memorial containing suggestions for neutralizing the Japanese advantage in muskets. The Korean bows did not have the range or the power of the Japanese muskets and could not stand up to them in set-piece battles. However, muskets had their own weaknesses:

> Although the musket is superior to the bow and arrow, it is slow and clumsy when loading powder and shot, lighting the match, and aiming and shooting. As for advancing and withdrawing at will, responding to opportunities with leisure or haste, being convenient for both infantry and cavalry, and being suitable for all situations, then it is not equal to the bow and arrow.[66]

The key for the Koreans, wrote Yu Song-nyong, would be to avoid set-piece battles and fight in terrain where the longer range of the musket would not come into play. They should take advantage of hilly or wooded terrain to ambush the Japanese, using the higher rate of fire of their bows at close range, but not allow the Japanese to close with their spears and swords. Korean partisans did apparently use similar tactics with success against the Japanese.

Yu Song-nyong was also concerned with neutralizing the Japanese advantage in close combat.[67] The Koreans had nothing that could match the Japanese swords, nor did they have time to train men in swordsmanship. Plenty of Japanese swords had been imported into Korea over the years, but the Koreans were not adept at using them. Yu Song-nyong's answer was to adopt volley fire for the Korean archers:

> If everyone fires at once, then although some of the bandits will be hit, the other bandits will be able to charge before they are able to draw another arrow. Volley fire is a way to prevent them from charging and to make the bandits unable to take advantage of our pause [in shooting]. If there are 100 archers, then they will be divided into 10 squads, with 10 men making up one squad. All of them will draw their bows, but in one squad three men will shoot first, then three men will shoot next, then four men will shoot next, so that the arrow nocks will follow one another without any gaps. Among 100 men there will always be 30 or 40 arrows fired in succession.[68]

Yu Song-nyong cited ancient Chinese precedent for volley fire, and indeed the idea was not new.[69]

In the same memorial, Yu Song-nyong was also very critical of the design of Korean fortifications. The Koreans had been known in the past, he said, for their skill at fortification, but the Japanese muskets rendered those fortifications obsolete:

> Today, the Japanese exclusively use muskets to attack fortifications. They can reach [the target] from several hundred paces away. Our country's bows and arrows cannot reach them. At any flat spot outside the walls, the Japanese will build earthen mounds and "flying towers." They look down into the fortifications and fire their bullets so that the people inside the fortifications cannot conceal themselves. In the end the fortifications are taken. One cannot blame [the defenders] for their situation.[70]

Not only were defenders vulnerable to musketfire – which explains why Pusan and other fortresses fell so quickly – but they were also vulnerable in other ways. Korean fortifications lacked bastions, and sometimes even battlements and moats, so besiegers could find shelter at the base of their walls. Yu Song-nyong recognized that Korea lacked the time and resources to rebuild its fortifications, but he hoped that supplying their garrisons with more firearms might compensate for some of the deficiencies. Time was short. "The Japanese will attack sooner or later," he warned.[71]

The Second Invasion of Korea

Yu Song-nyong was right. Hideyoshi was furious when he discovered that he had been duped by his own envoys, and he immediately ordered reinforcements be dispatched to Pusan. The Chinese quickly sent troops to support the Koreans. The Koreans hoped to avoid a repeat of the first invasion by stopping the Japanese reinforcements from reaching Pusan, but Yi Sun-sin was no longer in command of the fleet – political rivals had engineered his downfall in 1596, and one of them had taken charge of the fleet in his place. The Japanese won a tremendous victory over the Korean navy in the summer of 1597, and the way was open for the Japanese to advance out of Pusan.[72]

Their experience in Korea had only increased the Japanese appreciation for firearms. For example, the Tachibana contingent had been formed in 1591 with 300 cavalry and 1,100 infantry, including 200 musketeers; in 1597 it consisted of 212 cavalry and 1,153 infantry, including 350 musketeers. The proportion of cavalry fell and the proportion of musketeers rose.[73]

The Japanese armies advanced rapidly, taking key fortresses and inspiring panic among the Chinese and Korean commanders. The left wing of the Japanese army invaded the southwest corner of the peninsula, which had escaped the worst effects of the first invasion. Despite extensive modifications to the fortress at Namwon, the garrison was unable to hold out for more than a few days:

The Japanese vanguard of a hundred or more arrived under the fortifications. They fanned out and took cover in the fields in groups of three and five. They fired their muskets at the top of the fortifications for a while, then stopped. They left and then returned again. The men on the fortifications responded with [Chinese-style] "victory guns," and the Japanese main body sent out skirmishers from a distance to engage them. They advanced cautiously in waves, so the guns fired but did not hit them, while the Japanese bullets hit the men on the fortifications, many of whom fell dead.[74]

The Japanese occupied some ruined houses outside the walls. They spent a couple days preparing bundles of hay, then stacked these in the moat and against the walls while the fire from their muskets pinned down the defenders. Finally, they stormed the fortifications and put the defenders to the sword. The fortress held up the Japanese for no more than a week.[75]

Meanwhile, the right wing of the Japanese army drove north toward Seoul. The Chinese commander in Seoul almost abandoned the city before his superior came down from P'yongyang to take charge. The two sides fought to a bloody stalemate at Chiksan, south of Seoul, in the fall of 1597, and the Japanese drive was halted. On top of that, Yi Sun-sin had been rehabilitated and returned to command, and he won a decisive victory over the Japanese fleet at Myongnyang a week later. The Japanese were forced back on the defensive.[76]

The Japanese fell back on a line of fortresses that formed a perimeter around Pusan, anchored by Ulsan at one end and Sach'on at the other. The Chinese and Koreans mobilized an army of over 57,000 men, with more than 1,200 cannon, 118,000 fire-arrows, and innumerable smaller firearms, to strike at Ulsan in the winter of 1597–98. The initial assault failed to carry the Japanese fortifications in the face of Japanese bullets, arrows, and stones, and the Chinese and Koreans settled down to starve them out:

> At the foot of the hill were rotting fields; our soldiers had no place to plant their feet. The Japanese used their guns from the loopholes, and every shot struck its target.... If [the besiegers] lay prone the guns could not reach them easily; if they stood up they had to move in a crouch to avoid [being shot]. And those who lay prone suffered from the mud that covered their knees. Night and day they surrounded the fortress, and the ice and snow cracked their skin.[77]

Neither side was prepared for a siege, and the Japanese ran out of food and water within days. They held on, though, because they knew relief was at hand, and when it arrived the besiegers were too weak to resist. Ulsan did not fall, and Chinese sources admit to a loss of 20,000 men.[78]

A week after the battle was over, one of the Japanese commanders sent a letter to his father in Japan that read:

When troops come [to Korea] from the province of Kai, have them bring as
many guns as possible, for no other equipment is needed. Give strict orders
that all men, even the samurai, carry guns.[79]

The death of Hideyoshi in the eighth month of 1598 finally brought the
end in sight. As the Japanese made preparations to withdraw, the Chinese
and Koreans launched new attacks on their positions, but revenge was denied
them. Fighting with their backs to the wall, the Japanese repulsed attacks at
Sach'on and Sunch'on; once again, their fortifications and muskets gave them
the edge. Yi Sun-sin died in the last battle as his fleet harried the Japanese
withdrawal.[80]

The Japanese experience in Korea is yet another reminder, like the Chinese
experience in Vietnam, that advanced weaponry does not guarantee victory.
At the same time, it is also a sign of how quickly the Japanese had advanced
in the use of firearms. In the half century from 1542 to 1592, the Japanese
had made great strides in incorporating firearms into their armies. The muskets that the Japanese bought from the Portuguese in 1542 were relatively
advanced, but the Chinese had had access to the same weapons for about as
long, if not longer. The contrast is stark.

The Chinese made more use of cannon than the Japanese, but less use of
muskets. This put them at a disadvantage in the open, as when they out-
stripped their own cannon while pursuing the Japanese from P'yongyang in
1593. On the other hand, their cannon were not very impressive at attacking Japanese fortifications. Their one successful siege was at P'yongyang in
1593, where they broke through the Korean-built outer walls, but even there
they faltered in front of the Japanese-modified inner walls. In the fighting of
1598, the Chinese launched major attacks on Japanese-built fortifications
on at least three occasions, but without success.

For all that they were outgunned by the Japanese muskets, the Chinese
seem to have been less than completely impressed by them, at least as compared to the original product. Zhao Shizhen, writing at the end of the war
in 1598, found Ottoman muskets to be heavy and powerful, European ones
to be light and handy, and Japanese ones to be inferior to both. It is only
through constant practice, he wrote, that the Japanese became capable. Zhao
Shizhen spoke highly of the musket, but even at the end of the war with
the Japanese he did not envision an army organized and equipped like the
Japanese one.[81]

The single-minded intensity with which the Japanese pursued the musket
is sharply contrasted with Chinese experimentation. The musket was appropriate for Japanese warfare because Japanese warfare was very similar
to European warfare. The Chinese experience in Korea would have taught
them the importance of muskets in battles between large armies of opposing

infantry units, but the Chinese had little occasion to apply this lesson once the Japanese armies returned to Japan. Once the Japanese had withdrawn from Korea, the Chinese still had to face the old threat from the Mongols and the new threat from the Manchus. These threats could not be disposed of so easily.

Korea had close ties to China, and the Koreans tended to follow the Chinese model. Yu Song-nyong was familiar with the Chinese military classics, but he was also fond of quoting his near-contemporary, the Chinese general Qi Jiguang. The Koreans also made more use of cannon than did the Japanese, and while this may have been a disadvantage on land it probably contributed to the Korean success at sea. The Japanese might have addressed this weakness if other developments had not intervened to render the point moot.

The Tokugawa

Hideyoshi's death in 1598 cleared the way for Tokugawa Ieyasu, his old ally, to assume control. Ieyasu overcame a coalition of other warlords at the battle of Sekigahara in 1600 to solidify his position. Ieyasu had a better appreciation for large cannon than did Hideyoshi, and he took steps to build up his arsenal, buying some cannon from the English and the Dutch and ordering Japanese gunfounders to produce others. Some of these cannon were deployed at the two sieges of Osaka, in the winter of 1614 and the summer of 1615, when Ieyasu finally removed Hideyoshi's heir from the scene.[82]

Figure 7.1 is from a painted screen depicting some of the fighting outside of Osaka. There are few musketeers in this picture, as compared for example with the painted screen depicting the battle of Nagashino in 1575, and the number of bowmen still in the picture is surprising. The pikemen are not bunched together in tight formations, as they were in sixteenth-century Europe (see figure 3.1), but are standing in loose lines with room to use their weapons, more like the practice in seventeenth-century Europe. Most soldiers have swords on their belts, but they are fighting with pole-arms or missile weapons.[83]

The new regime, known as the Tokugawa *bakufu*, was headed by Ieyasu's descendants as *shoguns*, and ruled Japan down to 1868. Except for a pair of rebellions two centuries apart, in 1637–38 and 1837, there were no more battles in Japan for some 250 years. Ieyasu also instituted the "closed country" policy: The European presence in Japan was limited to a tiny Dutch outpost on an artificial island in Nagasaki harbor, and Chinese and Korean visitors also came under various restrictions. Ieyasu's descendants stuck to his policies down to the mid-1800s.

Nevertheless, contrary to popular belief, the Japanese never did "give up the gun." The misconception is based on a grievous misreading of Japanese history that is not accepted by any historians of Japan.[84] The Japanese continued to possess and produce firearms throughout the Tokugawa period. Just as there were different schools of fencing and sword-making there were also different schools of gunnery and gun-making, nearly 200 of them by the end of the Tokugawa period. Each lord was required to provide a certain number of soldiers with a certain number of guns from his domain – ranging from 235 men with 20 guns (8.5 percent) for a small domain rated at 1,000 *koku* to 2,155 men with 350 guns (16.2 percent) for a large one rated at 10,000 *koku* – in the event of a war. Prohibitions on ownership of weapons by commoners dating back to Hideyoshi's order in 1588 were enforced as well as they could be, which is to say only sporadically, but the prohibitions applied to all weapons, not just firearms. Firearms were not singled out. In fact, exceptions to the general prohibitions were made for firearms used for hunting and for guarding fields from wild animals. Large numbers of firearms remained in both official and private hands, just as they did in the Ottoman empire or in China.[85]

However, without the urgency imparted by warfare, fewer innovations were forthcoming. The Tokugawa tried to acquire mortars (capable of lobbing explosive shells at high angles over castle walls) from the Dutch to address some difficulties they had had with rebel fortresses in 1637–38, but the Dutch were not entirely cooperative and the Japanese eventually lost interest.[86] There was no pressure to create new firearms for military use and no cycle of mobilization and demobilization to pump them into society at large. Between the early 1600s and the mid-1800s, the focus shifted from military to sporting uses.[87] When someone decided to reprint an old Chinese firearms manual for a Japanese audience in 1808, this was his explanation:

> In Japan we have enjoyed peace for a long time. The samurai have mostly forgotten how difficult it is to protect one's achievements. They indulge in entertainment, and they only [fear] that there is not enough time [for it]. As for matters of military strategy and military discipline, they do not understand clearly what use they are, never mind about guns and cannon and firearms. Occasionally some will become involved in it, but from observing their performance, for the most part, if it is not bottomless empty boasting then it is like a child's game.[88]

FIGURE 7.1. Japanese battle scene from the siege of Osaka, 1614–15. Folding screen by Kuroda Nagamasa (1568–1623). Courtesy of Coll. Kuroda, Osaka-jo Tenshukaku, Osaka, Japan.

Japan's relative isolation ended in the mid-1800s. The British sent a fleet to China in 1840 to protect the illicit trade in opium, which the English were exporting to China from their colonies in India and Burma to address their unfavorable balance of trade. The Japanese viewed the Chinese defeat with alarm. Then the Americans sent a flotilla to Japan in 1853 to force the Japanese to open up their ports, in part to accommodate American whalers operating in the Pacific Ocean. The Japanese were powerless to resist.

The Tokugawa government recognized that Japan was in danger, and it responded accordingly, modernizing the armed forces and importing European firearms as rapidly as possible. However, some of the lords of the domains were able to acquire foreign weapons even faster, and a coalition of these lords overthrew the Tokugawa *shogun* in 1868 and established a new government in the name of the emperor. Although the leaders of the new Meiji government adopted the slogan "respect the emperor and expel the barbarians," the real power was kept in the hands of a small clique, the emperor remained a figurehead, and European technology was imported at an even faster clip. Within four decades Japan had become a military power to be reckoned with, defeating first the Chinese in 1894 and then the Russians in 1905. The Japanese were the first "Asian" power to defeat a European power in the "modern" period.[89]

These shifts were sudden but hardly very mysterious. When firearms were introduced in the 1540s, Japan was in the throes of civil war, and firearms spread quickly. After 1615, Japan was unified and there was no external threat. The Tokugawa political system dealt effectively with the samurai through various institutional arrangements, such as the requirement of alternate year residence in Edo and the holding of hostages.[90] Peasant unrest was met sometimes with concessions and sometimes with force, but in neither case was it allowed to grow to very serious proportions.[91] Japan was on the other side of the world from the imperial powers in Europe, so it escaped their notice until fairly late. After 1853, the existence of a new threat from the imperial powers could not be ignored, and the Japanese made prodigious efforts to rearm.

The simple fact of warfare did not by itself dictate the response to firearms. Warfare was as much a part of life in the Middle East or north China as it was in western Europe or Japan (before 1615). The response was shaped by the nature of warfare in each of these areas, however. Given how Japanese warfare resembled western European warfare, it is not surprising that the Japanese responded as enthusiastically to firearms as they did, at least as long as they remained at war.

8

Conclusion

Firearms were invented in China, probably in the 1100s. They spread to Europe and the Middle East by the 1300s, to India by the 1400s, and back to East Asia by the 1500s. The impact of firearms was nowhere greater than in Europe. By 1620, Francis Bacon could name gunpowder as one of the three discoveries that set his age apart from ancient times:

> It is well to observe the force and virtue and consequences of discoveries. These are to be seen nowhere more conspicuously than in those three which were unknown to the ancients, and of which the origin, though recent, is obscure and inglorious; namely, printing, gunpowder, and the magnet. For these three have changed the whole face and state of things throughout the world, the first in literature, the second in warfare, the third in navigation; whence have followed innumerable changes; insomuch that no empire, no sect, no star, seems to have exerted greater power and influence in human affairs than these mechanical discoveries.[1]

The development of firearms within the Oikoumene was affected by the degree to which an area was threatened by nomads instead of by infantry. Development was slower to the extent the threat came from nomads. Reducing chapters 2 through 7 into one simple table would give something like the following:

The Development of Firearms

		Significant Threat from Nomads?	
		Yes	No
Significant threat from infantry?	Yes	Intermediate (Ottomans, eastern Europe)	Rapid (western Europe, Japan before 1615)
	No	Slow (Middle East, India, China)	None (Japan after 1615)

Certainly, not every society responded to firearms precisely as the hypothesis might predict. Egypt and southern India might have done better than they did, since their exposure to invasion by steppe and desert nomads was relatively limited. The Mughals in northern India probably did better than one might expect, given their origins in Transoxania and Afghanistan. However, the point is not to go around the world and grade each area on how well it took advantage of firearms. The preceding chapters have already gone into some detail on each area. Rather, the point is that the strategic possibilities and constraints dictated by technology and geography establish baseline expectations from which the observed deviations are relatively small.

No other hypothesis accounts for the historical facts as closely. It should be apparent by now that Europe was not uniquely warlike, at least not compared to other parts of the Oikoumene. Japan after 1615 is the one area that did not see significant warfare, as the previous table indicates, and it experienced no significant development in firearms, as one would expect. However, no other part of the Oikoumene was free from warfare before 1700, by which time there was no question that Europe already had superior firearms.

Firearms were regulated or restricted by the Ottoman and Chinese empires, at least on paper. There is no reason to think that these restrictions were particularly effective in the Ottoman case. The Ottoman empire was wracked by rebellions in the early years of the 1600s in which demobilized infantrymen with firearms were conspicuous. If the Ottomans lost their edge in the 1600s, it was not because firearms were too tightly restricted. The Ming dynasty probably sacrificed some progress by restricting firearms in the 1400s, but it is likely that the restrictions were only effective because there was little demand for firearms in fifteenth-century China to begin with. The decision to make greater use of firearms in the 1500s was accompanied by a loosening of most of those restrictions. Better firearms must have become more freely available, but better firearms did not prevent the fall of the Ming dynasty in 1644. The Qing conquest of Mongolia in the 1690s and 1750s did not rely on the availability of better firearms either.

Finally, there is culture. There are two cases that are always cited for the proposition that certain people rejected firearms on cultural grounds. Upon closer examination, the Mamluk case turns out to be somewhat ambiguous. Although the Mamluks seem to have held a strong aversion to firearms, they also had little need for them before the 1500s, and when it became a matter of life or death, they were prepared on some level to adopt them to stave off the Ottoman conquest. Meanwhile, the Japanese case does not bear up under the slightest scrutiny. There is no more evidence of a cultural aversion to firearms among the Japanese than there is among the Europeans, and one would be hard pressed to find an historian of Japan knowledgeable in this period who believes that the Japanese actually "gave up the gun" in any meaningful sense.

The evidence for a cultural aversion to firearms among Europeans is, if anything, surprisingly strong. The association of firearms with Satan and the general disdain for missile weapons were both peculiar to Europe, whereas the cult of the horse was present in Europe but missing from China. If we were to rank which areas of the Oikoumene should have been most receptive to firearms on cultural grounds, Europe would not be high on the list, at least not in 1300. If European culture became more receptive to firearms over time, the question is why, and the best answer is that there was more incentive to use them.[2]

Firearms after 1700

The discussion of western European warfare in chapter 3 ended with two developments dating from the 1600s: the growth in armies and the spread of drill. These two developments gathered momentum after 1700.[3]

It took some time for European governments to develop the institutional means to recruit and train the necessary men. In the meanwhile, such organizational matters were handled indirectly, through the officers, with governments footing the bill. Regiments were bought and sold almost like private property. The colonel would expect to recoup his investment in purchasing a regiment by selling commissions to his officers and by selling equipment to his men. Each regiment had its own uniforms and even its own drills.[4]

European governments were slow to assume the responsibility of arming their soldiers as well. Soldiers brought their own weapons or purchased them from their officers; standardization was nonexistent. Although the French crown appointed commissioners and intendants in the 1600s to raise money, buy supplies, and review troops both on a province-by-province and a campaign-by-campaign basis, not until the 1700s did it take full responsibility for supplying weapons to its own forces.[5]

Although Venice and Istanbul had long had permanent naval facilities, the challenge of building and maintaining specialized gun-carrying sailing warships eventually forced the Atlantic and Baltic powers to follow suit. By 1700, for example, the British navy had permanent bases at Chatham, Portsmouth, and Plymouth equipped with dry docks, slips, storehouses, hospitals, and other facilities, not to mention the yards at Deptford and Woolwich on the Thames where ships were built.[6]

The growth in army size and military infrastucture eventually put greater demands on European governments in the 1700s, but whether it explains European military supremacy is another question. Viewed in comparative perspective, Europe was unexceptional. In terms of rate of growth, the Ottomans had gone from a standing army of 18,000 in 1527 to 76,000 in 1609; in terms of absolute size, the Ming dynasty already had over 1.2 million men in arms in 1392. As for centralization and standardization, it is odd how these are hailed as signs of progress in Europe when the same phenomena are blamed for lack of progress in the Ottoman and Ming empires.

What set the Europeans apart were training and discipline. European armies were among the most disciplined and professional in the world by 1700, whether compared to other powers in the Oikoumene or to the steppe and desert nomads. European armies not only had the best firearms, they also had a wealth of practical experience in techniques of training, organization, and supply that were fundamental to the effective deployment of firearms. It was not all that difficult for non-European armies to acquire advanced weapons, but it was much more difficult to introduce all the associated organizational changes.[7]

There is very little mystery concerning European dominance in firearms technology after 1700. Once the Europeans grabbed the lead in firearms technology, they never relinquished it. The Japanese ceased to compete in the early 1600s, although they caught up again quickly in the late 1800s. The Ottomans lagged behind Britain and France, but so did the rest of southern and eastern Europe to one degree or another. Although European descendants in America and other places remained competitive to a greater or lesser degree, practically no one else did.

Nothing changed in the 1700s or 1800s to slow Europe's headlong rush toward better firearms – quite the opposite. Conditions of warfare within Europe still favored the use of infantry. Their experience gave them an edge in developing institutions and organizations to handle the new weapons that they invented. Furthermore, Europe now had a clear lead in technology and innovation. From the 1600s on, every major innovation in firearms technology appeared first in Europe, beginning with the bayonet and the flintlock.

The bayonet, adopted in the late 1600s, transformed infantry tactics in the 1700s. The pike disappeared, and with it the distinction between pikemen and musketeers; every pikeman was his own musketeer and every musketeer his own pikeman. The efficiency of infantry doubled at one stroke, whether measured by firepower or by cold steel. The trade-off between pikemen (more tactical mobility, less firepower per soldier) and wagons (less tactical mobility, more firepower per soldier) was obviated, as bayonets combined the strengths of each without the weakness of either.

The flintlock, also adopted in the late 1600s, made the musket much easier to use by eliminating the burning "match" of the matchlock. Instead, the flintlock created a spark by striking flint against steel; the spark ignited the priming powder and the priming powder in turn ignited the main charge. The flintlock was much easier to use than the matchlock and therefore permitted a higher rate of fire. The flintlock was also much simpler and cheaper than the wheel lock, so it also replaced the wheel lock in pistols and carbines, although cavalry still continued to carry swords (sometimes even lances) for hand-to-hand combat.

The rifle was an even older invention than the bayonet or flintlock, but for a long time it was better suited for hunting than for warfare. The bullet fit tightly into the barrel and gripped the grooves that imparted the spin to it. The tighter fit gave the bullet greater force while the spin gave it greater accuracy. However, the tighter fit also made it all the more difficult to load the weapon from the muzzle, and what was gained in accuracy was more than lost in rate of fire. Rifles were little used in the 1700s except by skirmishers, or else by hunters and frontiersmen, who also needed to hit individual targets.[8]

Cannon changed little in design but improved markedly in quality. In 1715, Johann Maritz introduced new production techniques: by casting the cannon as a solid block and boring it out with a horizontal drill, it was possible to align the bore more exactly and improve reliability and accuracy. More exact alignment meant that less metal was used for the barrel, so the new cannon were also lighter and therefore more mobile as well. One of Maritz's sons was placed in charge of casting cannon for the royal arsenals in France, and his techniques spread throughout Europe.[9]

The tempo of invention accelerated in the 1800s. The percussion cap, invented in Scotland early in the century, replaced the flintlock: a sharp blow from the hammer of the gun ignited the percussion cap and in turn fired the gun. The hollow-base bullet (minié ball), introduced in France near the middle of the century, made the rifle easier to load: the lead bullet was slightly smaller than the bore of the barrel but expanded to grip the grooves when the force of the gunpowder compressed the hollow base. The paper cartridge made loading faster and simpler by reducing the number of steps involved. These were the weapons of the American Civil War.

Single-shot muzzle-loading rifles made traditional tactics obsolete. The unprecedented range and accuracy of these weapons forced infantry to spread out, to lie prone, to seek cover, and finally to dig in. Spreading out no longer made infantry vulnerable to cavalry changes because cavalry on horseback was too easy a target – it could not approach infantry without dismounting. Even infantry had to keep a safe distance from other infantry, and hand-to-hand combat became rare. Cavalry was relegated to a scouting role.

The need to take cover only became more urgent as the rate of fire increased. Samuel Colt patented his first revolver in 1836. The early breech-loading rifles, like the single-shot Prussian needle gun that appeared a few years later, still used paper cartridges, but brass cartridges made repeating rifles practical later in the century. Some repeating rifles were used in the American Civil War, and they became standard issue in European armies in the 1880s.

The brass cartridge also opened the way for the machine gun. Multibar-reled machine guns like the American Gatling gun and the French *mitrailleuse* appeared in the middle of the century, and Hiram Maxim invented the first single-barreled machine gun in 1884. The development of a stable and safe form of smokeless powder in France in 1886 contributed to the spread of machine guns, because smokeless powder left less residue to foul up the machinery and made automatic weapons more reliable.

The machine gun and barbed wire brought European armies to a defensive stalemate in World War I. Firepower had developed well beyond either protection or mobility, to the point where offensive action was almost suicidal. Where firearms had once ended the cavalry charge, they now ended the infantry advance as well. Heavy artillery and poison gas failed to break the stalemate; it was the introduction of tanks and airplanes during and after World War I that restored mobility to warfare.

The old gunpowder weapons – flamethrowers, rockets, mines, and bombs – were revived in the twentieth century. It is difficult to say whether any of them surpassed firearms in importance, but none of them were gunpowder weapons anymore, since they relied on jet fuel, rocket fuel, high explosives, or even nuclear weapons instead. These also tended to increase the gap between industrialized countries and nonindustrialized ones.

All this time, the rest of the world struggled to cope with the increased firepower of European armies. The firearms of the late 1800s made it possible for small numbers of European and European-trained soldiers to defeat much larger numbers of native soldiers outside the Oikoumene, whereas once-powerful empires within the Oikoumene struggled to adopt European weapons and institutions before it was too late.

The World after 1700

European superiority in firearms technology did not translate, initially, into territorial gains. European "empires" of the 1500s and 1600s were networks of trading posts that existed largely at the sufferance of the local rulers. The major exception was in the New World, where disease rendered the indigenous empires all but incapable of resistance. However, disease kept European imperialism in check in the tropics, and there were few direct clashes with the powers in the other parts of the Oikoumene, except with the Ottomans.

The matchlock-pike-cavalry-artillery model of the 1500s and 1600s was never really tested outside of Europe and the Maghrib. There were never more than a handful of European soldiers in the Americas or in the trading posts that dotted the coasts of the world's oceans. We could try to imagine the Swedish army of Gustavus Adolphus transported halfway around the world to fight the Mughals or Manchus, but the exercise is hardly more meaningful than imagining the Roman legions of Julius Caesar transported forward thirteen centuries to fight the Mamluks or Mongols. Whatever advantage may have existed would have been more than offset by the difficulties of projecting power over such distances.

The flintlock-bayonet-cavalry-artillery model of the 1700s, on the other hand, did prove its worth outside of Europe. The costs of transporting and supplying armies overseas were still prohibitive, but this model was applied by Europeans using native manpower in India, where Indian soldiers with European training overcame those without it. A little later in time and a little closer to home, a French army under Napoleon easily handled the descendants of the *mamluks* in Egypt in 1798. Such conflicts were not yet numerous, but they demonstrated the superiority of European techniques.

Otherwise, far from threatening the existence of the empires in the other regions of the Oikoumene, European firearms initially strengthened those empires against the steppe and desert nomads. Pastoral nomads in Iran and India enjoyed one last hurrah in the 1700s, when the Afghans destroyed the Safavid dynasty and crippled the Mughals. However, Gibbon could have been speaking for any of the civilizations of the Oikoumene in the late 1700s when he wrote that "Cannon and fortifications now form an impregnable barrier against the Tartar horse."[10]

Without industry, the nomads could not compete in this new arms race, and if the recurved composite bow still rivaled the matchlock in 1650, the same claim was harder to make with respect to the flintlock in 1750. There was some use of flintlocks among nomads, and among the cavalry that fought them, beginning in the 1700s, but nomads could produce neither guns nor ammunition. The rulers of the agrarianate states grew stronger and stronger, and even before railroads and telegraphs solved the problems of transportation and communication, the nomads were already doomed.[11]

Ironically, the rulers of these agrarianate states were often themselves the descendants of nomads. The Ottomans continued to rule down to the end of World War I, although they lost territory to imperial powers and separatist movements. The Safavids were followed by more Türkmen dynasties in Iran: the short-lived Afsharid (1736–96) and Zand (1751–94) dynasties, then the more stable Qajars (1779–1925). The Mughals (1526–1858) lost control of India in the 1700s, but many of the local rulers who replaced them were also Turks, at least until the British took over. The Manchu emperors of the Qing dynasty (1644–1911) in China were not nomads, strictly speaking, but otherwise they fit the profile.

The Manchus and the Russians between them managed to conquer the steppe before the end of the 1700s. The Turks kept their grip on the larger part of eastern and western Islamdom through the end of that century. However, when the Manchu and Turkish rulers of these empires faced the armed forces of European imperial powers in the 1800s, they were uniformly unsuccessful. None of them could keep up with Britain or France, or later with America or Germany, in military technology, especially after the Industrial Revolution.

Weaponry changed drastically in the 1800s. The armies at Waterloo (1815) were not so different from those at Blenheim (1704); the navies at Trafalgar (1805) would have been recognizable to the sailors at La Hogue (1692). However, looking back over the century that separated Waterloo from the Somme (1916), or Trafalgar from Jutland (1916), it is clear that the European military superiority that existed in 1800 was greatly magnified over the next 100 years by the Industrial Revolution. The repeating rifle and the machine gun, the dreadnought and the submarine, the tank and the airplane – these were all products of the Industrial Revolution.

The rest of the world did not stand still during the 1700s and 1800s. Even outside the Oikoumene, local armies were seldom more than one generation out of date, if only because European armies would unload surplus or obsolete weapons on the world market. African armies were not fighting machine guns with spears, but they were fighting flintlocks with matchlocks, breech-loading rifles with muzzle-loading muskets, or machine guns with single-shot rifles. Within the Oikoumene, some armies even had access to the most up-to-date weaponry, courtesy of arms merchants from one European power or another. However, the ability to purchase weapons did not translate simply into the ability to use them.[12]

Sooner or later, almost every territory in the world outside of Europe itself suffered one or more of the following fates: (1) its indigenous population was replaced by European immigrants (e.g., America, Argentina); (2) its indigenous population was ruled by European officials (e.g., Zaire, India);

(3) it was divided into spheres of influence by European powers (e.g., Iran, China); or (4) it was left as a buffer zone between rival European powers (e.g., Afghanistan, Thailand). There may be some debate as to where to place individual examples, but there are only a few places that never fell into any of these four categories.

Turkey and Japan both preserved their independence with only minor concessions, Turkey because it took so long for the European powers to absorb the rest of the Ottoman empire and Japan because it took so long for the European powers to reach it, but in both cases also because they were able to use that time to acquire the skills they needed to protect themselves. Japan even launched its own empire on the European model, in the process making a colony of Korea, one of the few places that had shared Japan's good fortune in escaping European attention. It may not be entirely coincidental that both Turkey and Japan were places that had had some success with firearms in the past.

The gap between European and non-European military capabilities reached its widest point after the Industrial Revolution, late in the 1800s, at the same time that most of the remaining independent powers were reduced to colonial status. Although the Industrial Revolution widened that gap, the gap was already in place before then. The European victories in India and Egypt in the 1700s, the difficulty experienced by other powers within the Oikoumene in adopting European firearms, and the relative success of Turkey and Japan all suggest that there was more to European military superiority than just hardware.[13]

European-trained and European-led armies routinely defeated other armies with even the same weapons. If Europeans trained their soldiers better, disciplined them more thoroughly, and supplied them more regularly, it was at least partially because they had more experience with the same or similar weapons. That expertise could not be duplicated overnight. This was military technology in the broader sense, including training, discipline, and organization – not just techniques for manufacturing weapons.

Wagons and Pikes

The line between success and failure with firearms within the Oikoumene corresponds closely to the line between two different schemes for protecting musketeers and artillery. Musketeers and artillery had to be protected somehow because they were neither trained nor equipped for hand-to-hand fighting. In western Europe and Japan, pikemen blocked opposing soldiers from approaching too close; in eastern Europe, the Middle East, India, and north China, musketeers and artillery took shelter behind wagons instead.

The regions where pikes predominated were also the regions where firearms were most effective. Was this mere coincidence? Probably not. But which was the cause and which the effect?

Like the salaries of Presbyterian ministers in Massachusetts and the price of rum in Havana,[14] both were effects of the same cause. In western Europe and Japan, where fighting ranged over thickly settled farmland, it was easier to support and supply large infantry units, because supplies could be obtained more readily. The rest of the Oikoumene had its densely populated areas as well, but the steppes and deserts where the nomads roamed offered little except pasturage, and armies operating there had to be lean and mobile. Wagons may not have moved much faster than infantry, but they consumed fewer supplies and carried more supplies themselves. Wherever it was difficult to find supplies to support infantrymen, the musketeers would have been reduced in number and the pikemen would have been replaced by wagons, in either case to reduce the number of mouths to feed.

It may be that pikemen were more effective on the battlefield than wagons. Wagons sacrificed tactical mobility for strategic mobility. They could move farther between battles, but on the battlefield they remained for all intents and purposes stationary. Since musketeers could not leave the shelter of the wagons, commanders could not bring their firepower to bear on the enemy, and they were relegated to a largely defensive role.[15] Pikemen could advance on the enemy, allowing the musketeers to bring their guns to bear. But as long as infantry existed primarily as an obstacle to enemy cavalry, wagons would have been nearly as good on the tactical level, and for armies that operated outside densely populated regions, wagons would have been better on the strategic level.

Wagons were used in warfare by peoples as diverse as the Russians, the Poles, the Hussites, the Hungarians, the Ottomans, the Mamluks, the Aqquyunlu, the Safavids, the Mughals, and the Chinese. In other words, wagons were used throughout the agricultural regions that bordered on the steppe and desert. The use of wagons in the Middle East instead of pikes is all the more remarkable when one considers that the wheel had disappeared from large parts of the Middle East since Roman times. Wagons were not a part of everyday life in the Middle East outside of Anatolia; the camel was such an economically efficient means of transportation that it had replaced the wagon within its natural habitat.[16]

Wagons were not the only inanimate objects used to protect musketeers and cannon. The Russians had wooden walls mounted on skis. The Russians and the Austrians both had long wooden beams studded with spikes; such devices were also found in other parts of Europe. The Mughals had some kind of wooden tripod, such as the ones Babur used before the battle of Khanua.

The Chinese had an array of instruments designed for these purposes. These devices might be seen as forerunners to barbed wire.[17]

Such devices were useful for defending fixed positions, but they also may have come in handy on long campaigns. Since one infantryman would consume 3 pounds of rations each day, he would consume the 30 pounds of rations in his knapsack plus another 150 pounds of supplies over the course of two months. If a device weighing less than 150 pounds could replace him, then it might have been worthwhile to carry the device rather than the supplies. Of course, any army short on manpower might have considered using such devices to bolster its strength even where supplies were not any particular problem.

Could it be that western Europeans and Japanese excelled with firearms *because* they utilized pikes? We cannot rule out the possibility, but this just begs the question of why the Europeans and Japanese used pikes while others did not. Certainly anyone who could make a spear could make a pike. Although some assign a critical role to Swiss culture in the early use of the pike in Europe, the cultural argument lets us down here too, since the Japanese came to use the pike independently. The use and nonuse of the pike present the same questions as the use and nonuse of the gun, and there is reason to think that the same logistical considerations lay behind both.

This observation about the choice between pikes and wagons fits well into (and helps to strengthen) the larger conclusion that there were two different styles of warfare in the Oikoumene during the early centuries of the invention and spread of firearms, if not before. The two styles of warfare corresponded to what we might call two zones of geography. Where there were technologically advanced agrarianate societies that were not threatened by steppe or desert nomads, we find the combination of firearms and pikemen, with an emphasis upon infantry (western Europe, Japan). Where there were technologically advanced agrarianate societies that were threatened by steppe or desert nomads, we find the combination of firearms and wagons, with an emphasis upon cavalry (eastern Europe, the Middle East, India, north China).

Firearms and Nomads

To complete the picture, we should add a third style of warfare, which corresponded to a third zone of geography: the light cavalry (primarily horse archers) of the pastoral nomads of the steppe and desert. There were other styles of warfare in the world during these centuries, such as that found in the forests and jungles of North and South America, Southeast Asia, and sub-Saharan Africa, but none of these posed any threat to the people of the

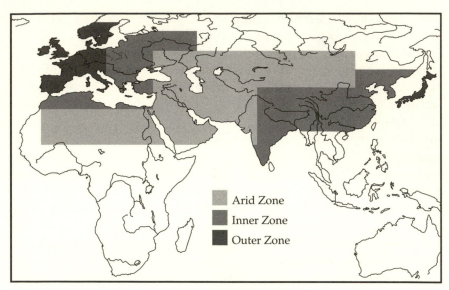

Map 6. Three Zones

Oikoumene, or to the pastoral nomads of the steppe and desert either for that matter.

We might call these three geographical zones the Arid Zone, the Inner Zone, and the Outer Zone (see map 6). The Arid Zone was discussed in chapter 1; it includes those areas bordering the Oikoumene that supported pastoral nomads. The Inner Zone includes those areas of the Oikoumene that were directly threatened by pastoral nomads, principally eastern Europe, the Middle East, India, and China. Note however that the Arid Zone cuts through the Inner Zone at the Middle East, such that there is no clean dividing line between the Arid Zone and the Inner Zone there. Finally, the Outer Zone includes those areas of the Oikoumene that were not directly threatened by pastoral nomads, principally western Europe and Japan. I call these "zones" rather than "regions" because neither the Inner Zone nor the Outer Zone was a contiguous or compact geographical area.[18]

One simple way to distinguish between the Inner Zone and the Outer Zone is to ask which areas of the Oikoumene were ruled by pastoral no-mads in 1288, the date of the first known firearm. Although the Mongol empire had broken apart or at least radically decentralized after the succes-sion crisis of 1260, the Mongols collectively controlled Korea, Manchuria, China, Transoxania, Iran, Iraq, Anatolia, and Russia, in addition to pretty much the entire steppe from Mongolia to the Ukraine. Meanwhile, Turkish sultans were ruling over very similar regimes in northern India, Egypt, and Syria, among other places. Southern India had escaped Turkish rule thus far but would eventually succumb to it as well, and the same might be said for the Maghrib and the Balkans. Not all of these areas remained under the rule of nomads in later centuries – China escaped in the 1300s, Russia in the 1400s – but even those areas remained threatened by them. Only western Europe and Japan had little to fear from nomads.

Before the development of firearms, the styles of warfare in the Inner Zone and the Outer Zone were quite similar to each other. Heavy cavalry dominated each one, in contrast to the light cavalry of the Arid Zone. The heavy cavalry of the Inner Zone was adapted to fighting the light cavalry of the Arid Zone, so it was more likely to carry bows and less likely to wear the heaviest armor. The heavy cavalry of the Outer Zone was adapted to overpowering infantry, so it relied more exclusively on hand-to-hand weapons like lances and swords and wore correspondingly greater protection. Still, the differences were small enough that the crusaders could adapt to warfare in Palestine and Syria, while the *mamluks* could engage the crusaders in hand-to-hand combat on fairly equal terms. The main difference was the growing role of infantry in both western Europe and Japan even before the introduction of firearms – this had no counterpart in the Inner Zone except perhaps in China, where south China was confronting north China between 1127 and 1276 with infantry, ships, and gunpowder weapons.

The introduction of firearms widened the divide between the styles of warfare in the Outer Zone and the Inner Zone because it put more power in the hands of infantry. Infantry was still of little use in the Inner Zone, because most areas in that zone were preoccupied with nomads, and infantry did not add enough in firepower to make up for what it sacrificed in mobility. Russia and the Ottoman empire were perhaps the two areas of the Inner Zone that had to cope with threats from both the Outer Zone and the Arid Zone. They both managed to use firearms fairly effectively. Neither Egypt nor Iran made comparable efforts, in spite of the Ottoman example. India and China faced no comparable threat from gunpowder infantry until the long arm of European imperialism reached them in the 1700s and 1800s. Japan might have presented the same challenge to China as western Europe did to Russia or the Ottoman empire, but it had the disadvantage of being an island group rather than a peninsula, and the logistical challenges of crossing the sea to fight against well-organized opponents were still insuperable in the 1500s and 1600s, as its invasions of Korea proved.

Unification halted firearms development in Japan in the 1600s, but firearms continued to improve in Europe. The heavy cavalry of the Inner Zone proved just as vulnerable to infantry with firearms as the heavy cavalry of the Outer Zone had been, but only the Mamluks in Egypt were close enough to infantry with firearms, in this case the Ottomans in Turkey, to be vulnerable to conquest in the 1500s. By contrast, the Safavids in Iran were able to use their light cavalry to stymie the Ottoman advance eastward. A Spanish or French army might have handled the Indians or Chinese with ease in the 1600s or 1700s, but the distances were so great that the point remains moot. Only in the 1800s did technology shorten those distances and allow power to be projected that far.

In a military sense, the weakness of most areas of the Oikoumene when faced with this new threat from European infantry stemmed directly or indirectly from their long preoccupation with the threat from steppe and desert nomads. They remained committed to cavalry as the best defense against nomads, never knowing how vulnerable it would be to infantry with firearms, or even imagining where such a threat might come from. When they did find out, it was too late.

Notes

Preface

1 Hodgson, *Rethinking world history*, p. 76.
2 Diamond, *Guns, germs, and steel*, pp. 53–57.
3 Ayalon, *Gunpowder and firearms*, p. 77.
4 Huang, *1587*, p. 171.

1. Introduction

1 Wei, "Heilongjiang"; Needham et al., *Science and civilisation in China*, vol. 5, pt. 7, pp. 290–94; Lu, Needham, and Phan, "The oldest representation of a bombard." For a description of the twelfth-century sculpture and the thirteenth-century firearm, see chapter 2, the section "The Invention of Firearms."

2 Qian, *Chengshou choulüe*, 5/18a–b (pp. 717–18). The last two sentences of the passage are taken almost word for word from Zhao, *Shenqi pu* 2/3a–b (p. 2681). When translating Chinese passages, where the text uses a round number of *li* simply to mean "a great distance," I convert *li* into leagues rather than miles (10 *li* equals 1 league equals 3 miles) to indicate that the distance is not meant to be taken literally.

3 Diamond, *Guns, germs, and steel*, pp. 35–191, offers one explanation why it was these regions that developed the most advanced technologies. Despite the title, the book has little to do directly with guns, however.

4 Black, *War and the world*, pp. 3–5, traces this idea back to Gibbon, who wrote: "In peace, the progress of knowledge and industry [in Europe] is accelerated by the emulation of so many active rivals: in war, the European forces are exercised by temperate and undecisive contests." Gibbon, *The decline and fall*, vol. 2, p. 441. There is a related argument, but one that stresses economic competition more than military competition, which goes something like this: European kingdoms allowed private ownership and production of firearms, while "Asian" empires stifled innovation by monopolizing them. This argument in its crudest form comes across as a projection of the Cold War on the past, with the Ottoman empire standing in for the USSR, and Ming dynasty China for the PRC. Kennedy, *The rise and fall of the great powers*, pp. 3–30, and McNeill, *The pursuit of*

power, pp. 24–116, are two of the better presentations of this argument. The principle itself is unobjectionable, but its factual basis as an historical matter is quite weak. At best, this argument has some validity for China in the 1400s; see chapter 6, "Institutional Change."

5 This argument has been anticipated by Esper, "Military self-sufficiency and weapons technology," p. 197 (see chapter 3, note 73), for Russia; by Matthee, "Unwalled cities and restless nomads," pp. 406–8 (see chapter 5, note 33), for Iran; by McNeill, *The age of gunpowder empires*, pp. 41–42, for China; and shortly before this manuscript was completed, by Allsen, "The circulation of military technology," p. 286.

6 The alternative to the universalistic explanation is the particularistic one. Every country, every society is different in one way or another. The more causal factors multiply, the easier it becomes to find a unique combination of otherwise common characteristics. The preference for a universalistic explanation over a particularistic one, or a more elegant explanation over a more cluttered one, is ultimately an aesthetic choice, as it is in (any) science. The elegant explanation always simplifies to some degree, and it can always be made more detailed by adding more complexity, but the additional complexity comes at a price. See also Slobodkin, *Simplicity and complexity.*

7 Hodgson, *The venture of Islam*, vol. 1, pp. 50 and 109–10. The same word is sometimes written "Ecumene" or "Oecumene" by other authors. Hodgson, *Rethinking world history*, pp. 8ff, heavily influenced much of the following. Hodgson takes the four-civilization scheme from McNeill, *The rise of the West.* Lewis, *Nomads and crusaders*, adopts a five-civilization scheme for the period 1000–1368, with "Byzantine-Russian" as the fifth, but this distinction is less useful for later centuries. Ostrowski, *Muscovy and the Mongols*, p. 31, would go the other way and adopt a three-civilization scheme, treating India as eclipsed by Islamic and Chinese civilization. I would not go quite that far, but I do include India in the chapter on "Eastern Islamdom," despite the four-civilization scheme, because it was largely conquered by Muslims after 1200 and for purposes of military history is usefully discussed in that context.

8 Hodgson, *The venture of Islam*, vol. 1, pp. 50 and 107–9.

9 There are serious problems with the term "East Asia," since "Asia" is such a pernicious concept; see March, *The idea of China*, pp. 23–45. However, the alternatives are just as bad.

10 McClellan and Dorn, *Science and technology in world history*, p. 105; Basalla, *The evolution of technology*, p. 102.

11 Hodgson, *The venture of Islam*, vol. 1, p. 456; Lewis, *The Muslim discovery of Europe*, p. 68; Lewis, *Race and slavery in the Middle East*, pp. 46–47; Chaudhuri, *Asia before Europe*, p. 67. Although Chinese art greatly influenced Iranian art from the Mongol period on, the Chinese reputation for artistry owed something to the legend of Mani as a master painter. See Schimmel, *A two-colored brocade*, pp. 120 and 149–50.

12 Hetoum, *A lytell cronycle*, p. 8. The original French text dates from around 1307; this English translation dates from around 1517.

13 Two books from 1998 take positions at the two ends of the spectrum: Landes, *The wealth and poverty of nations*, at the extreme Eurocentric end, and Frank, *ReOrient*, at the other. The latest major contribution to the debate at this writing

is Pomeranz, *The great divergence*, which argues that Europeans were not ahead in overall productivity in 1750 but that the core areas of northwestern Europe did have the best available technology in certain circumscribed fields by then (pp. 43–68).

It is important to distinguish between gaining or losing ground in relative terms and being ahead or behind in absolute terms, since the former would necessarily predate the latter, and possibly by a considerable length of time. Pacey, *Technology in world civilization*, p. 44, suggests that Europe was less advanced than either China or Islamdom in mechanical technology but was developing faster, and in new directions, by 1450.

In any event, the Eurocentric position does not make the problem go away. The earlier in time that a generalized European technological superiority gets pushed back, the easier it is to explain Europe's ultimate lead in firearms, but the harder it becomes to explain why it was the Chinese and not the Europeans who invented them in the first place.

14 Crosby, *The measure of reality*, fits eyeglasses and clocks into a broader scheme of new modes of perception in Europe after 1300.

15 Hodgson, *Rethinking world history*, pp. 269–70.

16 Hodgson, *The venture of Islam*, vol. 2, pp. 71–91.

17 Allsen, *Mongol imperialism*, describes the Mongol empire at its height under Möngke. Morgan, *The Mongols*, is the best general history.

18 The contemporary and mostly eyewitness accounts on which the following description is based are taken from European, Muslim, and Chinese sources: Carpini, *History of the Mongols*, pp. 5–8, 33–37, and 46–48; Polo, *The travels of Marco Polo*, vol. 1, pp. 251–52 and 261–63; Rubruck, *The journey of William of Rubruck*, pp. 93–96 and 100–103; Juvaini, *The history of the world-conqueror*, pp. 27–31; Meng, *Meng Da beilu*, p. 447; Xu, *Heida shilüe*, pp. 470–72 and 498–511.

19 Mongols occasionally dismounted to fight. Amitai-Preiss, *Mongols and Mamluks*, pp. 173 and 223; Amitai-Preiss, "Whither the Ilkhanid army?" p. 254. Chinese cavalrymen also dismounted at times while fighting on the steppe. See, for example, *Ming shilu*, Xianzong 24/4a (vol. 40, p. 467) (1465.12 *wuzi*), 36/8a (vol. 40, p. 719) (1466.11 *dingyou*), 81/9b (vol. 42, p. 1590) (1470.7 *jiachen*). On Mongol weapons, see also Reid, "Mongolian weaponry."

20 Rubruck, *The journey of William of Rubruck*, p. 220.

21 Fletcher, "The Mongols," pp. 15–16; Barfield, *The perilous frontier*; Di Cosmo, "State formation and periodization."

22 "Arab" and "Bedouin" were originally synonyms, but Arab has come to mean all the people who speak Arabic as a native tongue, whereas Bedouin has kept its original meaning as a name for the desert nomads of the Arabian Peninsula. Lewis, *The Arabs in history*, pp. 14–15; Hodgson, *The venture of Islam*, vol. 1, pp. 62–63.

23 On the differences between steppe and desert nomads, see, generally, Fletcher, "The Mongols"; Barfield, "Tribe and state relations"; Lindholm, "Kinship structure and political authority."

24 Bulliet, *The camel and the wheel*, pp. 95–100; Kennedy, *The armies of the caliphs*, pp. 10–11 and 23–27; Hill, "The role of the camel and the horse."

25 Lattimore, "The frontier in history," p. 487.

26 Keddie, "Is there a Middle East?" p. 269: "If there is one thing besides Islam that characterizes the Middle East as a unit, it is probably the uneasy but still adapted blend of pastoral nomadism and settled life which has been found with varying emphases in the whole area."

27 For historical perspectives on economic relations between agricultural and pastoral communities, see Fragner, "Social and internal economic affairs"; Mano, *Chuo Ajia no rekishi*, pp. 76–91.

28 Barfield, "Tribe and state relations," pp. 157–60; Smith, "Mongol nomadism and Middle Eastern geography," pp. 44–45.

29 Hodgson, *The venture of Islam*, vol. 2, pp. 78–85. Gunpowder did eventually help to shift the balance of power from the nomadic to the agrarianate, as Hodgson states, but the process was slow, and it took longer in Eastern Islamdom than in Western Islamdom.

30 Mano, *Chuo Ajia no rekishi*, pp. 53–60; Matthee, "Unwalled cities and restless nomads," pp. 402–4; Popper, *Egypt and Syria*, vol. 15, pp. 19–44, and maps. There were citadels in some European cities too, especially where the rulers were at odds with the populace; see, for example, Pepper and Adams, *Firearms & fortifications*, pp. 58–78, on the Spanish citadel in Siena, and Mallett, "Siegecraft in late fifteenth-century Italy," pp. 248–49, on the Florentine citadel in Volterra. One work from 1604 states that citadels were built for cities "when a conqueror, having won a great city, wants to assure it against the revolt of the inhabitants and to avoid the expense of such a large garrison that such a place would require." Errard, *La fortification reduicte en art*, p. 61.

31 Ibn Taghri-Birdi, *History of Egypt*, pt. 2, p. 47. Popper, *Egypt and Syria*, vol. 15, p. 81, notes how the Mamluks institutionalized the divide between city and citadel: "even a citadel situated within one of the larger capital cities was entirely independent of the provincial viceroy; it was one of the functions of the [viceroy] of the citadel to guard the interests of the Sultan as against the provincial viceroy."

32 On military slavery in Islam, see generally Pipes, *Slave soldiers and Islam*, pp. 3–102; Crone, *Slaves on horses*, pp. 74–91.

33 Perjés, "Army provisioning, logistics and strategy," pp. 4–5.

34 The calculations here are based primarily on Engels, *Alexander the Great*; Roth, *The logistics of the Roman army*; and Bachrach, "Animals and warfare." Horses could be raised so as to consume more grass and less grain, but grass was in shorter supply than grain in much of the Oikoumene, so stall-fed horses became dependent on a steady supply of grain, and that in large quantities. Harari, "Strategy and supply," pp. 320–24, suggests that stall-fed horses consumed more grain than could possibly have been transported by any means available in the 1300s, including sea or river transport.

35 Additional horses would increase that range, but horses were always in short supply. Two horses per man seems about right. Venetian light cavalry "lances" had two horses per man, the second horse being "a replacement plus baggage mount." Mallett, "Part I: c.1400–1508," p. 377. A Chinese detachment during the 1422 campaign in Mongolia comprised of 300 men and 600 horses carried twenty days' rations. *Ming shilu*, Yongle 250/2a (vol. 14, p. 2331) (1422.6 *gengyin*). In the latter case, assuming that each horse could carry 250 pounds, and assuming a total of 260 pounds for the rider (150 pounds), his equipment

(50 pounds), and his rations (60 pounds), each pair of horses could still carry up to 240 pounds of fodder, or 6 pounds for each of them for twenty days, a little low but still within tolerable limits.

36 Porters were used in preference to wagons by Alexander the Great, perhaps due to the lack of efficient harnessing in the ancient world. Engels, *Alexander the Great*, p. 17. Porters were also used in sixteenth-century Japan, possibly due to the rugged terrain. Fróis, *Européens & Japonais*, VII.40.

37 One German writer in 1621 estimated that one wagon was needed for every ten soldiers, but often the ratio was better than that, though probably seldom better than one wagon for every five soldiers, excluding wagons carrying siege equipment. Note that these figures do not take into account the hordes of civilian camp followers that accompanied most European armies. Tallett, *War and society in early-modern Europe*, pp. 54–55.

38 The logistical support for the 1410 and 1414 campaigns is described in some detail in the *Ming shilu* for those years. The account of the missed rendezvous begins at *Ming shilu*, Yongle 105/4b (vol. 12, p. 1364) (1410.6 *gengzi*). Alexander the Great relied on similar arrangements and almost lost his entire army in the Gedrosian Desert when his fleet failed to make the rendezvous. Engels, *Alexander the Great*, pp. 110–18.

39 Polo, *The travels of Marco Polo*, vol. 1, p. 260.

40 Piggott, *Wagon, chariot and carriage*, pp. 37–68; Drews, *The end of the Bronze Age*, pp. 104–63.

41 Drews, *The end of the Bronze Age*, pp. 164–67; Sima, *Shiji*, ch. 43, pp. 1806–11.

42 Michalak, "Sassanian heavy cavalry"; Haldon, *Warfare, state, and society*, pp. 128–34, 191–200, and 215–25.

43 Davis, *The medieval warhorse*; France, *Western warfare*, pp. 16–25. The number of men and horses in each "lance" varied greatly, from two to five or even more. Contamine, *War in the Middle Ages*, pp. 67–70 and 126–28. Where the men outnumbered the horses we know that the servants must have walked, but even where their numbers were equal the servants probably led the packhorses on foot. Although the knight traveled at the speed of infantry, he fought as cavalry on the battlefield; see note 47.

44 Smith, "'Ayn Jalut." For a lively account of battles with crusaders from the Arab point of view, see Hitti, *An Arab-Syrian gentleman and warrior*.

45 Graff, "Strategy and contingency"; Graff, *Medieval Chinese warfare*.

46 France, *Western warfare*, pp. 211–20; France, "Technology and success."

47 There is a distinction between men who fought on horseback and "cavalry," groups of men who fought on horseback. See, for example, Delbrück, *The dawn of modern warfare*, pp. 117–45. However, it is now believed that even European knights fought in groups as cavalry. See France, *Western warfare*, p. 156.

48 Nicolle, "Medieval warfare," pp. 584–85; Wink, *Al-Hind*, vol. 2, pp. 89–94; Smith, "Mongol society and military"; Adshead, *China in world history*, pp. 145–46 and 175; Jagchid and Banden, "Some notes on the horse-policy," pp. 255–63. For an argument that the Mongols shifted to heavy cavalry in Iran, see Martinez, "Some notes on the Il-Xanid army," but see Amitai-Preiss, "Whither the Ilkhanid army?" pp. 253–55, for an opposing view.

49 Paterson, "The archers of Islam," pp. 70–77, explains how the recurved composite bow was made.

50 If nomads felt confident enough to seek out battle with infantry or to attack fortifications manned by them, then something was seriously wrong, something beyond the power of muskets or cannon to redress. This was the case in sixteenth-century China; see chapter 6.

51 Esper, "The replacement of the longbow"; Parker, *The military revolution*, p. 17.

52 Qian, *Chengshou chouliie*, 5/10a (p. 701).

53 Hall, *Weapons and warfare in Renaissance Europe*, pp. 176–79. Carbines and pistols used wheel locks starting from the mid-1500s; see chapter 3, "Guns and Horses."

54 Illustrations of musketeers in the Islamic world show only one end of the match being kept lit, with the other end wrapped around the stock of the musket. This made the match easier to handle but increased the danger of it being extinguished.

55 Kist, "Commentary," pp. 39–42, translates the relevant passages from de Gheyn. This is the procedure for the arquebus. There is one extra step for the musket, when the rest is shifted from the right hand to the left hand, but otherwise the steps are basically the same. Note that de Gheyn starts with a soldier with a shouldered piece, so step 1 here is actually step 12 in the drill book. Also, de Gheyn includes steps for marching or standing guard that do not enter into the basic procedure for loading and firing described here.

56 Given a chance to load the musket and light the match ahead of time, it might have been possible to get off one shot from horseback before retiring to reload; Cook, *The hundred years war for Morocco*, pp. 205–7, describes a battle in 1545 where such tactics were used. However, the disadvantages would normally have outweighed the advantages by a wide margin.

57 Hall, *Weapons and warfare in Renaissance Europe*, pp. 134–56, has a detailed discussion of smoothbore ballistics.

58 Basalla, *The evolution of technology*, pp. 1–3, 21–63, and 135–43.

59 Gould, "The problem of perfection."

60 For example, the Mongols brought Chinese catapult operators to Iran in the 1250s and Muslim catapult operators to China in the 1270s, in each case so as to have the best available technology on hand. Allsen, "The circulation of military technology," pp. 265–72.

2. China to 1500

1 Gernet, *Daily life in China*, pp. 28–30. By contrast, Cairo had about 500,000 inhabitants (Baghdad had declined after the Mongol invasions), Venice no more than 160,000, and Paris maybe 80,000, in each case shortly before the Black Death. Abu-Lughod, *Before European hegemony*, pp. 98, 125, 196, and 212.

2 Rice was common in south China and among the elite in north China during the Yuan and Ming dynasties, but most people in north China still ate wheat, barley, millet, or sorghum as their staple food in the form of bread, noodles, or porridge. Mote, "Yüan and Ming," pp. 198–203. Soldiers probably did not eat rice, so the staple foods of Chinese and European armies were probably not that different, at least for Chinese armies in the north.

3 Barfield, *The perilous frontier*.

4 Johnston, *Cultural realism*, pp. 175–215 (quotes are from p. 187). The Ming emperors themselves did not necessarily share these views. The Yongle emperor saw both the Chinese and the Mongols as his rightful subjects; see Jin, "Beizheng lu" and "Beizheng houlu," for some indications of this attitude.

5 Barfield, *The perilous frontier*, argues that nomads before the Mongols did not seek to conquer China. If so, the Mongol conquest changed both Chinese and Mongol perceptions of what was likely or possible.

6 Needham et al., *Science and civilisation in China*, vol. 5, pt. 6, pp. 120–240.

7 Needham et al., *Science and civilisation in China*, vol. 5, pt. 4, pp. 179–200 and vol. 5, pt. 7, pp. 94–108.

8 Needham et al., *Science and civilisation in China*, vol. 5, pt. 7, pp. 111–26 and 147–92; Zeng, *Wujing zongyao* 11/23a–b (pp. 521–22), 12/50b–51a (pp. 622–23), 12/57a (p. 635), 12/59b (p. 640), 12/61a (p. 643).

9 The Chinese were also pioneers in the field of rocketry, but the potential for the rocket as a military weapon was not realized until the twentieth century, and rocketry contributed little if anything directly to the development of firearms. Needham et al., *Science and civilisation in China*, vol. 5, pt. 7, pp. 472–525. See also chapter 5, note 52.

10 Lu, Needham, and Phan, "The oldest representation of a bombard." The significance of the sculpture was first recognized by Professor Robin Yates.

11 Wei, "Heilongjiang"; Needham et al., *Science and civilisation in China*, vol. 5, pt. 7, pp. 290–94; *Yuanshi*, ch. 162, pp. 3797–98. The archeological report gives the figures in metric units: length of barrel 17.5cm, diameter of barrel 2.6cm, circumference of chamber 21cm, total length without handle 34cm, total weight without handle 3.55kg.

12 Maps 1 and 2 show the Yellow River emptying into the sea south of the Shandong peninsula, as it did after 1344. It shifted back to the north again in 1852.

13 Dreyer, *Early Ming China*, pp. 13–37; Dreyer, "Military origins of Ming China," pp. 44–72.

14 Dreyer, "The Poyang campaign," especially pp. 203–4.

15 Needham et al., *Science and civilisation in China*, vol. 5, pt. 7, pp. 295–96; Jiao, *Huolong shenqi zhenfa*, pp. 8–9. See also note 29.

16 *Ming shilu*, Hongwu 12/6b (vol. 1, p. 158) (1363.7 *bingxu*).

17 Dreyer, "The Poyang campaign."

18 Dreyer, *Early Ming China*, pp. 52–64; Dreyer, "Military origins of Ming China," pp. 88–98. On the Ming dynasty, see generally Twitchett and Mote, *The Cambridge history of China*, vols. 7–8.

19 Taylor, "Yüan origins of the wei-so system"; Dreyer, *Early Ming China*, pp. 76–87. "Brigade" is usually translated as "guard," from the literal meaning of the word *wei*, but I find this more misleading than useful, as there were imperial guards in the usual sense protecting the capital and the emperor. With this one exception I generally follow the translations for Chinese official titles given in Hucker, *A dictionary of official titles*. For the composition of companies, see *Ming shilu*, Hongwu 129/7a (vol. 5, p. 2055) (1380.1 *dingwei*); *Da Ming huidian* 192/1a (vol. 5, p. 2605).

20 *Mingshi*, ch. 89, pp. 2176–77.

21 Hucker, "Ming government," pp. 54–64. On eunuchs, see generally Tsai, *The eunuchs in the Ming dynasty*.

22 Serruys, "The Mongols in China: 1368–1398"; Serruys, "The Mongols in China: 1400–1450"; Robinson, *Bandits, eunuchs, and the son of heaven*, pp. 60–62.

23 On the Chinese recurved composite bow, see Needham et al., *Science and civilisation in China*, vol. 5, pt. 6, pp. 101–20.

24 Hucker, "Ming government," pp. 54 and 64–72; Waldron, *The Great Wall of China*, pp. 82–83; Elvin, *The pattern of the Chinese past*, pp. 97–101; Mote, *Imperial China*, pp. 743–46. Sweden's army was 5 percent of its population around 1710, and Prussia's 7 percent around 1760, to pick two extreme cases from Europe. Anderson, *War and society in Europe*, pp. 84–85 and 160.

25 Elvin, *The pattern of the Chinese past*, pp. 91–110. Most of the increase seems to have been on paper; however, see Huang, "Military expenditures in sixteenth-century Ming China."

26 Ban, *Hanshu*, ch. 46, pp. 2241–42.

27 There was an ancient rule of thumb: "If cavalry fights with infantry on flat terrain, then one cavalryman can match eight footsoldiers; if they fight on rough terrain, then one cavalryman can match four footsoldiers." *Liutao*, pp. 502–3. One sixteenth-century commander thought the true ratio more like one to ten. He, *Zhenji* 4/8a–b (pp. 797–98). An anonymous sixteenth-century author had a different view: "it just depends how you use them." Anonymous, *Caolu jinglüe* 5/15b (p. 232).

28 *Mingshi*, ch. 72, pp. 1759–60, ch. 74, pp. 1820–21, ch. 92, p. 2265; *Da Ming huidian* 192/1a–12b (vol. 5, pp. 2605–10), 193/1a–13a (vol. 5, pp. 2619–25).

29 Needham et al., *Science and civilisation in China*, vol. 5, pt. 7, pp. 24–33, discusses printed editions of this book at some length. None of the printed editions dates from before the 1500s at the earliest, and they mix material from the 1500s with material from the 1300s. In 1994, the People's Liberation Army published one of the surviving manuscripts in its fifty-volume series of classical Chinese military manuals, which I have used here. Although this manuscript cannot be dated, it does not seem to contain any material from the 1500s. See also Wang, *Zhongguo huoqi shi*, pp. 63–66.

30 Jiao, *Huolong shenqi zhenfa*, p. 51. The claim of 500 to 700 yards is rather dubious.

31 Surviving specimens include:
    1409 model: serial numbers 15238, 22058, 23283, 23625;
    1414 model: serial numbers 34519, 34606, 40554, 40868;
    1421 model: serial numbers 41277, 44854, 50115, 53041;
    1423 model: serial numbers 60231, 65623, 65876;
    1426 model: serial numbers 67299, 69246, 69958, 73294;
    1436 model: serial numbers 92088, 95464, 97640, 98612.
    Wang, *Zhongguo huoqi shi*, pp. 89–103. Note that Wang gives the serial number 5238 for one of the 1409 model guns, which would appear to be a typo for 15238, and 4854 for one of the 1421 model guns, which would appear to be a typo for 44854. The model years match up with the major campaigns of the Yongle reign and with the accessions of the Xuande and Zhengtong emperors. Most of the guns seem to have been produced in the third or ninth month of the year; the third lunar month usually corresponds to April or May, and the ninth to October or November.

32 Huang, *Taxation and government finance*, pp. 284–94; Huang, *1587*, pp. 160–62; Hucker, "Ming government," pp. 64–67; *Da Ming huidian* 192/13a–b (vol. 5, p. 2611).

33 *Ming shilu*, Yongle 15/6b–7a (vol. 9, pp. 280–81) (1402.12 *dingmao*).

34 Tani, "A study on horse administration," pp. 73–88; Tani, *Mindai basei no kenkyu*, pp. 143–61, 185–91, and 201–5; Rossabi, "The tea and horse trade"; Farmer, *Early Ming government*, pp. 66–70, 87–90, and 162–72.

35 Jagchid and Symons, *Peace, war, and trade*, pp. 79–113; Du and Bai, *Xi Menggu*, pp. 105–20.

36 Waldron, *The Great Wall of China*, pp. 72–73.

37 Langlois, "The Hung-wu reign," pp. 115–20; Dreyer, *Early Ming China*, pp. 71–73.

38 *Ming shilu*, Hongwu 71/1a (vol. 3, p. 1313) (1372.1 *gengxu*), 72/4b (vol. 3, p. 1332) (1372.2 *dingwei*), 73/2a (vol. 4, p. 1338) (1372.3 *dingmao*), 73/7b–8a (vol. 4, pp. 1348–49) (1372.5 *renzi*), 74/12b–13a (vol. 4, pp. 1358–59) (1372.6 *wuyin*), 74/19b–20a (vol. 4, pp. 1372–73) (1372.6 *jiachen*); *Mingshi*, ch. 2, pp. 26–28; Langlois, "The Hung-wu reign," pp. 128–29; Dreyer, *Early Ming China*, pp. 74–75. All dates given as "months" are lunar months.

39 Zhu, "Huang Ming zuxun" 5b–6a (pp. 1588–89).

40 *Ming shilu*, Hongwu 180/1a (vol. 6, p. 2721) (1387.1 *guichou*), 180/3a–b (vol. 6, pp. 2725–26) (1387.2 *jiashen*), 181/1a (vol. 6, p. 2731) (1387.3 *xinhai*), 182/2a–b (vol. 6, pp. 2741–42) (1387.5 *gengwu*), 182/4b (vol. 6, p. 2746) (1387.6 *dingyou*), 182/5b–6a (vol. 6, pp. 2748–49) (1387.6 *guimao, dingwei*), 182/7a–b (vol. 6, pp. 2751–52) (1387.6b *jiayin*); *Mingshi*, ch. 3, p. 44; Langlois, "The Hung-wu reign," pp. 157–58; Dreyer, *Early Ming China*, pp. 141–42.

41 *Ming shilu*, Hongwu 189/16a (vol. 7, p. 2861) (1388.3), 190/2a (vol. 7, p. 2865) (1388.4 *guichou* and *yimao*), 190/4b (vol. 7, p. 2870) (1388.4); *Mingshi*, ch. 3, p. 45; Langlois, "The Hung-wu reign," p. 159; Dreyer, *Early Ming China*, pp. 142–43.

42 Langlois, "The Hung-wu reign," p. 160.

43 See Tsai, *Perpetual happiness*, for the life of the Yongle emperor.

44 Farmer, *Early Ming government*.

45 Waldron, *The Great Wall of China*, pp. 76–81, suggests that the purpose was to save money, but the Yongle emperor spent more on his campaigns than he possibly could have saved.

46 Waldron, *The Great Wall of China*, pp. 61–62.

47 *Ming shilu*, Yongle 94/1a–b (vol. 12, pp. 1243–44) (1409.7 *guiyou*); 95/2b–3b (vol. 12, pp. 1258–60) (1409.8 *jiayin*); *Mingshi*, ch. 6, p. 87. On this campaign and the Yongle emperor's five campaigns in Mongolia, see Dreyer, *Early Ming China*, pp. 177–82.

48 Jin, "Beizheng lu"; *Ming shilu*, Yongle 97/1a–b (vol. 12, pp. 1279–80) (1409.10 *jihai*), 100/2a–b (vol. 12, pp. 1305–6) (1410.1 *renchen*), 101/4a (vol. 12, p. 1317) (1410.2 *dingwei*), 105/1b–2b (vol. 12, pp. 1358–60) (1410.6 *jiachen, dingwei*), 105/4b (vol. 12, p. 1364) (1410.6 *gengzi*), 106/1b (vol. 12, p. 1368) (1410.7 *renshen*), 106/3b (vol. 12, p. 1372) (1410.7 *renwu*); *Mingshi*, ch. 6, pp. 87–88. All references to tons are to U.S. ("short") tons, equal to 2,000 pounds.

49 Jin, "Beizheng houlu"; *Ming shilu*, Yongle 149/3a (vol. 13, p. 1739) (1414.3 *dinghai*), 152/1a (vol. 13, p. 1763) (1414.6 *jiachen*), 152/1b–2a (vol. 13, pp. 1764–65) (1414.6 *wushen*), 152/2a (vol. 13, p. 1765) (1414.6 *jiyou, gengxu*), 153/1b (vol. 13, p. 1772) (1414.7 *jichou*), 154/1a (vol. 13, p. 1775) (1414.8 *xinchou*); *Mingshi*, ch. 7, pp. 93–94.

50 *Ming shilu*, Yongle 246/1b–2a (vol. 14, pp. 2308–9) (1422.2 *yisi*), 247/2b (vol. 14, p. 2314) (1422.3 *wuyin*), 249/2b (vol. 14, p. 2324) (1422.5 *guiyou*), 250/1a (vol. 14, p. 2329) (1422.6 *renchen*), 250/2b–3a (vol. 14, pp. 2332–33) (1422.7 *jiwei*), 250/3b–4a (vol. 14, pp. 2334–35) (1422.7 *jisi*), 251/2a (vol. 14, p. 2348) (1422.9 *renxu*); *Mingshi*, ch. 7, pp. 101–2. The use of donkeys instead of horses or mules to pull the wagons should not affect the logistical calculations. Engels, *Alexander the Great*, pp. 14, 18, and 128–29. However, the ratio of wagons to supplies is double that in 1410, which is odd, unless they had switched to smaller wagons (substituting donkeys for horses?) since then.

51 *Ming shilu*, Yongle 261/2b (vol. 14, p. 2388) (1423.7 *wuxu*), 261/3a (vol. 14, p. 2389) (1423.7 *xinchou*), 262/1b (vol. 14, p. 2394) (1423.8 *gengshen*), 262/2b (vol. 14, p. 2396) (1423.8 *bingyin*), 263/1b (vol. 14, p. 2402) (1423.9 *guisi*), 264/1a–b (vol. 14, pp. 2405–6) (1423.10 *jiayin*), 265/1a (vol. 14, p. 2411) (1423.11 *jiashen*); *Mingshi*, ch. 7, p. 103.

52 Yang, "Beizheng ji"; *Ming shilu*, Yongle 269/1b–2a (vol. 14, pp. 2436–37) (1424.3 *wuyin*), 270/2a (vol. 14, p. 2447) (1424.4 *jiyou*), 271/3a (vol. 14, p. 2455) (1424.5 *bingshen*), 272/1b–2a (vol. 14, pp. 2462–63) (1424.6 *jiwei*), 272/2b (vol. 14, p. 2464) (1424.6 *guihai, jiazi*), 273/2a (vol. 14, p. 2469) (1424.7 *xinmao*); *Mingshi*, ch. 7, p. 104.

53 *Ming shilu*, Yongle 105/2b (vol. 12, p. 1360) (1410.6 *dingwei*).

54 *Ming shilu*, Yongle 152/1b (vol. 13, p. 1764) (1414.6 *wushen*).

55 Farmer, *Early Ming government*, p. 171.

56 On Vietnam, see generally Taylor, "The early kingdoms," pp. 137–53.

57 Zhu, "Huang Ming zuxun" 6b (p. 1590); Whitmore, *Vietnam, Ho Quy Ly, and the Ming*; Lo, "Intervention in Vietnam."

58 *Ming shilu*, Yongle 197/2a (vol. 13, p. 2063) (1418.2 *xinchou*); Yamamoto, *Betonamu-Chugoku kankeishi*, pp. 215–19.

59 *Ming shilu*, Yongle 233/1b (vol. 14, p. 2248) (1421.1 *jisi*); Yamamoto, *Betonamu-Chugoku kankeishi*, pp. 219–22.

60 *Ming shilu*, Xuande 22/12a–b (vol. 17, pp. 593–94) (1426.11 *yiwei*), 26/4b (vol. 17, p. 678) (1427.3 *jihai*); Yamamoto, *Betonamu-Chugoku kankeishi*, pp. 223–26; Lo, "Policy formulation and decision-making," pp. 56–60.

61 *Ming shilu*, Xuande 31/2a–3a (vol. 17, pp. 797–99) (1427.9 *yiwei*); Yamamoto, *Betonamu-Chugoku kankeishi*, pp. 227–39.

62 The Vietnamese apparently possessed some gunpowder weapons as well. Needham suggests that fire-lances may have been brought to Vietnam by Chinese soldiers fleeing from the Mongols in the late 1200s. Needham et al., *Science and civilisation in China*, vol. 5, pt. 7, pp. 310–13. Long after the fact, in the early 1700s, the editors of the dynastic history of the Ming wrote that the Chinese had learned about *shenji qiangpao* – a vague term that might mean anything from one specific gunpowder weapon to all gunpowder weapons in general – from the Vietnamese in the early 1400s and brought it back to China. *Mingshi*, ch. 89,

p. 2177 and ch. 92, p. 2264. This passage has given rise to no little confusion, leading some to believe that the Vietnamese made important contributions to Chinese firearms development, which is almost certainly not the case.

63 Miyazaki, *Tei Wa*, pp. 1–36; Chaudhuri, *Trade and civilisation*, pp. 50–55; Needham et al., *Science and civilisation in China*, vol. 5, pt. 9, pp. 418–33; Finlay, "The pilgrim art."

64 Lo, "The emergence of China as a sea power"; Polo, *The travels of Marco Polo*, vol. 1, pp. 31–38.

65 *Ming shilu*, Hongwu 70/7a–b (vol. 3, pp. 1307–8) (1371.12 *yiwei*); 139/7a (vol. 5, p. 2197) (1381.10 *jisi*); 205/4a (vol. 7, p. 3067) (1390.10 *yiyou*); 231/2a–b (vol. 8, pp. 3373–74) (1394.1 *jiayin*); 252/2b (vol. 8, p. 3640) (1397.4 *yiyou*). Compare this with the policies of the Mongol emperors of China, beginning with Khubilai, who strongly encouraged foreign trade. See Sugiyama, *Kubirai no chōsen*, pp. 184–241.

66 On Japanese reasons for sending tribute, see Grossberg, *Japan's renaissance*, pp. 33–37.

67 On Zheng He, see generally Miyazaki, *Tei Wa*; Levathes, *When China ruled the seas*. There are shorter accounts in Tsai, *Perpetual happiness*, pp. 197–208; Tsai, *The eunuchs in the Ming dynasty*, pp. 153–64; Needham et al., *Science and civilisation in China*, vol. 4, pt. 3, pp. 486–503; Dreyer, *Early Ming China*, pp. 198–203; Mills, "Introduction."

68 Levathes, *When China ruled the seas*, pp. 75–85; Needham, *Science and civilisation in China*, vol. 4, pt. 3, pp. 479–82. The actual size of the nine-masted treasure ships is disputed. The Chinese sources suggest something between 400 and 450 feet in length, but Sleeswyk, "The *liao* and the displacement," argues that wooden ships over 300 feet in length will break apart in even sheltered waters and suggests that the nine-masted treasure ships were 200 feet in length, based on figures that he interprets as their displacement.

69 Quoted in Mao and Li, *Ming Chengzu*, p. 254. The stelae erected by Zheng He are described in Levathes, *When China ruled the seas*, pp. 169–70.

70 For a cross-section of different opinions on the reasons for the voyages and the reasons for their discontinuation, see Tsai, *Perpetual happiness*, p. 208; Levathes, *When China ruled the seas*, pp. 88–89 and 175–80; Mao and Li, *Ming Chengzu*, pp. 248–58; Dreyer, *Early Ming China*, pp. 198–99 and 232–33; Lo, "The decline of the early Ming navy."

71 As a young lad on the 1414 campaign, the future Xuande emperor won his grandfather's praise by his quick reflexes and accurate archery. *Ming shilu*, Yongle 149/4b (vol. 13, p. 1742) (1414.3 *gengzi*). As emperor, he led a force of imperial guards that defeated a band of Mongols, personally shooting three Mongols with his bow. *Ming shilu*, Xuande 47/2a (vol. 18, p. 1141) (1428.9 *yimao*). The Mongols broke and fled after a volley from the Chinese firearms. Although the sources do not say so explicitly, the gunners must have been mounted infantrymen (i.e., dragoons – see chapter 3). Note, however, that this engagement occurred near the border, and it only occurred because the Mongols chose to fight. Even after riding all night, the imperial guards were still some twenty-odd miles from the Mongols when they were spotted, and it was the Mongols who initiated the battle.

72 Mote, "The T'u-mu incident," pp. 243–67.

73 It is unlikely that Esen ever expected to capture Beijing. When the *khaghan* balked at raiding China in 1447, Esen reportedly replied: "If Your Highness will not do it, I will do it myself. Even if we cannot take the great walled cities, we can keep the fields from being cultivated, keep the people from catching their breath, and get a lot of loot. That will be enough to show for it." *Ming shilu*, Zhengtong 160/6b (vol. 29, p. 3118) (1447.11 *dingwei*), quoted in Du and Bai, *Xi Menggu*, p. 100.

74 De Heer, *The care-taker emperor.*

75 Waldron, *The Great Wall of China*, pp. 91–103.

76 On horses, see the sources in note 34. On the Mongols in China after Tumu, see Robinson, "Politics, force and ethnicity in Ming China."

77 Waldron, *The Great Wall of China*, pp. 103–7.

78 Mote, "The T'u-mu incident," pp. 267–72.

3. Europe

1 Hale, *The civilization of Europe*, pp. 3 and 25–27.

2 Braudel, *The Mediterranean*, vol. 1, pp. 85–102.

3 Quoted in Piggott, *Wagon, chariot and carriage*, p. 69.

4 Jardine and Brotten, *Global interests*, pp. 132–83.

5 Bartlett, *The making of Europe*; France, *Western warfare*, pp. 77–127.

6 On the compass, see Needham et al., *Science and civilisation in China*, vol. 4, pt. 1, pp. 239–314, especially pp. 245–49; on the sternpost rudder, see Needham et al., *Science and civilisation in China*, vol. 4, pt. 3, pp. 627–56, especially pp. 635–38.

7 Allsen, "The circulation of military technology," pp. 272–82; DeWeese, "The influence of the Mongols."

8 Hall, "Introduction," pp. xxiii–xxv; Hall, *Weapons and warfare in Renaissance Europe*, pp. 42–43; DeVries, *Medieval military technology*, p. 143; Partington, *A history of Greek fire and gunpowder*, pp. 42–90.

9 Curiously, the fire-lance had appeared in the Middle East no later than 1294, but it is not attested in Europe until 1396. By contrast, firearms had appeared in Europe by 1326, but are not attested in the Middle East until 1342. Needham et al., *Science and civilisation in China*, vol. 5, pt. 7, pp. 259–60; Iqtidar Alam Khan, "The role of the Mongols"; Iqtidar Alam Khan, "The coming of gunpowder."

10 Hetoum, *A lytell cronycle*, p. 8. Note that the Armenians were Mongol vassals at this point.

11 Hall, *Weapons and warfare in Renaissance Europe*, pp. 43–44; DeVries, *Medieval military technology*, pp. 144–45.

12 Rogers, "The military revolutions of the Hundred Years War," pp. 58–64; Morillo, "Guns and government." Morillo points to Japan, where improvements in administrative efficiency in the 1400s preceded the introduction of firearms in the 1500s, as proof that government, not guns, was responsible for the rise of infantry. However, the introduction of pikes in Japan in the 1300s suggests that the rise of infantry in Japan may have preceded both guns and government. See chapter 6, the section "Japan." The role of government is open to question even

in Europe, where institutional continuity was supplied by mercenary bands, not by government units, well into the 1600s. Jones, "The professionalisation of the French army," pp. 150–51; Parrott, "Strategy and tactics," pp. 240–42. In any event, the importance of the knight on horseback in medieval warfare may have been exaggerated. See France, *Western warfare*, pp. 53–76 and 150–86; France, "Recent writing on medieval warfare," pp. 445–50. This has little effect on my argument one way or another, although the recent emphasis on the continued importance of infantry does strengthen the contrast between Europe and places like the Middle East, India, or China.

13   Hall, *Weapons and warfare in Renaissance Europe*, pp. 45–57; DeVries, "The impact of gunpowder weaponry," p. 229.

14   Contamine, *War in the Middle Ages*, p. 138; Delbrück, *The dawn of modern warfare*, p. 30; DeVries, *Medieval military technology*, pp. 146 and 151; Hale, "Gunpowder and the Renaissance," pp. 394–98; Murrin, *History and warfare in Renaissance epic*, pp. 123–37.

15   Morgan, *The Mongols*, pp. 56–57; Partington, *A history of Greek fire and gunpowder*, pp. 91–97. "Tatars" is used in this book as the name of the Eastern Mongols during the Ming dynasty (see chapter 2), reflecting contemporary Chinese usage, and as the name of certain groups of steppe nomads adjacent to Russia (see the section "Eastern Europe"), reflecting contemporary Russian usage.

16   Hall, *Weapons and warfare in Renaissance Europe*, pp. 58–66 and 74–79; DeVries, "Gunpowder and early gunpowder weapons," pp. 128–31.

17   Hall, *Weapons and warfare in Renaissance Europe*, pp. 114–30; Rogers, "The military revolutions of the Hundred Years War," pp. 64–76; DeVries, "The impact of gunpowder weaponry"; Cook, *The hundred years war for Morocco*, pp. 119–27; Mallett, "Siegecraft in late fifteenth-century Italy."

18   Hall, *Weapons and warfare in Renaissance Europe*, pp. 107–14. The word "laager" comes into English by way of South Africa, where the Boers had the practice of circling their wagons for protection.

19   Hall, *Weapons and warfare in Renaissance Europe*, pp. 67–104; Hall, "The corning of gunpowder."

20   Hall, *Weapons and warfare in Renaissance Europe*, pp. 176–79; Guilmartin, *Gunpowder and galleys*, pp. 274–76.

21   Parrott, "Strategy and tactics," pp. 242–44; Parker, *The military revolution*, pp. 57–60.

22   Anderson, *War and society in Europe*, pp. 88–89. Raids could weaken an enemy by pillaging his countryside, but a raid could not easily be converted into a siege, because raiding parties lacked the necessary logistical support. Harari, "Strategy and supply," p. 332. Nomads probably benefited more than agrarianate powers from a strategy of raiding, because they were less vulnerable to retaliation in kind and stood a better chance of gaining the upper hand in the long run.

23   Parker, *The military revolution*, pp. 9–10; Pepper and Adams, *Firearms & fortifications*, pp. 10–11.

24   Van Creveld, *Technology and war*, pp. 90–92; Tallett, *War and society in early-modern Europe*, pp. 21–33; Eltis, *The military revolution in sixteenth-century Europe*, pp. 43–51.

25 Williams, *A briefe discourse of warre*, p. 32.

26 Lynn, *Giant of the Grand Siècle*, pp. 538–46, discusses the *petite guerre* in Europe, much of which was associated with gathering or guarding supplies.

27 Parrott, "Strategy and tactics," pp. 231–32, argues that pike tactics evolved over the course of the 1500s. The close formations of the early 1500s gave way to the more open formations of the early 1600s, where each pikeman had more room to wield his weapon. Compare this illustration with Figure 7.1, showing Japanese pikemen in loose order.

28 Machiavelli, *The art of war*, p. 183.

29 Pepper and Adams, *Firearms & fortifications*; Parker, *The military revolution*, pp. 10–13 and 24–32. Elements of the style can be found as early as the 1450s. Mallett, "Siegecraft in late fifteenth-century Italy," p. 247.

30 Arnold, "Fortifications and the military revolution"; Thompson, "'Money, money, and yet more money!'"; Black, *European warfare*, pp. 67–86.

31 Michael Roberts originally singled out the spread of volley fire and military drill at the beginning of the 1600s as the significant part of the "military revolution" in his 1955 lecture (revised as an article and reprinted as Roberts, "The military revolution, 1560–1660"). Geoffrey Parker modified and expanded the argument in his 1988 book on the subject (Parker, *The military revolution*, first edition 1988), shifting the emphasis more to the *trace italienne* in the process. Parker's argument in turn stimulated a great deal of debate (see Rogers, *The military revolution debate*, 1995). Virtually every book on this period of military history to appear since the early 1990s has a discussion of the military revolution thesis, often highly critical (e.g., Black, *A military revolution?* 1991; Black, *European warfare*, 1994; Eltis, *The military revolution in sixteenth-century Europe*, 1995; Hall, *Weapons and warfare in Renaissance Europe*, 1997; Lynn, *Giant of the Grand Siécle*, 1997; Phillips, *The Anglo-Scots wars*, 1999). Parker has responded to some of these criticisms in the second edition of his book (1996) and elsewhere ("In defense of *The military revolution*," 1995). Parker's work is exceptional in dealing with military change across the world, and the military revolution thesis has been applied outside of Europe, sometimes to explain analogous changes (Cook, *The hundred years war for Morocco*, 1994), sometimes to explain why analogous changes never took place (see Black, *War in the early modern world*, 1999).

   However, the military revolution debate is largely irrelevant to the question addressed here. The difference between Europe and China, to pick one contrasting pair, was the prevalence of infantry and siege warfare in the former and cavalry warfare in the latter. Whether it was the pike or the cannon or the *trace italienne* or volley fire or the bayonet or the flintlock that most changed European warfare, no one disputes that European warfare was characterized by infantry and by sieges. I find the "punctuated equilibrium" model suggested by Rogers ("The military revolutions of the Hundred Years War," pp. 76–77) the most convincing, because I find it difficult to give priority to any of the changes in European warfare between 1300 and 1700 aside from chronological priority. None of the later ones would have occurred without one or both of the two earliest ones, the infantry revolution (associated with the pike) and the artillery revolution (associated with the cannon). For example, the *trace italienne* was largely irrelevant wherever heavy cannon did not exist, such as China, because it provided no extra protection against most other techniques of siege warfare, such as starvation. If most of the Oikoumene missed out on the later stages of the military revolution, it was because they never passed through the earlier stages.

32 Gottfried, *The Black Death*.

33 Machiavelli, *The art of war*, p. 125. See also Luttwak, *The grand strategy of the Roman empire*, pp. 45–46.

34 Hetoum, *A lytell cronycle*, p. 64.

35 Machiavelli, *The art of war*, p. 54.

36 Morgan, *The Mongols*, pp. 139–41.

37 On mounted archers and crossbowmen, see Contamine, *War in the Middle Ages*, pp. 129–30. On dragoons, for China see *Ming shilu*, Xuande 59/8a (vol. 19, p. 1409) (1429.11 *guimao*) ("1,000 cavalrymen, 1,000 infantrymen, and 250 mounted gunners, each with gun"); for Iran see Minorsky, *Tadhkirat al-muluk*, pp. 32–33; for Morocco see Cook, *The hundred years war for Morocco*, pp. 205–7; for Russia see Hellie, *Enserfment and military change in Muscovy*, p. 162; for Hungary see Kelenik, "The military revolution in Hungary," pp. 131–34; and for Venice see Hale, "Part II: 1509–1617," pp. 377–79.

38 Williams, *A briefe discourse of warre*, pp. 30–33; Love, "'All the King's horse-men'"; Duffy, *The military experience in the Age of Reason*, p. 116. By the American Civil War, all cavalry were dragoons in reality, if not in name, because rifles made it too dangerous to fight on horseback.

39 Hall, *Weapons and warfare in Renaissance Europe*, pp. 190–200; Delbrück, *The dawn of modern warfare*, pp. 41–42 and 122–38; Duffy, *The military experience in the Age of Reason*, p. 228.

40 It was a common complaint that pistols encouraged cavalrymen to fire ineffectively at a distance instead of charging at the enemy: "Out of a hundred pistolers, twentie nor scarce tenne at the most doo neither charge pistoll, nor enter a [enemy] squadron as they should, but commonlie and lightly alwaies they discharge their pistols, eight and fiue score off, and so wheele about." Williams, *A briefe discourse of warre*, p. 34. See also Hall, *Weapons and warfare in Renaissance Europe*, pp. 195–96.

41 Errard, *La fortification reduicte en art*, p. 5; Chandler, *Marlborough as military commander*, p. 226; Snyder, *The Marlborough Godolphin correspondence*, vol. 2, pp. 1033–34; Murray, *The letters and dispatches*, vol. 4, pp. 124 and 126.

42 Guilmartin, *Gunpowder and galleys*, especially pp. 39–41 and 157–75. Swivel guns were small breech-loading cannon used as antipersonnel weapons. Surviving Danish swivel guns are about 6 feet in length, with a bore between 1.25 and 3.75 inches, and fired iron balls weighing up to 3 pounds. See Howard, "Early ship guns, part I" and "Early ship guns, part II"; Vogt, "Saint Barbara's legion," pp. 179–80.

43 Rose, *Medieval naval warfare*.

44 Glete, *Warfare at sea*, pp. 17–39; Parker, "The *Dreadnought* revolution of Tudor England"; Rodger, "The development of broadside gunnery"; Rodger, *The safeguard of the sea*, pp. 61–72 and 204–21.

45 Martin and Parker, *The Spanish Armada*, especially pp. 195–225.

46 Anderson, *War and society in Europe*, p. 141; Lynn, *Giant of the Grand Siècle*, p. 509.

47   Anderson, *War and society in Europe*, p. 95; Rodger, "The development of broadside gunnery"; Lynn, *Giant of the Grand Siècle*, pp. 508–9. One has to wonder whether the 27,000 men embarked on Zheng He's fleets were an asset or a liability. Could he have achieved the same results with less cost by greater use of cannon? The circumstances were so different that there is no easy answer. His mission was to impress rulers in the South Seas, for which he needed a sizeable landing force.

48   Crosby, *Throwing fire*, pp. 104–5.

49   Heath, *Bow versus gun*, pp. xi–xiii; Smythe, *Certen discourses*, 20b–22b; Esper, "The replacement of the longbow," pp. 383–89. Similar arguments in favor of archers were made in France as late as 1660 and in America as late as the 1770s – though ultimately without success. There were also fitful attempts to bring back the pike. See Black, *European warfare*, p. 50; Black, *A military revolution?* p. 61; Lynn, "French opinion and the military resurrection of the pike."

50   Heath, *Bow versus gun*, p. xiii; Barwick, *A breefe discourse*, 17a–18b. Williams for one clearly agreed with Barwick: see *A briefe discourse of warre*, pp. 35–41, the sections entitled "To prooue Musketiers the best small shot that euer were inuented" and "To prooue Bow-men the worst shot vsed in these daies."

51   Latham and Paterson, *Saracen archery*, pp. 138 and 142. It takes an arrow less than two seconds to fly seventy-five yards.

52   Tallett, *War and society in early-modern Europe*, p. 23. Eighteenth-century infantrymen with flintlocks might manage two shots per minute with a misfire about once every five shots.

53   Latham and Paterson, *Saracen archery*, p. 138; Paterson, "The archers of Islam," p. 83.

54   Duffy, *The military experience in the Age of Reason*, p. 207; Guilmartin, *Gunpowder and galleys*, p. 149. Paterson, "The archers of Islam," p. 84, suggests that a good archer should never miss a man-sized target at sixty yards.

55   Eltis, *The military revolution in sixteenth-century Europe*, pp. 7–19, argues for the primacy of firearms on the inability of arrows to penetrate the best plate armor, but he only addresses Europe. Thornton, *Africa and Africans*, pp. 113–14, points out that penetrating power was "more than offset by the disadvantages of the slow rate of fire" in Africa, where soldiers generally did not wear armor, except in special circumstances such as naval warfare.

56   Farmers do not practice archery the way that hunters do, and England was unusual in having a culture of archery for as long as it did. On the decline of the longbow in England, see Esper, "The replacement of the longbow," pp. 390–93. There were peasant archery societies in China before the Mongol conquest. See Ma Duanlin, *Wenxian tongkao*, ch. 156, pp. 1360–61. The Mongols prohibited or discouraged the Chinese population from bearing weapons, but archers from Xuzhou and Baoding are still listed among the "special forces" during the Ming dynasty – see chapter 6, the section "Japanese Pirates."

57   Lynn, "Recalculating French army growth." There is a more specific argument that the *trace italienne* was responsible for the increase in army size. Parker, *The military revolution*, pp. 13–14 and 24–26. However, this argument has come under attack. Lynn, "The *trace italienne* and the growth of armies," pp. 172–74; Hall, "The changing face of siege warfare." In any event, growth in army size was not unique to Europe; see chapter 8, the section "Firearms After 1700."

For two perspectives on the political effects of army growth, see Tilly, *Coercion, capital, and European states*; Downing, *The military revolution and political change.*

58 Kist, "Commentary"; Parker, *The military revolution*, pp. 18–24. See, however, González de León, "'Doctors of the military discipline,'" p. 73.

59 McNeill, *Keeping together in time.*

60 Since Hungary and the Balkans turned into a battleground between the Habsburg and Ottoman empires, their fate diverged from that of Poland and Russia, and they are discussed in chapter 4. See, however, McNeill, *Europe's steppe frontier*, for a unified treatment of this region.

61 Wimmer, "L'infanterie dans l'armée polonaise," pp. 78–87; Majewski, "The Polish art of war." The editors' introduction to Majewski's article neatly summarizes the Polish dilemma: "This then was the basic dichotomy in the Polish military situation – the mobile cavalry armies needed to deal with Tatar raids were useless against fixed fortifications, while the infantry and artillery which were vital to any siege were ineffective in the vast open steppes where distance and an elusive enemy rendered them superfluous." Fedorowicz et al., *A republic of nobles*, p. 180.

62 On Russia, see generally Halperin, *Russia and the Golden Horde*; Crummey, *The formation of Muscovy*; Hellie, "Warfare."

63 See Ostrowski, *Muscovy and the Mongols*, pp. 155–56.

64 Alef, "Muscovite military reforms."

65 Collins, "The military organization." See also Fletcher, *Of the Russian commonwealth*, pp. 191–95.

66 Shaw, "Southern frontiers of Muscovy," pp. 119–24; Hellie, *Enserfment and military change in Muscovy*, pp. 174–80; Davies, "Village into garrison"; O'Rourke, *Warriors and peasants.*

67 Keep, *Soldiers of the Tsar*, pp. 13–55; Hellie, *Enserfment and military change in Muscovy*, pp. 21–48.

68 Fletcher, *Of the Russian commonwealth*, p. 183.

69 Ostrowski, *Muscovy and the Mongols*, pp. 50–52.

70 Quoted in Hellie, *Enserfment and military change in Muscovy*, p. 155.

71 Esper, "Military self-sufficiency and weapons technology," pp. 187–89; Hellie, *Enserfment and military change in Muscovy*, pp. 152–60.

72 Esper, "Military self-sufficiency and weapons technology," pp. 194–96.

73 Fletcher, *Of the Russian commonwealth*, p. 186. Esper, "Military self-sufficiency and weapons technology," p. 197: "Russia could not maintain simultaneously a massive cavalry force along its steppe frontier and a large infantry army equipped with firearms for use against its western neighbors."

74 Esper, "Military self-sufficiency and weapons technology," pp. 192–94; Keep, *Soldiers of the tsar*, pp. 60–73; Hellie, *Enserfment and military change in Muscovy*, pp. 161–64.

75 Hellie, *Enserfment and military change in Muscovy*, p. 164. Fletcher, *Of the Russian commonwealth*, pp. 185–86, describes the portable walls.

76 Kortepeter, *Ottoman imperialism during the Reformation*, pp. 25–34 and 107–14.

77 Hellie, *Enserfment and military change in Muscovy*, pp. 181–225; Keep, *Soldiers of the tsar*, pp. 80–87.

78 The distances and times from Beijing to Outer Mongolia were about twice as great. Compare the 20,000 tons mentioned here to the 15,600 tons needed for the first Yongle campaign in Mongolia in 1410, the 28,900 tons needed for the third campaign in 1422, and the 35,000 tons that would have been needed to support 150,000 men operating in the Ordos in the late 1400s.
79 Stevens, *Soldiers on the steppe*, pp. 111–21.
80 Cardan, *The book*, pp. 189–90.
81 Hassig, *Mexico and the Spanish conquest*; Hassig, "War, politics and the conquest of Mexico"; Guilmartin, "The military revolution," pp. 308–13; Guilmartin, "Technology and asymmetrics," pp. 45–49; Clendinnen, "'Fierce and unnatural cruelty.'"
82 McNeill, *Plagues and peoples*, pp. 176–207; Cook, *Born to die*; Crosby, *Ecological imperialism*.
83 Malone, *The skulking way of war*; Starkey, *European and Native American warfare*.
84 Scammell, *The first imperial age*, pp. 72–74; Fowler, "The Great Plains," pp. 6–12.
85 McDermott, *A guide to the Indian wars*, pp. 1–90; Perry, "Warfare on the pampas." The comparison between Mongolia and the Great Plains was suggested by Lattimore, "The frontier in history," p. 487, n. 15.
86 Hodgson, *The venture of Islam*, vol. 1, pp. 57–60, coined the term "Islamdom" by analogy to "Christendom."

4. Western Islamdom

1 Dunn, *The adventures of Ibn Battuta*.
2 al-Hassan, "Iron and steel technology"; Hill, *Islamic science and engineering*, pp. 216–19; al-Hassan and Hill, *Islamic technology*, pp. 115–17 and 251–58; Partington, *A history of Greek fire and gunpowder*, pp. 197–207.
3 Partington, *A history of Greek fire and gunpowder*, pp. 202–3; Needham et al., *Science and civilisation in China*, vol. 5, pt. 7, p. 259; Iqtidar Alam Khan, "The role of the Mongols," pp. 35–38; Iqtidar Alam Khan, "The coming of gunpowder," pp. 35–39.
4 For alternatives, see Canfield, *Turko-Persia in historical perspective*, pp. 1–34; Haneda, "Toho Isuramu sekai no seiritsu"; Haneda, *Mosuku ga kataru Isuramushi*, pp. 165–69.
5 On the early Ottoman empire, see generally Inalcik, *The Ottoman empire*; Imber, *The Ottoman empire*; Kafadar, *Between two worlds*.
6 Petrović, "Fire-arms in the Balkans," traces the spread of firearms. A Turkish chronicler of the late 1400s states in his account of the Ottoman army at Kossovo in 1389 that "the gunner Haydar was in the center because he was a complete master at firing guns." Neşri, *Kitab-ı cihan-nüma*, vol. 1, p. 282. Another (though slightly earlier) Turkish chronicler of the late 1400s states in his account of the siege of Constantinople in 1396–97 that "They set up mangonels from a good many spots," then adds as an aside, "At that time there were not many cannon; great numbers of cannon existed in the time of Sultan Murat [r. 1421–44 and 1446–51], son of Sultan Mehmet Han." 'Aşıkpaşazade, *Tevarih-i al-i 'Osman*, p. 66. The latter in particular is rather dubious evidence. On the

difficulties inherent in using these sources, see Kafadar, *Between two worlds*. Uzunçarşılı cited these instances in 1944 and added a third not supported by any citation (*Osmanlı devleti teşkilâtından kapukulu ocakları*, vol. 2, p. 35), but Wittek cast doubt on all three in 1956 and concluded that the Ottomans did not use firearms before 1400 (Ayalon, *Gunpowder and firearms*, pp. 141–42). Heywood, writing in 1980, supports Wittek's conclusions, which he suggests were largely the work of V. J. Parry ("Notes on the production," pp. 2–6). There has been not much movement since then, and Halaçoğlu still cited all three instances in his 1995 survey of early Ottoman institutions (*XIV–XVII. yüzyıllarda Osmanlılarda devlet teşkilâtı ve sosyal yapı*, pp. 53–54). The only really new material was a Bulgarian manuscript cited by Petrović in 1975 for the siege of 1396–97 ("Fire-arms in the Balkans," p. 175). However, Bartusis stated in 1992 that the manuscript describes firearms being used by certain "Franks" defending the city, not by the Ottomans besieging it (*The late Byzantine army*, p. 336). The evidence for firearms at Ankara in 1402 is very indirect: the report of a Spanish ambassador to the court of Temür might be read to imply that Temür captured gunmakers from the Ottomans, but as explained in chapter 5, note 2, the word used (*ballesteros*) could as easily mean "crossbowmen."

7 Bartusis, *The late Byzantine army*, pp. 336–41; Barbaro, *Diary of the siege of Constantinople*; Jones, *The siege of Constantinople*.

8 Guilmartin, "Ideology and conflict," p. 737.

9 Gibbon, *The decline and fall*, vol. 3, p. 686; Brummett, *Ottoman seapower and Levantine diplomacy*, pp. 27–87; Isom-Verhaaren, "An Ottoman report about Martin Luther"; Inalcik, "The socio-political effects."

10 Inalcik, *The Ottoman empire*, pp. 76–88.

11 Inalcik, "The socio-political effects," p. 204; Imber, *The Ottoman empire*, pp. 269–70. The Hungarians undoubtedly learned this from the Hussites – see chapter 3, "The Introduction of Firearms."

12 Uzunçarşılı, *Osmanlı devleti teşkilâtından kapukulu ocakları*, vol. 2, p. 97; Halaçoğlu, *XIV–XVII. yüzyıllarda Osmanlılarda devlet teşkilâtı ve sosyal yapı*, p. 54.

13 Fodor, "Making a living on the frontiers"; Inalcik, "The military and fiscal transformation," pp. 283–311; Inalcik, "The socio-political effects," pp. 195–202; Parry, "La manière de combattre," pp. 218–19.

14 Inalcik, *The Ottoman empire*, pp. 110–18. There were also cavalrymen without revenue assignments who fought as volunteers, in hopes of earning a revenue assignment or at least gathering booty. These faded away after 1595, their role taken over by Tatars. Imber, *The Ottoman empire*, pp. 260–65.

15 On Ottoman-Crimean relations see Kortepeter, *Ottoman imperialism during the Reformation*; on Ottoman-Kurdish relations see Özoğlu, "State-tribe relations."

16 Murphey, *Ottoman warfare*, pp. 35–49.

17 Murphey, *Ottoman warfare*, pp. 65–103.

18 Parry, "Materials of war in the Ottoman empire"; Ágoston, "Ottoman gunpowder production in Hungary"; Ágoston, "Gunpowder for the sultan's army." Bronze (copper and tin) was more common for military uses, even though brass (copper and zinc) was more common for nonmilitary uses, suggesting some European influence in the casting of cannon. Williams, "Ottoman military technology," p. 365.

19 Inalcik, "The military and fiscal transformation," pp. 283–311; Inalcik, "The socio-political effects," pp. 195–202; Jennings, "Firearms, bandits, and gun-control."

20 Imber, "The navy of Süleyman the Magnificent"; Imber, *The Ottoman empire*, pp. 287–317; Imber, "The reconstruction of the Ottoman fleet"; Grant, "Rethinking the Ottoman 'decline,'" pp. 184–90.

21 Szakály, "Nándorfehérvár."

22 Perjés, *The fall of the medieval kingdom of Hungary*, pp. 173–272.

23 Oman, *A history of the art of war*, pp. 666–77.

24 Hegyi, "The Ottoman network of fortresses"; Ágoston, "The costs of the Ottoman fortress-system."

25 Pálffy, "The border defense system."

26 Kelenik, "The military revolution in Hungary."

27 Finkel, *The administration of warfare*, pp. 7–20; Kortepeter, *Ottoman imperialism during the Reformation*, pp. 123–210. The four fortresses were Bihács (1592), Győr (1594), Eger (1596), and Kanizsa (1600), although Győr was retaken by the Habsburgs in 1598. Note that the Ottomans had also captured Esztergom (1543) and Szolnok (1552) earlier in the century.

28 Schmidt, "The Egri campaign of 1596."

29 Parry, "La manière de combattre," pp. 224–25. For Hungarian wagon laagers in 1526 see Perjés, *The fall of the medieval kingdom of Hungary*, pp. 238–39 and 265. The ratio of musketeers to pikemen among the French and Walloon mercenaries in the Habsburg army suggests that they may have been intended for deployment behind wagon laagers.

30 Inalcik, "The socio-political effects," pp. 199–202; Jennings, "Firearms, bandits, and gun-control." Recall how the Russians had the same problem in the Thirteen Years' War with Poland and resorted to drafting peasants.

31 Parry, "La manière de combattre," pp. 218–35.

32 Parry, "La manière de combattre," pp. 235–56; Black, *European warfare*, pp. 11–15 and 204–6.

33 On Ottoman seapower, in addition to the sources cited in note 20, see generally Brummet, *Ottoman seapower and Levantine diplomacy*, pp. 89–121; Kahane, Kahane, and Tietze, *The Lingua Franca in the Levant*, pp. 3–45; Hess, "The Ottoman conquest of Egypt"; Hess, "The evolution of the Ottoman seaborne empire."

34 Pryor, *Geography, technology, and war*; Guilmartin, *Gunpowder and galleys*.

35 Uzunçarşılı, *Osmanlı devletinin merkez*, p. 512; Bostan, *Osmanlı bahriye teşkilâtı*, pp. 84–85. "Cannon" is *top*, "culverin" is *darbzen* (also *zarbzan*), and "swivel gun" is *prangı*, as indicated in the text.

36 Oman, *A history of the art of war*, pp. 634–48.

37 Guilmartin, *Gunpowder and galleys*, pp. 176–93; Oman, *A history of the art of war*, pp. 708–17.

38 Oman, *A history of the art of war*, pp. 723–29.

39 Guilmartin, *Gunpowder and galleys*, pp. 236–50; Oman, *A history of the art of war*, pp. 729–34.

40 Imber, "The reconstruction of the Ottoman fleet"; Oman, *A history of the art of war*, pp. 734–37.

41 Guilmartin, *Gunpowder and galleys*, pp. 39–41 and 262–73.

42 Brummett, *Ottoman seapower and Levantine diplomacy*, pp. 171–74; Guilmartin, *Gunpowder and galleys*, pp. 7–15.
43 Busbecq, *The Turkish letters*, pp. 123–24.
44 Busbecq, *The Turkish letters*, p. 123.
45 Busbecq, *The Turkish letters*, p. 123. In other words, not only was the excuse ridiculous, but it was so lame that the ministers, despite their anger, and despite the solemnity of the occasion, could not help laughing at it. This story is quoted, without the punch line, in Jennings, "Firearms, bandits, and gun-control," p. 341.
46 Ágoston, "Ottoman artillery and European military technology"; Heywood, "The activities of the state cannon-foundry," pp. 214–15; Murphey, *Ottoman warfare*, pp. 109–11.
47 Imber, *The Ottoman empire*, pp. 273–74; Lewis, *The Muslim discovery of Europe*, pp. 223–27; Grant, "Rethinking the Ottoman 'decline,'" pp. 181–84; Mallett, "Part I: c.1400–1508," p. 84; Boxer, "Asian potentates and European artillery," p. 157; Boxer, "Notes on early European military influences," p. 73; Eltis, *The military revolution in sixteenth-century Europe*; Phillips, *The Anglo-Scots wars*, pp. 66 and 75. Nor were renegades always fated to live out the rest of their lives in Islamdom, never to return home; see Matar, *Turks, Moors, and Englishmen*, pp. 44–63.
48 Grant, "Rethinking the Ottoman 'decline.'"
49 Busbecq for one put a less negative spin on Ottoman borrowing when he wrote: "For no other nation has shown less reluctance to adopt the useful inventions of others; for example, they have appropriated to their own use large and small cannons and many other of our discoveries." Busbecq, *The Turkish letters*, p. 135. On the "Schooles of Warre," see Tallett, *War and society in early-modern Europe*, p. 41.
50 I follow common practice in using the word *mamluk* in lower case to refer to slave soldiers and "Mamluk" in upper case to refer to the rulers of Egypt and Syria (themselves *mamluks*) from 1260 to 1517. On the Mamluks, see generally Holt, *The age of the Crusades*; Irwin, *The Middle East in the Middle Ages*; Petry, *Protectors or praetorians?*
51 Smith, "'Ayn Jalut"; Amitai-Preiss; *Mongols and Mamluks*, pp. 26–48.
52 Ayalon, "The Muslim city," pp. 319–20. Popper, *Egypt and Syria*, vol. 15, p. 47, gives the figure of 686 miles, accurate to within 10 percent, for the road from Cairo to Aleppo. Mamluk raids toward the south did open the way for Bedouin nomads to migrate up the Nile River valley in the 1300s, destroying the Nubian kingdom of Maqurra in the process, but the sultanate did not expand in that direction. Oliver, *Medieval Africa*, pp. 99–100.
53 Ayalon, "Studies on the structure," pp. 206–16.
54 Ayalon, *Gunpowder and firearms*, pp. 2–4 and 59. The cargo manifest of a Catalan ship bound for Alexandria in 1394 lists three bombards and forty stones. DeVries, "A 1445 reference to shipboard artillery," p. 820. This does not prove introduction from Europe, but it suggests it was a possibility. There is some controversy over the interpretation of terminology in dating the arrival of firearms. The Arabic term *naft* was used to mean "naphtha" before it came to mean "gunpowder." (Naphtha is a petroleum-based incendiary material similar to Greek fire.) Ayalon believes naphtha was obsolete by the 1200s and that practically

any occurrence of the word *naft* after that point meant firearms (*Gunpowder and firearms*, pp. 9–24). Popper believes *naft* sometimes still meant naphtha in the 1300s (Ibn Taghri-Birdi, *History of Egypt*, pt. 4, p. 104, n. 23 and pt. 5, p. 34, n. 5), but unfortunately he did not explain his critique in depth. Partington also questions whether Ayalon is correct in reading *naft* in all cases after 1360 as gunpowder or firearm, but admits that Ayalon might be correct "if knowledge of gunpowder reached the Arabs from China" (*A history of Greek fire and gunpowder*, pp. 195–97). I find Ayalon persuasive on this issue, particularly his point that *midfaʿ* and *mukhula* rarely appear together with *naft* before the 1300s (*Gunpowder and firearms*, pp. 17–21). Since the earliest mentions of firearms use the rather unambiguous terms *midfaʿ* and *mukhula* anyway (pp. 2–3), there seems no reason to doubt the dates given by Ayalon for the introduction of firearms to Egypt.

55 Ayalon, "Studies on the structure," pp. 204–22; Rabie, "The training of the Mamluk faris."

56 Ayalon, "Studies on the structure," pp. 448–59; Ayalon, "The wafidiya"; Haarmann, "Joseph's law."

57 Ayalon, "The auxiliary forces."

58 Ayalon, "The Muslim city," pp. 328–29.

59 Ayalon, *Gunpowder and firearms*, pp. 52–59; Levanoni, "Rank-and-file Mamluks versus amirs." This paragraph is an attempt to strike a balance between Smith and Amitai-Preiss; see Smith, "Nomads on ponies vs. slaves on horses," and Amitai-Preiss, "Whither the Ilkhanid army?" pp. 257–58.

60 Ayalon, "Studies on the structure," pp. 204, 222–28, 462–64, and 70–73; Ayalon, "Plague and its effects"; Ayalon, "Some remarks on the economic decline"; Ayalon, "Mamluk: military slavery," pp. 2–6; Petry, *Protectors or praetorians?* pp. 81–130.

61 Ayalon, "The Mamluks and naval power"; Chaudhuri, *Trade and civilisation*, p. 148; Pryor, *Geography, technology, and war*, pp. 132–34.

62 France, *Western warfare*, pp. 211–20.

63 Amitai-Preiss, *Mongols and Mamluks*; Amitai-Preiss, "Whither the Ilkhanid army?"; Irwin, *The Middle East in the Middle Ages*, pp. 46, 66–67, and 99–101; Smith, "Mongol society and military."

64 Ibn Taghri-Birdi, *History of Egypt*, pt. 4, pp. 65 and 104.

65 Har-El, *Struggle for domination*.

66 Ayalon, *Gunpowder and firearms*, pp. 63–66. Ayalon sees one camel for two men as a sign of the disregard and contempt for musketeers, but how many armies in Europe had one animal for every two infantrymen? I see the allocation of camels to infantry as an indication of the problems of moving bodies of infantry across stretches of desert in Egypt and Syria.

67 Ayalon, *Gunpowder and firearms*, pp. 66–71, 73–74, and 79; Lewis, *Race and slavery in the Middle East*, pp. 65–69. See note 78.

68 Ayalon, *Gunpowder and firearms*, pp. 71–83. Ayalon does not translate *al-tabaqa al-khāmisa*; Petry translates it as "the Fifth Corps." The Mamluks used *tabaqa* to mean "the school or barracks in which [a *mamluk*] received his recruit training," but the musketeers were not the fifth one of these; *khāmisa* is instead a reference to the unit's payday, which was not one of the four paydays on which other units were paid. Ayalon, *Gunpowder and firearms*, p. 71. The basic

meaning of *tabaqa* in Arabic is class, rank, degree, or level; if "fifth class" has a pejorative connotation in English, so much the better in this context.

69 Subrahmanyam, *The Portuguese empire in Asia*, p. 66; Hess, "The evolution of the Ottoman seaborne empire," pp. 1907–11; Brummet, *Ottoman seapower and Levantine diplomacy*, pp. 111–21.

70 Ibn Iyas, *An account*, p. 37.

71 Ibn Iyas, *An account*, pp. 41–45; Petry, *Protectors or praetorians?* pp. 24–26 and 54; Uzunçarşılı, *Osmanlı tarihi*, vol. 2, pp. 284–86; Stripling, *The Ottoman Turks and the Arabs*, pp. 43–48.

72 Ayalon, *Gunpowder and firearms*, p. 91. See note 78. Ayalon quotes many more such outlandish remarks.

73 Ibn Iyas, *An account*, pp. 54 and 88.

74 Ibn Iyas, *Bada'i' al-zuhur fi waqa'i' al-duhur*, vol. 5, p. 134; cf. Ibn Iyas, *An account*, pp. 100–1.

75 Ayalon, *Gunpowder and firearms*, pp. 85–86.

76 Ibn Iyas, *Bada'i' al-zuhur fi waqa'i' al-duhur*, vol. 5, p. 145; cf. Ibn Iyas, *An account*, pp. 111–12.

77 Ibn Iyas, *An account*, pp. 111–13; Uzunçarşılı, *Osmanlı tarihi*, vol. 2, pp. 288–90; Stripling, *The Ottoman Turks and the Arabs*, pp. 52–54.

78 This is of course the primary explanation advanced by Ayalon, the acknowledged expert on the *mamluk* system and the authority for the larger part of the account presented earlier, in his *Gunpowder and firearms in the Mamluk kingdom*. In addition to his primary explanation, Ayalon also gives six secondary explanations. Elements of my explanation appear among his secondary explanations, and at most I differ with the priority he assigns them.

Prejudice against firearms is hard to disentangle from other motives. If the *mamluks* objected to black musketeers being given place of pride in parades or being singled out for special honors, was it because they carried muskets or was it because they were black slaves? Ayalon himself commented that black slaves were "the most despised human element in the kingdom." Ayalon, *Gunpowder and firearms*, p. 66; see also Lewis, *Race and slavery in the Middle East*.

If the *mamluks* resented the musketeers of the fifth class and stole their pay, was it because they carried muskets or because they were paid money that might have gone to meeting arrears in pay owed to the *mamluks* themselves? In 1488, the *mamluks* robbed the governor-inspector who was on his way to recruit Bedouin tribal cavalry for the expedition against the Ottomans and stole all the money he was carrying – there is no question of prejudice against firearms here. Har-El, *Struggle for domination*, p. 168.

The *mamluks* were sent to Syria to fight the Ottomans while the musketeers were sent to the Indian Ocean to fight the Portuguese. Was it because there was more glory in fighting the Ottomans? Ayalon, *Gunpowder and firearms*, pp. 80–81. Not necessarily. The bow and the lance were not "obsolete weapons" in 1516, as Ayalon would have it, and it would have been folly to deploy cavalry on ships when war threatened on land. If the decision coincides with sound military judgment, what does it prove about social prejudice?

Ayalon puts too much weight on the fantastic ravings of Ibn Zunbul and others after Marj Dabiq. Ayalon, *Gunpowder and firearms*, pp. 86–97. Such pitifully transparent *ex post* justifications are not serious evidence for *ex ante* motivations. Although Ibn Zunbul denounces firearms as cowardly and base weapons that strike men unawares from afar (unlike bows?), the implication that *mamluks* were too scrupulous to use firearms is laughable. Cowardly and base acts litter Mamluk history, not excepting the battle of Marj Dabiq itself.

If such scruples had any effect at all, they should have militated against the use of firearms in coups, where leaders were competing for the allegiance of their fellow *mamluks*. Presumably, a leader might alienate his own supporters by taking actions that were widely viewed as incompatible with the dignity or reputation of his faction. Yet *mamluks* routinely used firearms against each other in such politically charged situations. See Ibn Taghri-Birdi, *History of Egypt*, pt. 1, pp. 36–39, 71–74, and 100–1; pt. 2, pp. 82 and 192–93; pt. 5, pp. 12, 34, 45, and 48; pt. 6, pp. 16 and 18.

Petry, *Protectors or praetorians?* pp. 191–96 suggests that Sultan al-Ghawri may have seen the fifth class as an instrument of autocracy and a counterweight to the *mamluks*. Certainly the sultan had different interests than the rest of the *mamluks*, any of whom would have been happy to replace him, so this suggestion is not implausible. However, it does suffer somewhat from the implicit assumption that musketeers could handle swordsmen in streetfighting. In the only instance where they actually fought in the streets of Cairo, the black musketeers were beaten badly by the royal *mamluks*. Ayalon, *Gunpowder and firearms*, pp. 69–71; Lewis, *Race and slavery in the Middle East*, pp. 68–69.

79 On the Maghrib, see generally Abun-Nasr, *A history of the Maghrib*.

80 Ibn Khaldun, *Kitab al-'ibar*, vol. 1, pp. 269–70; cf. Rosenthal, *The muqaddimah*, vol. 1, p. 302.

81 Cook, *The hundred years war for Morocco*, pp. 119–27. Some sources give very early dates for the use of firearms in Granada. See Partington, *A history of Greek fire and gunpowder*, pp. 190–95; al-Hassan, *Islamic technology*, pp. 112–15. The earliest dates are highly suspect. Some of them precede the earliest mention of firearms in Europe or the Middle East. Unless firearms were invented there, and there is no evidence for independent invention in Granada other than these dates, it is hard to see how firearms could have reached Granada without passing through Europe or the Middle East.

82 Hess, "Firearms and the decline"; Abun-Nasr, *A history of the Maghrib*, pp. 144–58 and 168–70.

83 Cook, *The hundred years war for Morocco*. Morocco was a popular destination for English adventurers in particular. Matar, *Turks, Moors, and Englishmen*, pp. 46–50 and 63–66.

84 On sub-Saharan Africa, see generally Oliver, *Medieval Africa*.

85 Thornton, *Warfare in Atlantic Africa*, pp. 19–40 and 75–97; Webb, *Desert frontier*, pp. 68–96; Elbl, "The horse in fifteenth-century Senegambia."

86 Thornton, *Warfare in Atlantic Africa*, pp. 5–6, 41–74, and 127–39; Smith, *Warfare & diplomacy*, pp. 80–86.

87 Thornton, *Warfare in Atlantic Africa*, pp. 99–125.

88 On eastern Africa, see generally Pearson, *Port cities and intruders*. Vasco da Gama encountered an Indian ship armed with guns at Malindi, in what is now Kenya, on the first voyage to India in 1498. Subrahmanyam, *The career and legend*, p. 120.

89 Smith, *Warfare & diplomacy*, pp. 65 and 85–86.

5. Eastern Islamdom

1   On Iran, see generally Morgan, *Medieval Persia*.
2   On Temür, see generally Manz, *The rise and rule of Tamerlane*. Adshead quotes the Spanish emissary Clavijo to suggest that Temür introduced firearms to Transoxania from Turkey, but Clavijo uses the word *ballesteros*, which could just as easily mean "crossbowmen." Adshead, *Central Asia in world history*, p. 123, quoting Clavijo, *Embassy to Tamerlane*, pp. 287–88. There is no evidence that Temür used firearms in any battle or siege, although there is evidence that might be interpreted to refer to other gunpowder weapons. Professor John E. Woods was very kind to share with me his work in progress on the history of firearms in Iran and Central Asia, which examines this evidence in detail.
3   On the Aqquyunlu and Qaraquyunlu, see generally Woods, *The Aqquyunlu*; Roemer, "The Türkmen dynasties."
4   Woods, *The Aqquyunlu*, pp. 90 and 114–20.
5   Minorsky, *Persia*, p. 36; Woods, *The Aqquyunlu*, pp. 134, 138, and 143.
6   On the Safavids, see generally Savory, *Iran under the Safavids*; Roemer, "The Safavid period."
7   Quoted in Gandjei, "Turkish in the Safavid court of Isfahan," p. 314. See also note 11.
8   Haneda, *Le chah et les Qizilbas*, pp. 48–61 and 144–215. See Savory, *History of Shah 'Abbas the Great*, vol. 2, pp. 852, 856, 860, and 874, for examples of auxiliaries from the early 1600s.
9   Savory, *Iran under the Safavids*, p. 44; Savory, "The Sherley myth," p. 75; Khandamir, *Tarikh-i habib al-siyar*, vol. 2, pp. 580 and 583; Boxer, "Asian potentates and European artillery," pp. 156–57; Bacqué-Grammont, *Les Ottomans*, pp. 158–74. Bacqué-Grammont suspects that Isma'il's 2,000 muskets and 40 cannon were just for show, to deter the Ottomans from attacking.
10 Minorsky, *Tadhkirat al-muluk*, pp. 32–33; Savory, *Iran under the Safavids*, pp. 78–82; Haneda, *Le chah et les Qizilbas*, pp. 208–15. The *ghulams* took over the duties of the bodyguard, and the quiver-bearers became indistinguishable from the tribal levies.
11 The Safavid shahs were avid hunters, and they organized great hunts in the Mongol fashion, where a ring of hunters surrounded the prey and drove them over the course of many days or weeks into a small killing zone. See, for example, Khandamir, *Tarikh-i habib al-siyar*, vol. 2, pp. 581, 587, and 595. The use of swords in hunting may seem fantastical, but these same sources also attest to that practice.
12 Haneda, *Le chah et les Qizilbas*, pp. 29–47, 173–74, and 191–93; Savory, *Iran under the Safavids*, p. 79.
13 Smith, "Mongol nomadism and Middle Eastern geography."
14 Most estimates of the Ottoman army are higher, but anything much higher than 70,000 is probably unrealistic; see chapter 4, the section "The Ottoman Military." The figure of 20,000 is the larger of the two estimates recorded in Haneda, *Le chah et les Qizilbas*, p. 41. In 1516, two years after the battle, an escaped prisoner reported to the Ottomans that Isma'il only had some 18,000 effectives. Bacqué-Grammont, *Les Ottomans*, pp. 178–85.

15 The commander responsible for the bad advice was Durmish Khan Shamlu. The story does not appear in the contemporary *Tarikh-i habib al-siyar*, but it seems credible. Khandamir was a native of Herat, and he composed the work in the years 1521–24, when Durmish Khan Shamlu was regent for the heir apparent Tahmasp in Herat; the preface to the work describes the arrival of Durmish Khan Shamlu as a turning point in the author's life. Quinn, *Historical writing*, pp. 15–16 and 41. (I have been unable to consult the other major contemporary source, Sadr al-Din Sultan Ibrahim Amini Haravi's *Futuhat-i shahi*, which has yet to be published.) However, Khandamir's son included the story in his own continuation to his father's history, completed in 1550. Amir Mahmud, *Zayl-i habib al-siyar*, p. 86. Amir Mahmud was writing during the reign of Tahmasp, who supposedly cursed the name of Durmish Khan whenever the battle of Chaldiran was mentioned. Savory, *Iran under the Safavids*, p. 41. The story found its way into later works, such as Hasan Beg Rumlu's *Ahsan al-tavarikh* (pp. 189–90), completed in 1578; Iskandar Beg Munshi's *Tarikh-i 'alam-ara-yi 'Abbasi* (vol. 1, p. 42) (cf. Savory, *History of Shah 'Abbas the Great*, vol. 1, p. 68), completed in 1629; and Bijan's *Jahan-gusha'i-yi khaqan-i sahibqiran* (see Sarwar, *History of Shah Isma'il Safawi*, p. 79), completed in the 1670s.

16 Bacqué-Grammont, *Les Ottomans*, pp. 147–57.

17 Busbecq, *The Turkish letters*, p. 110.

18 Savory, *Iran under the Safavids*, pp. 58–59; Roemer, "The Safavid period," pp. 241–44.

19 Savory, *Iran under the Safavids*, pp. 72–77; Roemer, "The Safavid period," pp. 257–58.

20 Savory, *Iran under the Safavids*, pp. 85–86; Savory, *History of Shah 'Abbas the Great*, vol. 2, pp. 826–31. Ottoman sources may tell a different tale. The *Tarih-i Naim* from the beginning of the 1700s states that 1,500 Ottomans fought 15,000 Safavids at this battle, and that while they were overwhelmed by superior numbers, "their caution and acuteness was such, that only ten or fifteen of them tasted the cup of martyrdom, a circumstance which seems truly wonderful." Naima, *Annals of the Turkish empire*, pp. 243–45.

21 Savory, *History of Shah 'Abbas the Great*, vol. 2, pp. 832–33, 841, and 873.

22 Iskandar Beg Munshi, *Tarikh-i 'alam-ara-yi 'Abbasi*, vol. 2, p. 645; cf. Savory, *History of Shah 'Abbas the Great*, vol. 2, p. 835.

23 Savory, *Iran under the Safavids*, pp. 86–87; Savory, *History of Shah 'Abbas the Great*, vol. 2, pp. 833–36 and 843–47.

24 Iskandar Beg Munshi, *Tarikh-i 'alam-ara-yi 'Abbasi*, vol. 2, p. 697; cf. Savory, *History of Shah 'Abbas the Great*, vol. 2, p. 889. Note that there was no expectation that the city itself would resist the Ottomans, but that 'Abbas did plan to defend the newly rebuilt citadel.

25 Savory, *Iran under the Safavids*, p. 87; Savory, *History of Shah 'Abbas the Great*, vol. 2, pp. 856–64, 874–76, and 886–98. Compare the account in the *Tarih-i Naim*, which states that the Ottomans woke up the next morning to find that the Safavids had carried away the Ottoman cannon while they were sleeping, and that virtually all of the Ottoman casualties were actually just former Celali rebels anyway. Naima, *Annals of the Turkish empire*, pp. 300–5.

26 Savory, *Iran under the Safavids*, pp. 88–91; Savory, *History of Shah 'Abbas the Great*, vol. 2, pp. 1253–60 and 1265–80.

27 Khandamir, *Tarikh-i habib al-siyar*, vol. 2, pp. 589–92 and 596–604; Savory, *Iran under the Safavids*, pp. 35–38.

28 Amir Mahmud, *Zayl-i habib al-siyar*, pp. 148–49; Hasan Beg Rumlu, *Ahsan al-tavarikh*, pp. 281–85. The *Ahsan al-tavarikh* (p. 281) says ʿ*arābahā-yi pur az zarbzan[-i] farangī*, or "wagons full of Frankish culverins," but the better reading is probably ʿ*arābahā-yi pur az zarbzan [va] farangī*. It is unlikely that *farangī* refers to Europeans here. See chapter 6, note 10.

29 McChesney, "The conquest of Herat." Some sources mention treachery as a secondary byproduct of the shortage of food. Assaults in the sixth and eight months of the siege had been driven back by Safavid musket fire, and one in the ninth month had briefly captured one tower.

30 Savory, *Iran under the Safavids*, pp. 83–84; Savory, *History of Shah ʿAbbas the Great*, vol. 2, pp. 741–60.

31 Savory, *History of Shah ʿAbbas the Great*, vol. 2, pp. 809–22. Roemer, "The Safavid period," p. 267, states that the Safavids "lost the greater part of their new artillery in the process," but unfortunately he cites no source.

32 Inalcik, "The socio-political effects," pp. 208–10. Vámbéry, *The travels and adventures*, contains the firsthand account of an Ottoman naval commander who scuttled his fleet on the coast of India (see the section "The Portuguese") and returned to Turkey by way of Transoxania in the mid-1550s. The Uzbeks already had firearms at that time.

33 Matthee, "Unwalled cities and restless nomads," p. 406: "Just as it made sense for Poland to strengthen her cavalry rather than her infantry and artillery against the horsemen of the Ukrainian steppes, and to concentrate on armies that could win battles rather than conduct sieges, so it made sense for the Safavids to concentrate on strengthening their cavalry and its traditional warfare."

34 Morgan, *Medieval Persia*, p. 90, stresses the resilience of nomadic confederations.

35 Arjomand, *The shadow of God*, pp. 110–12.

36 See Khandamir, *Tarikh-i habib al-siyar*, vol. 2, pp. 574, 579–80, 583, 588, and 591 for examples.

37 Matthee, "Unwalled cities and restless nomads."

38 Quoted in Lockhart, "The Persian army in the Safavi period," p. 90.

39 Minorsky, *Tadhkirat al-muluk*, p. 33; Matthee, "Unwalled cities and restless nomads," pp. 392–96.

40 The Ottoman–Safavid rivalry was one example of technological asymmetry, a topic that has attracted much attention lately. See Guilmartin, "Technology and asymmetrics." Technological asymmetry is usually discussed as a function of unequal development, but it does occur as a result of geographical asymmetry, as in the Battle of the Atlantic.

41 Gommans, "The silent frontier of South Asia," pp. 1–17; Wink, "India and the Turko-Mongol frontier," pp. 211–19.

42 Gommans, *The rise of the Indo-Afghan empire*, pp. 71–74; Wink, *Al-Hind*, vol. 2, pp. 83–94.

43 Wink, "India and the Turko-Mongol frontier," pp. 219–30.

44 Wink, *Al-Hind*, vol. 2, pp. 95–110; Digby, *War-horse and elephant*.

45 Kolff, *Naukar, Rajput & Sepoy*.

46 Wink, *Al-Hind*, vol. 2, pp. 111–49; Jackson, *The Delhi sultanate*, pp. 17–18. The conquest of northern India was completed by the Ghurids, who were actually

Tajiks – in other words, Iranians. However, like the Safavids, their army consisted largely of Turkish cavalry. Wink, *Al-Hind*, vol. 2, pp. 137–40.

47 Gommans, "The silent frontier of South Asia," pp. 17–22.

48 On the Delhi sultanate, see generally Jackson, *The Delhi sultanate*. The *mamluk* institution was weaker in India than in Egypt or Turkey: there were fewer of them, they lacked systematic training, and they shared power with freeborn ministers. Wink, *Al-Hind*, vol. 2, pp. 186–90.

49 Stein, *Vijayanagara*.

50 Stein, *Peasant state and society*, pp. 400–405; Digby, *War-horse and elephant*; Wink, *Al-Hind*, vol. 2, pp. 79–110; Polo, *The travels of Marco Polo*, vol. 1, pp. 83–84, and vol. 2, pp. 340, 395, and 438; Pires, *The Suma Oriental of Tome Pires*, pp. 17, 20–21, and 43–44; Barbosa, *The book of Duarte Barbosa*, pp. 178, 189, and 211; Nuniz, *Chronicle of Fernão Nuniz*, pp. 294 and 362; Albuquerque, *The commentaries*, p. 76. One of the princes of Jolof in west Africa in the same period also paid the Portuguese for both dead and live horses, for the same reason. Elbl, "The horse in fifteenth-century Senegambia," pp. 100–1.

51 Iqtidar Alam Khan, "Origin and development of gunpowder technology," pp. 20–26; Iqtidar Alam Khan, "The role of the Mongols"; Iqtidar Alam Khan, "The coming of gunpowder," pp. 39–44. In addition to sulfur, saltpeter, and charcoal, the ingredients recorded by Prataparudradeva include such oddities as orpiment, mercury, and cinnabar, all found in Chinese formulas as well. Gode, "The history of fire-works in India," pp. 42–44. The earliest Arab gunpowder formulas also contained similar ingredients: "The most notable feature of Hasan al-Rammah's work is the extensive use it makes of Chinese material." Partington, *A history of Greek fire and gunpowder*, p. 202.

52 Iqtidar Alam Khan, "Origin and development of gunpowder technology," pp. 26–29; Iqtidar Alam Khan, "The role of the Mongols," pp. 40–41. The idea of the rocket may have been borrowed by the Indians from the Chinese; the British borrowed the idea from the Indians at the end of the 1700s and used them, most famously, against the Americans at Fort McHenry in 1814. Black, *European warfare*, pp. 45–46; Olejar, "Rockets in early American wars."

53 Iqtidar Alam Khan, "Early use of cannon and musket"; Boxer, "Asian potentates and European artillery," pp. 158–59.

54 Barbosa, *The book of Duarte Barbosa*, pp. 132 and 165; Albuquerque, *The commentaries*, pp. 58, 65, 88–90, and 99; Pires, *The Suma Oriental of Tome Pires*, p. 77. Subrahmanyam, "State formation and transformation," p. 97, suggests that the importance of firearms is exaggerated even for the 1500s and 1600s, but Rao et al., *Symbols of substance*, pp. 220–41, shows that firearms were prevalent enough to make their presence felt in poetry and legend.

55 Barbosa, *The book of Duarte Barbosa*, pp. 119–20; Pires, *The Suma Oriental of Tome Pires*, pp. 34 and 52; Albuquerque, *The commentaries*, p. 96; Paes, *Narrative of Domingo Paes*, p. 267. The word for "musket" is some variation on the Turkish *tüfek*: *thuppaki* in Tamil (*Tamil Lexicon*, p. 1969) and *tupaki* in Telugu (Brown, *Dictionary Telugu-English*, p. 538). Similarly, the word for "cannon" is some variation on the Turkish *prangı*: *piranki* in Tamil (*Tamil Lexicon*, p. 2736) and *pirangi* in Telugu (Brown, *Dictionary Telugu-English*, p. 761).

56 Iqbal Ghani Khan, "Metallurgy in medieval India," pp. 72–77. Pacey, *Technology in world civilization*, pp. 26–33, suggests that India, together with Southeast

Asia, had a technology complex that did not favor machines or large-scale engineering works, especially as compared with China or Iran. However, any conclusions along these lines are necessarily very tentative.

57 "Cannon" is *top*; "culverin" is *zarbzan*; "swivel gun" is *farangī*.

58 Babur's memoirs recount this anecdote from a siege in Afghanistan in 1519: "Although the Bajauris had never seen firearms, they showed no fear at the sound of matchlocks, and even made fun of the noise with obscene gestures when they heard it." Babur, *Baburnama* 217a (Mano, p. 344; Thackston, p. 270), quoting Thackston translation. There is a ten-year lacuna in the memoirs before this year, encompassing the period when Babur may have first acquired firearms.

59 Babur, *Baburnama* 264a (Mano, p. 426; Thackston, p. 323), quoting Thackston translation. I have changed the translation of *Rūm* from "Anatolian" to "Ottoman" consistent with my translation of it elsewhere.

60 Babur, *Baburnama* 310b–311a and 322b–323a (Mano, pp. 495–96 and 511; Thackston, pp. 372 and 384–85), quoting Thackston translation. Note that Babur was not ashamed to give his gunners and musketeers credit for their accomplishments in battle, even in an official victory proclamation.

61 Babur, *Baburnama* 336b–337a and 370a–b (Mano, pp. 533–34 and 590–92; Thackston, pp. 399–400 and 434–36).

62 Babur, *Baburnama* 302a–b, 309a, 311a, 331b, and 352b (Mano, pp. 483, 493, 495, 561–62, and 595; Thackston, pp. 363, 371, 372, 395, and 417).

63 Streusand, *The formation of the Mughal empire*, pp. 51–57. For a description of the Mughal army under Akbar, see Monserrate, *The commentary of Father Monserrate*, pp. 68–90.

64 Streusand, *The formation of the Mughal empire*, pp. 57–69; Gommans, "Warhorse and gunpowder in India," pp. 114–15; McNeill, *The age of gunpowder empires*, p. 38.

65 Gommans, "Warhorse and gunpowder in India," pp. 107–9; Gommans, *The rise of the Indo-Afghan empire*; Gordon, *The Marathas*, pp. 37–41, 81–84, and 189–90. The Mughal royal army only covered about three miles a day in the 1600s, when it moved at all. Streusand, *The formation of the Mughal empire*, p. 64; Gommans, "Warhorse and gunpowder in India," p. 107. The same was true of the royal army of Vijayanagara in the 1500s. Barbosa, *The book of Duarte Barbosa*, pp. 227–28; Nuniz, *Chronicle of Fernão Nuniz*, pp. 316–18.

66 On the Portuguese in the Indian Ocean, see generally Boxer, *The Portuguese seaborne empire*; Subrahmanyam, *The Portuguese empire in Asia*; Barendse, *The Arabian seas*. On trade in the Indian Ocean before the Portuguese, see generally Abu-Lughod, *Before European hegemony*; Chaudhuri, *Trade and civilisation*; Chaudhuri, *Asia before Europe*. The seminal work on firearms technology and overseas expansion in general is Cipolla, *Guns, sails and empires*.

67 Subrahmanyam, *The career and legend*, pp. 128–30.

68 The bullion drain was so great that some Portuguese complained it was the Indians who discovered them instead of vice versa. Boxer, "Preface," p. xi. As much as a third or more of the total production of the mines in the New World may have found its way to East Asia, either directly by the Manila galleon or indirectly through Europe. Atwell, "Ming China and the emerging world economy," pp. 376–416.

69 Quoted in Parker, "The *Dreadnought* revolution of Tudor England," p. 276.

70 Correa, *The three voyages of Vasco da Gama*, pp. 367–68. The Calicut fleet had firearms too, but less powerful ones.

71 Pearson, *The Portuguese in India*, pp. 36–39; Subrahmanyam, *The political economy of commerce*, pp. 252–97.

72 On reasons for the rise of navies, see Glete, *Warfare at sea*, pp. 60–75. The suppression of piracy was a by-product of the existence of navies, but not a reason for their existence.

73 It is true that Indian ships were not sturdy enough to carry cannon, since their hulls were sewn rather than nailed together, but Indian shipwrights soon learned to build European designs. Chaudhuri, *Trade and civilisation*, pp. 140–41, and 148–51.

74 Commissariat, *A history of Gujarat*, vol. 1, discusses this period of Gujarat's history.

75 Özbaran, "Ottoman naval policy in the south"; Glete, *Warfare at sea*, pp. 76–89; Dames, "The Portuguese and the Turks in the Indian Ocean"; Vámbéry, *The travels and adventures*; Guilmartin, *Gunpowder and galleys*, pp. 7–15. The European naval powers used oared ships extensively themselves, but only as auxiliaries to the galleons; they could rarely take on galleons alone.

76 Oliver, *Medieval Africa*, pp. 123–27; Özbaran, "Ottoman naval policy in the south"; Commissariat, *A history of Gujarat*, vol. 1, pp. 337–39 and 441–48; Inalcik, "The socio-political effects," pp. 202–6. It can be difficult to separate mercenaries from official representatives. However, Mustafa Rumi Khan was the nephew of Salman Reis, who had commanded the Ottoman Red Sea fleet in 1517 and had participated in the Mamluk–Gujarati expedition of 1507 as well, and he apparently went to India at his father's behest. Khaja Safar was said to have had janissaries under his command.

77 Lenman, "The transition to European military ascendancy."

78 Boxer, "Anglo-Portuguese rivalry in the Persian Gulf."

79 On Southeast Asia, see generally Reid, *Southeast Asia*; Tarling, *The Cambridge history of Southeast Asia*. Emmerson, "'Southeast Asia,'" discusses the history of the term. This term raises the same problems as "East Asia" (see chapter 1, note 9), but there is no satisfactory alternative.

80 Reid, *Southeast Asia*, vol. 1, pp. 121–29.

81 Ma Duanlin, *Wenxian tongkao*, vol. 2, p. 2610.

82 Reid, *Southeast Asia*, vol. 1, pp. 106–19.

83 Reid, *Southeast Asia*, vol. 2, pp. 220–21; Andaya, "Interactions with the outside world," pp. 36–41.

84 Boxer, "Asian potentates and European artillery," pp. 160–64.

85 Subrahmanyam, *The Portuguese empire in Asia*, pp. 249–61; Lieberman, "Europeans, trade, and the unification of Burma." Note, however, that when a band of Portuguese adventurers tried to establish their own colony on the coast, they lacked the manpower to prevent Upper Burma from conquering Lower Burma, or even to defend themselves. Scammell, "Indigenous assistance," and Thompson, "The military superiority thesis," stress that Europeans were able to exploit local divisions in the societies they colonized and win over local allies to provide much-needed manpower, supplies, and information. This is certainly correct. However, there are innumerable examples where non-European powers took advantage of European rivalries too. If the consequences were different, it was

only because the European powers had seized the initiative and, more often than not, were fighting in someone else's land.

86 Andaya, "Interactions with the outside world," p. 46; Tana, "An alternative Vietnam?"; Cooke, "Regionalism and the nature of Nguyen rule," pp. 150–57; Pires, *The Suma Oriental of Tome Pires*, p. 115. Comments in the sources on the proficiency of local soldiers range from dismissive to respectful. See Boxer, "Asian potentates and European artillery," pp. 162–68; Reid, *Southeast Asia*, vol. 2, pp. 224–33. Andaya downplays the importance of firearms in transforming local warfare, stating that "these new guns were employed in traditional war tactics where the war elephant, pikes, swords, and spears were still the dominant weaponry" (p. 51), but the same could be said of sixteenth-century Europe, except for the elephants.

87 Andaya, "Interactions with the outside world," pp. 43–44; Reid, *Southeast Asia*, vol. 2, pp. 224–29. The musket and the swivel gun were also the most popular European weapons in China in the 1500s – see chapter 6, the section "Foreign Firearms."

88 Manguin, "The vanishing *jong*"; Reid, *Southeast Asia*, vol. 2, pp. 36–43; Andaya, "Interactions with the outside world," pp. 34–35. Portuguese galleys provoked similar admiration in China – see chapter 6, the section "Japanese Pirates."

89 Boxer, "The Achinese attack on Malacca."

6. China from 1500

1 See, for example, Qian, *Chengshou choulüe*, 5/18a–23b (pp. 717–28); Zhao, *Shenqi pu* 4/6a–b (p. 2708).

2 *Ming shilu*, Jiajing, 38/14a (vol. 72, p. 975) (1524.4 *jiwei*), 68/10b–11a (vol. 74, pp. 1562–63) (1526.9 *jihai*). The discovery of the sea route did not spell the end of the land route. Rossabi, "The 'decline' of the Central Asian caravan trade"; McNeill, "The eccentricity of wheels."

3 Ferguson, *Letters from Portuguese captives*, pp. 1–16 (quote on p. 1); Wills, "Relations with maritime Europeans," pp. 335–41.

4 For Chinese views of foreign weapons, see, for example, the sources cited in note 1. For foreign views of Chinese weapons, see Lach, *Asia in the making of Europe*, vol. 1, p. 787.

5 Yan, *Shuyu zhouzi lu*, ch. 9, p. 320.

6 Fok, "Early Ming images of the Portuguese." This rumor is reminiscent of the Arab belief that the crusaders were cannibals. Maalouf, *The Crusades through Arab eyes*, pp. 39–40. It is hard to believe that that reputation could have persisted for 400 years, but both the crusaders and the Portuguese were known by the same name, some variant of the Arabic root FRNJ. See note 10.

7 Yan, *Shuyu zhouzi lu*, ch. 9, pp. 321–22. The Chinese imagined that Portugal was located somewhere in the vicinity of Melaka. *Mingshi*, ch. 325, p. 8430. They also believed that the Portuguese were related to Javanese cannibals. Yan, *Shuyu zhouzi lu*, ch. 9, p. 320. The swivel gun was sometimes known as the "Javanese gun." Zhang, *Xiaoshan leigao* 9/9b (vol. 1272, p. 392). One of the letters written by Portuguese captives in China tells a different story about the introduction of the swivel gun. According to this source, a Christian Chinese who had

come back to China with the Portuguese fleet in 1521 claimed to know "how to make gunpowder, bombards and galleys," and did in fact make gunpowder and bombards for the emperor. Ferguson, *Letters from Portuguese captives*, pp. 116–17.

8 Ferguson, *Letters from Portuguese captives*, pp. 16–22.

9 Wang, *Zhongguo huoqi shi*, pp. 115–25. There are some indications that the swivel gun may have been known in China even before the Portuguese themselves first arrived. Needham et al., *Science and civilisation in China*, vol. 5, pt. 7, pp. 369–73. Wang rejects the evidence as weak and contradictory, but his conclusion is based partly on the presumption that the Chinese could only have obtained the swivel gun from the Portuguese, which overlooks the involvement of the Turks in India and the Indian Ocean. The Ottoman *prangı* may have reached the Indian Ocean before either Ottoman or Portuguese ships did. See note 10.

10 Zheng, *Chouhai tubian* 13/32b (p. 1257), Wang, *Dengtan bijiu*, huoqi 6b (p. 3916), and *Mingshi*, ch. 92, p. 2264, all insist that *folangji* was the name of a people, not of a gun, evidently because there was some confusion among Chinese of the time as to which was the original meaning. Pelliot, "Le Hoja et le Sayyid Husain," took the opposite view, that the gun reached China before the Portuguese did, and that the name *folangji* was applied first to the gun and then by extension to the people. However, neither explanation is correct.

We know from Chinese descriptions and pictures that the *folangji* was a breech-loading swivel gun. The Portuguese and Spanish called this kind of cannon a *verso*, undoubtedly because it was loaded from the back (the breech) rather than from the front (the muzzle). Guilmartin, *Gunpowder and galleys*, pp. 159–61. In Malay it was known as *rentaka* or *lantaka*. Andaya, "Interactions with the outside world," pp. 31 and 44–45; Mardsen, *A dictionary and grammar*, vol. 1, p. 150. None of these words is related to *folangji*.

The nearest cognates are found in Dravidian languages. Significantly, both Tamil and Telugu have similar but different words for "European" and "cannon": *paranki* as opposed to *pīranki* in Tamil (*Tamil Lexicon*, p. 2559) and *parangi* as opposed to *pīrangi* in Telugu (Brown, *Dictionary Telugu-English*, p. 715). Despite the false etymologies in these two dictionaries and elsewhere (e.g., Yule and Burnell, *Hobson-Jobson*, p. 353) that link these pairs of words together, it is highly unlikely there would be two separate words in these languages if they did not actually represent two separate loanwords.

Another cognate is found in northern India. Babur's gunners used a weapon that he called *farangī* in his memoirs, but Babur never described it. Bacqué-Grammont (p. 333) translates *farangī* as "couleuvrine," which is a kind of cannon. Thackston (p. 437) follows Beveridge (p. 667, n. 3) in treating *farangī* as a kind of catapult. Mano (p. 590, n. 1110) notes this interpretation but takes no position on it.

However, the word *farangī* appears elsewhere in Persian literature in its meaning as a weapon. Hasan Beg Rumlu uses *farangī* half a dozen times in his chronicle *Ahsan al-tavarikh*, four times in descriptions of Ottoman land battles (Marj Dabiq on pp. 205, 207, and 208 and Raydaniya on p. 214) and twice in accounts of Ottoman sea battles (Lepanto 1499 on p. 58 and Lepanto 1571 on p. 583).

The Ottoman name for the breech-loading swivel gun was *pranği*. It is the same weapon as the *folangji*, and the name is similar in sound to both *folangji* and *farangī*. Because the word is written differently in Ottoman (PRNGY) than in Persian (FRNGY), it must have been borrowed into Persian from Ottoman through the spoken language. Tamil and Telugu probably borrowed the word directly from the Ottomans, since the Tamil and Telugu versions are much closer to the original Ottoman than to the Persian.

The word *pranği* comes from the Italian *braga*, short for *pezzo a braga* or *petriera a braga*, a breech-loading wrought-iron stone-firing cannon. Kahane, Kahane, and Tietze, *The Lingua Franca in the Levant*, pp. 122–23. Italian *braga* (<Latin *braca*) is the singular for "pants" or "breeches." There is an obvious similarity between a breech-loader and half of a pair of pants, where the barrel of the cannon is like the leg of the pants. "Breech" in English is derived from a Germanic cognate of the Latin *braca*, both of which in turn are derived from the same Indo-European root.

On the other hand, *folangji* as the name of a people goes back to the Arabic *franj* or some variant thereof, and from there perhaps to the "Franks." Alternatively, it is possible that the Arabic *franj* originally referred to the "Varangians," the Viking palace guards in Constantinople, many of whom were Anglo-Saxon refugees from the Norman conquest in 1066. Logan, *The Vikings in history*, pp. 196–97; Bartusis, *The late Byzantine army*, pp. 271–76 and 281–83.

Therefore, it seems that *folangji* represents two different words, the name of a people *and* the name of a gun, with two different etymologies. The two words remained distinct in Ottoman, Tamil, and Telugu, but they merged together in Persian and in Chinese.

11　Needham et al., *Science and civilisation in China*, vol. 5, pt. 7, pp. 369–76; Qi, *Lianbing shiji*, zaji 5/20b–22b (pp. 642–46).

12　Hall, *Weapons and warfare in Renaissance Europe*, p. 93. Breech-loaders were later cast from iron even in Europe, because their high rate of fire made them useful in some situations.

13　Needham et al., *Science and civilisation in China*, vol. 5, pt. 7, pp. 429–55; Zhao, *Shenqi pu* 2/2a–3b (pp. 2680–81).

14　Yan, *Shuyu zhouzi lu*, ch. 9, p. 321 (emphasis added).

15　Zheng, *Chouhai tubian* 13/33a (p. 1258) (emphasis added). See also Needham et al., *Science and civilisation in China*, vol. 5, pt. 7, p. 376.

16　Huang, *1587*, pp. 156–88.

17　Qi, *Jixiao xinshu* 15/10b–11b (pp. 484–86). Needham et al., *Science and civilisation in China*, vol. 5, pt. 7, pp. 358–59, translates the passage from the 1584 edition rather than the earlier 1560 edition. Hall, "The corning of gunpowder," pp. 89–90 and n. 12, and *Weapons and warfare in Renaissance Europe*, p. 73 and n. 15, is misled into presuming that the earliest record in Chinese sources occurs in 1584 and that the Jesuits were responsible for introducing the technique. As explained here, the Chinese seem to have learned about corned powder in the early 1520s.

18　Udagawa, *Higashi Ajia*, pp. 354–74 and 439–47; Tanaka, *Wako*, p. 157. However, wagons were not adopted in Korea, perhaps because the terrain was too rugged. Udagawa, *Higashi Ajia*, pp. 100–7. The same was true of Japan.

19 Needham et al., *Science and civilisation in China*, vol. 5, pt. 7, pp. 335–37; Qi, *Lianbing shiji*, zaji 5/17a–20a (pp. 635–41).

20 Zhao, *Shenqi pu* 2/35a (p. 2697).

21 Needham et al., *Science and civilisation in China*, vol. 5, pt. 7, p. 220, suggests that the widespread use of bamboo in China was one inspiration for the invention of firearms. The design of this particular weapon tends to support this notion.

22 Wang, *Zhongguo huoqi shi*, pp. 141–42 and 153–59. It is worth noting in this regard that the Chinese had a long history of designing multiple-shot crossbows as well. See Needham et al., *Science and civilisation in China*, vol. 5, pt. 6, pp. 155–70.

23 Zhao, *Shenqi pu* 2/36a (p. 2697), 5/9b (p. 2724), 5/18a–b (p. 2728), 5/23a–b (p. 2730); Qi, *Jixiao xinshu* 15/1a (p. 464).

24 He, *Binglu* 11/36a–37a (pp. 653–54).

25 See chapter 3, the section "Guns and Bows."

26 Zhao, *Shenqi pu* 5/9b (p. 2724).

27 Zhao, *Shenqi pu* 2/23a and 25b and 4/9b–10a (pp. 2691–92 and 2710).

28 Zhao, *Shenqi pu* 4/16b–17a (pp. 2713–14).

29 Huang, 1587, pp. 160–76, presents a picture of the sixteenth-century Ming military as hopelessly primitive and backward. He emphasizes the breakdown of the official supply system but slights the informal mechanisms that arose in its place. Furthermore, a closer look at the supposed backwardness of the Ming military raises the question, backward compared to whom? Huang seems to be comparing sixteenth-century China with eighteenth-century Europe. Sixteenth-century European armies did not have standardized equipment supplied by centralized government arsenals.

30 Huang, "Military expenditures in sixteenth-century Ming China," pp. 40–43; Robinson, *Bandits, eunuchs, and the son of heaven*, pp. 71–91; Nimick, "Ch'i Chi-kuang and I-wu county."

31 Okuyama, "Mindai no hokuhen."

32 Tani, "A study on horse administration," pp. 92–94.

33 Robinson, *Bandits, eunuchs, and the son of heaven*, pp. 91–96. This is not to say that privately organized military units did not exist. See Robinson, pp. 81–88.

34 Wang, *Zhongguo huoqi shi*, pp. 72, 76, and 88–89.

35 Anonymous, *Caolu jinglüe* 1/5b (p. 12).

36 Huang, "The Liao-tung campaign of 1619," p. 47, also concludes that Qi Jiguang had firearms produced outside of the official workshops in Beijing, but he unaccountably presumes that they were produced under the old system, and from this concludes that the quality of the firearms must have been poor. Since Huang himself has shown in great detail elsewhere how the old system had broken down by the 1500s, it seems more reasonable to presume that the firearms were purchased, so there is no reason to think that the quality was necessarily poor.

37 Despite the suggestive term "fire wheel," this weapon does not appear to be a wheel lock. It appears instead that the *yang* mechanism would hold the match.

38 Tang, *Wubian* 5/10a–12a (vol. 13, pp. 729–33). *Tael* and *catty* are words of Malay origin traditionally used to translate the Chinese *liang* (1.3 ounces) and *jin* (1.3 pounds) respectively. See Yule and Burnell, *Hobson-Jobson*, pp. 175 and 888.

39 Hai, *Beiwang ji* 2/33b–35a (vol. 1286, pp. 50–51). Note that the magistrate, Hai Rui, was a notorious stickler for correct procedure. Huang, 1587, pp. 130–55.

40 Zhao, *Shenqi pu* 5/20b–21a (p. 2729).

41 Zhao Shizhen noted that "Gunpowder and bullets are not found in the market; who would dare to manufacture them privately?" Zhao, *Shenqi pu* 4/5a (p. 2708). However, this does not mean that inventors were forbidden, or even discouraged, from coming up with new weapons. There is a long history of inventions being presented to the emperor, and the prospect of a reward may have compensated for the lack of patent protection and the inability to pursue the private market. European governments provided similar inducements to investors in the form of prizes, as with the prize for the calculation of longitude.

42 Andaya, "Interactions with the outside world," pp. 2–5 and 22–24; Atwell, "Ming China and the emerging world economy"; Von Glahn, *Fountain of fortune*.

43 So, *Japanese piracy in Ming China*, pp. 1–50; Tanaka, *Wako*, pp. 11–129. Smuggling and piracy represented a continuum of responses to official restrictions on trade. The vigorous enforcement of state-imposed monopolies ratcheted up the level of violence and forced out the less heavily armed smugglers, but the resulting monopoly profits attracted more heavily armed pirates by compensating them for the greater costs and greater risks of competing by force. Pérotin-Dumon, "The pirate and the emperor."

44 Zheng, *Chouhai tubian* 13/3b–20a (pp. 1199–1232); Qi, *Jixiao xinshu* 18/12b–13a (pp. 636–39). The Fujian ship also carried 520 pounds of coarse gunpowder and 130 pounds of musket gunpowder, demonstrating that the Chinese were already producing different types of gunpowder for different purposes. See note 17.

45 Zheng, *Chouhai tubian* 13/33a (p. 1258).

46 Yan, *Shuyu zhouzi lu*, ch. 9, p. 321.

47 Zheng, *Chouhai tubian* 13/18a (p. 1228): "The boat is called the centipede boat, from its shape. Its design came from the southeastern barbarians. They use it particularly to carry swivel guns.... It is a special technique of the island barbarians. Its method was transmitted to China, and China has used it to control the barbarians."

48 Zheng, *Chouhai tubian* 12/2a–14b (pp. 1018–43).

49 Zheng, *Chouhai tubian* 11/76a–81a (pp. 963–73).

50 Hucker, "Hsü Tsung-hsien's campaign."

51 Huang, *1587*, pp. 160–74.

52 So, *Japanese piracy in Ming China*, pp. 50–202; Tanaka, *Wako*, pp. 131–60.

53 Struve, *The southern Ming*, pp. 154–66 and 178–93; Wills, *Pepper, guns and parleys*; Croizier, *Koxinga*.

54 Zheng, *Chouhai tubian* 12/4a (p. 1022), 12/9b (p. 1033).

55 Meskill, *Ch'oe Pu's diary*, is the story of a Korean official shipwrecked off the Chinese shore in 1488 that illustrates the casual violence of this frontier very well. After being robbed by pirates, Ch'oe Pu and his party barely escaped being lynched by the local Chinese inhabitants and murdered by the local Chinese soldiers as well.

56 Waldron, *The Great Wall of China*, pp. 110–12.

57 Geiss, "The Cheng-te reign"; Geiss, "The Leopard Quarter." See also Robinson, *Bandits, eunuchs, and the son of heaven*, for the Zhengde emperor's relationship with men of violence in the capital region.

58 Waldron, *The Great Wall of China*, pp. 122–39.

59 Waldron, *The Great Wall of China*, pp. 151–60.

60 Zheng, *Chouhai tubian* 12/13b (p. 1041). See Waldron, *The Great Wall of China*, pp. 194–226, on the myths surrounding the Great Wall.

61 Waldron, *The Great Wall of China*, pp. 150–51.

62 Momiyama, *Kan teikoku*, pp. 45–116. This could hardly have been a case of institutional continuity, since there was no Great Wall for long stretches of time between the Han and Ming dynasties, and much of what we know about the Han dynasty Great Wall comes from twentieth-century archeological excavations. Luttwak, *The grand strategy*, gives an account of Roman border defenses that is also quite similar in many respects; see especially pp. 61–80 and 130–45 for tactical and operational considerations.

63 Zhao, *Shenqi pu* 4/17a (p. 2714). One might have said "mobility" instead of "protection," but when Zhao Shizhen was writing in 1598, Chinese forces had their hands full simply not getting run over by Mongol cavalry.

64 *Mingshi*, ch. 92, p. 2266. This source is one of the many that pairs wagons with ships: "The Central Plain [of north China] uses wagon warfare, and the southeast uses ships and oars, and the two of them are the most critical in military affairs." See also Zhao, *Shenqi pu* 4/17a–18a (p. 2714); Qian, *Chengshou choulüe*, 5/14a (p. 709) (paraphrasing Zhao Shizhen). Both wagons and ships provided protection, and both mounted guns for offensive purposes. To the Chinese, wagons were the ships of the steppe.

65 Qi, *Lianbing shiji*, zaji 6/22a–26a (pp. 723–31).

66 Qi, *Lianbing shiji*, zaji 6/15a–21b (pp. 709–22); Huang, *1587*, p. 180. The "crouching tiger" cannon consisted of a two-foot-long barrel weighing about 47 pounds together with heavy hoops and spikes that were driven into the ground to hold the cannon in place and absorb the recoil. Qi, *Lianbing shiji*, zaji 5/24b–27b (pp. 650–56). It had no carriage or wheels, so it was light enough to carry on horseback, even though the powder and shot and all the associated equipment would have raised the total weight to several times the weight of the barrel, and it probably could be set up fairly easily. Qi Jiguang suggested that it be supplied with 30 stone shot and 900 lead shot, the latter probably being grapeshot for antipersonnel use. There was also a weapon known as the "beehive" that was similar in concept to the crouching tiger cannon. The beehive was light enough to be carried on a strap over the shoulder, and it was fixed in the ground by prongs when fired. It fired a single blast of 100 pellets, something like a Claymore mine in effect.

67 Qi, *Lianbing shiji*, zaji 6/9a–14b (pp. 697–708); Huang, *1587*, pp. 179–81.

68 Zhao, *Shenqi pu* 2/17a (p. 2688), has the "Picture of five men firing guns in rotation"; 4/19a (p. 2715) explains how it worked. Chinese crossbowmen had used volley fire in the 1000s. Zeng, *Wujing zongyao* 2/28b (p. 104). Qi Jiguang had suggested applying volley fire to muskets in 1560. Qi, *Jixiao xinshu* 2/4a–b (pp. 113–14).

69 Qi, *Lianbing shiji*, zaji 6/11b (p. 702).

70 Qi, *Lianbing shiji*, zaji 6/28b (p. 736).

71 Qi, *Lianbing shiji*, zaji 6/29b (p. 738).

72 Geiss, "The Chia-ching reign," pp. 476–78; Waldron, *The Great Wall of China*, pp. 185–87; Jagchid and Symons, *Peace, war, and trade*, pp. 86–103.

73 Jagchid and Symons, *Peace, war, and trade*, pp. 104–13.

74 Tani, "A study on horse administration," pp. 94–96.
75 See Huang, "Military expenditures in sixteenth-century Ming China," on personnel costs, and Waldron, *The Great Wall of China*, pp. 160–64, on walls. Huang, *Taxation and government finance*, puts the blame for budget deficits on the inflexibility of the bureaucracy.
76 Lorge, "War and warfare in China," argues that Chinese warfare changed little between 1450 and 1815. I see the early Qing armies as a combination of the cavalry of the early Ming armies and the firearms of the late Ming armies, so I agree that the change from the early Ming to the early Qing was not too great, even while I argue that the change from the early Ming to the late Ming was.
77 Di Cosmo, "Military aspects of the Manchu wars," pp. 351–54.
·78 Wakeman, *The great enterprise*, vol. 1, pp. 23–86; Huang, "The Liao-tung campaign of 1619."
79 Boxer, "Portuguese military expeditions," pp. 108–9.
80 *Ming shi*, ch. 325, p. 8437; Huang, "Sun Yuanhua," p. 227; Wang, *Zhongguo huoqi shi*, pp. 224–28. The Dutch were called the "red-haired barbarians."
81 Boxer, "Portuguese military expeditions"; Huang, "Sun Yuanhua."
82 Huang, "Sun Yuanhua," pp. 234–36; Wang, *Zhongguo huoqi shi*, pp. 228–30.
83 Boxer, "Portuguese military expeditions"; Huang, "Sun Yuanhua," pp. 237–254; Wang, *Zhongguo huoqi shi*, pp. 230–33. Wang says it was 2,000 muskets.
84 Parsons, *Peasant rebellions*; Wakeman, *The great enterprise*, vol. 1, pp. 225–318.

The mutinies and rebellions of the 1630s and 1640s were not the only incidents of civil disorder under the Ming, of course. On banditry and rebellion in the Ming, see generally Robinson, *Bandits, eunuchs, and the son of heaven*; Tong, *Disorder under heaven*. Tong counted 630 incidents of banditry or rebellion over the 277 years of the Ming dynasty, with close to two-thirds of them (413) consisting of predatory banditry, and over four-fifths of them (522) occurring after 1506. Most incidents occurred during one of three peaks: the reign of the Zhengde emperor between 1505 and 1521 (the period discussed by Robinson), the Japanese piracy of the mid-1500s (discussed earlier), and the rebellions that brought down the dynasty (discussed here).

In the early stages of their activities (banditry and rebellion were treated as earlier and later stages of the same phenomenon), bandits rarely challenged government troops or attacked major cities. They had no incentive to fight except when cornered, and as a general rule they seem to have kept horses for quick get-aways. In the advanced stages of their activities, rebels did engage in battles and sieges, providing some scope for the deployment of firearms against them, but by that point they would already have sapped the dynasty's strength from within and undermined its ability to produce more or better firearms.

85 Parker, *The military revolution*, pp. 143–44, suggests that Chinese city walls were too massive for cannon to make any impression on them, and "That may be why indigenous heavy artillery never really developed there." It is more likely that the Chinese did not develop heavy cannon because there were no walled cities for them to attack, and that they did not develop a counterpart to the *trace italienne* because no one was pointing heavy cannon at their walled cities either. The walls of Beijing may have been built on a monumental scale for political effect, but otherwise there is no reason to think that Chinese city walls were particularly thick.

86 Perdue, "Culture, history, and imperial Chinese strategy"; Waley-Cohen, "Religion, war, and empire-building"; Snellgrove and Richardson, *A cultural history of Tibet*, pp. 197–201.

87 Perdue, "Military mobilization"; Perdue, "Fate and fortune in Central Eurasian warfare."

7. Korea and Japan

1 On Korea, see generally Lee, *A new history of Korea*.

2 Jeon, *Science and technology in Korea*, pp. 233–57.

3 Ho, *Choson sidae*, pp. 5–7.

4 Henthorn, *Korea*; Ho, *Choson sidae*, pp. 7–8. Korean sailors and soldiers participated in the Mongol invasions of Japan in 1274 and 1281, but the evidence for gunpowder weapons in those invasions is now disputed; see note 21.

5 Quoted in Ho, *Choson sidae*, p. 9. "Councilor" is *chech'uhoe*.

6 Jeon, *Science and technology in Korea*, pp. 185–87 and 207–11; Ho, *Choson sidae*, pp. 9–22.

7 Jeon, *Science and technology in Korea*, pp. 187–205; Ho, *Choson sidae*, pp. 21–22, 27–28, 44–45, and 187–88; Udagawa, *Higashi Ajia*, pp. 290–302.

8 Ho, *Choson sidae*, pp. 187–88, accepts the story in the sources, but the evidence cited in the following paragraph suggests the story is false.

9 Udagawa, *Higashi Ajia*, p. 339. The inscription on the breech is in Chinese, and the date in the inscription uses the reign name of the Chinese emperor, but the Koreans kept official records in Chinese and followed the Chinese calendar, so this tells us nothing either way. However, the date is written with a combination of reign name and cyclical characters, which seems more typical of Korean than Chinese; Chinese firearms tend to bear the reign name and the reign year. Furthermore, whereas the name of the craftsman can be read in either Korean or Chinese, the surname is very common in Korea and quite rare in China.

10 Ho, *Choson sidae*, pp. 141, 178, 187–88, and 252.

11 On early Japanese warfare, see generally Farris, *Heavenly warriors*; Friday, *Hired swords*. For the Chinese system from which the Japanese borrowed, see Graff, *Medieval Chinese warfare*.

12 Farris, *Heavenly warriors*, pp. 16 and 101–3; Varley, *Warriors of Japan*, pp. 5 and 13–17; Wilson, "The way of the bow and arrow," pp. 187–88. The sixteenth-century Portuguese Jesuit Luís Fróis remarked that "Our horses are very beautiful; those of Japan are much inferior to them." Fróis, *Européens & Japonais*, VIII.1. Horses in Europe were specially bred for size and strength to support the weight of armor. Davis, *The medieval warhorse*.

13 Farris, *Heavenly warriors*, pp. 104–13; Friday, *Hired swords*, pp. 45–56.

14 Farris, *Population, disease, and land*.

15 Nishigaya, *Jokaku*, pp. 46–71.

16 Yamamura, "The growth of commerce."

17 Nishigaya, *Jokaku*, pp. 82–101. Errard noted in 1604 that princes in Europe planned cities around fortresses to "render that place capable of containing the number of subjects that he will be advised, lodged in length and in breadth, enough to accommodate there a garrison sufficient to resist the efforts of his enemies." Errard, *La fortification*, p. 61.

18 Nishigaya, *Jokaku*, pp. 102–7. The entrepôt cities were too useful to the warlords to be destroyed, and the urban institutions in the Kyoto marketing network generally survived under Nobunaga and Hideyoshi. Wakita, "The social and economic consequences," pp. 110–21. However, the great cities of the 1600s and 1700s like Edo and Osaka generally developed out of castle towns. Nakai and McClain, "Commercial change and urban growth," pp. 519–38.

19 Varley, *The Onin War*; Shinji, "Ashigaru"; Ono, *Nihon heino shiron*, pp. 143–49.

20 Suzuki, "Yari"; Ono, *Nihon heino shiron*, pp. 98–102; Arai Hakuseki, *Honcho gunki ko*, ch. 7, pp. 343–44. The crossbow had been introduced to Japan from China, via Korea, in the 600s, but it fell out of use in the 900s as infantry was de-emphasized. Farris, *Heavenly warriors*, pp. 113–16.

21 For an argument that Chinese-style firearms had been introduced to Japan in earlier centuries, see Hora, *Teppo*, pp. 36–56. The only evidence for the use of gunpowder weapons in the Mongol invasions of Japan is a picture of a bombshell in a Japanese scroll that was apparently added some time after the scroll was completed. See Conlan, *In little need of divine intervention*, pp. 12 and 73.

22 Murai, "Teppo denrai saiko"; Hora, *Teppo*, pp. 3–12. The year 1543 is given in the *Teppoki*, the basic source for the introduction of firearms to Tanegashima, written at the beginning of the 1600s. The year 1542 is given in a Portuguese work from 1563. Galvano, *The discoveries of the world*, pp. 229–30. The latter not only is more contemporary but also fits in better with other evidence about the parties involved.

23 For an argument that European-style firearms had been introduced to Japan by pirates in earlier years, see Udagawa, *Teppo denrai*, pp. 11–15.

24 Hora, *Teppo*, pp. 154–60. The phenomenon of warrior-monks is well known. The usual term is *sōhei*, but Fróis knew them as *nengoros*: "Our monks always desire peace, and wars are more repugnant to them than anything else; the *nengoros* make a profession of war, and their services are hired by lords for combat." Fróis, *Européens & Japonais*, IV.10. In Tokugawa times there was still a company of musketeers known as the Negoro-gumi.

25 Morris, "The city of Sakai"; Hora, *Teppo*, pp. 160–70. The other center of firearms production in the Tokugawa period, aside from Sakai, was Kunitomo village in Omi province. It is not clear whether Kunitomo was an important center in the 1500s, however, as the only source on the early history of Kunitomo is late and unreliable. See Hora, *Teppo*, pp. 178–205.

26 Udagawa, *Teppo denrai*, pp. 25–30.

27 Elisonas, "Christianity and the daimyo."

28 Udagawa, *Teppo denrai*, pp. 18–23, 30–36, and 38–52. It may seem odd that people gave away these new weapons so freely, but probably no one yet realized just how revolutionary they would be, and their diplomatic value initially outweighed their military value. Still, no one seems to have given them away to neighbors either. It had been many centuries since Japan had been united, and Kyoto must have seemed very far away from Kyushu, far enough that the gift would not come back to haunt the giver.

29 On Nobunaga, see generally Lamers, *Japonius tyrannus*.

30 Ota, *Shinchoko ki* (shukan), pp. 22, 26, and 49; Nishigaya, *Kosho Oda Nobunaga jiten*, pp. 97–98.

31   Ota, *Shinchoko ki* (shukan), pp. 36–37. Literally, "the firearms were fired one after another." Fujimoto, *Nobunaga*, pp. 226–28, argues that this was Nobunaga in person firing the muskets as his attendants loaded and handed them to him, much like the arrangement in Figure 6.3.

32   Ota, *Shinchoko ki* (shukan), p. 70.

33   Ota, *Shinchoko ki* (shukan), pp. 72–73.

34   Ota, *Shinchoko ki* (shukan), p. 73. The reference to "fascines two and three deep" is actually a quote from a fourteenth-century literary work, the *Taiheiki*, so it may not be meant literally in this case.

35   Fujimoto, *Nobunaga*, pp. 69–132; Owada, *Sengoku*, pp. 35–53.

36   During the campaign in Omi province in 1570, Hideyoshi wrote a letter to a Sakai merchant demanding supplies of gunpowder and saltpeter. Berry, *Hideyoshi*, p. 45.

37   Fujimoto, *Nobunaga*, pp. 133–66; Ota, *Shinchoko ki* (ch. 3), p. 110. Nobunaga was reinforced by another 3,000–4,000 troops under Tokugawa Ieyasu shortly before the battle who are not counted in the 10,000 mentioned here. They defeated 8,000 men under Asakura Yoshikage and 5,000 men under Asai Nagamasa at the battle of Anegawa.

38   Ota, *Shinchoko ki* (ch. 3), p. 114. Since the figure of 20,000 would include both infantry and cavalry, the proportion of musketeers among the infantry would be higher than 15 percent.

39   Ota, *Shinchoko ki* (ch. 3), pp. 113–14.

40   Brown, "The impact of firearms"; Lamers, *Japonius tyrannus*, p. 75, quoting a letter from Luís Fróis on the destruction of the Enryakuji (I changed "harquebusiers" to "musketeers" and "bonzes" to "monks" in the quote); Ota, *Shinchoko ki* (ch. 7), pp. 174–75; Fujimoto, *Nobunaga*, pp. 167–89.

41   Fujimoto, *Nobunaga*, pp. 191–235; Owada, *Sengoku*, pp. 99–115; Ota, *Shinchoko ki* (ch. 8), pp. 181–85. What was once the usual account of this battle was based on Ose Hoan's *Shincho ki*, a novelistic work written decades after Nobunaga's death, which claimed that Nobunaga deployed 3,000 firearms and that he ordered them to fire in three volleys of 1,000 firearms each. Ose, *Shincho ki* (ch. 8), vol. 2, pp. 83–84. This is the account that eventually found its way into Perrin, *Giving up the gun*, p. 19, and Parker, *The military revolution*, p. 140. However, the earlier and more reliable *Shinchoko ki* by Ota Gyuichi, one of Nobunaga's attendants, only mentions 1,000 firearms and says nothing of volley fire. See the discussions in Fujimoto, *Nobunaga*, pp. 59–67 and 223–35; Owada, *Sengoku*, pp. 110–15; Suzuki, *Teppo*, pp. 72–94. (Berry, *Hideyoshi*, p. 45, n. 12, conflates the two sources; it was Ose Hoan who wrote around 1600 and was prone to poetical fancies.) Note that the figure of 1,000 is not the number of firearms in Nobunaga's army at the battle of Nagashino but rather the number of musketeers detached from their units and deployed by Nobunaga under the special command of five officers at the start of the battle. Significantly, the detachment of 4,000 men that Nobunaga had sent around the Takeda army the day before the engagement (to relieve Nagashino castle) contained the pick of Ieyasu's archers and musketeers as well as 500 musketeers from Nobunaga's own bodyguard. Ota, *Shinchoko ki* (ch. 8), p. 182.

42   Parts of this print are reproduced in Perrin, *Giving up the gun*, p. 21, and in Parker, *The military revolution*, cover and p. 141. The print is discussed in Fujimoto, *Nobunaga*, pp. 237–50.

43 Ota, *Shinchoko ki* (ch. 11), pp. 248 and 255; Lamers, *Japonius tyrannus*, pp. 155–56; Fujimoto, *Nobunaga*, pp. 253–73. Udagawa, *Higashi Ajia*, pp. 212–15, suggests that the cannon on these ships were swivel guns, but the evidence is inconclusive. The Jesuit letter translated by Lamers and quoted in the text speaks of *tres tiros de artelharia grossa* ("three pieces of heavy ordnance"), *alguns tiros pequenos* ("a few small pieces"), and later in the same letter, *espingardas grandes* ("large muskets"), none of which are obviously swivel guns. *Cartas qve os padres*, vol. 1, 415b.

44 On Hideyoshi, see generally Berry, *Hideyoshi*.

45 Suzuki, *Teppo*, pp. 45–140, *pace* Berry, *Hideyoshi*, p. 45.

46 Owada, *Sengoku busho*, pp. 17–20; Ikegami, *The taming of the samurai*; Fróis, *Européens & Japonais*, VII.42: "Among us, treason is rare and very blameworthy; in Japan, it is something so common that one is hardly ever surprised by it."

47 Nishigaya, *Jokaku*; Fujiki, *Zohyotachi no senjo*, pp. 149–77.

48 Fróis, *Européens & Japonais*, VII.20.

49 Nobunaga massacred the men, women, and children in the True Pure Land strongholds in the Nagashima Delta in 1574. Aside from the True Pure Land, other cases of stubborn resistance were the product of unusual circumstances. With Ieyasu's garrison at Nagashino castle, for example, the position of the river made escape difficult; Ieyasu had a representative at the castle to make negotiations awkward; Ieyasu held a number of hostages from the families of the commanders; and the commander of the garrison had betrayed Katsuyori once before. Fujimoto, *Nobunaga*, pp. 201–4.

50 Yamamura, "The growth of commerce," pp. 376–81.

51 Fróis, *Européens & Japonais*, VII.39. See also Fujiki, *Zohyotachi no senjo*, pp. 3–6 and 15–89, who discusses this quote from another angle.

52 Coaldrake, "Introduction," p. 16. The construction of large castles also got a boost from Hideyoshi's decree allowing each domain to possess only a single castle. Not surprisingly, lords of domains concentrated on making that one castle as lavish and imposing as possible. Parker, *The military revolution*, pp. 142–43, makes much the same argument for Japan that he does for China (see chapter 6, note 85), that Japanese castles were so large and strong that there was no point in trying to acquire cannon to use against them. However, Tokugawa Ieyasu made efforts to purchase and to produce large cannon in the early 1600s, when the majority of these castles were being completed, suggesting that the construction of larger castles encouraged the acquisition of larger cannon. Far from being "impregnable until the age of aerial bombardment," as Parker suggests, they would have been highly vulnerable to siege mortars with explosive shells, such as the kind the Dutch brought to Japan in the mid-1600s. If the Japanese did not show too great an interest in Dutch siege mortars in the mid-1600s, it was probably because the country seemed securely at peace, as in fact it was (see note 84).

53 Elisonas, "The inseparable trinity," pp. 265–71.

54 Kitajima, *Toyotomi Hideyoshi*, pp. 34–39; Hora, *Teppo*, pp. 335–37; Udagawa, *Teppo denrai*, p. 83.

55 Elisonas, "The inseparable trinity," pp. 271–76; Kitajima, *Toyotomi Hideyoshi*, pp. 39–83.

56 Yu, *Soe munjip* 16/23b–24a (p. 283). See also Udagawa, *Higashi Ajia*, pp. 288–90.

57 Quoted in Brown, "The impact of firearms," p. 240.

58 Yi, *Yi Ch'ungmugong chonso* tosol/7a–10b (pp. 50–51), 2/19b–20a (p. 81), and
    10/4b (p. 277); Arima, *Chosen'eki suigunshi*, pp. 35–38 and 79–81; Kitajima,
    Toyotomi Hideyoshi, pp. 100–112.

59 Elisonas, "The inseparable trinity," pp. 276–80; Kitajima, *Toyotomi Hideyoshi*,
    pp. 84–100 and 113–22.

60 Yu, *Chingbirok* 2/2b (p. 518); Kitajima, *Toyotomi Hideyoshi*, pp. 122–27.
    Sunzi warned against backing an enemy into a corner where he had no choice
    but to fight.

61 Elisonas, "The inseparable trinity," pp. 280–81; Kitajima, *Toyotomi Hideyoshi*,
    pp. 127–38.

62 Elisonas, "The inseparable trinity," pp. 281–85; Kitajima, *Toyotomi Hideyoshi*,
    pp. 139–80.

63 Jeon, *Science and technology in Korea*, pp. 205–6.

64 Yu, *Soe munjip* 7/16b (p. 128).

65 See Hora, *Teppo*, pp. 353–62, for Korean efforts to produce better guns.

66 Yu, *Soe munjip* 14/4b (p. 239).

67 Swords and firearms are complementary weapons, despite the arguments in
    Perrin, *Giving up the gun*. The Chinese and the Koreans had so much trouble
    against the Japanese because the Japanese were proficient with *both* the sword
    and the musket. For the Chinese see Zhao, *Shenqi pu* 5/4b–6a (pp. 2721–22);
    for the Koreans see Yu, *Soe munjip* 14/4a–4b (p. 239) and 14/14b (p. 244).
    It was the bow that was replaced by firearms, not the sword. The sword
    may have been in competition with the pike, but that is a different story.
    Udagawa, *Teppo denrai*, p. 174. As far as that is concerned, it seems that
    the sword had already been replaced by the pike as the primary weapon for
    hand-to-hand combat before firearms were ever introduced to Japan. Suzuki,
    Katana, pp. 54–109. This was largely the case in western European warfare
    as well, proponents of the sword (for example, Machiavelli, *The art of war*,
    pp. 44–52) notwithstanding. If swords became more popular in the Tokugawa
    period, it was probably because they were easy to carry in public and handy to
    use in brawls, although even then they were not always the weapon of choice.
    See, for example, Katsu, *Musui's story*, pp. 43–60.

68 Yu, *Soe munjip* 14/15a (p. 245).

69 Yu Song-nyong must have been working from memory, because the ancient
    Chinese precedent he cited said nothing about volley fire. The story involved
    Chinese cavalrymen on the steppe who ran out of arrows while surrounded
    by Xiongnu. The Chinese commander had his men draw their bows while
    he picked off some of the Xiongnu with whatever arrows he had left. The
    Xiongnu were fooled into withdrawing. Ban, *Hanshu*, ch. 54, p. 2445. For
    actual precedents see chapter 6, note 68.

70 Yu, *Soe munjip* 14/12a–12b (p. 243).

71 Yu, *Soe munjip* 14/8b–9a (pp. 241–42) and 14/13b (p. 244). Literally, "if not
    in the morning then in the evening."

72 Elisonas, "The inseparable trinity," pp. 285–86; Kitajima, *Toyotomi Hideyoshi*,
    pp. 180–91.

73 Hora, *Teppo*, pp. 362–63.

74 Yu, *Soe munjip* 16/22a (p. 282).

75 Yu, *Soe munjip* 16/21b–23a (pp. 282–83).

76 Elisonas, "The inseparable trinity," pp. 286–87; Kitajima, *Toyotomi Hideyoshi*, pp. 191–214.

77 Zhuge, *Liangchao pingrang lu*, vol. 2, p. 158.

78 Elisonas, "The inseparable trinity," p. 287; Kitajima, *Toyotomi Hideyoshi*, pp. 222–39; Zhuge, *Liangchao pingrang lu*, vol. 2, pp. 145–61.

79 Quoted in Brown, "The impact of firearms," p. 241.

80 Elisonas, "The inseparable trinity," pp. 288–90; Kitajima, *Toyotomi Hideyoshi*, pp. 239–58.

81 Zhao, *Shenqi pu* 4/6a–b (p. 2708). Ottoman muskets were generally more powerful than European ones. Murphey, *Ottoman warfare*, p. 111.

82 Hora, *Teppo*, pp. 241–58.

83 See chapter 3, note 27 for the evolution of European pike tactics. The clouds, incidentally, are a Japanese artistic convention. Although a seventeenth-century battlefield would have been covered with smoke, there is no reason to think that they were meant to represent gunsmoke.

84 The source of this myth is Perrin's 1979 book *Giving up the gun*. Like the myth of the Great Wall of China (Waldron, *The Great Wall of China*, pp. 194–226), or the myth of Captain Cook (Obeyesekere, *The apotheosis of Captain Cook*), it did not even originate with the people whose mentality it purports to illustrate. Perrin's argument is not taken seriously by specialists in this period of Japanese history, Japanese or otherwise. When *Giving up the gun* was translated into Japanese in 1984, the Japanese translator himself commented in his postscript: "This book does not take as its goal the empirical examination of the events of the past." Quoted in Udagawa, *Teppo denrai*, p. 174. If historical inaccuracy is ignored for the sake of the message, writes Udagawa, then it is not clear what the message gains from being placed in an historical setting. Udagawa, *Teppo denrai*, pp. 174–75. Suzuki is characteristically more blunt: "This view is completely wrong." Suzuki, *Teppo*, p. 202. Although praising Perrin for his enthusiasm and style, Totman also comments that "we can lament the making of a bad argument because it precludes the development of a good one and serves the author's cause poorly." Totman, "Review," p. 599. The most persuasive argument is the obvious one: "Guns went out of style because war ended. Had it continued, the use of guns would have continued." Totman, "Review," p. 600. Unfortunately, Perrin's work is still cited all too frequently by historians who, like Perrin, do not read Japanese and are unfamiliar with Japanese history.

85 Tokoro, *Hinawaju*, pp. 63–83; Suzuki, *Teppo*, pp. 202–5. *Koku* is a unit of rice.

86 Boxer, "Notes on early European military influences," pp. 73–87.

87 Tokoro, *Zukai koju jiten*, p. 88.

88 Zhao, *Shenqi pu* preface/4a–b (p. 2645).

89 Beasley, *The rise of modern Japan*, pp. 1–158; Ralston, *Importing the European army*, pp. 142–72.

90 Bolitho, *Treasures among men*, pp. 1–41.

91 Bix, *Peasant protest in Japan*; Vlastos, *Peasant protests and uprisings*.

8. Conclusion

1 Bacon, *Novum organum*, book I, aphorism 129, quoted in Needham et al., *Science and civilisation in China*, vol. 1, p. 19, and vol. 5, pt. 7, p. xxx. Note

that Bacon chose the same three inventions that Cardano did half a century earlier – if he did not mention exploration separately, it is only because it was one consequence of the compass.

2 This is how I understand Kafadar's comment that sometimes "cultural history is only an epistemological path and not a causal statement." Kafadar, *Between two worlds*, p. 58. What evidence is there that Europeans were culturally predisposed to favor firearms other than the very use of firearms that is supposedly being explained?

3 Black (in *A military revolution?* and *European warfare*) has argued that the "military revolution" should be dated to the period after 1650 in large part for these reasons. As mentioned earlier (see chapter 3, note 31), the argument in this work is unaffected by this question, because most of the Oikoumene never went through the infantry revolution and artillery revolution that preceded all the other stages of military change in Europe. Still, Black's work shows why the view that European military superiority depended primarily on the Industrial Revolution (see the section "The World after 1700") is untenable.

4 Anderson, *War and society in Europe*, pp. 45–50.

5 Lynn, *Giant of the Grand Siècle*, pp. 86–97 and 180–83.

6 Coad, *The royal dockyards*. The demands of administering these facilities called for specialized government offices. The Board of Admiralty, responsible for naval strategy and tactics, acquired permanent headquarters in 1695. The Navy Board, responsible for building and maintenance, posted commissioners at each of the major bases by 1700. The Bureau of Ordnance supplied the guns, first through purchase from private manufacturers, after 1717 also from the Royal Arsenal at Woolwich.

7 Ralston, *Importing the European army*.

8 Black, *European warfare*, pp. 38–43.

9 Jackson and de Beer, *Eighteenth century gunfounding*, pp. 16–17 and 72–74; Black, *European warfare*, pp. 43–45.

10 Gommans, *The rise of the Indo-Afghan empire*; Gibbon, *The decline and fall*, vol. 2, p. 442.

11 On nomads using firearms, Matthee, "Unwalled cities and restless nomads," pp. 406–7, mentions Uzbeks, the Tatars of Daghestan, Lezgis, Baluchis, and Afghans. The agrarianate states that benefited from the shift in the balance of power have been called the "gunpowder empires." Hodgson, *The venture of Islam*, vol. 3; McNeill, *The age of gunpowder empires*. The term has come under criticism when applied to the Mughals. Streusand, *The formation of the Mughal empire*, pp. 10–13 and 66–69; Eaton, *The rise of Islam and the Bengal frontier*, pp. 151–53. It seems even less applicable to the Safavids. It certainly should not be taken to imply that the Ottoman, Safavid, and Mughal empires relied solely on firearms, even in military affairs.

12 Vandervort, *Wars of imperial conquest in Africa*; Headrick, *The tools of empire*.

13 Curtin, *The world and the West*, pp. 19–37, does not see a gap appearing before the mid-1800s. It may be better to say that only in the mid-1800s did the gap become so wide that it dwarfed by comparison the disadvantages of long distances, numerical inferiority, and the like.

14 This is the famous example from Huff, *How to lie with statistics*, p. 90. Salaries of Presbyterian ministers and the price of rum in Havana both went up over time along with rising price levels worldwide.

15 Babur's account of the battle of Khanua suggests otherwise (see chapter 5, the section "The Mughals"), but it is hard to see how the wagons might have been moved if they were tied together with wooden shields, or how the musketeers could have left the shelter of the wagons safely.

16 Bulliet, *The camel and the wheel*, pp. 7–27; McNeill, "The eccentricity of wheels." As noted in chapter 1, steppe nomads used wagons whereas desert nomads did not. McNeill, *Keeping together in time*, p. 186, n. 55, speculates about "a long-standing tradition of cart warfare on the Eurasian steppes," but it seems unlikely that steppe nomads used wagons while fighting on any regular basis. Certainly when Chinese armies came upon Mongol baggage trains, the Mongols did not hesitate to abandon them.

17 Fletcher, *Of the Russian commonwealth*, pp. 185–86; Parry, "La manière de combattre," pp. 236–37; Babur, *Baburnama* 311a (Mano, p. 496; Thackston, p. 372); Wang Minghe, *Dengtan bijiu*, yingqi 2a–8a (pp. 3891–903).

18 The Inner Zone and Outer Zone might almost be called the "Wagon Zone" and the "Pike Zone" since, as explained in the section "Wagons and Pikes," there is a strong correlation with the use of pikes or wagons. However, there were large areas within the Inner Zone where wagons were not used, especially south China and Korea, because there were too many rivers or mountains. Therefore, inner and outer seemed more appropriate. Viewed from the usual mental vantage point of English-speaking historians, the labels for inner and outer may appear reversed, but viewing the Oikoumene as a whole, it makes sense to look at western Europe and Japan as the outer areas.

Bibliography

Abu-Lughod, Janet L. *Before European hegemony: The world system* A.D. *1250–1350.* Oxford: Oxford University Press, 1989.

Abun-Nasr, Jamil M. *A history of the Maghrib in the Islamic period.* Cambridge: Cambridge University Press, 1987.

Adshead, S. A. M. *Central Asia in world history.* London: MacMillan, 1993.

———. *China in world history.* New York: St. Martin's Press, 1988.

Ágoston, Gábor. "The costs of the Ottoman fortress-system in Hungary in the sixteenth and seventeenth centuries," in Géza Dávid and Pál Fodor, eds. *Ottomans, Hungarians, and Habsburgs in Central Europe: The military confines in the era of Ottoman conquest.* Leiden: Brill, 2000.

———. "Ottoman artillery and European military technology in the fifteenth and seventeenth centuries," *Acta Orientalia Academiae Scientiarum Hungaricae* 47 (1994a): 15–48.

———. "Ottoman gunpowder production in Hungary in the sixteenth century: The *baruthane* of Buda," in Géza Dávid and Pál Fodor, eds. *Hungarian-Ottoman military and diplomatic relations in the age of Süleyman the Magnificent.* Budapest: Hungarian Academy of Sciences, 1994b.

———. "Gunpowder for the sultan's army: New sources on the supply of gunpowder to the Ottoman army in the Hungarian campaigns of the sixteenth and seventeenth centuries," *Turcica* 25 (1993): 75–96.

D'Albuquerque, Afonso. *The commentaries of the great Afonso Dalboquerque, second viceroy of India,* vol. 2. Translated by Walter De Gray Birch. London: Hakluyt Society, 1877.

Alef, Gustave. "Muscovite military reforms in the second-half of the fifteenth century," *Forschungen zur osteuropäischen Geschichte* 18 (1973): 73–108, reprinted in *Rulers and nobles in fifteenth-century Muscovy.* London: Variorum, 1983.

Allsen, Thomas T. "The circulation of military technology in the Mongolian empire," in Nicola Di Cosmo, ed. *Warfare in Inner Asian history (500–1800).* Leiden: Brill, 2002.

———. *Mongol imperialism: The policies of the Great Qan Möngke in China, Russia and the Islamic lands, 1251–1259.* Berkeley: University of California Press, 1987.

Amīr Mahmūd-i Khāndamīr. *Tārīkh-i Shāh Ismāīl va Shāh Tahmāsp-i Safavī (Zayl-i habīb al-siyar).* Edited by Muhammad 'Alī Jarrāhī. Tehran: Nashr-i Gustara, 1991.

Amitai-Preiss, Reuven. "Whither the Ilkhanid army? Ghazan's first campaign into Syria (1299–1300)," in Nicola Di Cosmo, ed. *Warfare in Inner Asian history (500–1800).* Leiden: Brill, 2002.

———. *Mongols and Mamluks: The Mamluk-Īlkhānid war, 1260–1281.* Cambridge: Cambridge University Press, 1995.

Andaya, Leonard Y. "Interactions with the outside world and adaptation in Southeast Asian society, 1500–1800," in Nicholas Tarling, ed. *The Cambridge history of Southeast Asia, volume one, part two: From c.1500 to c.1800.* Cambridge: Cambridge University Press, 1999.

Anderson, M. S. *War and society in Europe of the Old Regime 1618–1789.* Montreal: McGill-Queen's University Press, 1998 [1988].

Anonymous. *Caolu jinglüe.* Daoguang edition. In *Zhongguo bingshu jicheng,* vol. 37. Beijing: Jiefang jun, 1994.

Arai Hakuseki. *Honchō gunki kō.* 1709. In *Arai Hakuseki zenshū,* vol. 6. Tokyo: Yoshikawa Hanshichi, 1907.

Arima Seiho. *Kahō no kigen to sono denryū.* Tokyo: Yoshikawa kōbunkan, 1962.

———. *Chōsen'eki suigunshi.* Tokyo: Umi to sora sha, 1942.

Arjomand, Said Amir. *The shadow of God and the hidden Imam: Religion, political order, and societal change in Shi'ite Iran from the beginning to 1890.* Chicago: University of Chicago Press, 1984.

Arnold, Thomas F. "Fortifications and the military revolution: The Gonzaga experience, 1530–1630," in Clifford J. Rogers, ed. *The military revolution debate: Readings on the military transformation of early modern Europe.* Boulder: Westview, 1995.

'Āşıkpaşazāde. *Tevārīh-i āl-i 'Osmān'dan 'Āşıkpaşazāde tarīhi.* Istanbul: Matbaa-i 'Āmire, 1914.

Atwell, William. "Ming China and the emerging world economy, c.1470–1650," in Denis Twitchett and Frederick W. Mote, eds. *The Cambridge history of China, volume 8: The Ming dynasty, part 2.* Cambridge: Cambridge University Press, 1998.

Ayalon, David. "The auxiliary forces of the Mamluk sultanate," in *Der Islam: Zeitschrift für Geschichte und Kultur des islamischen Orients 65.* Berlin: Walter de Gruyter, 1988, reprinted in *Islam and the Abode of War: Military slaves and Islamic adversaries.* London: Variorum, 1994a.

———. "Mamlūk: Military slavery in Egypt and Syria," in *Islam and the Abode of War: Military slaves and Islamic adversaries.* London: Variorum, 1994b.

———. "Some remarks on the economic decline of the Mamlūk sultanate," *Jerusalem Studies in Arabic and Islam* 16 (1993): 108–24, reprinted in *Islam and the Abode of War: Military slaves and Islamic adversaries.* London: Variorum, 1994c.

———. *Gunpowder and firearms in the Mamluk kingdom: A challenge to a mediaeval society.* London: Frank Cass, 1978 [1956].

———. "The Mamluks and naval power," *Proceedings of the Israel Academy of Sciences and Humanities* 1 (1965): 1–12, reprinted in *Studies on the Mamlūks of Egypt (1250–1517).* London: Variorum, 1977a.

———. "The Muslim city and the Mamluk military aristocracy," *Proceedings of* the Israel Academy of Sciences and Humanities 2 (1968): 311–29, reprinted in *Studies on the Mamlūks of Egypt (1250–1517)*. London: Variorum, 1977b.

———. "Plague and its effects upon the Mamluk army," *Journal of the Royal Asiatic Society* (1946): 67–73, reprinted in *Studies on the Mamlūks of Egypt (1250–1517)*. London: Variorum, 1977c.

———. "Studies on the structure of the Mamluk army," *Bulletin of the School of Oriental and African Studies* XV (1953): 203–28 and 448–76, and XVI (1954): 57–90, reprinted in *Studies on the Mamlūks of Egypt (1250–1517)*. London: Variorum, 1977d.

———. "The wafidiya in the Mamluk kingdom," *Islamic Culture* 25 (1951): 81–104, reprinted in *Studies on the Mamlūks of Egypt (1250–1517)*. London: Variorum, 1977e.

Bābur, Zahīr al-Dīn Muhammad. *Bāburnāma*. Text: Mano Eiji. *Bāburunāma no kenkyū*, vol. 1, kōteihon. Kyoto: Shōkadō, 1995. Translations: (1) Mano Eiji. *Bāburunāma no kenkyū*, vol. 3, yakuchū. Kyoto: Shōkadō, 1998. (2) Wheeler M. Thackston. *The Baburnama: Memoirs of Babur, prince and emperor*. Oxford: Oxford University Press, 1996. (3) Jean-Louis Bacqué-Grammont. *Le livre de Babur: Mémoires du premier Grand Mogol des Indes (1494–1529)*. Paris: Collection Orientale de L'Imprimerie Nationale, 1985. (4) Annette S. Beveridge. *The Bābur-Nāma*. London: Luzac & Co., 1922.

Bachrach, Bernard S. "Animals and warfare in early medieval Europe," *Settimane di Studio del Centro Italiano di sull'alto Medioevo* 31 (1985): 707–51, reprinted in *Armies and politics in the early medieval West*. London: Variorum, 1993.

Bacqué-Grammont, Jean-Louis. *Les Ottomans, les Safavides et leurs voisins – contributions à l'histoire des relations internationales dans l'Orient islamique de 1514 à 1524*. Istanbul: Nederlands Historisch-Archaeologisch Instituut, 1987.

Ban Gu. *Hanshu*. Beijing: Zhonghua, 1992 [1962].

Barbaro, Nicolò. *Diary of the siege of Constantinople*. 1453. Translated by J. R. Melville Jones. New York: Exposition Press, 1969.

Barbosa, Duarte. *The book of Duarte Barbosa: An account of the countries bordering on the Indian Ocean and their inhabitants, written by Duarte Barbosa and completed about the year 1518* A.D. Liechtenstein: Kraus Reprint Society [Hakluyt Society], 1967 [1918].

Barendse, R. J. *The Arabian seas: The Indian Ocean world of the seventeenth century*. London: M. E. Sharpe, 2002.

Barfield, Thomas J. "Tribe and state relations: The Inner Asian perspective," in Philip S. Khoury and Joseph Kostiner, eds. *Tribes and state formation in the Middle East*. Berkeley: University of California Press, 1990.

———. *The perilous frontier: Nomadic empires and China*. Cambridge: Basil Blackwell, 1989.

Bartlett, Robert. *The making of Europe: Conquest, colonization and cultural change, 950–1350*. Princeton: Princeton University Press, 1993.

Bartusis, Mark C. *The late Byzantine army: Arms and society, 1204–1453*. Philadelphia: University of Pennsylvania Press, 1992.

Barwick, Humfrey. *A breefe discourse, concerning the force and effect of all manuall weapons of fire*. 1594, reprinted in E. G. Heath. *Bow versus gun*. East Ardsley: EP Publishing, 1973.

Basalla, George. *The evolution of technology.* Cambridge: Cambridge University Press, 1988.

Beasley, William G. *The rise of modern Japan.* 2d ed. New York: St. Martin's Press, 1995.

Berry, Mary Elizabeth. *Hideyoshi.* Cambridge: Harvard University Press, 1982.

Bix, Herbert P. *Peasant protest in Japan.* New Haven: Yale University Press, 1986.

Black, Jeremy. *War and the world: Military power and the fate of continents, 1450–2000.* New Haven: Yale University Press, 1998.

———. *European warfare, 1660–1815.* New Haven: Yale University Press, 1994.

———. *A military revolution? Military change and European society 1550–1800.* Atlantic Highlands, NJ: Humanities Press International, 1991.

Black, Jeremy, ed. *War in the early modern world 1450–1815.* London: UCL Press, 1999.

Bolitho, Harold. *Treasures among men: The fudai daimyo in Tokugawa Japan.* New Haven: Yale University Press, 1974.

Bostan, İdris. *Osmanlı bahriye teşkilâtı: XVII. yüzyılda tersâne-i âmire.* Ankara: Türk tarih kurumu basımevi, 1992.

Boxer, Charles Ralph. "Notes on early European military influences in Japan, 1543–1853," *Transactions of the Asiatic Society of Japan,* 2nd ser., 8 (1931): 67–93, reprinted in Douglas M. Peers, ed. *Warfare and empires: Contact and conflict between European and non-European military and maritime forces and cultures.* Aldershot: Variorum, 1997.

———. "Portuguese military expeditions in aid of the Mings against the Manchus, 1621–1647," *T'ien Hsia Monthly* 7/1 (1938): 24–36, reprinted in *Estudos para a História de Macau, Séculos XVI a XVIII,* vol. 1. Lisbon: Fundação Oriente, 1991.

———. "The Achinese attack on Malacca in 1629, as described in contemporary Portuguese sources," in John Bastin and R. Roolvink, eds. *Malayan and Indonesian studies: Essays presented to Sir Richard Winstedt on his 85th birthday.* Oxford: Clarendon Press, 1964. Reprinted in *Portuguese conquest and commerce in Southern Asia, 1500–1750.* London: Variorum, 1985a.

———. "Anglo-Portuguese rivalry in the Persian Gulf, 1615–1635," in Edgar Prestage, ed. *Chapters in Anglo-Portuguese relations.* Watford: Voss & Michael, 1935. Reprinted in *Portuguese conquest and commerce in Southern Asia, 1500–1750.* London: Variorum, 1985b.

———. "Asian potentates and European artillery in the 16th–18th centuries: A footnote to Gibson-Hill," *Journal of the Malaysian Branch of the Royal Asiatic Society* XXXVIII (1966): 156–72. Reprinted in *Portuguese conquest and commerce in Southern Asia, 1500– 1750.* London: Variorum, 1985c.

———. "Preface," in *Portuguese conquest and commerce in Southern Asia, 1500–1750.* London: Variorum, 1985d.

———. *The Portuguese seaborne empire 1415–1825.* London: Hutchinson, 1977 [1969].

Braudel, Fernand. *The Mediterranean and the Mediterranean world in the age of Philip II.* Translated by Siân Reynolds. New York: Harper & Row, 1972 [1966].

Brown, Charles Philip. *Dictionary Telugu-English.* 2d ed. New Delhi: Asian Educational Services, 1979 [1903].

Brown, Delmer M. "The impact of firearms on Japanese warfare, 1543–98," *Far Eastern Quarterly* 7 (1948): 236–53.

Brummett, Palmira. *Ottoman seapower and Levantine diplomacy in the age of discovery*. Albany: State University of New York, 1994.

Bulliet, Richard W. *The camel and the wheel*. New York: Columbia University Press, 1990 [1975].

Busbecq, Ogier Ghiselin de. *The Turkish letters of Ogier Ghiselin de Busbecq, Imperial Ambassador at Constantinople 1554–1562*. Translated by Edward Seymour Forster. Oxford: Clarendon Press, 1968 [1927].

Canfield, Robert L., ed. *Turko-Persia in historical perspective*. Cambridge: Cambridge University Press, 1991.

Cardan, Jerome. *The book of my life (De propria vita)*. Translated by Jean Stoner. New York: E. P. Dutton & Co., 1930 [1575].

Carpini, John of Plano. *History of the Mongols*. In Christopher Dawson, ed. *Mission to Asia*. Toronto: University of Toronto, 1980. (*The Mongol mission*. London: Sheed and Ward, 1955.)

Cartas qve os padres e irmãos da Companhia de Iesus escreuerão dos reynos de Iapão & China aos da mesma Companhia da India, & Europa, des do anno de 1549 atè o de 1580. Euora: Por Manoel de Lyra, 1598.

Chandler, David. *Marlborough as military commander*. 2d ed. London: B.T. Batsford, 1979.

Chaudhuri, K. N. *Asia before Europe: Economy and civilisation of the Indian Ocean from the rise of Islam to 1750*. Cambridge: Cambridge University Press, 1990.

———. *Trade and civilisation in the Indian Ocean: An economic history from the rise of Islam to 1750*. Cambridge: Cambridge University Press, 1986 [1985].

Cipolla, Carlo M. *Guns, sails and empires: Technological innovation and the early phases of European expansion 1400–1700*. New York: Pantheon Books, 1965.

Clavijo, Ruy González de. *Embassy to Tamerlane 1403–1406*. Translated by Guy Le Strange. New York: Harper & Brothers, 1928.

Clendinnen, Inga. "'Fierce and unnatural cruelty': Cortés and the conquest of Mexico," in Stephen Greenblatt, ed. *New World encounters*. Berkeley: University of California Press, 1993.

Coad, Jonathan G. *The royal dockyards 1690–1850: Architecture and engineering works of the sailing navy*. Aldershot: Scolar Press, 1989.

Coaldrake, William H. "Introduction," in Motoo Hinago, *Japanese castles*. Tokyo: Kodansha International, 1986.

Collins, L. J. D. "The military organization and tactics of the Crimean Tatars, 16th–17th centuries," in V. J. Parry and M. E. Yapp, eds. *War, technology, and society in the Middle East*. London: Oxford University Press, 1975.

Commissariat, M. S. *A history of Gujarat, including a survey of its chief architectural monuments and inscriptions*. Bombay: Longmans, Green & Co., 1938.

Conlan, Thomas D. *In little need of divine intervention: Takezaki Suenaga's scrolls of the Mongol invasions of Japan*. Ithaca: Cornell University East Asia Program, 2001.

Contamine, Philippe. *War in the Middle Ages*. Translated by Michael Jones. Oxford: Basil Blackwell, 1984 [1980].

Cook, Noble David. *Born to die: Disease and New World conquest, 1492–1650*. Cambridge: Cambridge University Press, 1998.

Cook, Weston F. Jr. *The hundred years war for Morocco: Gunpowder and the military revolution in the early modern Muslim world*. Boulder: Westview Press, 1994.

Cooke, Nola. "Regionalism and the nature of Nguyen rule in seventeenth-century Dang Trong (Cochinchina)," *Journal of Southeast Asian Studies* 29 (1998): 122–61.

Correa, Gaspar. *The three voyages of Vasco da Gama and his viceroyalty.* Translated by Henry E. J. Stanley. New York: Burt Franklin, 1963 [1869].

Croizier, Ralph C. *Koxinga and Chinese nationalism: History, myth, and the hero.* Cambridge: Harvard University Press, 1977.

Crone, Patricia. *Slaves on horses: The evolution of the Islamic polity.* Cambridge: Cambridge University Press, 1980.

Crosby, Alfred W. *Throwing fire: Projectile technology through history.* Cambridge: Cambridge University Press, 2002.

———. *The measure of reality: Quantification and Western society, 1250–1600.* Cambridge: Cambridge University Press, 1997.

———. *Ecological imperialism: The biological expansion of Europe, 900–1900.* Cambridge: Cambridge University Press, 1993 [1986].

Crummey, Robert O. *The formation of Muscovy 1304–1613.* London: Longman, 1987.

Curtin, Philip D. *The world and the West: The European challenge and the overseas response in the Age of Empire.* Cambridge: Cambridge University Press, 2000.

Da Ming huidian. Shen Shixing. 1576 ed. Taipei: Xinwenfeng, 1976.

Dames, M. Longworth. "The Portuguese and the Turks in the Indian Ocean in the sixteenth century," *Journal of the Royal Asiatic Society of Great Britain and Ireland* (1921): 1–28.

Davies, Brian. "Village into garrison: The militarized peasant communities of southern Muscovy," *Russian Review* 51 (1992): 481–501.

Davis, R. H. C. *The medieval warhorse: Origin, development, and redevelopment.* London: Thames and Hudson, 1989.

De Heer, Ph. *The care-taker emperor: Aspects of the imperial institution in fifteenth-century China as reflected in the political history of the reign of Chu Ch'i-yü.* Leiden: E. J. Brill, 1986.

Delbrück, Hans. *The dawn of modern warfare.* Translated by Walter J. Renfroe Jr. Lincoln: University of Nebraska, 1990 [original 1920, translation 1985].

DeVries, Kelly Robert. "Gunpowder and early gunpowder weapons," in Brenda J. Buchanan, ed. *Gunpowder: The history of an international technology.* Bath: Bath University Press, 1996.

———. "The impact of gunpowder weaponry on siege warfare in the Hundred Years War," in Ivy A. Corfis and Michael Wolfe, eds. *The medieval city under siege.* Woodbridge: The Boydell Press, 1995.

———. *Medieval military technology.* Lewiston, NY: Broadview Press, 1992.

———. "A 1445 reference to shipboard artillery," *Technology and Culture* 31 (1990): 818–29.

DeWeese, Devin. "The influence of the Mongols on the religious consciousness of thirteenth century Europe," *Mongolian Studies* 5 (1978–79): 41–78.

Di Cosmo, Nicola. "Military aspects of the Manchu wars against the Čaqars," in Nicola Di Cosmo, ed. *Warfare in Inner Asian history (500–1800).* Leiden: Brill, 2002.

———. "State formation and periodization in Inner Asian history," *Journal of World History* 10 (1999): 1–40.

Diamond, Jared. *Guns, germs, and steel: The fates of human societies.* New York: W. W. Norton & Company, 1997.

Digby, Simon. *War-horse and elephant in the Delhi sultanate: A study of military supplies.* Oxford: Orient Monographs, 1971.

Downing, Brian M. *The military revolution and political change: Origins of democracy and autocracy in early modern Europe.* Princeton: Princeton University Press, 1992.

Drews, Robert. *The end of the Bronze Age: Changes in warfare and the Catastrophe ca. 1200 B.C.* Princeton: Princeton University Press, 1993.

Dreyer, Edward L. "Military origins of Ming China," in Denis Twitchett and Frederick W. Mote, eds. *The Cambridge history of China, volume 7: The Ming dynasty, part 1.* Cambridge: Cambridge University Press, 1988.

———. *Early Ming China: A political history, 1355–1435.* Stanford: Stanford University Press, 1982.

———. "The Poyang campaign, 1363: Inland naval warfare in the founding of the Ming dynasty," in Frank A. Kiernan and John K. Fairbank, eds. *Chinese ways in warfare.* Cambridge: Harvard University Press, 1974.

Du Rongkun and Bai Cuiqin. *Xi Menggu shi yanjiu.* Urumqi: Xinjiang Renmin, 1986.

Duffy, Christopher. *The military experience in the Age of Reason.* Ware: Wordsworth, 1998 [1987].

Dunn, Ross E. *The adventures of Ibn Battuta: A Muslim traveler of the 14th century.* Berkeley: University of California Press, 1986.

Eaton, Richard M. *The rise of Islam and the Bengal frontier, 1204–1760.* Berkeley: University of California Press, 1993.

Elbl, Ivana. "The horse in fifteenth-century Senegambia," *The International Journal of African Historical Studies* 24 (1991): 85–110.

Elisonas, Jurgis. "Christianity and the daimyo," in John W. Hall, ed. *The Cambridge history of Japan: Volume 4, early modern Japan.* Cambridge: Cambridge University Press, 1991a.

———. "The inseparable trinity: Japan's relations with China and Korea," in John W. Hall, ed. *The Cambridge history of Japan: Volume 4, early modern Japan.* Cambridge: Cambridge University Press, 1991b.

Eltis, David. *The military revolution in sixteenth-century Europe.* New York: Barnes & Noble, 1998 [1995].

Elvin, Mark. *The pattern of the Chinese past: A social and economic interpretation.* Stanford: Stanford University Press, 1973.

Emmerson, Donald K. "'Southeast Asia': What's in a name?" *Journal of Southeast Asian Studies* 15 (1984): 1–21.

Engels, Donald W. *Alexander the Great and the logistics of the Macedonian army.* Berkeley: University of California Press, 1978.

Errard de Bar-le-Duc, Jean. *La fortification reduicte en art et demonstree par J. Errard de Bar-le-Duc.* Frankfurt-am-Main, 1604.

Esper, Thomas. "Military self-sufficiency and weapons technology in Muscovite Russia," *Slavic Review* 28 (1969): 185–208.

———. "The replacement of the longbow by firearms in the English army," *Technology and Culture* 6 (1965): 382–93.

Farmer, Edward L. *Early Ming government: The evolution of dual capitals.* Cambridge: Harvard University Press, 1976.

Farris, William Wayne. *Heavenly warriors: The evolution of Japan's military, 500–1300*. Cambridge: Harvard University Press, 1992.

———. *Population, disease, and land in early Japan, 645–900*. Cambridge: Harvard University Press, 1985.

Fedorowicz, J. K. et al., eds. *A republic of nobles: Studies in Polish history to 1864*. Cambridge: Cambridge University Press, 1982.

Ferguson, Donald. *Letters from Portuguese captives in Canton, written in 1534 and 1536, with an introduction on Portuguese intercourse with China in the first half of the sixteenth century*. Bombay: Education Society, 1902.

Finkel, Caroline. *The administration of warfare: The Ottoman military campaigns in Hungary, 1593–1606*. Vienna: VWGÖ, 1988.

Finlay, Robert. "The pilgrim art: The culture of porcelain in world history," *Journal of World History* 9 (1998): 141–87.

Fletcher, Giles. *Of the Russian commonwealth*. 1591. Edited by Lloyd E. Berry and Robert O. Crummey, *Rude & barbarous kingdom: Russia in the accounts of sixteenth-century English voyagers*. Madison: University of Wisconsin Press, 1968.

Fletcher, Joseph. "The Mongols: Ecological and social perspectives," *Harvard Journal of Asiatic Studies* 46 (1986): 11–50.

Fodor, Pál. "Making a living on the frontiers: Volunteers in the sixteenth-century Ottoman army," in Géza Dávid and Pál Fodor, eds. *Ottomans, Hungarians, and Habsburgs in Central Europe: The military confines in the era of Ottoman conquest*. Leiden: Brill, 2000.

Fok, K. C. "Early Ming images of the Portuguese," in Roderich Ptak, ed. *Aspects in history and economic history, sixteenth and seventeenth centuries*. Stuttgart: Franz Steiner Verlag Wiesbaden, 1987. Reprinted in Anthony Disney, ed. *Historiography of Europeans in Africa and Asia, 1450–1800*. Aldershot: Variorum, 1995.

Fowler, Loretta. "The Great Plains from the arrival of the horse to 1885," in *The Cambridge history of the native peoples of the Americas, volume 1: North America, part 2*. Cambridge: Cambridge University Press, 1988.

Fragner, Bert. "Social and internal economic affairs," in Peter Jackson and Laurence Lockhart, eds. *The Cambridge history of Iran, volume 6: The Timurid and Safavid periods*. Cambridge: Cambridge University Press, 1986.

France, John. "Recent writing on medieval warfare: From the fall of Rome to c.1300," *Journal of Military History* 65 (2001): 441–73.

———. *Western warfare in the age of the Crusades, 1000–1300*. Cornell: Cornell University Press, 1999.

———. "Technology and success of the First Crusade," in Yaacov Lev, ed. *War and society in the eastern Mediterranean, 7th–15th centuries*. Leiden: E. J. Brill, 1997.

Frank, Andre Gunder. *ReOrient: Global economy in the Asian age*. Berkeley: University of California Press, 1998.

Friday, Karl F. *Hired swords: The rise of private warrior power in early Japan*. Stanford: Stanford University Press, 1992.

Fróis, Luís. *Européens & Japonais: Traité sur les contradictions & différences de mœurs, écrit par le R.P. Luís Fróis au Japon, l'an 1585*. Translated by Xavier de Castro. Paris: Chandeigne, 1998.

Fujiki Hisashi. *Zōhyōtachi no senjō – chūsei no yōhei to doreikari*. Tokyo: Asahi, 1995.

Fujimoto Masayuki. *Nobunaga no Sengoku gunjigaku*. Tokyo: Yōsensha, 1997 [1992].

Galvano, Antonio. *The discoveries of the world from their first original unto the year of Our Lord 1555*. New York: Burt Franklin [Hakluyt Society], 1971 [1601].

Gandjei, Tourkhan. "Turkish in the Safavid court of Isfahān," *Turcica* 21–23 (1991): 311–18.

Geiss, James. "The Cheng-te reign, 1506–1521," in Denis Twitchett and Frederick W. Mote, eds. *The Cambridge history of China, volume 7: The Ming dynasty, part 1*. Cambridge: Cambridge University Press, 1988a.

———. "The Chia-ching reign, 1522–1566," in Denis Twitchett and Frederick W. Mote, eds. *The Cambridge history of China, volume 7: The Ming dynasty, part 1*. Cambridge: Cambridge University Press, 1988b.

———. "The Leopard Quarter during the Cheng-te reign," *Ming Studies* 24 (1987): 1–38.

Gernet, Jacques. *Daily life in China on the eve of the Mongol invasion 1250–1276*. Translated by H. M. Wright. Stanford: Stanford University Press, 1962.

Gheyn, Jacob de. *The exercise of armes for calivres, muskettes, and pikes*. Translated with commentary by J. B. Kist. New York: McGraw-Hill, 1971 [1607].

Gibbon, Edward. *The decline and fall of the Roman empire*. New York: Random House, n.d.

Glete, Jan. *Warfare at sea, 1500–1650: Maritime conflicts and the transformation of Europe*. London: Routledge, 2000.

Gode, P. K. "The history of fire-works in India between A.D. 1400 and 1900," in *Studies in Indian cultural history, vol. II*. Poona: Prof. P. K. Gode Collected Works Publication Committee, 1960.

Gommans, Jos J. L. *The rise of the Indo-Afghan empire, c.1710–1780*. Delhi: Oxford University Press, 1999a.

———. "Warhorse and gunpowder in India c.1000–1850," in Jeremy Black, ed. *War in the early modern world 1450–1815*. London: UCL Press, 1999b.

———. "The silent frontier of South Asia, c. A.D. 1100–1800," *Journal of World History* 9 (1998): 1–23.

González de León, Fernando. "'Doctors of the military discipline': Technical expertise and the paradigm of the Spanish soldier in the early modern period," *Sixteenth Century Journal* 27 (1996): 61–85.

Gordon, Stewart. *The new Cambridge history of India, II.4: The Marathas 1600–1818*. Cambridge: Cambridge University Press, 1993.

Gottfried, Robert S. *The Black Death: Natural and human disaster in medieval Europe*. New York: The Free Press, 1983.

Gould, Stephen Jay. "The problem of perfection: Or how can a clam mount a fish on its rear end?" in *Ever since Darwin: Reflections in natural history*. New York: Penguin Books, 1977.

Graff, David A. *Medieval Chinese warfare, 300–900*. London: Routledge, 2002a.

———. "Strategy and contingency in the Tang defeat of the Eastern Turks, 629–630," in Nicola Di Cosmo, ed. *Warfare in Inner Asian history (500–1800)*. Leiden: Brill, 2002b.

Grant, Jonathan. "Rethinking the Ottoman 'decline': Military technology diffusion in the Ottoman empire, fifteenth to eighteenth centuries," *Journal of World History* 10 (1999): 179–201.

Grossberg, Kenneth Alan. *Japan's Renaissance: The politics of the Muromachi bakufu.* Cambridge: Harvard University Press, 1981.

Guilmartin, John Francis, Jr. "Technology and asymmetrics in modern warfare," in Lloyd J. Matthews, ed. *Challenging the United States symmetrically and asymmetrically: Can America be defeated?* Carlisle: U.S. Army War College, 1998.

———. "The military revolution: Origins and first tests abroad," in Clifford J. Rogers, ed. *The military revolution debate: Readings on the military transformation of early modern Europe.* Boulder: Westview, 1995.

———. "Ideology and conflict: The wars of the Ottoman Empire, 1453–1606," *Journal of Interdisciplinary History* 18 (1988): 721–47.

———. *Gunpowder and galleys: Changing technology and Mediterranean warfare at sea in the sixteenth century.* Cambridge: Cambridge University Press, 1974.

Haarmann, Ulrich. "Joseph's law – the careers and activities of Mamluk descendants before the Ottoman conquest of Egypt," in *The Mamluks in Egyptian politics and society.* Edited by Thomas Philipp and Ulrich Haarmann. Cambridge: Cambridge University Press, 1998.

Hai Rui. *Beiwang ji.* In *Siku quanshu,* vol. 1286. Taipei: Taiwan shangwu, 1983.

Halaçoğlu, Yusuf. *XIV–XVII. yüzyıllarda Osmanlılarda devlet teşkilâtı ve sosyal yapı.* Ankara: Türk tarih kurumu basımevi, 1995.

Haldon, John. *Warfare, state, and society in the Byzantine world, 565–1204.* London: UCL Press, 1999.

Hale, John Rigby. *The civilization of Europe in the Renaissance.* New York: Atheneum, 1994.

———. "Part II: 1509–1617," in J. R. Hale and M. E. Mallett, eds. *The military organization of a Renaissance state: Venice c.1400 to 1617.* Cambridge: Cambridge University Press, 1984.

———. "Gunpowder and the Renaissance: An essay in the history of ideas," in *Renaissance war studies.* London: Hambledon, 1983 [1965].

Hall, Bert S. "Introduction," in J. R. Partington, ed. *A history of Greek fire and gunpowder.* Baltimore: Johns Hopkins University Press, 1999 [1960].

———. *Weapons and warfare in Renaissance Europe: Gunpowder, technology, and tactics.* Baltimore: Johns Hopkins University Press, 1997.

———. "The corning of gunpowder and the development of firearms in the Renaissance," in Brenda J. Buchanan, ed. *Gunpowder: The history of an international technology.* Bath: Bath University Press, 1996.

———. "The changing face of siege warfare: Technology and tactics in transition," in Ivy A. Corfis and Michael Wolfe, eds. *The medieval city under siege.* Woodbridge: The Boydell Press, 1995.

Halperin, Charles J. *Russia and the Golden Horde: The Mongol impact on medieval Russian history.* Bloomington: Indiana University Press, 1987 [1985].

Haneda Masashi. *Mosuku ga kataru Isuramushi.* Tokyo: Chūō kōronsha, 1994.

———. "Tōhō Isurāmu sekai no seiritsu," in Suzuki Tadashi, ed. *Pakusu Isuramika no seiki.* Tokyo: Kōdansha, 1993.

———. *Le chah et les Qizilbas: Le systeme militaire safavide.* Berlin: K. Schwarz, 1986.

Har-El, Shai. *Struggle for domination in the Middle East: The Ottoman-Mamluk war, 1485–1491.* Leiden: E. J. Brill, 1995.

Harari, Yuval Noah. "Strategy and supply in fourteenth-century western European invasion campaigns," *Journal of Military History* 64 (2000): 297–334.

Hasan Beg Rūmlū. *Ahsan al-tavārīkh*. Edited by 'Abd al-Husayn Navā'ī. Tehran: Chāpkhāna-i Haydarī, 1978.

al-Hassan, Ahmad Y. "Iron and steel technology in medieval Arabic sources," *Journal for the History of Arabic Science* 2 (1978): 31–52.

al-Hassan, Ahmad Y., and Donald R. Hill. *Islamic technology: An illustrated history*. Cambridge: Cambridge University Press, 1986.

Hassig, Ross. "War, politics and the conquest of Mexico," in Jeremy Black, ed. *War in the early modern world 1450–1815*. London: UCL Press, 1999.

———. *Mexico and the Spanish conquest*. London: Longman, 1994.

He Liangchen. *Zhenji*. Qing edition. In *Zhongguo bingshu jicheng*, vol. 25. Beijing: Jiefang jun, 1994.

He Rubin. *Binglu*. In *Siku jinhuishu congkan*, ser. 3, vol. 9. Beijing: Beijing, 1997.

Headrick, Daniel R. *The tools of empire: Technology and European imperialism in the nineteenth century*. Oxford: Oxford University Press, 1981.

Heath, E. G. *Bow versus gun*. East Ardsley: EP Publishing, 1973.

Hegyi, Klára. "The Ottoman network of fortresses in Hungary," in Géza Dávid and Pál Fodor, eds. *Ottomans, Hungarians, and Habsburgs in Central Europe: The military confines in the era of Ottoman conquest*. Leiden: Brill, 2000.

Hellie, Richard. "Warfare, changing military technology, and the evolution of Muscovite society," in John A. Lynn, ed. *Tools of war: Instruments, ideas, and institutions of warfare, 1445–1871*. Chicago: University of Illinois Press, 1990.

———. *Enserfment and military change in Muscovy*. Chicago: University of Illinois Press, 1971.

Henthorn, William E. *Korea: The Mongol invasions*. Leiden: E. J. Brill, 1963.

Hess, A. C. "The Ottoman conquest of Egypt (1517) and the beginning of the sixteenth-century world war," *International Journal of Middle East Studies* 4 (1973): 55–76.

———. "Firearms and the decline of Ibn Khaldun's military elite," *Archivum Ottomanicum* 4 (1972): 173–201.

———. "The evolution of the Ottoman seaborne empire in the age of the oceanic discoveries, 1453–1525," *The American Historical Review* 75 (1970): 1892–919.

Hetoum. *A lytell cronycle: Richard Pynson's translation (c 1520) of La fleur des histoires de la terre d'Orient (c 1307)*. Edited by Glenn Burger. Toronto: University of Toronto, 1988.

Heywood, Colin. "The activities of the state cannon-foundry (Tophāne-i 'Āmire) at Istanbul in the early sixteenth century according to an unpublished Turkish source," in *Writing Ottoman history: Documents and interpretations*. Aldershot: Variorum, 2002a.

———. "Notes on the production of fifteenth-century Ottoman cannon," in *Writing Ottoman history: Documents and interpretations*. Aldershot: Variorum, 2002b.

Hill, Donald R. *Islamic science and engineering*. Edinburgh: Edinburgh University Press, 1993.

———. "The role of the camel and the horse in the early Arab conquests," in V. J. Parry and M. E. Yapp, eds. *War, technology, and society in the Middle East*. London: Oxford University Press, 1975.

Hitti, Philip K. *An Arab-Syrian gentleman and warrior in the period of the Crusades: Memoirs of Usāmah Ibn-Munqidh.* Princeton: Princeton University Press, 1987 [1929].

Hŏ Sŏn-do. *Chosŏn sidae pyŏnggi sa yŏngu,* Seoul: Iljogak, 1994.

Hodgson, Marshall G. S. *Rethinking world history: Essays on Europe, Islam, and world history.* Cambridge: Cambridge University Press, 1993.

———. *The venture of Islam: Conscience and history in a world civilization.* 3 vols. Chicago: University of Chicago, 1974.

Holt, Peter Malcolm. *The age of the Crusades: The Near East from the eleventh century to 1517.* London: Longman, 1986.

Hora Tomio. *Teppō: Denrai to so no eikyō.* Kyoto: Shibunkaku, 1991.

Howard, Frank. "Early ship guns, part II: Swivels," *The Mariner's Mirror* 73 (1987): 49–55.

———. "Early ship guns, part I: Built-up breech-loaders," *The Mariner's Mirror* 72 (1986): 439–53.

Huang, Ray. *1587, a year of no significance: The Ming dynasty in decline.* New Haven: Yale University Press, 1981a.

———. "The Liao-tung campaign of 1619," *Oriens Extremus* 28 (1981b): 30–54.

———. *Taxation and government finance in sixteenth-century Ming China.* Cambridge: Cambridge University Press, 1974.

———. "Military expenditures in sixteenth-century Ming China," *Oriens Extremus* 17 (1970): 39–62.

Huang, Yi-Long. "Sun Yuanhua (1581–1632): A Christian convert who put Xu Guangqi's military reform policy into practice," translated by Peter Engelfriet, in Catherine Jami et al., eds. *Statecraft and intellectual renewal in late Ming China: The cross-cultural synthesis of Xu Guangqi (1562–1633).* Leiden: E. J. Brill, 2001.

Hucker, Charles O. "Ming government," in Denis Twitchett and Frederick W. Mote, eds. *The Cambridge history of China, volume 8: The Ming dynasty, part 2.* Cambridge: Cambridge University Press, 1998.

———. *A dictionary of official titles in imperial China.* Stanford: Stanford University, 1985.

———. "Hsü Tsung-hsien's campaign against Hsü Hai, 1556," in Frank A. Kiernan and John K. Fairbank, eds. *Chinese ways in warfare.* Cambridge: Harvard University Press, 1974.

Huff, Darrell. *How to lie with statistics.* New York: W. W. Norton & Co., 1954.

Ibn Iyās, Muhammad Ibn Ahmad. *Badā'i 'al-zuhūr fi waqā'i 'al-duhūr.* Text: Muhammad Mustafā, ed. 5 vols. Cairo, al-Hay'at al-Misrīyat al-ʿĀmma lil-Kitāb, 1984. Translation: W. H. Salmon. *An account of the Ottoman conquest of Egypt in the year* A.H. 922(A.D. 1516), *translated from the third volume of the Arabic chronicle of Muhammed Ibn Ahmed Ibn Iyās, an eyewitness of the scenes he describes.* Westport, CT: Hyperion Press, 1981 [1921].

Ibn Khaldūn, 'Abd al-Rahmān Abū Zayd. *Kitāb al-ʿibar.* Text: M. Quatremère. *Prolégomènes d'Ebn-Khaldoun.* 3 vols. Paris, Libraire de l'Institut Impérial de France, 1858. Translation: Franz Rosenthal. *The muqaddimah: An introduction to history.* 3 vols. New York: Pantheon Books, 1958.

Ibn Taghrī-Birdī, [Abu'l-Mahasin]. *History of Egypt 1382–1469 A.D. Translated from the Arabic annals of Abu 'l-Mahasin Ibn Taghrī Birdī.* 8 vols. Translated by William Popper. Berkeley: University of California Press, 1954–63.

Ikegami, Eiko. *The taming of the samurai: Honorific individualism and the making of modern Japan*. Cambridge: Harvard University Press, 1995.

Imber, Colin H. *The Ottoman empire, 1300–1650*. New York: Palgrave Macmillan, 2002.

———. "The reconstruction of the Ottoman fleet after the battle of Lepanto, 1571–1572," in *Studies in Ottoman history and law*. Istanbul: Isis Press, 1996.

———. "The navy of Süleyman the Magnificent," *Archivum Ottomanicum* 6 (1980): 211–82.

Inalcik, Halil. "The military and fiscal transformation in the Ottoman empire, 1600–1700," *Archivum Ottomanicum* 6 (1980): 283–337.

———. "The socio-political effects of the diffusion of fire-arms in the Middle East," in V. J. Parry and M. E. Yapp, eds. *War, technology, and society in the Middle East*. London: Oxford University Press, 1975.

———. *The Ottoman empire: The classical age 1300–1600*. Translated by Norman Itzkowitz and Colin Imber. London: Weidenfeld and Nicolson, 1973.

Iqbal Ghani Khan. "Metallurgy in medieval India – 16th to 18th centuries," in Aniruddha Roy and S. K. Bagchi, eds. *Technology in ancient & medieval India*. Delhi: Sundeep Prakashan, 1986.

Iqtidar Alam Khan. "The coming of gunpowder to the Islamic world and north India: Spotlight on the role of the Mongols," *Journal of Asian History* 30 (1996a): 27–45.

———. "The role of the Mongols in the introduction of gunpowder and firearms in South Asia," in Brenda J. Buchanan, ed. *Gunpowder: The history of an international technology*. Bath: Bath University Press, 1996b.

———. "Early use of cannon and musket in India: A.D. 1442–1526," *Journal of the Economic and Social History of the Orient* XXIV (1981): 146–64.

———. "Origin and development of gunpowder technology in India: A.D. 1250–1500," *The Indian Historical Review* IV (1977): 20–29.

Irwin, Robert. *The Middle East in the Middle Ages: The early Mamluk sultanate 1250–1382*. Carbondale: South Illinois University Press, 1986.

Iskandar Beg Munshī. *Tārīkh-i ʿĀlamārā-yi ʿAbbāsī*. ed. Īraj Afshār. 2d ed. 2 vols. Tehran: Amīr Kabīr, 1971.

İsom-Verhaaren, Christine. "An Ottoman report about Martin Luther and the Emperor: New evidence of the Ottoman interest in the Protestant challenge to the power of Charles V," *Turcica* 28 (1996): 299–317.

Jackson, Melvin H. and Carel de Beer. *Eighteenth century gunfounding: The Verbruggens at the Royal Brass Foundry, a chapter in history of technology*. Newton Abbot: David & Charles, 1973.

Jackson, Peter. *The Delhi sultanate: A political and military history*. Cambridge: Cambridge University Press, 1999.

Jagchid, Sechin and C. R. Bawden. "Some notes on the horse-policy of the Yüan dynasty," *Central Asiatic Journal* 10 (1965): 246–68.

Jagchid, Sechin and Van Jay Symons. *Peace, war, and trade along the Great Wall: Nomadic-Chinese interaction through two millennia*. Bloomington: Indiana University Press, 1989.

Jardine, Lisa and Jerry Brotton. *Global interests: Renaissance art between east & west*. Ithaca: Cornell University Press, 2000.

Jennings, R. C. "Firearms, bandits, and gun-control: Some evidence on Ottoman policy towards firearms in the possession of *reaya*, from judicial records of Kayseri, 1600–1627," *Archivum Ottomanicum* 6 (1980): 339–58.

Jeon, Sang-woon. *Science and technology in Korea: Traditional instruments and techniques*. Cambridge: MIT Press, 1974.

Jiao Yu. *Huolong shenqi zhenfa*. 1412. In *Zhongguo bingshu jicheng*, vol. 17. Beijing: Jiefang jun, 1993.

Jin Youzi. "Beizheng lu." 1410. In Deng Shilong, comp. *Guochao diangu*, vol. 1. Beijing: Beijing daxue, 1993a.

—— "Beizheng houlu." 1414. In Deng Shilong, comp. *Guochao diangu*, vol. 1. Beijing: Beijing daxue, 1993b.

Johnston, Alastair Iain. *Cultural realism: Strategic culture and grand strategy in Chinese history*. Princeton: Princeton University Press, 1995.

Jones, Colin. "The Military Revolution and the professionalisation of the French army under the Ancien Régime," in Clifford J. Rogers, ed. *The military revolution debate: Readings on the military transformation of early modern Europe*. Boulder: Westview, 1995.

Jones, J. R. Melville, tr. *The siege of Constantinople 1453: Seven contemporary accounts*. Amsterdam, Hakkert, 1972.

Juvaini, 'Ala-ad-Din 'Ata-Malik. *The history of the world-conqueror*. Translated by John A. Boyle. Manchester: Manchester University Press, 1958.

Kafadar, Cemal. *Between two worlds: The construction of the Ottoman state*. Berkeley: University of California Press, 1995.

Kahane, Henry, Renée Kahane, and Andreas Tietze. *The Lingua Franca in the Levant: Turkish nautical terms of Italian and Greek origin*. Urbana: University of Illinois Press, 1958.

Katsu Kokichi. *Musui's story: The autobiography of a Tokugawa samurai*. Translated by Teruko Craig. Tucson: University of Arizona Press, 1993 [1988].

Keddie, Nikki R. "Is there a Middle East?" *International Journal of Middle East Studies* 4 (1973): 255–71.

Keep, John L. H. *Soldiers of the tsar: Army and society in Russia, 1462–1874*. Oxford: Oxford University Press, 1985.

Kelenik, József. "The military revolution in Hungary," in Géza Dávid and Pál Fodor, eds. *Ottomans, Hungarians, and Habsburgs in Central Europe: The military confines in the era of Ottoman conquest*. Leiden: Brill, 2000.

Kennedy, Hugh. *The armies of the caliphs: Military and society in the early Islamic state*. London: Routledge, 2001.

Kennedy, Paul M. *The rise and fall of the great powers: Economic change and military conflict from 1500 to 2000*. New York: Random House, 1987.

Khāndamīr, Ghiyās al-Dīn b. Humām al-Dīn al-Husaynī. *Tārīkh-i habīb al-siyar fī akhbār-i afrād-i bashar*. Translated by Wheeler M. Thackston. *Habibu's-siyar*. 2 vols. Cambridge: Harvard University Department of Near Eastern Languages and Civilizations, 1994.

Kist, J. B. "Commentary," in Jacob de Gheyn, ed. *The exercise of armes for calivres, muskettes, and pikes*. New York: McGraw-Hill, 1971 [1607].

Kitajima Manji. *Toyotomi Hideyoshi no Chōsen shinryaku*. Tokyo: Yoshikawa Kōbunkan, 1995.

Kolff, Dirk H. A. *Naukar, Rajput and Sepoy: The ethnohistory of the military labour market in Hindustan, 1450–1850.* Cambridge: Cambridge University Press, 1990.

Kortepeter, Carl Max. *Ottoman imperialism during the Reformation: Europe and the Caucasus.* New York: New York University Press, 1972.

Lach, Donald F. *Asia in the making of Europe, vol. 1: The century of discovery.* Chicago: Chicago University Press, 1994 [1965].

Lamers, Jereon Pieter. *Japonius tyrannus: The Japanese warlord Oda Nobunaga reconsidered.* Leiden: Hotei Publishing, 2000.

Landes, David S. *The wealth and poverty of nations: Why some are so rich and some so poor.* New York: W. W. Norton & Co., 1998.

Langlois, John D. Jr. "The Hung-wu reign, 1368–1398," in Denis Twitchett and Frederick W. Mote, eds. *The Cambridge history of China, volume 7: The Ming dynasty, part 1.* Cambridge: Cambridge University Press, 1988.

Latham, J. D. and W. F. Paterson. *Saracen archery: An English version and exposition of a Mameluke work on archery (ca. A.D. 1368).* London: The Holland Press, 1970.

Lattimore, Owen. "The frontier in history," in *Studies in frontier history: Collected papers 1928–1958.* London: Oxford University Press, 1962.

Lee Ki-baik. *A new history of Korea.* Translated by Edward W. Wagner. Cambridge: Harvard-Yenching Institute, 1984.

Lenman, Bruce P. "The transition to European military ascendancy in India, 1600–1800," in John A. Lynn, ed. *Tools of war: Instruments, ideas, and institutions of warfare, 1445–1871.* Chicago: University of Illinois Press, 1990.

Levanoni, Amalia. "Rank-and-file Mamluks versus amirs: New norms in the Mamluk military institution," in Thomas Philipp and Ulrich Haarmann, eds. *The Mamluks in Egyptian politics and society.* Cambridge: Cambridge University Press, 1998.

Levathes, Louise. *When China ruled the seas: The treasure fleet of the dragon throne, 1405–1433.* Oxford: Oxford University Press, 1994.

Lewis, Archibald. *Nomads and crusaders A.D. 1000–1368.* Bloomington: Indiana University Press, 1988.

Lewis, Bernard. *Race and slavery in the Middle East: An historical inquiry.* Oxford: Oxford University Press, 1990.

———. *The Muslim discovery of Europe.* New York: W. W. Norton, 1982.

———. *The Arabs in history.* New York: Harper & Row, 1966.

Lieberman, Victor B. "Europeans, trade, and the unification of Burma, c.1540–1620," *Oriens Extremus* 27 (1980): 203–26.

Lindholm, Charles. "Kinship structure and political authority: The Middle East and Central Asia," in *Comparative Studies in Society and History* 28 (1986): 334–355.

Liutao. Song ed. In *Zhongguo bingshu jicheng*, vol. 1. Beijing: Jiefang jun, 1987.

Lo, Jung-pang. "Intervention in Vietnam: A case study of the foreign policy of the early Ming government," *Ts'ing-hua Journal of Chinese Studies* 8 (1970): 154–82.

———. "Policy formulation and decision-making on issues respecting peace and war," in Charles O. Hucker, ed. *Chinese government in Ming times – seven studies.* New York: Columbia University Press, 1969.

———. "The decline of the early Ming navy," *Oriens Extremus* 5 (1958): 149–68.

————. "The emergence of China as a sea power during the late Sung and early Yüan periods," *Far Eastern Quarterly* 14 (1955): 489–503.

Lockhart, Laurence. "The Persian army in the Safavī period," *Der Islam* 34 (1959): 89–98.

Logan, F. Donald. *The Vikings in history.* 2d ed. London: Routledge, 1991.

Lorge, Peter. "War and warfare in China 1450–1815," in Jeremy Black, ed. *War in the early modern world 1450–1815.* London: UCL Press, 1999.

Love, Ronald S. "'All the King's horsemen': The equestrian army of Henry IV, 1585–1598," *Sixteenth Century Journal* 22 (1991): 510–33.

Lu Gwei-djen, Joseph Needham and Phan Chi-hsing. "The oldest representation of a bombard," *Technology and Culture* 29 (1988): 594–605.

Luttwak, Edward N. *The grand strategy of the Roman empire: From the first century A.D. to the third.* Baltimore: Johns Hopkins University Press, 1976.

Lynn, John A. *Giant of the Grand Siècle: The French army, 1610–1715.* Cambridge: Cambridge University Press, 1997.

————. "Recalculating French army growth during the *Grand Siècle*, 1610–1715," in Clifford J. Rogers, ed. *The military revolution debate: Readings on the military transformation of early modern Europe.* Boulder: Westview, 1995a.

————. "The *trace italienne* and the growth of armies: The French case," in Clifford J. Rogers, ed. *The military revolution debate: Readings on the military transformation of early modern Europe.* Boulder: Westview, 1995b.

————. "French opinion and the military resurrection of the pike, 1792–1794," *Military Affairs* 41 (1977): 1–7.

Ma Duanlin. *Wenxian tongkao.* 1322. Beijing: Zhonghua, 1991 [1986].

Maalouf, Amin. *The Crusades through Arab eyes.* Translated by Jon Rothschild. New York: Schocken Books, 1984.

Machiavelli, Niccolò. *The art of war.* 1521. Translated by Ellis Farneworth. New York: Da Capo, 1990.

Majewski, Wieslaw. "The Polish art of war in the sixteenth and seventeenth centuries," in J. K. Fedorowicz et al., eds. *A republic of nobles: Studies in Polish history to 1864.* Cambridge: Cambridge University Press, 1982.

Mallett, Michael. "Siegecraft in late fifteenth-century Italy," in Ivy A. Corfis and Michael Wolfe, eds. *The medieval city under siege.* Woodbridge: Boydell Press, 1995.

————. "Part I: c.1400–1508," in J. R. Hale and M. E. Mallett, eds. *The military organization of a Renaissance state: Venice c.1400 to 1617.* Cambridge: Cambridge University Press, 1984.

Malone, Patrick M. *The skulking way of war: Technology and tactics among the New England Indians.* New York: Madison Books, 1991.

Manguin, Pierre-Yves. "The vanishing *jong*: Insular Southeast Asian fleets in trade and war (fifteenth to seventeenth centuries)," in Anthony Reid, ed. *Southeast Asia in the early modern era: Trade, power, and belief.* Ithaca: Cornell University Press, 1993.

Mano Eiji. *Chūō Ajia no rekishi: Sōgen to oashisu no sekai.* Tokyo: Kōdansha, 1977.

Manz, Beatrice Forbes. *The rise and rule of Tamerlane.* Cambridge: Cambridge University Press, 1989.

Mao Peiqi and Li Zhuoran. *Ming Chengzu shilun.* Taipei: Wenjin, 1994.

March, Andrew L. *The idea of China: Myth and theory in geographic thought*. New York: Praeger, 1974.

Mardsen, William. *A dictionary and grammar of the Malayan language*. 2 vols. Oxford: Oxford University Press, 1984 [1812].

Martin, Colin and Geoffrey Parker. *The Spanish Armada*. London: Hamish Hamilton, 1988.

Martinez, A. P. "Some notes on the Īl-Xānid army," *Archivum Eurasiae Medii Aeivi* 6 (1986): 129–242.

Matar, Nabil. *Turks, Moors, and Englishmen in the Age of Discovery*. New York: Columbia University Press, 1999.

Matthee, Rudi. "Unwalled cities and restless nomads: Firearms and artillery in Safavid Iran," in *Safavid Persia: The history and politics of an Islamic society*. Edited by Charles Melville. London: I. B. Tauris & Co., 1996.

McChesney, Robert D. "The conquest of Herat 995–6/1587–8: Sources for the study of Safavid/Qizilbash–Shibānid/Ūzbak relations," in Jean Calmard, ed. *Etudes Safavides*. Paris: Institut Français de Recherche en Iran, 1993.

McClellan, James E. III, and Harold Dorn. *Science and technology in world history: An introduction*. Baltimore: Johns Hopkins University Press, 1999.

McDermott, John D. *A guide to the Indian wars of the West*. Lincoln: University of Nebraska Press, 1998.

McNeill, William H. *Keeping together in time: Dance and drill in human history*. Cambridge: Harvard University Press, 1995.

———. *The age of gunpowder empires 1450–1800*. Washington: American Historical Association, 1989a.

———. *Plagues and peoples*. New York: Anchor Books, 1989b [1976].

———. "The eccentricity of wheels, or Eurasian transportation in historical perspective," *The American Historical Review* 92 (1987): 1111–16.

———. *The pursuit of power: Technology, armed force, and society since A.D. 1000*. Chicago: University of Chicago Press, 1982.

———. *Europe's steppe frontier 1500–1800*. Chicago: University of Chicago Press, 1964.

———. *The rise of the West: A history of the human community*. Chicago: University of Chicago Press, 1963.

Meng Gong. *Meng Da beilu*. In Wang Guowei, ed. *Menggu shiliao sizhong*. Taipei: Zhengzhong, 1989 [1926].

Meskill, John, tr. *Ch'oe Pu's diary: A record of drifting across the sea*. Tucson: University of Arizona Press, 1965.

Michalak, Mirostaw. "The origins and development of Sassanian heavy cavalry," *Folia Orientalia* 24 (1987): 73–86.

Mills, J. V. G. "Introduction," in Ma Huan. *Ying-yai sheng-lan: "The overall survey of the ocean's shores."* Translated by J. V. G. Mills. Cambridge: Cambridge University Press, 1970.

Mingshi. Zhang Tingyu. 28 vols. Beijing: Zhonghua, 1987 [1974].

Ming shilu. 183 vols. Taipei: Zhongyang yanjiuyuan lishi yuyan yanjiusuo, 1961.

Minorsky, Vladimir, tr. *Tadhkirat al-mulūk: A manual of Safavid administration (circa 1137/1725)*. Cambridge: E. J. W. Gibb Memorial Trust, 1980 [1943].

———. *Persia in* A.D. *1478–1490: An abridged translation of Fadlullāh b. Rūzbihān Khunjī's Tārīkh-i ʿAlam-ārā-yi Amīnī.* London: Royal Asiatic Society of Great Britain and Ireland, 1957.

Miyazaki Masakatsu. *Tei Wa no nankai dai ensei – Eirakutei no sekai chitsujo saihen.* Tokyo: Chūkō shinsho, 1997.

Momiyama Akira. *Kan teikoku to henkyō shakai – Chōjō no fūkei.* Tokyo: Chūō kōron shinsha, 1999.

Monserrate. *The commentary of Father Monserrate, S. J., on his journey to the court of Akbar.* 1591. Translated by J. S. Hoyland, annotated by S. N. Banerjee. London: Oxford University Press, 1922.

Morgan, David. *The Mongols.* Oxford: Blackwell, 1993 [1986].

———. *Medieval Persia 1040–1797.* New York: Longman, 1988.

Morillo, Stephen. "Guns and government: A comparative study of Europe and Japan," *Journal of World History* 6/1 (1995): 75–106.

Morris, V. Dixon. "The city of Sakai and urban autonomy," in George Elison and Bardwell L. Smith, eds. *Warlords, artists, & commoners: Japan in the sixteenth century.* Honolulu: University Press of Hawaii, 1981.

Mote, Frederick W. *Imperial China 900–1800.* Cambridge: Harvard University Press, 2000.

———. "Yüan and Ming," in K. C. Chang, ed. *Food in Chinese culture: Anthropological and historical perspectives.* New Haven: Yale University Press, 1977.

———. "The T'u-mu incident of 1449," in Frank A. Kiernan and John K. Fairbank, eds. *Chinese ways in warfare.* Cambridge: Harvard University Press, 1974.

Murai Shōsuke. "Teppō denrai saikō," in *Tōhōgaku ronshū: Eastern Studies fiftieth anniversary volume.* Tokyo: Tōhō Gakkai, 1997.

Murphey, Rhoads. *Ottoman warfare, 1500–1700.* London: UCL Press, 1999.

Murray, [General Sir] George, ed. *The letters and dispatches of John Churchill, First Duke of Marlborough, from 1702 to 1712.* 5 vols. New York: Greenwood Press, 1968 [1845].

Murrin, Michael. *History and warfare in Renaissance epic.* Chicago: University of Chicago Press, 1997 [1994].

Naima [Mustafa Naim]. *Annals of the Turkish empire from 1591 to 1659 of the Christian era.* Translated by Charles Fraser. New York: Arno Press, 1973 [1832].

Nakai Nobuhiko and James L. McClain. "Commercial change and urban growth in early modern Japan," in John W. Hall, ed. *The Cambridge history of Japan: Volume 4, early modern Japan.* Cambridge: Cambridge University Press, 1991.

Needham, Joseph. *The development of iron and steel technology in China.* Cambridge: The Newcomen Society, 1964 [1958].

Needham, Joseph, et al. *Science and civilisation in China.* Cambridge: Cambridge University Press, 1954–.

Neşri [Mehmet]. *Kitāb-ı cihan-nümā.* 2 vols. Ankara: Türk tarih kurumu basımevi, 1995.

Nicolle, David. "Medieval warfare: The unfriendly interface," *Journal of Military History* 63 (1999): 579–600.

Nimick, Thomas G. "Ch'i Chi-kuang and I-wu county," *Ming Studies* 34 (1995): 17–29.

Nishigaya Yasuhiro. *Kōshō Oda Nobunaga jiten.* Tokyo: Tōkyōdō, 2000.

———. *Jōkaku (Nihonshi shōhyakka 24).* Tokyo: Kondō shuppansha, 1988.

Nuniz, Fernão. *Chronicle of Fernão Nuniz.* In Robert Sewell. *A forgotten empire: Vijayanagara.* Delhi: Government of India, 1962 [1884].

Obeyesekere, Gananath. *The apotheosis of Captain Cook: European mythmaking in the Pacific.* Princeton: Princeton University Press, 1992 (new afterword, 1997).

Okuyama Norio. "Mindai no hokuhen ni okeru gunshi no getsuryō ni tsuite," in Nakayama Hachirō et al., eds. *Mindaishi ronsō.* Tokyo: Kyūko shoin, 1990.

Olejar, Paul D. "Rockets in early American wars," *Military Affairs* 10 (1946): 16–34.

Oliver, Roland and Anthony Atmore. *Medieval Africa 1250–1800.* Cambridge: Cambridge University Press, 2001.

Oman, Charles. *A history of the art of war in the sixteenth century.* New York: E. P. Dutton, [1937].

Ono Takeo. *Nihon heinō shiron.* Tokyo: Yūhikaku, 1938.

O'Rourke, Shane. *Warriors and peasants: The Don Cossacks in late imperial Russia.* New York: St. Martin's Press, 2000.

Ose Hoan. *Shinchō ki.* Edited by Matsuzawa Chisato. 2 vols. Tokyo: Koten bunko, 1982.

Ostrowski, Donald. *Muscovy and the Mongols: Cross-cultural influences on the steppe frontier, 1304–1589.* Cambridge: Cambridge University Press, 1998.

Ōta Gyūichi. *Shinchōkō ki.* Edited by Okuno Takahiro and Iwasawa Yoshihiko. Tokyo: Kadogawa, 1969.

Owada Tetsuo. *Sengoku jū daikassen no nazo: Sakusen, jindate, yōhei – jitsu wa kō datta.* Tokyo: PHP, 1995.

———. *Sengoku bushō.* Tokyo: Chūō Kōronsha, 1990 [1981].

Özbaran, Salih. "Ottoman naval policy in the south," in Metin Kunt and Christine Woodhead, eds. *Suleyman the Magnificent and his age: The Ottoman empire in the early modern world.* London: Longman, 1995.

Özoğlu, Hakan. "State-tribe relations: Kurdish tribalism in the 16th- and 17th-century Ottoman empire," *British Journal of Middle Eastern Studies* 23 (1996): 5–27.

Pacey, Arnold. *Technology in world civilization: A thousand-year history.* Cambridge: MIT Press, 1990.

Paes, Domingo. *Narrative of Domingo Paes.* In Robert Sewell. *A forgotten empire: Vijayanagara.* Delhi: Government of India, 1962 [1884].

Pálffy, Géza. "The origins and development of the border defense system against the Ottoman empire in Hungary (up to the early eighteenth century)," in Géza Dávid and Pál Fodor, eds. *Ottomans, Hungarians, and Habsburgs in Central Europe: The military confines in the era of Ottoman conquest.* Leiden: Brill, 2000.

Parker, Geoffrey. "The *Dreadnought* revolution of Tudor England," *The Mariner's Mirror* 82 (1996): 269–300.

———. "In defense of *The military revolution*," in Clifford J. Rogers, ed. *The military revolution debate: Readings on the military transformation of early modern Europe.* Boulder: Westview, 1995.

———. *The military revolution: Military innovation and the rise of the West, 1500–1800.* Cambridge: Cambridge University Press, 1988.

Parrott, David A. "Strategy and tactics in the Thirty Years' War: The 'military revo-lution,'" in Clifford J. Rogers, ed. *The military revolution debate: Readings on the military transformation of early modern Europe*. Boulder: Westview, 1995.

Parry, V. J. "La manière de combattre," in V. J. Parry and M. E. Yapp, eds. *War, technology, and society in the Middle East*. London: Oxford University Press, 1975.

———. "Materials of war in the Ottoman empire," in M. A. Cook, ed. *Studies in the economic history of the Middle East from the rise of Islam to the present day*. London: Oxford University Press, 1970.

Parsons, James Bunyan. *Peasant rebellions of the late Ming dynasty*. Tucson: University of Arizona Press, 1970.

Partington, J. R. *A history of Greek fire and gunpowder*. Baltimore: Johns Hopkins University Press, 1999 [1960].

Paterson, W. P. "The archers of Islam," *Journal of the Economic and Social History of the Orient* 9 (1966): 69–87.

Pearson, M. N. *Port cities and intruders: The Swahili coast, India, and Portugal in the early modern era*. Baltimore: Johns Hopkins University Press, 1998.

———. *The new Cambridge history of India, I.1: The Portuguese in India*. Cambridge: Cambridge University Press, 1987.

Pelliot, Paul. "Le Hoja et le Sayyid Husain de l'histoire des Ming," *T'oung Pao* 38 (1948): 81–92.

Pepper, Simon and Nicholas Adams. *Firearms & fortifications: Military architecture and siege warfare in sixteenth-century Siena*. Chicago: University of Chicago Press, 1986.

Perdue, Peter C. "Fate and fortune in Central Eurasian warfare: Three Qing emperors and their Mongol rivals," in Nicola Di Cosmo, ed. *Warfare in Inner Asian history (500–1800)*. Leiden: Brill, 2002.

———. "Culture, history, and imperial Chinese strategy: Legacies of the Qing conquests," in Hans van de Ven, ed. *Warfare in Chinese history*. Leiden: Brill, 2000.

———. "Military mobilization in seventeenth and eighteenth-century China, Russia, and Mongolia," *Modern Asian Studies* 30 (1996): 757–93.

Perjés, Géza. *The fall of the medieval kingdom of Hungary: Mohács 1526–Buda 1541*. Translated by Mário D. Fenyő. Highlands Lakes, NJ: Atlantic Research and Publications, 1989 [1977].

———. "Army provisioning, logistics and strategy in the second half of the 17th century," *Acta Historica Academiae Scientiarum Hungaricae* 16 (1970): 1–51.

Pérotin-Dumon, Anne. "The pirate and the emperor: Power and the law on the seas, 1450–1850," in James D. Tracy, ed. *The political economy of merchant empires*. Cambridge: Cambridge University Press, 1991.

Perrin, Noel. *Giving up the gun: Japan's reversion to the sword, 1543–1879*. Boston: David R. Godine, 1979.

Perry, Richard D. "Warfare on the pampas in the 1870s," *Military Affairs* 36/2 (1972): 52–58.

Petrović, Djurdjica. "Fire-arms in the Balkans on the eve of and after the Ottoman conquests of the fourteenth and fifteenth centuries," in V. J. Parry and M. E. Yapp, eds. *War, technology, and society in the Middle East*. London: Oxford University Press, 1975.

Petry, Carl F. *Protectors or praetorians? The last Mamlūk sultans and Egypt's waning as a great power.* Albany: State University of New York Press, 1994.

Phillips, Gervase. *The Anglo-Scots wars, 1513–1550: A Military history.* Woodbridge: Boydell Press, 1999.

Piggott, Stuart. *Wagon, chariot and carriage: Symbol and status in the history of transport.* New York: Thames and Hudson, 1992.

Pipes, Daniel. *Slave soldiers and Islam: The genesis of a military system.* New Haven: Yale University Press, 1981.

Pires, Tomé. *The Suma Oriental of Tome Pires: An account of the East, from the Red Sea to Japan, written in Malacca and India in 1512–1515.* Edited by Armando Cortesao. New Delhi: Asian Educational Services, 1990.

Polo, Marco. *The travels of Marco Polo: The complete Yule-Cordier edition.* 2 vols. Translated by Henry Yule, edited by Henri Cordier. New York: Dover, 1993 [1920].

Pomeranz, Kenneth. *The great divergence: China, Europe, and the making of the modern world economy.* Princeton: Princeton University Press, 2000.

Popper, William. *Egypt and Syria under the Circassian sultans 1382–1468: Systematic notes to Ibn Taghrî Birdî's Chronicles of Egypt.* 2 vols. Berkeley: University of California Press, 1955–57.

Pryor, John H. *Geography, technology, and war: Studies in the maritime history of the Mediterranean, 649–1571.* Cambridge: Cambridge University Press, 1988.

Qi Jiguang. *Lianbing shiji.* Qing edition. In *Zhongguo bingshu jicheng,* vol. 19. Beijing: Jiefang jun, 1994a [1571].

———. *Jixiao xinshu.* Jiaqing edition. In *Zhongguo bingshu jicheng,* vol. 18. Beijing: Jiefang jun, 1994b [1560].

Qian Zhan. *Chengshou choulüe.* 1644 edition. In *Zhongguo bingshu jicheng,* vol. 37. Beijing: Jiefang jun, 1994.

Quinn, Sholeh A. *Historical writing during the reign of Shah 'Abbas: Ideology, imitation and legitimacy in Safavid chronicles.* Salt Lake City: University of Utah Press, 2000.

Rabie, Hassanein. "The training of the Mamlūk fāris," in *War, technology, and society in the Middle East.* V. J. Parry and M. E. Yapp, eds. London: Oxford University Press, 1975.

Ralston, David B. *Importing the European army: The introduction of European military techniques and institutions into the extra-European world, 1600–1914.* Chicago: University of Chicago Press, 1990.

Rao, Velcheru Narayana, David Shulman, and Sanjay Subrahmanyam. *Symbols of substance: Court and state in Nāyaka period Tamilnadu.* Delhi: Oxford University Press, 1992.

Reid, Anthony. *Southeast Asia in the age of commerce, 1450–1680.* 2 vols. New Haven: Yale University Press, 1988 and 1993.

Reid, Robert W. "Mongolian weaponry in *The Secret History of the Mongols.*" *Mongolian Studies* 15 (1992): 85–95.

Roberts, Michael. "The military revolution, 1560–1660," reprinted in Clifford J. Rogers, ed. *The military revolution debate: Readings on the military transformation of early modern Europe.* Boulder: Westview, 1995.

Robinson, David M. *Bandits, eunuchs, and the son of heaven: Rebellion and the economy of violence in mid-Ming China.* Honolulu: University of Hawai'i Press, 2001.

———. "Politics, force and ethnicity in Ming China: Mongols and the abortive coup of 1461," *Harvard Journal of Asiatic Studies* 59 (1999): 79–123.

Rodger, N. A. M. *The safeguard of the sea: A naval history of Britain, 660–1649.* New York: W. W. Norton & Co., 1998.

———. "The development of broadside gunnery, 1450–1650," *The Mariner's Mirror* 82 (1996): 301–24.

Roemer, H. R. "The Safavid period," in Peter Jackson and Laurence Lockhart, eds. *The Cambridge history of Iran, volume 6: The Timurid and Safavid periods.* Cambridge: Cambridge University Press, 1986a.

———. "The Türkmen dynasties," in Peter Jackson and Laurence Lockhart, eds. *The Cambridge history of Iran, volume 6: The Timurid and Safavid periods.* Cambridge: Cambridge University Press, 1986b.

Rogers, Clifford J. "The military revolutions of the Hundred Years War," in Clifford J. Rogers, ed. *The military revolution debate: Readings on the military transformation of early modern Europe.* Boulder: Westview, 1995.

Rose, Susan. *Medieval naval warfare 1000–1500.* London: Routledge, 2002.

Rossabi, Morris. "The 'decline' of the Central Asian caravan trade," in James D. Tracy, ed. *The rise of merchant empires: Long-distance trade in the early modern world, 1350–1750.* Cambridge: Cambridge University Press, 1990.

———. "The tea and horse trade with Inner Asia during the Ming," *Journal of Asian History* 4 (1970): 136–68.

Roth, Jonathan P. *The logistics of the Roman army at war (264 B.C.–A.D. 235).* Leiden: Brill, 1999.

Rubruck, William of. *The journey of William of Rubruck.* In Christopher Dawson, ed. *Mission to Asia.* Toronto: University of Toronto, 1980. (*The Mongol mission.* London: Sheed and Ward, 1955.)

Sarwar, Ghulām. *History of Shāh Ismāʿīl Safawī.* New York: AMS Press, 1975 [1939].

Savory, Roger M. "The Sherley myth," *Iran. Journal of the British Institute of Persian Studies* 5 (1967): 73–81, reprinted in *Studies on the history of Safawid Iran.* London: Variorum, 1987.

———. *Iran under the Safavids.* Cambridge: Cambridge University Press, 1980.

———. *History of Shah ʿAbbas the Great.* 2 vols. Boulder: Westview Press, 1978.

Scammell, G. V. *The first imperial age: European overseas expansion c.1400–1715.* London: Routledge, 1992 [1989].

———. "Indigenous assistance in the establishment of Portuguese power in Asia in the sixteenth century," *Modern Asian Studies* 14 (1980): 1–11.

Schimmel, Annemarie. *A two-colored brocade: The imagery of Persian poetry.* Chapel Hill: University of North Carolina Press, 1992.

Schmidt, Jan. "The Egri campaign of 1596; military history and the problem of sources," in Andreas Tietze, ed. *Habsburgisch-osmanische Beziehungen.* Vienna: Verlag des Verbandes der wissenschaftlichen Gesellschaften Österreichs, 1985.

Serruys, Henry. "The Mongols in China during the Hongwu period (1368–1398)," in *Mélanges chinois et bouddhiques* 11 (1959).

———. "The Mongols in China: 1400–1450," *Monumenta Serica* 27 (1968): 233–305, reprinted in *The Mongols and Ming China: Customs and history.* London: Variorum, 1987.

Shaw, Dennis J. B. "Southern frontiers of Muscovy, 1550–1700," in James A. Bater and R. A. French, eds. *Studies in Russian historical geography*, vol. 1. New York: Academic Press, 1983.

Shinji Yoshimoto. "Ashigaru," in *Kokushi daijiten*, vol. 1. Tokyo: Yoshikawa kōbunkan, 1979.

Sima Qian. *Shiji*. Beijing: Zhonghua, 1985 [1982].

Sleeswyk, André Wegener. "The *liao* and the displacement of ships in the Ming navy," *The Mariner's Mirror* 82 (1996): 3–13.

Slobodkin, Lawrence B. *Simplicity and complexity in games of the intellect*. Cambridge: Harvard University Press, 1992.

Smith, John Masson Jr. "Mongol nomadism and Middle Eastern geography: Qīshlāqs and tümens," in Reuven Amitai-Preiss and David O. Morgan, eds. *The Mongol empire and its legacy*. Leiden: Brill, 1999.

———. "Nomads on ponies vs. slaves on horses," *Journal of the American Oriental Society* 118 (1998): 54–62.

———. "Mongol society and military in the Middle East: Antecedents and adaptations," in Yaacov Lev, ed. *War and society in the eastern Mediterranean, 7th–15th centuries*. Leiden: E. J. Brill, 1997.

———. "'Ayn Jālūt: Mamlūk success or Mongol failure?" *Harvard Journal of Asiatic Studies* 44 (1984): 307–45.

Smith, Robert S. *Warfare & diplomacy in pre-colonial West Africa*. 2d ed. Madison: University of Wisconsin Press, 1989.

Smythe, [Sir] John. *Certen discourses concerning the formes and effects of divers sorts of weapons*. 1590, reprinted in E. G. Heath. *Bow versus gun*. East Ardsley: EP Publishing, 1973.

Snellgrove, David and Hugh Richardson. *A cultural history of Tibet*. 2d ed. Boston: Shambhala, 1995.

Snyder, Henry L., ed. *The Marlborough Godolphin correspondence*. 3 vols. Oxford: Clarendon Press, 1975.

So Kwan-wai. *Japanese piracy in Ming China during the 16th century*. Lansing: Michigan State University Press, 1975.

Starkey, Armstrong. *European and Native American warfare, 1675–1815*. Norman: University of Oklahoma Press, 1998.

Stein, Burton. *The new Cambridge history of India, I.2: Vijayanagara*. Cambridge: Cambridge University Press, 1989.

———. *Peasant state and society in medieval south India*. Oxford: Oxford University Press, 1980.

Stevens, Carol Belkin. *Soldiers on the steppe: Army reform and social change in early modern Russia*. DeKalb: Northern Illinois University Press, 1995.

Streusand, Douglas E. *The formation of the Mughal empire*. Delhi: Oxford University Press, 1999 [1989].

Stripling, George William Frederick. *The Ottoman Turks and the Arabs 1511–1574*. Philadelphia: Porcupine Press, 1977 [1942].

Struve, Lynn A. *The southern Ming 1644–1662*. New Haven: Yale University Press, 1984.

Subrahmanyam, Sanjay. *The career and legend of Vasco da Gama*. Cambridge: Cambridge University Press, 1997.

———. *The Portuguese empire in Asia, 1500–1700: A political and economic history*. London: Longman, 1993.

————. *The political economy of commerce: Southern India 1500–1650.* Cambridge: Cambridge University Press, 1990.

————. "State formation and transformation in early modern India and Southeast Asia," in *India and Indonesia during the Ancien Regime.* Leiden: E. J. Brill, 1989.

Sugiyama Masaaki. *Kubirai no chōsen – Mongoru kaijō teikoku e no michi.* Tokyo: Asahi, 1995.

Suzuki Keizō. "Yari," in *Kokushi daijiten,* vol. 14. Tokyo: Yoshikawa kōbunkan, 1993.

Suzuki Masaya. *Katana to kubitori – Sengoku kassen isetsu.* Tokyo: Heibonsha, 2000.

————. *Teppō to Nihonjin: "Teppō shinwa" ga kakushite kita koto.* Tokyo: Yōsensha, 1997.

Szakály, Ferenc. "Nándorfehérvár, 1521: The beginning of the end of the medieval Hungarian kingdom," in Géza Dávid and Pál Fodor, eds. *Hungarian-Ottoman military and diplomatic relations in the age of Süleyman the Magnificent.* Budapest: Hungarian Academy of Sciences, 1994.

Tallett, Frank. *War and society in early-modern Europe, 1495–1715.* London: Routledge, 1992.

Tamil Lexicon. New Delhi: Asian Educational Services, 1982 [1924–36].

Tana, Li. "An alternative Vietnam? The Nguyen kingdom in the seventeenth and eighteenth centuries," *Journal of Southeast Asian Studies* 29 (1998): 111–21.

Tanaka Takeo. *Wakō – umi no rekishi.* Tokyo: Kyōikusha, 1982.

Tang Shunzhi. *Wubian.* Wanli edition. In *Zhongguo bingshu jicheng,* vol. 13–14. Beijing: Jiefang jun, 1989.

Tani Mitsutaka. *Mindai basei no kenkyū.* Kyoto: Tōyōshi kenkyūkai, 1972.

————. "A study on horse administration in the Ming period," *Acta Asiatica* 21: 73–97 (1971).

Tarling, Nicholas, ed. *The Cambridge history of Southeast Asia, volume one.* Cambridge: Cambridge University Press, 1999.

Taylor, Keith W. "The early kingdoms," in Nicholas Tarling, ed. *The Cambridge history of Southeast Asia, volume one: From earliest times to c.1800.* Cambridge: Cambridge University Press, 1992.

Taylor, Romeyn. "Yüan origins of the wei-so system," in Charles O. Hucker, ed. *Chinese government in Ming times – Seven studies.* New York: Columbia University Press, 1969.

Thompson, I. A. A. "'Money, money, and yet more money!' Finance, the fiscal-state, and the military revolution: Spain 1500–1650," in Clifford J. Rogers, ed. *The military revolution debate: Readings on the military transformation of early modern Europe.* Boulder: Westview, 1995.

Thompson, William R. "The military superiority thesis and the ascendancy of western Eurasia in the world system," *Journal of World History* 10 (1999): 143–78.

Thornton, John K. *Warfare in Atlantic Africa, 1500–1800.* London: UCL Press, 1999.

————. *Africa and Africans in the making of the Atlantic world, 1400–1680.* Cambridge: Cambridge University Press, 1990.

Tilly, Charles. *Coercion, capital, and European states,* A.D. *990–1990.* Oxford: Basil Blackwell, 1990.

Tokoro Sōkichi. *Hinawajū.* Tokyo: Yūzankaku, 1993 [1969].

————. *Zukai kojū jiten.* Tokyo: Yūzankaku, 1987.

Tong, James W. *Disorder under heaven: Collective violence in the Ming dynasty.* Stanford: Stanford University Press, 1991.

Totman, Conrad. "Review," *Journal of Asian Studies* 39 (1980): 599–601.

Tsai, Shih-shan Henry. *Perpetual happiness: The Ming emperor Yongle.* Seattle: University of Washington Press, 2001.

————. *The eunuchs in the Ming dynasty.* Albany: State University of New York Press, 1996.

Twitchett, Denis and Frederick W. Mote, eds. *The Cambridge history of China, volume 8: The Ming dynasty, part 2.* Cambridge: Cambridge University Press, 1998.

————. *The Cambridge history of China, volume 7: The Ming dynasty, part 1.* Cambridge: Cambridge University Press, 1988.

Udagawa Takehisa. *Higashi Ajia heiki kōryūshi no kenkyū: Jūgo kara jūnana seiki ni okeru heiki no juyō to denpa.* Tokyo: Yoshikawa kōbunkan, 1993.

————. *Teppō denrai – heiki ga kataru kinsei no tanjō.* Tokyo: Chūō kōronsha, 1990.

Uzunçarşılı, İsmail Hakkı. *Osmanlı tarihi.* 4 vols. Ankara: Türk tarih kurumu basımevi, 1994 [1943].

————. *Osmanlı devletinin merkez ve bahriye teşkilâtı.* Ankara: Türk tarih kurumu basımevi, 1988 [1948].

————. *Osmanlı devleti teşkilâtından kapukulu ocakları.* 2 vols. Ankara: Türk tarih kurumu basımevi, 1988 [1944].

Vámbéry, Arminius. *The travels and adventures of the Turkish admiral Sidi Ali Reis in India, Afghanistan, Central Asia, and Persia, during the years 1553–1556.* Lahore: Al-Biruni, 1975 [1899].

van Creveld, Martin. *Technology and war from 2000 B.C. to the present.* London: Brassey's, 1991.

Vandervort, Bruce. *Wars of imperial conquest in Africa, 1830–1914.* Bloomington: Indiana University Press, 1998.

Varley, H. Paul. *Warriors of Japan as portrayed in the war tales.* Honolulu: University of Hawaii Press, 1994.

————. *The Ōnin War: History of its origins and background with a selective translation of The Chronicle of Ōnin.* New York: Columbia University Press, 1967.

Vlastos, Stephen. *Peasant protests and uprisings in Tokugawa Japan.* Berkeley: University of California Press, 1986.

Vogt, John. "Saint Barbara's legion: Portuguese artillery in the struggle for Morocco, 1415–1578," *Military Affairs* 41 (1977): 176–82.

Von Glahn, Richard. *Fountain of fortune: Money and monetary policy in China, 1000–1700.* Berkeley: University of California Press, 1996.

Wakeman, Frederic Jr. *The great enterprise: The Manchu reconstruction of imperial order in seventeenth-century China.* 2 vols. Berkeley: University of California Press, 1985.

Wakita Osamu. "The social and economic consequences of unification," translated by James L. McClain, in John W. Hall, ed. *The Cambridge history of Japan: Volume 4, early modern Japan.* Cambridge: Cambridge University Press, 1991.

Waldron, Arthur. *The Great Wall of China: From history to myth.* Cambridge: Cambridge University Press, 1990.

Waley-Cohen, Joanna. "Religion, war, and empire-building in eighteenth-century China," *The International History Review* 20 (1998): 336–52.

Wang Minghe. *Dengtan bijiu.* 1599. In *Zhongguo bingshu jicheng,* vol. 20–24. Beijing: Jiefang jun, 1990.

Wang Zhaochun. *Zhongguo huoqi shi.* Beijing: Junshi kexue, 1991.

Webb, James L. A. Jr. *Desert frontier: Ecological and economic change along the western Sahel, 1600–1850.* Madison: University of Wisconsin Press, 1995.

Wei Guozhong. "Heilongjiang Achengxian Panlachengzi chutu di tong huochong," *Wenwu* 1973/11: 52–54.

Whitmore, John K. *Vietnam, Ho Quy Ly, and the Ming (1371–1421).* New Haven: Yale University Press, 1985.

Williams, Alan. "Ottoman military technology: The metallurgy of Turkish armor," in Yaacov Lev, ed. *War and society in the eastern Mediterranean, 7th–15th centuries.* Leiden: E. J. Brill, 1997.

Williams, [Sir] Roger. *A briefe discourse of warre.* In John X. Evans, ed. *The works of Sir Roger Williams.* Oxford: Oxford University Press, 1972.

Wills, John E. Jr. "Relations with maritime Europeans, 1514–1662," in Denis Twitchett and Frederick W. Mote, eds. *The Cambridge history of China, volume 8: The Ming dynasty, part 2.* Cambridge: Cambridge University Press, 1998.

———. *Pepper, guns and parleys: The Dutch East India Company and China 1622–1681.* Cambridge: Harvard University Press, 1974.

Wilson, William Ritchie. "The way of the bow and arrow: The Japanese warrior in *Konjaku monogatari,*" *Monumenta Nipponica* 28 (1973): 177–233.

Wimmer, Jan. "L'infanterie dans l'armée polonaise aux XVe–XVIIIe siècles," translated by Roger Posnic, in Witold Bieganski et al., eds. *Histoire militaire de la Pologne: Problèmes choisis.* Warsaw: Ministère de la Défense Nationale, 1970.

Wink, André. "India and the Turko-Mongol frontier," in Anatoly M. Khazanov and André Wink, eds. *Nomads in the sedentary world.* Richmond: Curzon Press, 2001.

———. *Al-Hind: The making of the Indo-Islamic world.* 2 vols. Leiden: E. J. Brill, 1990 and 1997.

Woods, John E. *The Aqquyunlu: Clan, confederation, empire.* 2d ed. Salt Lake City: University of Utah Press, 1999.

Xu Ting. *Heida shilüe.* In Wang Guowei, ed. *Menggu shiliao sizhong.* Taipei: Zhengzhong, 1989 [1926].

Yamamoto Tatsurō. *Betonamu-Chūgoku kankeishi – Kyokushi no taitō kara Shin-Butsu sensō made.* Tokyo: Yamakawa shuppansha, 1975.

Yamamura, Kozo. "The growth of commerce in medieval Japan," in Kozo Yamamura, ed. *The Cambridge history of Japan, vol. 3, medieval Japan.* Cambridge: Cambridge University Press, 1990.

Yan Cungjian. *Shuyu zhouzi lu.* 1574. Beijing: Zhonghua, 1993.

Yang Rong. "Beizheng ji." 1424. In Deng Shilong, comp. *Guochao diangu,* vol. 1. Beijing: Beijing daxue, 1993.

Yi Sun-sin. *Yi Ch'ungmugong chŏnsŏ.* 1795 ed. Seoul: Sŏngmungak, 1989.

Yu Sŏng-nyong. *Sŏe munjip pu Chingbirok.* Seoul: Sŏnggyunguan tehakkyo tedong munhwa yŏnguwŏn, 1958.

Yuanshi. Toto. 15 vols. Beijing: Zhonghua, 1987 [1976].

Yule, Henry and A. C. Burnell. *Hobson-Jobson: The Anglo-Indian dictionary*. Ware: Wordsworth Editions, 1996 [1886].

Zeng Gongliang. *Wujing zongyao*. Wanli edition. In *Zhongguo bingshu jicheng*, vol. 3–5. Beijing: Jiefang jun, 1988.

Zhang Yue. *Xiaoshan leigao*. In *Siku quanshu*, vol. 1272. Taipei: Taiwan shangwu, 1983.

Zhao Shizhen. *Shenqi pu*. 1598 (1808 Japanese edition). In *Wakokuhon Min Shin shiryō shū*, vol. 6. Edited by Nagasawa Kikuya. Tokyo: Koten kenkyūkai, 1974.

Zheng Ruozeng. *Chouhai tubian*. 1562 ed. In *Zhongguo bingshu jicheng*, vol. 15–16. Beijing: Jiefang jun, 1990.

Zhu Yuanzhang, "Huang Ming zuxun," in *Mingchao kaiguo wenxian*. 4 vols. Taipei: Taiwan xuesheng, 1970.

Zhuge Yuansheng. *Liangchao pingrang lu*. 1606 edition. In *Renchen zhi i shiliao huiji*. Beijing: Quanguo tushuguan wenxian suowei fuzhi zhongxin, 1990.

Index